URNING

Urning

Queer Identity in the German Nineteenth Century

DOUGLAS PRETSELL

UNIVERSITY OF TORONTO PRESS

Toronto Buffalo London

© University of Toronto Press 2024
Toronto Buffalo London
utorontopress.com
Printed in the USA

ISBN 978-1-4875-5560-3 (cloth)   ISBN 978-1-4875-5561-0 (EPUB)
                                  ISBN 978-1-4875-5563-4 (PDF)

Library and Archives Canada Cataloguing in Publication

Title: Urning : queer identity in the German nineteenth century /
    Douglas Pretsell.
Names: Pretsell, Douglas, author.
Description: Includes bibliographical references and index.
Identifiers: Canadiana (print) 20230533795 | Canadiana (ebook) 20230533809 |
    ISBN 9781487555603 (hardcover) | ISBN 9781487555634 (PDF) |
    ISBN 9781487555610 (EPUB)
Subjects: LCSH: Gay men – Germany – Identity – History – 19th century. |
    LCSH: Gay activists – Germany – History – 19th century.
Classification: LCC HQ76.2.G4 P74 2024 | DDC 306.76/62094309034 – dc23

Cover design: Val Cooke
Cover image: Anselm Feuerbach, *Männlicher Halbakt* / Axis Images /
Alamy Stock Photo

We wish to acknowledge the land on which the University of Toronto Press
operates. This land is the traditional territory of the Wendat, the Anishnaabeg,
the Haudenosaunee, the Métis, and the Mississaugas of the Credit First Nation.

University of Toronto Press acknowledges the financial support of the
Government of Canada, the Canada Council for the Arts, and the Ontario Arts
Council, an agency of the Government of Ontario, for its publishing activities.

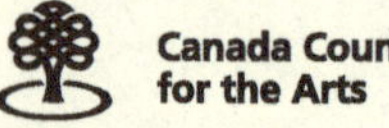

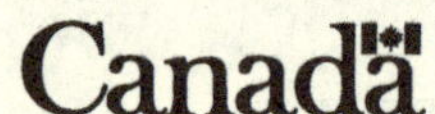

Dedicated to the memory of
ROBERT DEAM TOBIN
1961–2022

Contents

Acknowledgments

It is a testament to the advances in digitization of archives across Europe that I could embark on a book that was based on nineteenth-century German correspondence, hard-to-obtain literature, and official documents. Even a decade ago, it would have been impossible for a scholar located in Australia to have collected and compiled the materials that appear in this book.

I gathered the urning letters by visiting archives and emailing others to retrieve digital copies. The archive of these letters was then published in 2020 in a critical edition titled *The Correspondence of Karl Heinrich Ulrichs, 1846–1894*.[1] I am thankful to the following archives for their cooperation: Bundesarchiv des Deutschen Reiches, Bayerische Staatsbibliothek München, Deutsches Literaturarchiv Marbach (Cotta-Archiv), Freies Deutsches Hochstift/Frankfurter Goethe-Museum, Geheimes Staatsarchiv Preußischer Kulturbesitz, Universitätsbibliothek Giessen, Goethe und Schiller Archiv Frankfurt, National Széchényi Library (Hungary), Niedersächsisches Landesarchiv, Österreichisches Staatsarchiv, Staatsarchiv Bremen, Staatsbibliothek zu Berlin, Kantonsbibliothek Vadiana (St. Gallen), Herzog August Bibliothek Wolfenbüttel, Monacensia im Hildebrandhaus (Münchner Stadtbibliothek), Stadtarchiv Braunschweig, Universität Heidelberg, Universität Leipzig, Humboldt Universität, Universität Göttingen, and Stadtarchiv Uslar.

My thanks go to the interlibrary loan team at La Trobe University Library who retrieved many obscure digitized documents from the libraries of Europe. Some nineteenth-century published texts are thankfully now available in free digitized form on the internet, and I sourced many documents from the Internet Archive (archive.com), Project Gutenberg, the Hathi Trust, the Wellcome Library, the Bibliothèque nationale de France Catalogue Général, the OPACPlus search engine at the Bayerische Staatsbibliothek, the Österreichisches Staatsarchiv, the Zentralbibliothek Zürich, and Google Books. The Kalliope-Verbund search engine from the Staatsbibliothek zu Berlin was a valuable starting point to identify letters held in archives across Germany, and the Subito search engine identified library holdings of hard-to-find books. I sourced historic newspaper articles from Zefys Zeitungsinformationssystem, the British Newspaper Archive, and e-newspaperarchives.ch, and German police notices from adelsquellen.de. To confirm births, deaths, and marriage documents I used ancestry.com.

Spidery nineteenth-century Gothic (Fraktur) copperplate can be a challenge to transcribe, and I am especially thankful to Rolf Thalmann in Basel, Switzerland, who diligently and efficiently transcribed hundreds of letters of variable quality. Barbara Hein and Johanna Riese gave some initial help transcribing two letters. Thanks to Camille Nurka for her tireless work proofreading and to Rolf Thalmann and Sarah Jäckel for proofing the German. Several others deserve a mention for helping me along the way. Klaus Müller, Helmut Neuhold, and René Hornung each read and commented on early versions of three chapters. Rolf Thalmann, Jörg Hutter, Jens Dobler, Francesca Campani, Manfred Herzer, Ralf Dose, Hannes Sulzenbacher, Philipp Hofstetter, and Kyle Frackman each helped retrieve letters and obscure texts.

I am also grateful to the La Trobe University History Department, including Dr. Timothy Jones, Dr. Liz Conor, Dr. Claudia Haake, Prof. Katie Holmes, and Prof. Adrian Jones for their editorial input and timely counsel at various points. Several people deserve thanks for encouraging me to take the steps into scholarly historical study. Daryl Scott Lindsey encouraged me to write about Ulrichs over coffee in Berlin in the summer of 2010. Aimée Samuels-Meens helped me explore sustainable ways to make this happen in 2016. Prof. Edward Hollis in Edinburgh advised and encouraged me to write.

The Australian Commonwealth funded the research and writing of this book, and grants from the School of Humanities and Social Sciences Internal Research Grant Scheme and the La Trobe University Social Research Assistance Platform funded transcription and archive costs.

Finally, this book was written through Australia's worst ever fire season and 259 days of COVID-19 lockdown in Melbourne. It was also written while I was mourning the deaths of three close relatives and one dear friend. My thanks go to my long-suffering husband, Peter, who shared the grief and has put up with all my late nights translating, writing, and editing. I could not have finished this book without his patient, uncomplaining support.

Notes on Terminology

This book is about the men who called themselves "urnings," a neologism proposed for same-sex-attracted men by Karl Heinrich Ulrichs in 1864.[1] I have preferenced the original German rendering of this word rather than the English translation "uranian," which was introduced by John Addington Symonds in the 1890s and bore different nuances of meaning. The only exception to this general usage is in the final chapter on Symonds.

Of course, urning was not the only word circulating in Germany in the period under consideration. In 1869, Karl Friedrich Otto Westphal, the director of mental and nervous diseases at the Charité Hospital in Berlin, coined the clinical term *conträre Geschlechtsempfindung* (contrary sexual feeling).[2] The first appearance of the word "homosexual" was in a letter that Karl Maria Kertbeny sent to Karl Heinrich Ulrichs in 1868.[3] Although "homosexual" was used in print several times, it did not become common until Richard von Krafft-Ebing started using it in *Psychopathia Sexualis*.[4] Initially, these three words had different, albeit overlapping, meanings; in practice, however, they were used interchangeably in the psychiatric and sexological literature. There is no evidence, though, that the two other terms were used widely as self-descriptors in the period under discussion. Letters, autobiographic texts, and contemporary literature show that it was the word "urning" that was used for the purpose of self-description.[5] It may be that, particularly after the controversial trials of 1868–9 (see chapter 3), widespread media dissemination and public discussion of the "urning" category led to that word being used even by men who had not read Ulrichs's texts.

Prior to Ulrichs's intervention, sexuality was imperfectly located by terminology relating to specific sexual acts: *pederast/sodomit* (anal intercourse) and *Knabenschänder* (boy molester). There was no word at all for the same-sex-attracted person who did not engage in any sexual act or for those who only practised mutual masturbation. Such individuals were invisible to the discourses of the day. The imprecision of these earlier terms and the diversity of options post-1864 led to a particular terminological difficulty in describing same-sex-attracted men over the whole period. So, this book uses "same-sex-attracted" to account for individuals living at a time when there was no terminology but also to describe individuals over a longer period when various terms were in use. Similarly, "queer" is used in this book as a general descriptor for the period before terminology as well as for the longer period through successive language transition. Previously, "queer" was considered an anachronistic term that would not have been comprehensible to men living in Germany in the nineteenth century. However, in more recent historiography there has been a discursive shift in usage.[6] Whereas in preceding decades, the word had an epoch-specific role in rejecting liberal humanism vis-à-vis "queer theory," it is now increasingly used by Anglo-American historians in a different sense to suggest an expansive or inclusive approach towards sexual and gender diversity. There is also an increasing tendency among historians to use the word "queer" in a more genealogical sense to account for sexual and gender categories imperfectly located within or before periods when identities began to take on more modern definitions. It is with those more recent historiographical definitions in mind that "queer" is used in the title and occasionally throughout this book.

URNING

The Age of the Urning

It was only when I was about 30 years old that I came across the writings of Numa (Ulrichs) and I cannot describe what a relief it was for me to learn that there were many other men who were just as sexually inclined as I was, and that what I felt sexually was not an aberration but a special sexual disposition inherent in me by nature. For the first time I experienced the pleasure of finding sexual satisfaction through direct contact with a man's body. I no longer tried in vain to fight against a deeply implanted disposition and since I let my urning nature run free, I am happier, healthier and more efficient![1]

The above passage was written in 1885 by an independently wealthy forty-eight-year-old scientific writer in a letter to the psychiatrist Richard von Krafft-Ebing. This man recounted his early sense of sexual drive towards handsome men, especially young officers "in tight-fitting trousers and tightly laced uniforms," his failed attempts at coitus with a woman, his largely sexless marriage, and, although he was masculine in appearance and demeanour, his incipient effeminate tastes for needlework and weeping in theatres. However, the watershed moment when he made sense of and reordered his whole sexual being came through his engagement with the works of Karl Heinrich Ulrichs. Ulrichs, a lawyer from the Kingdom of Hanover, wrote and published twelve pamphlets between 1864 and 1879 arguing for the rights of men he called "urnings." He defined the urning as a man who was sexually attracted to his own sex and sexually repelled by the opposite sex. Many of Ulrichs's readers, such as this man, took on the description of the urning in his books as a personal identity. For this man, it was not just encountering the neologism "urning" that changed his life; it was also the realization through his reading that he had a "special sexual disposition" inherent in him and that this was shared by a whole class of men just like him. Suddenly all the facets of his sexual being had come together to form a single identity. The effect on his life was transformative.

Ulrichs was not the first to publish a plea for the rights of same-sex-attracted men. Heinrich Hössli, a milliner in Glarus, Switzerland, had done so earlier, in 1836–8.[2] Nor was Ulrichs the first to propound a new biological theory with its own nomenclature. Claude-François Michéa in 1849 had described the *philopede* in the forensic literature and backed that categorizing terminology with a scientific explanation.[3] But although they were pioneers, neither Hössli nor Michéa inspired readers to adopt a new terminology or identity.[4] Ulrichs's writings did just that: during the 1860s, Ulrichs's concept of identity, articulated in print, manifested itself as a new personage in German society.

The search for the discursive turn that transformed the status of sex and sexuality historically has been satirized by Eve Kozovsky Sedgwick as the "Great Paradigm Shift."[5] This book makes the case for locating the origin of modern sexual categories and identities in Germany in 1864, the place and the year that Ulrichs started publishing his pamphlets. For the next thirty-three years, same-sex-attracted men in the German-speaking world referred to themselves as "urnings" to the exclusion of any other terminology. In 1897, when Magnus Hirschfeld convened the inaugural meeting of the world's first queer rights organization, the Wissenschaftlich-humanitäres Komitee (Scientific Humanitarian Committee), he could do so because men calling themselves urnings had prepared the way in the preceding decades. The men who called themselves urnings in the years up to 1897 inaugurated a strikingly modern sensibility about sex and sexuality. Urnings were not a passive and transient audience; in fact, they actively engaged with Ulrichs through correspondence.

This is a history constructed from the words that self-identifying urnings wrote about themselves. Drawing directly from the correspondence that urning readers sent to Ulrichs, the research presented in this book aims to reconstruct their world. German historians had already found some of the correspondence and published some of it in facsimile.[6] Over several years I was able to add to this reserve by excavating fragments of letters from Ulrichs's writings, visiting and securing digital copies from archives in Germany and Hungary, and contacting other archives in Germany, Austria, and Switzerland to secure digital copies via email. By the time I finished, I had assembled an archive of more than four hundred letters. With the help of a transcriber, I translated the letters, publishing the majority of these in 2020 as *The Correspondence of Karl Heinrich Ulrichs, 1846–1894*.[7] That collection of translated letters forms the core archive used in this book.

Published autobiographical accounts, including autobiographical psychiatric case studies as well as the memoirs of several elderly urnings written at the turn of the century, augmented the archive of letters. I translated the autobiographical case studies contained in the works of Richard von Krafft-Ebing in a second critical edition of sources published in 2023 as *Queer Voices in the Works of Richard von Krafft-Ebing, 1883–1901*.[8] Finally, there was an "invisible archive" of letters now lost, described but not quoted in other sources. The analysis of these autobiographical and epistolary sources, which carry the voices of urnings, delivers insights that are substantially different from those found in historical studies that rely only on the published works of elite writers. The analysis reveals what is apparently a dynamic and motivated cadre of self-identifying urnings, some of whom corresponded with Ulrichs, carried out widespread community building, engaged with the scientific discourse, worked behind the scenes to improve the lot of fellow urnings, and translated and reinterpreted Ulrichs's ideas for an international audience. As the research progressed, the men who followed Ulrichs emerged, revealing the details of their lives and their contributions to the furtherance of the urnings' cause.

This book, the result of all that research, is a history from below that seeks to understand and describe the world of men who called themselves urnings in nineteenth-century German-speaking Europe. However, before proceeding, it is worth considering what social, scientific, and political considerations made 1860s Germany the optimal period for the transmission of modern sexual identities. There were conditions in 1860s Germany that supported the emergence of modern, self-aware individuals comfortable with their urning sexual identity. There are reasons to believe that neither the timing nor the place was at all accidental. Ulrichs was a remarkable man and the originator of transformative ideas on sexuality, but he would not have achieved a breakthrough transmission of his ideas had the circumstances not been optimal.

Ulrichs's Germany

When Ulrichs launched his campaign in the 1860s, the country we now call Germany was a fragmented polity, largely non-urbanized and pre-industrial, and thus quite distinct from its urbanized industrial neighbours.[9] The German states had taken a different route to modernization, pursuing it largely through a massive expansion and transformation of their universities so that they came to resemble modern research institutions.[10] No other nation was taking a similar path.[11] Karl Marx observed in 1844 that although the Germans were backward industrially and in practical political development, they were far advanced in their progressive philosophical outlook.[12] This was most evident in the dominant class of university-educated men, the *Bildungsbürgertum*, who played such a leading role in the revolutions of 1848.[13] The revolutions involved all classes of Germans, but many of their leaders, such as Rudolf Virchow, were liberal academics and scientists who saw their involvement in revolution as an extension of their intellectual practice.[14] That scientists were at the forefront of political and legal reform was a feature of this period in German history and was reflected in the enhanced status of both the individuals and their scientific ideas.[15] Ultimately the political outcomes of the 1848 revolutions foundered on a fundamental polarization between progressives, who favoured a broad democratic union that included Austria (*Großdeutsche Lösung*), and conservatives, who favoured a smaller autocratic state dominated by Prussia (*Kleindeutsche Lösung*).[16] However, few people doubted that unification in some form was inevitable now that the German states were already drawing together economically and politically under a loose Confederation Parliament in Frankfurt.[17]

The German Confederation comprised thirty-nine kingdoms, princely states, archduchies, bishoprics, and free cities, including the regional powers Prussia and Austria.[18] The imminence of political reorganization offered tantalizing prospects for reform, in that the unified German state, however it was configured, would have to establish a new legal code. This had implications for sexual law reform as each of the thirty-nine states had its own legal system and some of them had no antisodomy law. Bavaria had repealed its antisodomy laws with Paul Johann Anselm Ritter von Feuerbach's thoroughly modern legal code of 1813.[19] Based on that code, the states of Württemberg (1839), Brunswick (1840), Hanover (1840), and Thuringia (1852) reformed their own criminal laws to remove sodomy as a crime. However, whereas the Bavarian legal code removed all prohibitions on "unnatural sex," most of the others retained some exceptions.[20] Most of the rest of the German states followed versions of the archaic *Constitio Carolina* of the Holy Roman Empire, which ostensibly required the death penalty for sodomy.[21] Prussia and Austria had reformed a little but retained antisodomy laws. Josef II's *Strafgesetzbuch* (1787) for Habsburg territories had ended the death penalty for male and female same-sex behaviour, instead punishing it with hard labour.[22] Paragraph 143 of Prussia's *Allgemeine Landrecht* of 1794 dropped any prohibition against same-sex sexual expression among women; however, it punished "unnatural fornication, whether between persons of the male sex or of humans with beasts," with between one and four years' imprisonment.[23] In general, prosecutions for sodomy were infrequent even in places like Berlin, where there was a strong police presence. Even in mid-1860s Berlin there were only two to three prosecutions per year.[24] In Prussia, it was only anal intercourse that was specifically prohibited by law, not other sexual acts, and it was notoriously difficult to secure a conviction. Published crime statistics over the next decades suggested to the German public that sexual crime was an increasing problem even though those statistics were largely an artefact of an increase in police ranks and the expansion of categories for prosecution.[25] The few cases that did reach the courts were open to public scrutiny, and some of those cases led to sensational trials that were widely covered in newspapers.[26] These high-profile trials fostered a grubby trade in blackmail. At this point in history, most same-sex-attracted men were unlikely to be prosecuted but feared the public shame from exposure that blackmail threatened. Graham Robb's insight into nineteenth-century England is also true about Germany: same-sex-attracted people at that time "lived under a cloud but it seldom rained."[27]

In 1862, only a small proportion of Germans lived in cities or large towns.[28] The overwhelming majority still lived in small towns, in villages, or in the open countryside. In the same period, the Great Powers of Europe were urbanizing quickly. For example, in 1862 fully one fifth of the United Kingdom's inhabitants lived in cities.[29] Germany would not begin to reshape itself as an urbanized state until the 1870s. Prior to the 1860s, only the cities of Berlin and Vienna experienced any growth. Berlin grew rapidly, from a population of about 400,000 in the 1840s to 865,000 by 1871.[30] The cosmopolitan and anonymous nature of big-city life allowed subcultures to emerge. Reports from as early as 1782 suggest that specialized clubs for same-sex-attracted men were in operation.[31] In 1837, the Berlin police arrested Friedrich Wadzeck for running a kind of "pederast's brothel."[32] Beginning around that time, a sexual subculture became more evident and a target for those in the administration concerned about the city's moral health. In an analysis of prostitution in Berlin, the man who was to become Berlin's chief of police only two years later, Wilhelm Stieber, wrote anonymously in 1846: "There are formal areas of the city which form the gathering places of such atrocities (in particular, the chestnut grove behind the new guardhouse and the carp pond in the Tiergarten are to be emphasised in this respect), and not a few people, especially common soldiers, who make a trade out of it, are sought out here."[33]

Berlin also had the beginnings of a homosocial scene, with dedicated venues touting their business in the 1860s. As Hugo Friedländer, reflecting on his youth, wrote in 1914: "At that time, Berlin was not yet a cosmopolitan city; small-town, cosy conditions prevailed, which did not remain without influence on the intercourse among the homosexuals. It was very cosy in the homosexual pubs, since almost all the people knew each other. At the balls, the most cheerful merriment prevailed. It was like being at a big family ball."[34]

Over the next three decades as Germany urbanized, homosocial infrastructures emerged in other places as well.[35] Vienna had seen a growth rate similar to that of Berlin, and, like Berlin, that growth spurred the emergence of a queer demimonde. By the mid-nineteenth century, the Spittelberg Quarter had emerged as a centre for the sex trade, with establishments catering to same-sex-attracted men.[36] The Prater, the Rathauspark, and the Volksgarten had sections that were used as cruising areas.[37] The amusement arcade Eldorado, on Petersplatz, and the Universum pleasure garden were known as romping grounds for same-sex-attracted men.[38] Finally, the ancient but fashionably rebuilt Brünnlbad became, in the 1860s, a renowned meeting place.[39] Later on, the Zentralbad, opened in 1889, would become the preferred bathhouse for same-sex-attracted men.[40]

Outside the cities, opportunities to meet, socialize, and have sex with like-minded individuals were considerably more limited. In garrison towns, however, transactional *Soldatenliebe* (soldier love) was a subcultural feature of this period. Even before the revolutions of 1848, many German states had developed large standing armies in the expectation of instability and conflict. These soldiers were mostly young, underpaid men garrisoned in towns where it was possible for them to supplement their wages through prostitution. Ulrichs was himself attracted to soldiers and considered this sexual predilection to be "dominant in Germany."[41] The widespread availability of soldier-prostitutes in towns across Germany meant that some men became exclusively attracted to men in uniform.

Attitudes towards sexually active "pederasts" (sodomites) were universally hostile even in those states that had decriminalized such activities and in cities that had emerging subcultures.[42] One thousand years of legal and religious prohibition had left a deep mark on society. However, attitudes towards non-normative gender presentation and same-sex sensuality were not always as clearly negative. In part, this was an artefact of how pre-industrial Germany was socially organized and the consequent status of German manhood. Industrializing and urbanizing nations like France and Britain had already moved towards a social structure in which hegemonic bourgeois masculinity dictated sharply separate spheres for the sexes. In Germany, where urban industrialization came late, this change would not occur in any meaningful way until well into the 1870s. In the 1860s, German manhood was still a contested space.[43] In that decade, older Enlightenment concepts of German manhood coexisted with more modern bourgeois sensibilities. The older Enlightenment models of masculinity valorized homosociality, reflecting a tradition of idealized male–male friendship that some have characterized as a "queer proto-identity."[44] In addition, widespread military deployment had introduced a militaristic-gentry masculine identity, one that stemmed from older *Junker* (Prussian) or *Adel* (Austrian) classes of the minor nobility that valorized the "whole man" as a military adventurer.[45] These pre-bourgeois admixtures of revolutionary, military, and older aristocratic forms of masculinity, with their subformations of bohemian licence and libertinage, coexisted alongside the more urban, middle-class "whole man" masculinity in the decades leading up to the 1860s, and both were still present alongside new bourgeois sensibilities in that decade, during which boundaries between public and private were still porous, people married late, and the liberal-nationalist political class favoured a more egalitarian balance between the sexes.[46] The consequence was that no model of masculinity was hegemonic in this decade and there was room for alternative models to emerge within the margins of multiple competing masculinities.

Ulrichs and his followers drew on prevalent discourses of homosociality, Greek and Roman classicism, and newer discourses of medical science when forming new structures of identity.[47] The aftermath of the revolution in the 1850s meant that political activity was subdued, but this started to change in the 1860s, at which time a politicized class inclined towards activism began to emerge.[48] With unification in the air, debates over an appropriate legal system for the future state came to the fore. One of the existing legal codes, or a new legal code based on them, would become the law of the land. The decade saw advances by trade unions and the formal organization of a national feminist association and the Social Democratic Party.[49] The early part of the 1860s was thus an optimally strategic time for a German political intervention on behalf of urnings; it was also the time when such an intervention would attract the most attentive urning audience. The rights of workers and women became prevailing discourses of the age, as did, with Ulrichs's advocacy, the rights of same-sex-attracted men. Ulrichs seized his opportunity to contest the space.

Early in 1862, Ulrichs withdrew himself from paid employment in order to write two pamphlets arguing for the human rights of same-sex-attracted men.[50] He gave these pamphlets Latin names, *Vindex* and *Inclusa*, and published them under a pseudonym, Numa Numantius. In these pamphlets he proposed the neologism "urning" to describe a class of men who were attracted to their own sex. This first account provided a biological explanation and positioned the urning as an individual with the body of a man but the love-drive of a woman. This was a third gender model of sexuality that approximated what Eve Sedgwick has characterized as a "minoritizing" identity.[51] Sedgwick famously identified two concepts of sexuality that have prevailed over time, a "universalizing" definition that stressed that all people were capable of any sexual behaviour and that sexual behaviour could be modified, and a "minoritizing" definition where sexual orientation was conceived as fixed for life and limited to a particular group. Ulrichs by writing his pamphlets had launched the urning as a new, minoritized sexual identity. Right from the start, he sent copies of his pamphlets to influential groups, including prominent psychiatrists, and in due course some psychiatrists started to write on the subject as well. They used their own terminologies, but the ideas were substantially the same. Soon after he published his first two pamphlets, encouraged by the letters he received from readers, Ulrichs wrote three more. He would go on to write twelve pamphlets in all between 1864 and 1880 in which he presented ever more elaborate versions of the urning identity based on the accounts in letters he received from readers. The outline of the urning character that Ulrichs presented in print had, for his readers, become a name and a sexual identity. In time, the term urning and the sexual identity attached to it would circulate beyond this readership. Although it differed in several respects from our twenty-first-century queer sensibilities, the urning identity was nevertheless the first modern same-sex sexual identity. Arguably, this development in sexual ontology fomented by Ulrichs's pamphlet activism approximated the social transition first identified and proposed by Michel Foucault in 1976.

Foucault's Proposition

Michel Foucault famously identified the discursive shift around sexuality that occurred in the final decades of the nineteenth century in volume 1 of his *History of Sexuality*.[52] The main passage in that volume relating to the "invention" of the homosexual has become well known:

> As defined by the ancient civil or canonical codes, sodomy was a category
> of forbidden acts; their perpetrator was nothing more than the juridical
> subject of them. The nineteenth-century homosexual became a personage,
> a past, a case history, and a childhood, in addition to being a type of life,
> a life form, and a morphology, with an indiscreet anatomy and possibly a
> mysterious physiology. Nothing that went into his total composition was
> unaffected by his sexuality. It was everywhere present in him: at the root

of all his actions because it was their insidious and indefinitely active principle; written immodestly on his face and body because it was a secret that always gave itself away. It was consubstantial with him, less as a habitual sin than as a singular nature. We must not forget that the psychological, psychiatric, medical category of homosexuality was constituted from the moment it was characterized – Westphal's famous article of 1870 on "contrary sexual sensations" can stand as its date of birth – less by a type of sexual relations than by a certain quality of sexual sensibility, a certain way of inverting the masculine and the feminine in oneself. Homosexuality appeared as one of the forms of sexuality when it was transposed from the practice of sodomy onto a kind of interior androgyny, a hermaphrodism of the soul. The sodomite had been a temporary aberration; the homosexual was now a species.[53]

Foucault was making important new observations about a real shift in discourse over the century. The nineteenth century opened with the churches dominating the terms of sexual discourse, and their focus was on individual acts as sins. By the end of the century, psychiatric pioneers were articulating new discourses of sexual orientation. Sexuality as an organizational concept emerged from this discursive shift, and the production of the homosexual identity was one of several outcomes. At the same time, Foucault noted the independent self-definition of same-sex-attracted individuals. The appearance of the "homosexual," he wrote, "also made possible the formation of a 'reverse' discourse: homosexuality began to speak on its own behalf, to demand that its legitimacy or 'naturality' be acknowledged, often in the same vocabulary, using the same categories by which it was medically disqualified."[54]

Foucault was referring here to how individuals took on these identities after the psychiatric discourse had produced them. He clarified this point in an interview he gave shortly after publishing the first volume of *The History of Sexuality*:

All you have to do is look at the notion of homosexuality in 1870 to see, if you will, that the great debate on homosexuality, and against the segregation of homosexuality, took off in the next twenty years and to realize that there was an absolutely correlative phenomenon to all this: it was an attempt to imprison people within this notion of homosexuality, and naturally they fought back – people like Gide, like Oscar Wilde, like Magnus Hirschfeld, and so on.[55]

Unfortunately, in the decade that followed Foucault's groundbreaking work, comments such as that one led to the erroneous conclusion

by some historians that the homosexual had no independent concep-
tual existence until he was codified by psychiatry.[56] These accounts
relegated Ulrichs and the men who followed him to footnotes or presented them only in passing as irrelevant oddities.[57] So pervasive was
this early historiographical neglect that in more recent works focusing
on the period, it has become a trope of the genre to address the "Foucauldian problem."[58] The following discussion will suggest a way to accommodate the important points Foucault was making and adapt them
to an understanding of queer identity formation in the period before
psychiatry turned its gaze to the homosexual.

It is important to be completely clear about what Foucault was proposing. In fact, he wrote comparatively little about homosexuality, and
what he did write amounted to initial impressions from a perusal of the
literature. At the time he was writing the first volume of *History of Sexuality* (first published in 1976), historical investigations of the homosexual nineteenth century were in their infancy.[59] Foucault's genealogical
analysis specifically identified a change in the modes of disqualifica-
tion – from religious/legal to psychiatric – encountered in published
works during this period.[60] In context, this was a surprisingly astute
observation. Scholarly writing does undergo a change in focus, from
the policing and prosecution of sexual acts to literature concerned with
the inner lives of individuals with a fixed identity in the final decades
of the nineteenth century.[61] However, this was not his only speculation
about the long history of sexuality, and it was never intended to be his
last word on the origins of homosexuality.

Foucault revised and reworked many of his ideas over the course of
his writing, including his ideas about the origins of sexual categories.
For example, in an earlier work, *Madness and Civilization*, he located the
origin of homosexuality in the seventeenth century.[62] In his original outline for *The History of Sexuality*, he envisaged several volumes, one of
which would focus entirely on the "Perversions." Foucault did not keep
to that outline, focusing instead on classical Greece and Rome in the two
volumes he had completed by the time of his death in 1984. There are
indications that his thinking was in transition in his final years. Within
months of the publication of *History of Sexuality*, volume 1, his position
on the periodization of homosexual origins became much more nuanced,
particularly after he read John Boswell's pioneering work on the Vatican
archives.[63] It is probable that had he lived to write the volume on "Perversions" in the late 1980s, a fuller account of the history of homosexuality would have emerged, more anchored in historical analysis. There are
some indications in his later publications that his ideas were evolving. In
the second volume of *History of Sexuality*, Foucault came back to his ideas

on the origins of homosexuality. It seems that he anticipated a longer historical process: "In nineteenth-century texts there is a stereotypical portrait of the homosexual or invert … One could doubtless trace the long history of this image (to which actual behaviours may have corresponded, through a complex play of inductions and attitudes of defiance)."[64] His ideas about the formation of queer identities were also in a state of transition during this period.

Foucault in his later works was preoccupied with the subjectification and inscription of "docile bodies." However, an undue focus on that sits uneasily with the question of resistance – which was arguably the main driver, and object, of all his writings.[65] There are reasons to believe that he would have taken a different path through subjectification and personal agency had he come back to the subject of homosexuality in his subsequent work. In a seminar delivered at the University of Vermont in the autumn of 1982, Foucault gave an indication of where his thinking was heading: "Perhaps I've insisted too much on the technology of domination and power. I am more and more interested in the interaction between oneself and others and in the technologies of individual domination, the history of how an individual acts upon himself in the technology of self."[66]

Foucault's thinking in the 1980s became more focused on the creative processes of self-invention that he observed in contemporary gay culture.[67] Perhaps if he had been aware of Ulrichs and the men who called themselves urnings, he would have been similarly impressed with their creative reworking of their own *technology of self*. It is conceivable that had he then written a more rigorously researched volume on the "Perversions," he would have examined the emerging scholarship to build a more complex picture.

Speculating on unwritten intentions is not an end in itself, and there is still much to be gained from Foucault's analytical approach when investigating new material. While the "urning" that emerged in the 1860s as "a personage, a past, a case history, and a childhood"[68] was certainly a social identity that can be understood through a Foucauldian lens, Foucault's later ideas about the technology of self and individuation, though they lack the theoretical concreteness of his earlier work, may be of use. However, Foucault was a cultural theorist, not a social historian, and the sources he used from the published record tended to be at least one step removed from the men who were living in the nineteenth century with the new forms of sexual identity. An epistolary history focused specifically on the autobiographical accounts of urning men – which is what this book is – has the potential to answer and correct some of the impressions raised by Foucault's theorizations about sexuality.

Methods: The Analysis of Letters and Autobiography

By publishing his ideas and terminology in twelve pamphlets, Ulrichs opened up a discursive field in the public sphere and initiated the emergence of a grassroots community of same-sex-attracted men across the German-speaking world and beyond. Many of his initial readers responded to the pamphlets with letters; he then published extracts from those letters in his next pamphlets. This discursive loop of correspondence and quotation constituted what Nancy Fraser has called a "subaltern counter-public."[69] Through the medium of correspondence, the men who self-identified as urnings circulated counter-discourses through which they could entertain and rehearse their identities, interests, and needs without being censured by the liberal bourgeois public sphere in 1860s Germany. An epistolary history derived from these sources delivers a historical narrative substantially different from those that rely solely on published elite texts. The disinterested dissection of Ulrichs's theories as just one in a succession of textual impressions instead becomes a highly personalized response to those same ideas from men who took them on as social identities. The impact of Ulrichs's intervention is measured first by the responses from men who engaged directly with it and for whom it had the greatest meaning. Later, some of these men became rounded out as characters in their own right propounding the urning cause in their own ways. In this way, the period between Ulrichs's activism and 1897, when Magnus Hirschfeld inaugurated a more formal movement – for so long a neglected period of queer history – is repopulated and reanimated and can be better understood.

Ulrichs and the urnings were not unique in using correspondence subversively. In the late eighteenth century, a homosocial epistolary tradition flourished in literary circles around the celebrated art historian Johann Joachim Winckelmann.[70] The constellation of correspondence forming around Ulrichs was less concerned with homosociality. In fact, Ulrichs kept strictly to a rule that the network of correspondence should not be a vehicle for sexual contact.[71] Instead, Ulrichs's correspondents shared their self-understanding, experience, news, and insights in a serious engagement with the urning cause. They also shared publications: Ulrichs's correspondents alerted him to the works of Johann Ludwig Casper and Heinrich Hössli, and others sent scientific papers and details of scholarly lectures and made sure his pamphlets were stocked in libraries in Vienna, Zurich, and London. In that sense, the community of correspondence was more like that of the mimeograph-sharing "Samizdat" dissidents of the twentieth-century Soviet Union.

The letters Ulrichs received from his readers serve as a starting point to gauge his impact on and the reaction of the men who self-described as urnings. Many of the physical letters themselves have not survived. This is particularly true of the urning letters sent to Ulrichs in response to his writings that are the focus of the earlier chapters in this book. All that remains of those letters are passages selected by him to illustrate points in his pamphlets. Ulrichs often presented these passages as anonymous fragments devoid of their epistolary context. While it is possible that Ulrichs faithfully transcribed each fragment from a letter he had received, it is also possible that he "corrected" or reworded some of these. If so, what editorial criteria did he apply? When evaluating the licence he took when rewriting his correspondence for publication, it is worth remembering that these letters were only a tiny fraction of the ones he received.[72] Clearly there is no way to be confident there was no curation or editorial interference with letter contents, and that should make us wary of treating these letters as providing direct and unmediated access to the entire truth.

This prompts us to ask certain questions. What criteria did he apply when selecting the letters he cited? Almost certainly he quoted from the letters that best illustrated the points he wanted to make, but what was the nature of the correspondence he did *not* use? Very few of the quoted letters come from masculine individuals, and Ulrichs did allude to the fact that some masculine men objected to his ideas. Very early on, a masculine urning from central Germany met Ulrichs socially. When Ulrichs recounted his ideas about the femininity of urnings, the man got quite upset and indignantly declared, "We are men!"[73] This prompts us to ask whether Ulrichs was deliberately excluding critical letters from masculine urnings. Ulrichs later referred to a "party of Grumblers" among his correspondents and how one particular "detractor from Munich" pursued him with letters into Italian exile. Although these letters were not quoted from directly and have not survived, Ulrichs did not stint from acknowledging the masculine discourse and accommodating it in a modification of his theory.

Ulrichs did not write an autobiography, although he did scatter biographical details here and there throughout his works. However, he was entirely open about his own sexual nature, so his description of the urning inadvertently became a challenge to his readers to examine and account for themselves. In this way, Ulrichs inaugurated what was to become a tradition of autobiographical empiricism that would characterize urning advocacy in the decades to follow.[74] While it is tempting to see the autobiographical letters as "truthful" historical accounts, some caution should prevail. The first letter quoted gave explicit permission for publication, but was this the case with every letter reproduced? And if the letter writers were writing specifically for publication, how does that shape our interpretation of these as historical documents? Where the letters include autobiographical elements, one should approach these as retrospective accounts where a linear chronology starts and ends at the finish.[75] They were not detailed blow-by-blow eyewitness accounts but instead "fictionalized" models of elements and features of the narrator's life. The "autobiographical" letters in most cases therefore tell us more about self-perception and self-presentation than about verifiable events.[76] Reading the letters with these considerations in mind, it is possible nevertheless to draw certain conclusions about the impact of Ulrichs's ideas.

Chapters

This book charts the history of the urning as a category of identity from 1864, tracing the men who embraced that identity in the years that followed, and concludes in 1897, when Magnus Hirschfeld launched the Wissenschaftlich-humanitäres Komitee. Part One of the book, chapters 1 to 4, covers the years up to 1870 during which Ulrichs was highly active and the dominant theorist of urning Germany. Part Two, chapters 5 to 8, covers the years 1871 to 1897 during which Ulrichs stepped back and the agency of other urnings came to the fore.

Chapter 1 outlines the life of Karl Heinrich Ulrichs, the first urning, and describes his pioneering campaign. Ulrichs was an original theorist and one of the first queer activists. His campaign to end the persecution of urnings ostensibly failed. However, in proposing a neologism and a "third sex" model of sexuality, Ulrichs inaugurated an ontological turn that would transform queer society.

Chapter 2 focuses on the men who read Ulrichs's pamphlets and responded by writing to him. Ulrichs introduced a new name and the outline of an identity, but it was only through the reception of this by others that it became a collective identity. The intense networking through correspondence that marks this period lays to rest any sense that Ulrichs's campaign was lonely and monomaniacal. For several years, he acted as a spokesperson for an ever-growing circle of urning followers. Using the letters that Ulrichs reproduced in his pamphlets and some of Ulrichs's own descriptions, this chapter maps out nine character types apparent in the 1860s and the years that followed. This character typology will serve as a heuristic for understanding each of the urnings profiled in the chapters that follow.

Chapter 3 profiles the sensational trials of Friedrich Feldtmann in Bremen and Carl Zastrow in Berlin, held in 1867 and 1869 respectively. Both these trials generated a media firestorm and captured the public imagination, for these two defendants were the first two individuals other than Ulrichs to use the word "urning" to describe themselves publicly. In so doing, they propelled Ulrichs and his theories into the public gaze, so that the urning became a universal public identity appraised by the wider population. But at the same time, as Scott Spector writes, the Zastrow trial ensured that the urning became linked to notions of violence and sexual horror in the public consciousness. That trial coincided with deliberations on a unified legal code for Germany; thus, it appears that an early manifestation of the twentieth century's culture wars ensured that the authorities retained the antisodomy law in the new code.

Chapter 4 focuses on two groups of same-sex-attracted men in the urban setting who had established a *modus operandi* independent of Ulrichs and who did not necessarily respond positively to his message. In the larger cities, communities of cross-dressing men and masculine men who hid their orientations but transacted sex in secret had been a feature of the urban environment well before Ulrichs's activism. They wrote letters to Ulrichs but were among the least receptive to his epistemic politics. One such correspondent was Karl Maria Kertbeny, an erstwhile masculine supporter who became a disaffected rival. Ulrichs also received several accounts of cross-dressing from urnings in London and Vienna; however, these correspondents cared more about their escapades than about the rights of urnings.

Part Two of this book covers the years after the German Empire had been united under Prussian rule. Ulrichs stepped back from overt activism and, in 1880, left for Italy. In his place, other urnings took up Ulrichs's activist banner. Chapter 5 tells the remarkable story of a young man who studied at Ulrichs's feet and then took his ideas, and his pamphlets, back to Switzerland. Jakob Rudolf Forster first encountered Ulrichs in Stuttgart in 1878 and became an ardent acolyte. He then returned to Zurich to put what he had learned into action. He was repeatedly thrown into prison for his efforts over ten years of state persecution. Forster was particularly notable for his indefatigability. His fostering of a networked urning community in Zurich was possibly a mode of grassroots activism in which others across Germany and Austria were also engaged, although they have not left written traces. Forster was unusual in that he wrote about his efforts in his autobiography, which is the main source for this chapter.

Chapter 6 turns to the engagement between Ulrichs and his urning followers with Germany's "new psychiatry" and positions this as the longest-running urning campaign, spanning four decades. Ulrichs captured the attention of psychiatrists in the 1860s. In the 1870s, psychiatrists began studying same-sex sexuality. Taking their lead from Ulrichs, a small group of urnings lobbied the Viennese psychiatrist Richard von Krafft-Ebing in the 1880s and 1890s. The analysis in this chapter focuses on the agency of these individuals, who sent Krafft-Ebing their sexual autobiographies in the hope of changing his mind about the pathological nature of the urning disposition.

By the mid-1880s, Berlin was home to a growing and increasingly visible urning scene that had started to attract the attention of the city police. Chapter 7 focuses on Adolf Glaser, a writer and publisher who had had his own tangle with the police. Glaser cultivated a friendship with the senior officer responsible for the policing of urnings: Leopold von Meerscheidt-Hüllessem. Over the course of the next decade, Glaser encouraged his friend to become an ally to Berlin's urnings and redirect police resources to the prosecution of blackmailers. Glaser's influential friendship serves as an early example of police liaison as a campaign tactic.

Chapter 8 centres on the eminent English man of letters and avid follower of Walt Whitman, John Addington Symonds, who had come across Ulrichs's writings, among other sexological texts, while writing a sexual autobiography. Symonds synthesized a new uranian theory in a privately printed polemic that brought together Ulrichs's minoritized identity with Hellenism and Whitman's masculine comradely adhesion. After visiting Ulrichs in Aquila, he collaborated with Henry Havelock Ellis and Edward Carpenter on the first work of English sexology. The result was a modified homosexual identity that was subsequently promulgated in England and the English-speaking world by Edward Carpenter.

Finally, in the conclusion to this book there is a discussion of the social and linguistic changes that brought the Age of the Urning to a close. Magnus Hirschfeld convened the first meeting of the Wissenschaftlich-humanitäres Komitee (WhK), and masculinists critiqued the "third sex" model of sexuality. In the years that followed, Kertbeny's neologism "homosexual" displaced "urning" as the preferred nomenclature.

After the conclusion, a timeline of events iterates all the events described in the eight chapters of this book. The chapters span a period of thirty-three years, with each chapter centring on only a few years within that time period. Since there are overlaps in the time period of each chapter, the timeline breaks events down to single years so that the reader can temporally locate the chapters and their content at a glance.

The picture that emerges from an examination of Ulrichs's correspondence and related documents is of a community of same-sex-attracted men in the German-speaking world who had taken on the urning identity. For almost four decades, "urning" was the principal word they used to describe themselves. It survived into the early years of the twentieth century, when other terms eclipsed it. Ultimately, the men who called themselves urnings prepared the way for the development of Hirschfeld's WhK in 1897. Ulrichs reshaped and complexified the urning identity through engagement with his followers. In time, competing models from Kertbeny and Symonds joined Ulrichs's urning. Ulrichs's closest urning followers comprised a small group of men committed to his sociopolitical thesis and a wider group of individuals who were happy – publicly or privately – to own the urning identity. Although the geopolitical and legal situation made it impossible for them to coalesce into a formal activist association, they maintained networks of correspondence and friendships that allowed a limited capacity for activism. The revolution in personal sexual identity that Ulrichs had sparked proved to be a means for urnings to carve out a quasi-public existence. These men might not have been formally organized, but they were developing skills and preparing the ground for the next generation of activists. This is their history.

PART ONE

1862–1871

Part One of this book covers the period when Ulrichs was most active in his advocacy for urning rights. These chapters discuss how urnings from across Germanic Europe responded enthusiastically to Ulrichs's writings and engaged in the articulation of the urning identity. While two sensational trials engaged public interest, the urban subcultures of masculine men and cross-dressers were less enthusiastic about Ulrichs's campaign.

The First Urning: Karl Heinrich Ulrichs, 1825–1895

The last two centuries saw efforts to abolish the persecution of heresy and witchcraft. In our century, indeed, in our decade, efforts will be made to abolish the persecution of man-manly love.[1]

The first man to adopt a minoritized sexual identity and call himself an "urning" was Karl Heinrich Ulrichs. In doing so, he inaugurated an ontological turn that would transform queer history. Although this was probably the most important development resulting from Ulrichs's works, it was not one he had intended. Ulrichs deployed his "urning" neologism and described its properties as a strategic device in order to argue for the human rights of a "third sex" minority. His initial intention was to change the minds of lawyers, legislators, and doctors. Ulrichs's campaign was both timely and impactful, although it failed in its primary objective, which was to abolish the "persecution of man-manly love." Even so, it would be impossible to evaluate the "Age of the Urning" without first considering the man who made it all possible. This chapter focuses on the life and work of Ulrichs and the context of his intervention.

The Early Years

Karl Heinrich Ulrichs was born in 1825 at Westerfeld near Aurich in the East Friesland region of the Kingdom of Hanover. He apparently had a happy early childhood.[2] Ulrichs's father died on 24 August 1835 when his son was just ten years old. This was a traumatic event for one so young. Soon after, in the spring of 1836, his mother sold the Westerfeld estate and moved the family to Burgdorf, 300 kilometres away, on the other side of the kingdom.[3] Ulrichs's maternal relatives were religious.

His grandfather and most of his uncles were Lutheran pastors, and his sisters would both go on to marry churchmen. They appear to have been a loving family who supported Ulrichs throughout his school years.[4]

Ulrichs trained as a lawyer at the Universities of Göttingen and Berlin. He had been aware of his sexual orientation since he was a teenager, but it was probably during his student years in Berlin that he became sexually active. Ulrichs's earliest fantasies were "about some splendid 20- or 22-year-old soldier."[5] He seems to have been sexually focused exclusively in this direction, and Berlin offered plenty of opportunities for him to satisfy his desires. After graduation, in 1848, Ulrichs joined the Royal Hanoverian Civil Service as a lawyer. That same year, revolutionary disturbances in cities across German-speaking Europe ushered in reforms that brought liberals to power. A confederal German National Assembly convened in Frankfurt. Unhappy in his first position, Ulrichs yearned for a post with the newly elected parliament. In January and February of 1849, he travelled to Frankfurt and applied, unsuccessfully, "to federal ministers Gagern and Mohl for a position in the federal service."[6]

The early promise of this revolutionary period soon faded. The resulting instability and fear of future conflict meant that most of the German states recruited standing armies, which were garrisoned in towns and cities across the region. In towns where soldiers were garrisoned, transactional *Soldatenliebe* (soldier love) was a subcultural feature of this period. Ulrichs apparently transacted soldier assignations discreetly while employed as a lawyer. After six years in state service, on 30 November 1854, Ulrichs's sexual secret was revealed and his legal career came to an abrupt end.[7] Rumours of his sexuality were circulating, possibly because of a failed blackmail attempt, and Ulrichs resigned his position to avoid the consequences.[8] This episode impeded Ulrichs's subsequent efforts to find employment and may have been a motivator for his later activism.

Ulrichs went first to his pastor and his mother in Burgdorf and then on to his sister Dorothea and her husband, Pastor Grupen, in Dassel, near Göttingen.[9] This appears to have been a watershed moment for Ulrichs – a dark night of his soul during which he agonized about who he was and what that meant. Returning to Burgdorf, Ulrichs spent several years acting as a defence advocate for the poor in the courts and as a freelance legal and legislative correspondent for what was to become Germany's leading newspaper, the *Allgemeine Zeitung*. From 1859 to early 1863, he served as the private secretary to Justin Freiherr von Linde, a conservative politician who represented Liechtenstein,

Reuss-Greiz, and Hesse-Homburg in the Confederation Parliament in Frankfurt.

During this period of employment, Ulrichs acquired valuable skills in political lobbying. For example, he wrote and published a long treatise in two parts on the post office monopoly.[10] This was an important issue of his day, and Ulrichs would have made sure his pamphlets were in the hands of all the parliamentarians who mattered. Similarly, in 1862 he wrote and published a thirty-six-page essay on the Greater Germany solution.[11] These published works were Ulrichs's first polemic legal/political works, and it is likely that he promoted them to the audiences of legislators they were intended for and that he made use of them for lobbying purposes. The lobbying of legal authorities and legislatures would play a large part in Ulrichs's later activism on behalf of urnings.

Hubert Kennedy positions the events of the summer of 1862 as pivotal in Ulrichs's life, for that is when he turned to campaigning on behalf of man-manly love.[12] He had attended a political event in a journalistic capacity where he encountered the charismatic social democrat Johann Baptist von Schweitzer. Shortly afterwards, Schweitzer was arrested in the Mannheim Palace Park and charged with a same-sex sexual crime.[13] Ulrichs wrote two letters to Schweitzer while he was in initial detention with written defences for his trial; one of the letters got through, but the authorities confiscated the other.[14] This event appeared to have spurred Ulrichs to begin his campaign.

The Activist Years

Ulrichs wrote his works against the backdrop of a seismic geopolitical realignment in central Europe. When he started his campaign, the Kingdom of Hanover was an independent state in loose confederal association with thirty-nine kingdoms, princely states, archduchies, bishoprics, and free cities, including the regional powers: Prussia and Austria.[15] This political arrangement was a compromise, and by the 1860s most people believed that unification of the German states was inevitable. The approaching political reorganization offered tantalizing prospects for reform, given that the new, unified state would have to craft a new legal code. This was of specific interest to Ulrichs, as each of the thirty-nine states had its own legal system and some of them had no antisodomy law – including the Kingdom of Hanover, where Ulrichs began his campaign. Even in the states where it was illegal, the laws were inconsistent. For example, Paragraph 143 of the Prussian legal code proscribed only specific sexual acts; thus "pederasty" applied only to anal intercourse between men, leaving all other same-sex sexual acts unpunished. Any attempt to unify Germany under a new legal code would draw primarily on the reformed codes, and the plurality of options meant that the new central government would have to make a decision as to whether to retain an antisodomy law. Ulrichs probably perceived that there was a very real prospect for reform and that the time was optimal for a carefully executed campaign.[16]

Ulrichs spent the closing months of 1862 informing his relatives about what he was planning to write; in the early months of 1863, he wound up his affairs in Frankfurt.[17] In deference to his relatives and their misgivings, Ulrichs would use the pseudonym "Numa Numantius" for his first five pamphlets.[18] Ulrichs's publications on man-manly love would vary in length – from his first, *Vindex*, at 28 pages, to his seventh, *Memnon*, at 184 pages. But they were all pamphlets, not books, and he would deploy them following a pamphleteering strategy while at the same time his publisher sold them in bookshops.

At the time he launched his campaign, Ulrichs had not widely networked with any subculture of same-sex-attracted men. He had lived in small towns and modestly sized cities that probably had little or no same-sex subculture. He transacted his sexual experiences with soldiers, and the need for discretion to avoid blackmailable situations would probably not have led to him socializing with other men with the same tastes. If Ulrichs knew other same-sex-attracted men before 1862, he did not mention any. In a letter to his sister dated September 1862, he confessed, "I know only very few."[19] Three months later, in a letter to his uncle regarding his ideas about sexuality, Ulrichs wrote: "All the Uraniers I have asked [about six Uraniers] are in agreement here, and all the rest will probably agree."[20] As he was living in Frankfurt at the time, it would not be unreasonable to assume that these men also lived there. It appears that Ulrichs observed and interrogated six other uraniers in preparation for his writings – he had to be sure that his own disposition as he theorized it reflected the dispositions of other same-sex-attracted men. The interviews with these men revealed broad agreement:

That the individual Uranier had been attracted by the sight of handsome young men even in his earliest youth will by no means have escaped an attentive observer; just as the sight of blooming girls, irresistible to other young men, left him completely cold. Furthermore, that even in the period of his youth his character, his career ambitions, games, etc., and his bearing in manners, gestures and movements in many cases were not male, but female.[21]

In his second pamphlet, *Inclusa*, Ulrichs made note of the feminine nature he had observed in his six urnings: "Only in 1862 did I pick it up again, namely because I had the opportunity to observe other Urnings: I noticed their feminine habits again and again, even if they were different in certain traits."[22]

It seems extraordinary that Ulrichs wanted to speak for a whole community of men despite his limited experience of them. Indeed, it is possible that his initial theory was coloured by the small sample size he was working with. Ulrichs wrote his first two pamphlets under the impression that all urnings were effeminate. If the six urnings he had chosen to observe and interrogate before writing were more overtly effeminate than the norm, this could have led him to exaggerate this facet in his initial theories.[23] Ulrichs initially suggested that he himself had a feminine character, and he recounted instances from his youth and early adulthood to corroborate this.[24] However, he admitted later that this was "weakly marked" and that his brother-in-law had told him, "I have never noticed this about you."[25] Hirschfeld later wrote that Nicolò Persichetti, the Marquis of Musti'ola, who had known Ulrichs in person, had told him that "he did not appear feminine in any way."[26]

Ulrichs also argued that the preferred partner of the urning was a "dioning" man. Dioning was the word Ulrichs used to describe a man who was attracted only to the opposite sex. The thrust of Ulrichs's argument that urnings were a third sex axiomatically led him to generalize that the natural partner of the urning was a dioning.[27] Ulrichs's own sexual experience was mostly through the transactional soldier trade, so one would have to assume that this was the same for his six urning contacts. It is therefore possible that Ulrichs's six subjects were also soldier-lovers. Perhaps he even recruited them through one of his soldier-trade contacts. In whatever manner Ulrichs came to know these men, they were the first other people to take on the urning identity and express their support for him. These six men were, in the first instance, the men he would struggle to liberate: "I believe that I owe it to my poor, in my opinion guiltless, fellow comrades to publish. Several of them, to whom I have communicated my ideas, consider publication to be absolutely necessary."[28]

Ulrichs decided to focus his campaign on a classic pamphleteering strategy. This had been an established form of political activism in Germany since the Protestant Reformation and the introduction of the printing press. A campaign of printed tracts mailed to political targets had often proved highly effective. Ulrichs wrote his first two pamphlets, *Vindex* and *Inclusa*, in a style he was familiar with as a lawyer. He styled them as the opening address of a prosecutor before a court in a case where his non-urning readers were at the same time defendant, judge, and jury.[29] In the introduction and conclusions to each section, he addressed his readers directly, appealing to them to make an unbiased examination of the arguments he had just deployed. It reads curiously now, but it was a style that was familiar to the lawyers and legislators among his readers. Ulrichs deployed two different legal arguments in these pamphlets: a classical liberal demand for the repeal of unjust laws, and an anthropological argument in which the creation of a fixed innate urning nature was used to argue that urning sex could never be construed as "unnatural."[30] Since the Prussian law proscribed "unnatural" sex, deployment of the natural urning made strategic sense, and it was through this anthropological argument that the urning identity was first articulated in print.[31] Ulrichs published these two pamphlets in 1864.

Encouraged by the letter responses to these first pamphlets, Ulrichs planned three more, which he published in 1865.[32] His writings outlined theories of a fixed, innate, and natural urning identity. Ulrichs's idiosyncratic stylistic approach saw his prose populated with quotations from classical literature, his own poetry, snippets from ancient history, jurisprudence, theology, excerpts from letters sent by his urning readers, and urning-related news from across the German-speaking world and beyond. These first five pamphlets were a set – his publisher issued an edition of all five together a few years later. Emboldened by the number of people writing to him and their enthusiasm, Ulrichs started drafting plans for the formation of a "Federation of Urnings"[33] and a periodical magazine to be called *Uranus*.[34] His plans at this stage suggest either that he was wildly overoptimistic or that he was genuinely responding to the volume of enthusiastic support he was receiving from his readers. His efforts were short-lived – neither the federation nor the magazine proceeded, as events overtook both. In 1866 the German–Danish War engulfed all the states in northern Germany.

Prussia annexed Hanover in September, imposing martial law and driving the Hanoverian royal family into exile.[35] Ulrichs, an ardent royalist, convened public meetings in Burgdorf at which he rallied the local opposition to the Prussian occupation, advocated for a united Germany and the restoration of the monarchy, and supported candidates in the forthcoming elections who were opposed to the occupation.[36] Consequently, the Prussian authorities arrested him in January 1867 and detained him in the fortress at Minden. He was released without charge; however, a search of his apartment in April 1867 uncovered incriminating material.[37] The authorities also discovered copious material relating to Ulrichs's campaign for urning rights: piles of his pamphlets, long lists of correspondents with names and addresses, and several manuscripts for new publications.[38] Ulrichs was again arrested and imprisoned at Minden, this time from 24 April to 5 July.[39] During this second incarceration, the Prussians made sure the press revealed that Ulrichs was the real name of Numa Numantius, the notorious advocate of urning rights.[40] However, they were unable to prosecute Ulrichs because Hanover had no antisodomy law and because the other charges had no substance, so he was released on 5 July 1867 with the "obligation to take his residence outside the province or at Hildesheim."[41] Ulrichs chose to leave Hanover, never to return, and settled instead in Würzburg, Bavaria, where there was no antisodomy law.

His arrests did not quell his activism. A little over a month after his release, Ulrichs was in Munich at the Congress of German Jurists. On 29 August, he climbed to the speaker's box in the main hall of the Odeon Theatre to address five hundred of Germany and Austria's most illustrious lawyers, judges, and legal scholars, as well as some parliamentarians and one Bavarian prince.[42] This was an unparalleled opportunity to appeal directly to all those with influence over any reform process. Ulrichs was only able to read his opening arguments before cries for adjournment by some of the delegates drove him from the stage. Before he was silenced, he had been able to make clear that he was pleading on behalf of "a group of men which is discriminated against *on no ground for unjust* criminal prosecution because nature *which creates and governs mysteriously* has implanted in this group a sexual nature that is inconsistent with the common one."[43] The calls for adjournment came mainly from individuals on the governing council and their supporters. These were individuals who had read the original submission from Ulrichs and fully understood what it was they were trying to silence. However, as Ulrichs noted with appreciation, there were also many voices in the hall raised in his favour.[44]

This was the very first time an urning had made his case openly in a public forum. Ulrichs's unashamed public attempt to protest was a victory in and of itself. By appearing in person as a self-confessed urning, against vocal attempts to silence him by a determined group, Ulrichs had made his point more eloquently than he could have done simply by speaking his case. The attempt to silence him demonstrated amply his point that it was narrow prejudice and not legal rectitude that ensured the continuance of this legal injustice. An eyewitness who spoke to Ulrichs after his protest wrote: "He was not dissatisfied with the result, i.e., he expected nothing else. He was of the opinion that the breach had been made."[45]

On his return to Würzburg, Ulrichs resumed his pamphlet activism. In September and October 1867 he wrote a full account of the event in Munich, which had been the first public protest on behalf of men who were sexually oriented towards their own sex. It was published with no pseudonym and under his own name in early 1868 as *Gladius Furens*.[46] Ulrichs concluded this pamphlet by asserting that this protest was just the first of what would, in time, be a great many public protests against the injustice of legal prohibition: "As long as this love publicly exists in the penal code, as long as state prosecutors and the courts emphasize the fact, lovers of this kind may open public channels in their behalf to come before the forum and to enter their protest and to establish their petition of rights."[47]

Ulrichs sent five hundred copies of *Gladius Furens* to the members of the Association of Jurists, including judges, legal academics, and legislators. Four of these men acknowledged receipt with thanks, four returned their copies, and the rest remained unacknowledged.[48] Ulrichs was already working on his most important pamphlet, *Memnon*, which would be published in two volumes with the final iteration of his urning theory in 1868.

By 1869, Ulrichs was again receiving a large volume of letters. By then, the public press was discussing his ideas, sometimes approvingly, and his campaign was arguably at its peak. He was probably also receiving some unwelcome attention now that his works were becoming better known. Two hostile medical reviews of which Ulrichs was apparently unaware had previously been published in the psychiatric journal *Der Irrenfreund* within months of publication of the first pamphlets.[49] In 1869 another review appeared in the Viennese *Medizinische Presse* in which the author claimed "in certain cases there is the condition of unaccountability, in which the Urning finds himself, and for which Ulrichs makes a plea."[50] That same year an anonymous pamphlet, titled "Das Paradoxon der Venus Urania" and later revealed to be the work of University of Würzburg professor Alois Geigel, started appearing in bookshops.[51] This was a relatively sophisticated attack on Ulrichs's theories, which Geigel criticized as unforgivably dualist. Geigel wasn't entirely against Ulrichs's theories, but the tone of the pamphlet was often witheringly hostile. "Mr Ulrichs has decidedly not been favored by fate, one way or the other," he wrote. "He should have been born either in the year 2000, when one will perhaps be so advanced to bless uranian marriages, or some centuries before our time, when nobody was so presumptuous as to doubt that the sun moves around the earth."[52]

Geigel closed with a plea to Ulrichs "to leave our 'young Dionings' untouched" and accused Ulrichs of claiming "they did no wrong when they quenched the lust of an old sinful 'Urning'!"[53] This was not the first time that Ulrichs had been challenged in those terms. Rudolf Virchow previously wrote to Ulrichs to ask, "Do you not realise you assail the dignity of the person when you use him in some business for which he is by nature not destined?"[54] Ulrichs positioned the dioning as the principal love interest of the urning because transactional sex with soldiers was what he knew best, but, as a tacit argument in favour of prostitution, it was the weakest part of his theory in the eyes of conservatives. Conservative attitudes towards Ulrichs himself were also far from flattering. Looking back on his student years in Würzburg, the conservative Catholic politician Johann Thaler reminisced during a speech in Parliament on 31 May 1905:

> One of the main representatives of the new teaching is Ulrichs, a former Hanoverian assessor. He speaks for the first time of "Urnings," of which he was one himself. I knew him personally when I studied in Würzburg. There he was with a pale face and shaky knees running around the city, and, gentlemen of the left, you will not give much attention to what I thought, but I give you the assurance: if I imagine a bejesus, then all I need is to remember the former Hanoverian assessor, the Urning Ulrichs, how he looked hollow and shy with his stick under his arm, lonely, sneaking around in the streets.[55]

Nor were some on the political left any more supportive of Ulrichs's arguments. Karl Marx sent a copy of Ulrichs's pamphlet *Incubus* to Friedrich Engels in 1869; Engels replied on 22 June with contempt that "these are extremely unnatural revelations; the paederasts are beginning to count themselves."[56] The hostility from certain parties was probably countered from Ulrichs's perspective by the good wishes of some of his supporters. However, there is little doubt that by 1869, with his pamphlets beginning to gain popularity (and notoriety) in wider circles, he was being confronted by significant criticism.

Ulrichs's campaign reached its pinnacle in 1869. That same year saw a number of other important developments. Ulrichs's works were attracting more positive and negative attention partly as a result of the sensational trial of Carl von Zastrow in Berlin.[57] Ulrichs, seeking to capitalize on the attention, published two more pamphlets in quick succession.[58] That same year, a psychiatrist named Carl Friedrich Otto Westphal published a paper about "conträre Sexualempfindung" (contrary sexual feeling). Ulrichs had lobbied Westphal, and the psychiatrist quoted from Ulrichs's works extensively in his paper. Karl Maria Kertbeny, who had been a correspondent of Ulrichs's as well as a potential rival, published two anonymous publications in 1869 using his alternative neologism, "homosexual."[59] It was also in 1869 that the Prussian Justice Minister considered whether to include an antisodomy law in the new German legal code. Ulrichs's ideas were by this time receiving widespread attention. Unfortunately, not all that attention was positive. In an early example of the culture wars that were to characterize queer rights in the twentieth century, conservative religious organizations raised their voices against legal reform.[60] The Justice Minister decided to retain the antisodomy law. When Prussia extended rule over the remaining German states except Austria in 1871, the antisodomy law, Paragraph 175, became the law of the new German empire.[61]

Ulrichs moved to Stuttgart after unification. Perhaps because a Prussian-style legal code had been adopted in 1872, he stopped publishing his urning works and published books of poetry instead.[62] He did, however, convene meetings of a close cadre of activists. Ulrichs published his final pamphlet, *Critische Pfeile*, in 1879; the following year, he gave up the fight and walked over the Alps into Italian exile. After a few years in Naples, he settled in Aquila, where he published a Latin newspaper, *Alaudae*. Ulrichs died at Aquila in 1895.

Conclusion

Karl Heinrich Ulrichs believed in his exile that his campaign had been for nothing. In one of his final letters, he wrote to a friend back in Germany: "It is the writings, the writings, that have brought me to the beggar's staff by bringing me nothing."[63] It is true that his campaign had failed to change the law and that, at least in the short term, it had failed to end the persecution of urnings. In exile, he had been neglected by his urning comrades and possibly had no appreciation of the impact his ideas had on a generation of same-sex-attracted men. One could argue that Ulrichs's legacy was the minoritized, "third sex" personal identity and of the men who defined themselves as urnings.

As the originator of the "urning" terminology, Ulrichs disseminated ideas and tactics that were entirely original, and his bravery in mounting the campaign is without question. Without his intervention, there would have been no other people calling themselves urnings, and the spread of this terminology and the ideas underpinning it fomented a modern sexual sensibility among his followers. His articulation of a modern minoritized sexual identity and the transmission of that identity to his readers was a critical early stage in sexual modernity. The next chapter turns to the initial group of men who received and responded to his ideas. These individuals revealed themselves through the letters they sent Ulrichs, which he then reproduced in his pamphlets. These men were the first generation of urnings.

Chapter Two

From Page to Personhood: The Transmission of *Urningtum*, 1864–1868[*]

The urning, embodied not only as a theoretical construction, but also in real people, appeared as a new social character.[1]

Something extraordinary happened after the publication of *Vindex* and *Inclusa* in 1864. An ontological turn began to transform the ways some people viewed their sexual selves. Although it happened specifically in Germany in the 1860s, this development would have international ramifications in the coming century. In the opening pages of the pamphlet *Vindex*, Ulrichs introduced the neologism "urning" to describe a man with a sexual drive directed only toward the same sex and who was not aroused sexually by the opposite sex.[2] The same-sex-attracted men who read and responded to Ulrichs's pamphlets took up the neologism and forged from it a minoritized personal identity. Sexuality was no longer defined by actions, tastes, crimes, or sins. It had become a definition of their whole being, one that informed sexual *and* non-sexual behaviour and united them as a brotherhood. Having first been described on paper, the urning would over time became flesh and blood as a social personage. This transmission of a social construction from page to personhood was both striking and specific.

The pamphlets were not intended for a readership of like-minded men; even so, the majority of letters sent in response via the publisher came from same-sex-attracted men who found the theories a compelling reflection of their own lives. The first urning readers were men browsing in

---

[*] In his books, Ulrichs attached the suffix "-tum" to the noun "urning" to produce the word *Urningtum*, meaning the totality of the urning world, in an analogous way to *Christentum* (Christendom) or *Judentum* (Judaism).

bookshops. The bookseller and publisher of the pamphlets, H. (Heinrich) Matthes, had shops in the major towns and cities of Germany. H. Matthes also produced a catalogue, mailed to subscribers, that listed Ulrichs's pamphlets alongside all the other recent releases.[3] The pamphlets had Latin titles, but the German subtitles proclaimed that they were about "man-manly sexual love" (*mannmännliche Geschlechtsliebe*). A title of this kind would have startled any same-sex-attracted man who noticed it on the shelf in a bookshop or in a catalogue listing. Several readers who sent letters to Ulrichs made it clear that they saw themselves in the traits he associated with the urning. This chapter will focus on the letters he received from same-sex-attracted men who had taken on the urning neologism as a personal identity. These men called themselves urnings. They negotiated the parameters of their new identities and applied them to their unique life settings.

The Letters

Reader correspondents could respond quickly to the publications because railway expansion had dramatically improved the speed and efficiency of the postal service.[4] Large-scale industrialization and urban growth came late to Germany, but the German states had begun expanding the railway network in the 1830s. By 1850, there were 6,000 miles of track connecting all the main German towns and cities.[5] Each correspondent would have first established contact by writing to the publisher, H. Matthes, who would then forward the letters.[6]

Ulrichs was pleasantly surprised to receive letters from his readers, and he would refer to them, quote from them, and use them to illustrate his points in subsequent pamphlets. His correspondence was probably far more extensive than the extent of letters reproduced in his pamphlets would indicate. In 1867, the authorities confiscated a quantity of this correspondence: the letters from Berlin alone came from around 150 individuals.[7] Given this, is reasonable to assume that in 1864 and 1865 he received correspondence from at least several hundred individuals from across the German states. The authorities confiscated all the letters Ulrichs received before his arrest and never returned them;[8] those he received in the years after his arrest have also not survived.[9] The quoted letters that appeared from the third pamphlet, *Vindicta*, to the last pamphlet, *Critische Pfeile*, are all that remains of that correspondence.

In total, Ulrichs's pamphlets quoted from 154 individual letters, of which eighty-two were from sixty-six individual urnings.[10] The other seventy-two letters came from sixty-three individual dionings, including seventeen lawyers, twenty-four doctors, two Catholic bishops, two

Protestant ministers, three government officials, one publisher, one librarian, a philosopher, an archivist, a Berlin university professor, and ten interested dioning readers.[11] The content of the urning letters was often presented as short passages or fragments devoid of their original epistolary context. A handful of letters were presented in what may have been near-complete form; the preamble to the first letter claimed that the author had given explicit permission to publish. The identities of urning correspondents were not disclosed, although sometimes, when available, the age and location of the writer were provided, along with the date the letter was sent. In thirteen letters, the correspondent gave his age: eight were in their twenties, three were in their thirties, one was forty, and one called himself "middle-aged." Fifty-nine letters indicated the location of the writer; most of these had been sent by individuals residing in the German and Austrian states. There was strong representation from the large population centres of Berlin (7 letters) and Vienna (6).[12] However, most of the letters – forty-six in total – came from towns of fewer than 150,000 or from rural areas.[13] From outside Germany/Austria, there were letters from London (6), Paris (3), Moscow (3), St. Petersburg (3), Switzerland (3), Bohemia (1), Hungary (1), and the Adriatic coast (1). Ulrichs quoted some correspondents on more than one occasion from letters sent on different dates, suggesting an ongoing reciprocal correspondence. Some correspondence indicated that the writer was responding to a letter. There was no indication that Ulrichs met any of these individuals in person in the 1860s, so the relationships he had with them were probably mostly epistolary.[14]

Ulrichs sorted the responses he received into categories of variation in sexuality and gender expression. Responses from his readers revealed multiple additional nuances to the urning identity. Ulrichs understood that a "future researcher will discover an underlying law for this apparent chaos of varieties" and fully expected his ideas on identity to be challenged and revised in coming years.[15] Nonetheless, the most remarkable thing about this engagement in the process of self-definition was that the men who had contributed to the expansion of Ulrichs's theories went on to take the name and its definitions as a personal sexual identity. The urning had progressed from paper to personhood.

The Urning Identity

Ulrichs's works had a transformative personal effect on the men who engaged with his model of identity. Initially, this was limited to the subset of same-sex-attracted men who read and engaged with the articulation of the urning nature in his pamphlets. In time, the changes would have more far-reaching effects on a much wider population. To fully assess the broader implications of this discursive shift, one must first examine what preceded it. Eve Sedgwick, in a passage about the changing perceptions of sexuality in the eighteenth and nineteenth centuries, contrasted the two styles of sexual definition that coexisted at multiple points during the period when sexual modernity was taking shape as definitions that were either universalizing or minoritizing.[16] That is, there were definitions of sexuality that stressed that all people were capable of any sexual behaviour and that sexual behaviour could be modified (universalizing), and others that defined sexual orientation as fixed for life and limited to a particular group (minoritizing). The definitions that preceded Ulrichs's intervention were mostly of the universalizing kind. Prior to 1864, little had been written about deviant sexuality. Temporal and canonical law were focused entirely on the commission of certain sexual acts and the still prevalent Enlightenment conception of sexuality that characterized it as a taste or inclination. These were both universalizing definitions that saw deviant sexuality as excessive or non-normative behaviour that should be corrected or minimized.[17] The mutability of universalizing definitions of sexuality made them inherently unstable as a basis for personal sexual identities.

So the question is, how did same-sex-attracted men define themselves in the immediate period before Ulrichs proposed his alternative minoritizing identity? Living as we do in an era saturated with discourses of sexuality and gender, it is perhaps difficult to imagine what it was like to make sense of one's sexual self in a period when there were no written words or public examples to follow. Yet it was still possible. Particularly in the urban centres of the period there were sexual subcultures that allowed some individuals to assertively articulate their complete sexual selves. Shortly before Ulrichs started writing, a German man living in Italy wrote an autobiographical account of his sexuality and sent it as a letter to the forensic examiner Johann Ludwig Casper.[18] The strong sense of sexual self expressed in this letter is disarming when you consider that this man managed to articulate it without any of the various neologisms that were poised to appear. The absence of available terminology meant that this man referred to his particular inclination/disposition (*Neigung*) as a sexual attraction towards men and a sexual disinterest in women. Although this account was published by Casper under the headline "Self-Confessions of a Pederast," its author was careful to distance himself from the practice of pederasty (sodomy) and the use of that terminology for himself – "I abhor this tendency as do others."[19] He was also able to identify other individuals with the same inclination: "Benevolent nature has given us a certain instinct which unites us, as a brotherhood; we find each other in a moment, it is hardly a glance of the eye, like an electric shock, and with some caution has never deceived me."[20]

His confident assertion of his sexual self was the outcome of a succession of events that he described in his account. Up to the age of nineteen, he was aware of a mysterious difference in himself but innocent of its nature. It was in this state that a friend took him to a brothel at the age of eighteen, where he experienced a feeling of deep disgust. For one year, he repeatedly visited the brothel, but he could only achieve coitus by thinking of his attractive male friends. The experience left him demoralized and disgusted with himself. He then wrote of his first sexual encounter in the Tiergarten, Berlin's main cruising area. During this encounter, his sexual partner informed him that there were many others with the same inclination. In his second encounter in the Tiergarten, eight days later, he met a man who became his lover for some time. The writer then wrote of his lover's death and burial. Following this death, perhaps as a result of scandal or blackmail, the writer was driven into unwelcome exile. He travelled to London, Paris, Italy, and Vienna, where "everywhere I found us miserable."[21] As an attractive man he had little difficulty in finding sexual and social contacts in the years that followed: "On the Righi, in Palermo, in the Louvre, in the Scottish Highlands, in Petersburg, yes, when landing in Barcelona, I found people I had never seen before, who in a second were spellbound to me, I to them – can that be a crime?"[22]

This account made an assertive emancipatory case from an Enlightenment perspective positing that sexual orientation was a taste he shared with certain other men. This man's inchoate personal sexual identity comprised a strong sexual self-knowledge born of experience, a loose fellowship with other sexually active men, and an ability to recognize the look of desire in other men. It was an identity embedded in universalizing discourses, but at the same time it appeared to anticipate a more fixed minoritized existence. The man does not make any explicit statements about the nature of his sexual identity, but he conveyed an implicit sense that his sexuality was an established state that he could not change through personal exertion, and he recognized that this state existed in others he met.

We should be wary of concluding that this man's strong sense of sexual self was a widely shared attribute. Casper wrote that from his knowledge of pederasts in the Berlin court system, he had not come across any with similar "noble natures."[23] Casper's *pederast* was socially and financially independent, an educated man of the higher classes. His sexual enlightenment had been mediated through encounters in the Tiergarten and Berlin's homosocial subculture. Such atomized brotherhoods of the Tiergarten had been a feature of the city for many years, and, according to Hugo Friedländer, they were beginning to coalesce in small "cozy" venues catering to them on the eastern edge of the park in the 1860s.[24] It is also possibly true that this man's inchoate sense of sexual self was just one of a variety of personal self-rationalizations that coexisted in Berlin in this period before the emergence of a unifying sexual discourse. These could have manifested themselves in something similar to the multiple social worlds defined by race, class, cultural style, or sexual praxis that George Chauncey found in early twentieth-century New York.[25]

Berlin's relatively plentiful sexual and social possibilities were out of reach to most Germans, around 96 per cent of whom lived in towns of fewer than 100,000.[26] In those non-urban settings, the prospects for same-sex-attracted people to meet were limited. Larger towns where garrisons had been established offered opportunities for transactional sex with soldiers looking for additional income. For men whose moral scruples or lack of ready cash precluded transactional sexual encounters, the options were limited. Many would have succumbed to family or community pressure to marry. The reality probably was that acquiring a strongly assertive sense of sexual selfhood was out of reach for most people outside of Berlin. Nor was being a city dweller necessarily a guarantor of sexual enlightenment; for those of less elevated classes, family pressure to marry or the lack of social or financial independence limited the opportunities to discover and explore their sexual selves. Prior to Ulrichs's intervention, assertive sexual selfhood was likely a rare commodity, and even for those who did achieve it, the process may have taken many years of heartache and uncertainty.

Ulrichs arrived at his own strong sense of sexual self in several stages of realization, including a period of transactional sex with soldiers, which culminated in his resignation from the legal service to avoid exposure in 1854. It is probable that in the ensuing years, his own sexuality was a matter very much in his thoughts, as it was the reason given by his former employers for repeatedly intervening to prevent him practising law in Hanover. His first attempt to write on the subject in 1861 came after he found more secure employment as a parliamentary secretary and freelance journalist in Frankfurt. At that point, he tried to explain his sexuality as a form of "passive animal magnetism."[27] In Frankfurt, Ulrichs began to meet others who shared his inclinations, and he noticed that each of them had a feminine nature.[28] In late 1862, Ulrichs wrote four letters to his relatives in which he first articulated his emerging ideas about sexuality and announced his plans to write and publish works on the subject. We can assume that Ulrichs finished asserting his own sense of sexual self by coming out to his relatives.

The urning that Ulrichs described in his first two pamphlets was a strategic identity crafted for rhetorical purposes in a legal disquisition. That was not how it was received. The outline of identity and the properties he invested in it became for Ulrichs's readers the definition and parameters of a new, sexually modern social identity. His pamphlets attracted an audience of same-sex-attracted men, something that Ulrichs may not have anticipated. The liberating experience of seeing oneself described in print for the first time made some of these men especially disposed to taking on *Urningtum* as a personal identity. However, it would be an error to characterize Ulrichs's urning social identity solely as an outward expression of inward truths. Rather, this was an identity whose central parameters reconfigured the whole conception of sexuality and sexual selfhood. There were three defining characteristics to the urning identity.

First, Ulrichs elevated sexual desire to the very core of identity.[29] It was the defining classificatory element for the whole being of the individual and not just a peripheral trait, a taste or a tendency. As noted earlier, sexuality up to that point had been conceived of in Enlightenment discourses as a "universal" taste that any individual could have towards their own sex, while legal and theological texts defined individuals by their sexual acts. By contrast, the urning identity defined the individual as a separate being minoritized by the orientation of his sexual desire. The urning was characterized specifically by his sexual orientation whether it was expressed or not and whether he was even aware of it or not. This was an important break with past practice. Even the isolated virgin, without the opportunity for sexual outlet, could claim the urning identity as a self-definition.

Second, Ulrichs framed his anthropological argument in *Inclusa*, his second pamphlet, around an embryological origin.[30] Sexuality was physically embodied as a germ in the embryo that would give rise to the individual's love drive. Usually, a male embryo would develop with a male love drive and a female embryo with a female love drive. By contrast, in the urning, a male embryo developed with a female love drive.[31] Ulrichs was positioning the urning as a biologically delineated third sex whose female love drive oriented him towards dioning men – a kind of psychological hermaphrodite. This embryological argument might seem arcane today but was consistent with an emerging Darwinian discourse popularly disseminated in the works of Ernst Haeckel and others.[32] The biological origin established several qualities and parameters for the urning identity. The urning was a natural phenomenon created in the womb. His sexual orientation was not a matter of choice or amenable to therapeutic reshaping. The urning disposition was innate and fixed for life. Accepting this argument was a key step on the path to self-acceptance. In addition, in constructing the biological argument and its binary configuration Ulrichs positioned the only possible love interest for the urning as the dioning and not other urnings – Ulrichs declared that opposites attract, and the female love drive of the urning was oriented towards an individual with a male love drive.[33] This seemingly logical consequence of the binary embryological argument would prove controversial among those of his correspondents who had found partners among other urnings.

Third, Ulrichs's limited observation of his six urning friends had convinced him that the presence of the female love drive at the core of the urning's being gave rise to certain feminine tastes and mannerisms. In its first iteration, the urning was conceived as gently effeminate.[34] However, Ulrichs prefigured more intense forms of gender nonconformity by illustrating his arguments with two proto-trans examples: Susskind Blank, a Jewish tailor in Dessau who lived as a woman and petitioned the state to be recognized as such, and the Roman emperor Antoninus Heliogabalus, who asked one of his lovers to call him My Lady rather than My Lord.[35] Ulrichs later used the Latin aphorism *anima muliebris virili corpore inclusa* (a woman's soul within a male body) to express this part of his theory. This component of the theory will be referred to in the chapters that follow as the "anima thesis."[36] Ulrichs's focus on the feminine in the urning made his model distinct from later models of same-sex orientation and has led some scholars to position Ulrichs as an early trans advocate.[37] While that may be true up to a point, gender was always subordinate to sexual orientation as a secondary characteristic of the urning. It also proved to be the most controversial element of the identity among Ulrichs's readers.

The letters Ulrichs received after he started publishing his pamphlets speak to the impact his ideas had on same-sex-attracted men. The responses from younger men, married men, and men located outside of Berlin were the most effusive and grateful. These were the men most in need of sexual guidance. For these men, the urning identity gave them a name for a sexual selfhood they had yet to achieve. That such an identity existed revealed what otherwise might have remained mysterious through years of heartache and sexual/social praxis. The urning identity allowed even the isolated virgin to attain a modicum of sexual self-knowledge. This made the urning identity an attractive proposition for this group and led them to accept a third-sex, minoritized model of sexuality with the orientation of sexual desire as its defining characteristic.

Unsurprisingly, the least responsive group were the ones who did not benefit from Ulrichs's insights – the older men in Berlin who had already achieved sexual self-acceptance. For these men, Ulrichs's works offered a new terminology to describe a level of knowledge they had already attained. Ulrichs's strongest following, at least in this first wave of identity formation, came from the men who benefited most from the urning identity and for whom it was a lifeline. Like the man quoted at the start of the introduction to this book, they could be satisfied in no longer having "in vain to fight against a deeply implanted disposition" and rejoice that since they had taken on the urning identity they were "happier, healthier and more efficient!"[38]

Ulrichs had drawn from his own experience as a self-confessed urning and on his observations of six other urning men.[39] When the urning first appeared in print, it presented an unstable counter-normative discourse. It acquired strength and stability as more and more men read about it and applied the name and identity to themselves. However, Ulrichs's readers did not meekly accede to the urning ideology; instead, they contested its parameters and properties. Readers disputed Ulrichs's assumption that the dioning was the only natural sexual partner of the urning and wrote instead of their sexual relationships with other urning men. Some correspondents indicated that they were attracted to both sexes, and Ulrichs called these men *Uranodionings* (bisexuals).[40] Other correspondents wrote about their gendered characters. Ulrichs at first wrote of the effeminacy of urnings as if that was the only possibility. However, he heard from men who did not consider themselves feminine. He also received many letters from men whose effeminacy extended to transvestism and who were considerably more effeminate than Ulrichs had originally envisaged. Ulrichs proposed a continuum from the effeminate urning or *Weibling* to the masculine urning or *Mannling*.[41] Those whose gendered behaviour fell between these two poles he referred to as intermediate urnings.[42] Gender presentation was not central to the definition of the urning, but it occupied a more prominent position than it does in more contemporary sexual identities.[43] In addressing the engaged responses from his urning readers, Ulrichs developed a more nuanced model of identity in two further iterations, one in his fourth pamphlet, *Formatrix* (1865), and the final one in his seventh pamphlet *Memnon* (1868). By the time he had finished, the urning was no longer a single type of person but a class of diverse types with the orientation of sexual desire as a unifying property. The urning that emerged from this discursive engagement was a layered and segmented social identity that extended and reconfigured how same-sex-attracted individuals saw themselves and their fellow urnings from the 1860s onwards in Germany.

This was the point in time that Foucault identified as presenting a distinctly new discourse that revised and replaced older categories. However, it was not "the psychological, psychiatric, medical category of homosexuality" that was axiomatic in this discursive shift.[44] Instead, the urning was a product of its own subjects, a sexual self-definition. Rather than aligning with Foucault's construction of a "reverse discourse" deploying "the same categories by which it was medically disqualified," the urning emerged as a new discourse grounded in lived experience a full six years before psychiatry started formulating sexual categories. It is more productive, therefore, to consider the category of urning as an example of Foucault's later utopian construction of sexual identity as "the interaction between oneself and others and in the technologies of individual domination" and the creative construction of how "an individual acts upon himself in the technology of self."[45] While Foucault's later theorizing has some merit, it was never fully articulated as a theory of the construction of social sexual identities.

One more recent theoretical position that can enhance our understanding of the advent of the urning identity and its impact on German society is José Esteban Muñoz's conception of utopian futurity.[46] The urning identity embodied an anticipated relational future that did not yet exist. Even the isolated young man alone with Ulrichs's pamphlets, engaging with the urning technology of self, was joined in a utopian brotherhood with all other urnings. In that sense, it was an identity that, as Jean-Luc Nancy put it, was a "singular plurality."[47] The urning identity was first and foremost a personal identity, but it was also a utopian identity that foregrounded future delineations of community and movement. Ulrichs anticipated this utopian future and outlined a pathway towards it through living in the open as a happy, healthy urning: "As Urnings, we should and must represent ourselves openly. Only then will we overcome ourselves in human society with our feet firmly planted on the ground; otherwise, we never will."[48]

Ulrichs himself embodied a second element of utopian futurity in the urning identity. Through his tireless efforts to advance the urning cause in print and through his actions, he prefigured the proto-activist urge among some of his followers, but there were limits to its reach.[49] The identity may have been personally transformative, but it did not radically change broader social prejudices and prohibitions. It is likely that at least for young men, the newfound identity may have predicated certain decisions that could result in changes to their own circumstances. For example, they could have felt empowered to refuse family pressure to marry, or they could have opted to study or work away from home in a city environment more conducive to an urning lifestyle. As George

Chauncey observed, "the history of gay resistance must be understood to extend beyond formal political organizing to include the strategies of everyday resistance that men devised to claim space for themselves in the midst of a hostile society."[50] In time, once a critical mass of individuals were calling themselves urnings and relating to one another as an emerging community, this urge to improve circumstances would manifest itself in more overt acts of proto-activism. The second part of this book examines several instances of urning proto-activism in the 1880s and 1890s, which foregrounded and arguably made possible the more formal activism that would follow at the turn of the century.

The urning identity, a minoritized third-sex model of identity with its incipient utopian futurity of relational openness and anticipated proto-activism, was something new and modern. Crucially, it elevated the orientation of sexual desire to a central defining characteristic of the individual. From the moment it was first articulated, it was on the move. Initially, the men who called themselves urnings were just those who had read Ulrichs's works. By the end of the decade, scientific writers and the mass media were spreading the ideas further. In time the identities would be passed from individual to individual, lover to lover, without the medium of written discourse. The terminology itself did not survive long into the twentieth century, and the identity would be modified to accommodate cultural, political, and linguistic settings of the future. However, the minoritized social identity with orientation of sexual desire at its core, which Ulrichs launched upon the world in 1864, would also be the scaffold that future queer identities employed: homosexual, homophile, *Schwul*/gay.[51] The sexually modern urning identity would become a standard that was replicated and modified in a cascade of future queer identities in the years to come.[52]

A Brotherhood of Urnings

The urning identity had passed from paper to personhood but not yet to the public sphere. It is likely that most urnings kept their urning nature private and would not have made public declarations.[53] The consequences for those who took on the urning identity depended very much on their life situations. In the 1860s there was no formal organization, nor, at least initially, was there evidence of other urnings stepping forward. At this stage it would not be appropriate to call the urnings a movement or even a community. They were, if anything, a sequestered brotherhood.

There is nevertheless some evidence of urning social gatherings being held shortly after the publication of Ulrichs's first pamphlets. He reported one of these in his fifth pamphlet; as he did not indicate it as news from correspondence, it was possibly an event that he had attended himself: "A large Uranian coffee social took place in January 1865 in Frankfurt-am-Main. Approximately fourteen Urnings attended. A few of them had also brought their lovers, Austrian and Prussian soldiers."[54]

The sequestration of urning life in the 1860s makes it hard to gauge or quantify the uptake of the urning terminology as a personal identity in this early period. However, the use of Ulrichs's terminology by his correspondents is a measure of sorts. Of the eighty-two urning letters that Ulrichs quoted from, thirty-five used the urning terminology. By contrast, only nine of seventy-two letters from dionings used the word "urning," and in that case, they did so after 1869, when the terminology had entered wider public discourse.

Urning society, while not formally configured or closely networked, can be ascertained in part from the letters themselves. Many of the letters reveal characteristics of the men who wrote them. It is possible to use these along with portraits of urning life by Ulrichs and later writers[55] to chart a typology of significant characters in the urning world. Klaus Müller charted a similar typology in his examination of Krafft-Ebing's autobiographical case studies. Müller recognized that the autobiographical sexual case studies behaved more like fictional prose: "This was not only contoured in the "factual reports," the staging of the self was more clearly expressed by the narrative attitude, the position towards the fictional reader, the stylistic borrowings from the most diverse genres."[56]

If the accounts are treated as if they were narrative fictions rather than factual historical records, it is possible to excavate characters through analysis of the texts themselves. This can be extended to the urning letters Ulrichs received, since the autobiographical accounts contained in these are read as the way the author self-conceives rather than as accurate first-person accounts. By aggregating this material, it is possible to analyse the common properties, character clues, and biographical tropes that, taken together, form the cast of urning characters.

A thematic analysis of the sources reveals nine broad groups of men who took up or engaged with the new urning identity or who existed on the boundaries of the urning world: the ordinary urning, the consummate weibling, the discreet professional, the isolated urning, the married man, the social cross-dresser, the ambivalent mannling, the soldier, and the blackmailer. As a rubric for understanding and navigating the world of urnings in the 1860s, these characters have some utility.[57]

1. *The Ordinary Urning*

The defining feature of the ordinary urning was less his character than his uncomplicated response to Ulrichs's pamphlets. He was the reader most likely to embrace the urning identity. He was probably sexually active and did not have a high-profile position that could introduce greater risk through exposure. Ulrichs did not describe them as such, but "ordinary urnings" were the group he was probably closest to. Ulrichs's first six urning friends from Frankfurt – the "guiltless fellow comrades" who urged him to publish his ideas – might be considered the initial ordinary urnings.[58] The ordinary urning was often a young intermediate or only slightly masculine or feminine individual living in a city or large town who had managed to find a means to fulfil his sexual instinct. It would be an error to assume that the ordinary urning was more likely to be effeminate; rather, he was inclined to be relaxed about any association with effeminacy. There were also a few who otherwise considered themselves more strongly gendered as mannlings or weiblings. Among the other types, they were the individuals most likely to take on the urning identity and back Ulrichs's activism or – in one or two cases – mount their own campaigns.

2. *The Consummate Weibling*

Ulrichs's initial postulation that the urning was a female soul in a male body (the anima thesis) meant that his message had a special resonance with effeminate weiblings. For some of these, the sense of their inner female nature went a lot further than mere effeminacy and may have approximated what would later be described in the early twentieth century as a "transsexual" identity (or more recently, a transgender or gender-diverse identity).[59] Ulrichs forthrightly and inclusively deployed these proto-trans examples, with the result that he is seen today as an early transgender ally. For any individuals among his readers with a strong inner female sensibility, this must have been a great comfort even when they maintained their inner female nature in private.

3. *The Discreet Professional*

A subset of Ulrichs's close followers comprised discreet professionals who were older and in positions of importance. Although no less supportive of Ulrichs's cause, their contribution to the effort was necessarily of a different kind. Ulrichs wrote that several of his correspondents were important men: "Prussian and Bavarian judges in active service to the state ... businesspeople, factory owners ... and the aristocracy."[60] Ulrichs did not identify these men by profession even when he quoted from their letters. He only once noted that a correspondent came from a position of influence and authority.[61]

4. *The Isolated Urning*

Those who were isolated were perhaps the individuals most in need of Ulrichs's urning writings. These were men of all ages who opted to stay chaste and unmarried and who suppressed their inner lives out of fear of humiliation or prosecution. This was, of course, not a lived experience unique to the 1860s. They lived in an age when most men married late and those who did not face family pressure could remain unmarried without too many problems. Although they predominated in regions outside the main cities, it is probable that some lived in highly urbanized environments. These isolated men were unable to mix with other urnings and may not have known of other possibilities until they read Ulrichs's pamphlets.

5. *The Married Man*

In Germany during the 1860s, there were some urning men who had come under concerted social and familial pressure to marry. Some of these men were uranodionings (bisexuals) who could reconcile their sexuality with marriage. However, there were also urnings who had succumbed to overwhelming familial pressure and had married despite having no sexual inclination for women. Ulrichs noted that "many unfortunate urnings of our century ... living in isolation, are pressured into marriage with a woman by persuasion and by so-called 'standards' (There are hundreds of such marriages in Germany!)."[62] Sometimes the pressure came from family, but not always. The tragedy was double: a woman deceived, and a man traumatized in the pursuit of unachievable heteronormativity.[63] In Germany, the rights of women within marriages were limited, but it was at least easier for a woman to sue for divorce than in other countries.[64] The outlook for the men, unless they were released through bereavement or divorce, was probably bleak. Those who were sexually active with men would have to have been so adulterously, making them vulnerable to blackmailers.

6. *The Social Cross-Dresser*

In the 1860s, there was a subset of city-dwelling, effeminate urnings who adopted female attire as part of a subcultural practice of female impersonation. Female impersonation in the late nineteenth century was partly an artefact of older traditions of sexual and gender non-conformity and gender "passing." However, this was overlaid with more recent notions of theatricality and urban modernity.[65] Social cross-dressers were protean figures. Their public manifestations were an overt statement of sexual availability to the initiated, a message that was at the same time submerged and obscured for everybody else. Female impersonation in public offered challenges to "easy notions of binarity," disrupting conceptions of both gender and sexual orientation.[66] Few of the weiblings who cross-dressed lived their whole lives in women's clothing – the cross-dressing was a periodic performance for young men whose figures and feminine personalities were suited to a convincing female impersonation. These cross-dressing young men for the most part occupied the hedonistic niche that large Western cities today similarly afford "scene queens." In that sense, these cross-dressing young men were distinct from the consummate weiblings described earlier and their transvestism was not an expression of deeper gender dissonance.

7. *The Ambivalent Mannling*

Ulrichs called masculine urnings "mannlings," and there were several of these among his closest colleagues. However, a small group of city-dwelling mannlings showed themselves resistant to the urning label and were inclined to criticize Ulrichs from the sidelines. These men had arrived at a sense of sexual self in the urban subcultural context and so were less enthusiastic about Ulrichs's new terminology. It is unlikely that they used either "urning" or "mannling" to describe themselves. They did, however, engage critically with Ulrichs in correspondence, and for the purposes of this typology, they constitute their own character type.

8. *The Soldier*

Ulrichs's original model for the urning posited that his sexual and love partners were dioning men. This was because Ulrichs, and presumably the urnings he consulted, shared a sexual preference for soldiers. Soldier-love (*Soldatenliebe*) was widespread in late nineteenth-century

Germany.[67] The appeal of soldiers to urnings was that they had youth, strong physiques, fitness and health, and alluring uniforms. Also, the stereotype of the soldier was masculine and adventurous, and, since he lived in an all-male environment away from the family home, he was an object of desire for urnings.[68] While it was almost certainly true that most soldiers who engaged with urnings were in fact dionings, the widespread conscription of a whole generation of young men in the 1860s must have meant there were some with a predisposition towards their own sex. These individuals either had become sexually awakened in all-male regimental company or had dabbled in soldier prostitution and realized they had a taste for other men.

9. The Blackmailer

Many of Ulrichs's correspondents either were victims of blackmail or knew of others who were. It is unlikely, although possible, that some of Ulrichs's readers were blackmailers themselves. Some blackmailers certainly identified as urnings, although there were also dionings among them. One can gauge the sheer scale of the problem with blackmail from a typology of seven kinds of blackmailer that Ulrichs extracted from the countless letters he had received on the subject.[69] Reports of blackmail saturate Ulrichs's pamphlets. It was the single biggest complaint of urnings in the German states and in Austria in the 1860s and 1870s, and it would continue to be a problem in the ensuing decades. Ulrichs tried to think of practical solutions. In 1869, upon hearing that the Berlin police maintained a list of 3,000 urnings, Ulrichs suggested that urnings start sending the details of blackmailers to them.[70] They could do so anonymously to avoid making themselves the object of police inquiries. There is no evidence that any of his correspondents started doing this, and it is possible that Ulrichs placed a little too much stock in the goodwill of the police.

These character classifications were not intended to be discrete identities, and there were some very significant overlaps among them: the "ordinary urning" was an "everyman" character defined by his response to the urning identity and thus overlapped with almost all the character types; some of the mannlings had been soldiers; some of the isolated urnings would over time, accept their identities; and a small minority of each type would be victims, or perpetrators, of blackmail. These stereotyped characters do not constitute the whole picture – everyone classified in this model had unique life circumstances and personal qualities that made them very much more complex than their typological groupings. Even so, these categories serve as a reference point for the individuals whose life stories are profiled in richer detail in the chapters that follow.

Conclusion

The urning began in 1864 as an abstract entity in print and then proceeded from page to personhood. By the end of the decade, men across the German-speaking world were calling themselves urnings. The urning, with his self-crafted identity, was a significant cultural development in the 1860s, even if numbers were small. Ulrichs and his correspondents had accomplished together the intellectual articulation of a broad, inclusive sexual identity. In the decades that followed, the numbers of men calling themselves urnings would grow, and some of these would own their urning identities publicly.

The next chapter introduces two urnings who made public confessions in the 1860s. Up until the late 1860s, Ulrichs's campaign had been a lonely one, for he was the only individual (as far as we know) who had publicly identified as an urning. That was all about to change. Unlike Ulrichs, however, these urnings made their public declarations in unhappy circumstances. Their trials were watershed events that took the urning message to new levels of public awareness.

Chapter Three

Two Trials: Sensation, Horror, and the Urning in the Public Sphere, 1867–1870

Is it so difficult to understand that the scandal is caused much less by the action itself than by what is made of it, that the parents of the scandal are the gossip and the sensation for which the injured bed-secret alone pays the alimony?[1]

When Magnus Hirschfeld wrote the above in the early twentieth century, he was looking back over several decades of sensational trials. The scandals that arose around each case not only amplified the public discourse on sexuality but also drew in prurient fantasies of "degeneration, atavism and violence."[2] This was a feature of each case, but the two trials profiled here, held in 1867 and 1869, specifically linked the new public discourse of urning sexuality with degeneracy, depravity, and bloodlust in a pivotal year for Karl Heinrich Ulrichs's campaign for law reform.

In the early years of the urning movement, only Ulrichs had a public profile as an urning man. This made him the *de facto* urning spokesman – a situation that was unsustainable. If the urning communities were to survive and advocate for their own rights, others would have to step forward and add their names to the cause. Ulrichs's first five pamphlets had generated considerable correspondence but no critical mass of urnings stepping forward to demand their own rights.

In 1867, Ulrichs would be arrested and banished after Prussia's annexation of most of the north of Germany in the wake of the Austro-Prussian War of 1866. The North German Confederation, established through the annexation of territories with extant legal codes, began the process of forging a new legal code that would cover the whole territory. Ulrichs did not want the Prussian model of criminal law to prevail, and indeed, it was not a foregone conclusion that all the provisions in Prussian law would carry over into the new state.

Regarding several parts of the criminal law, the new authorities recognized that the multitude of options meant they needed to be reviewed. The antisodomy law, Paragraph 143 of the Prussian code, was one such law, as Hanover and Brunswick had no antisodomy laws. In the initial provisional penal code, Paragraph 143 became Paragraph 152. Deliberations now began, with legislators and legal scholars discussing the way forward. Ulrichs, now resident in Würzburg, Bavaria, must have realized that his campaign would have to shift focus to the drafting of the new, unified penal code.

It seems that Ulrichs was still the only urning to have made a public declaration. Two others were about to join him, although the circumstances of their public declarations were not of their choosing. Their sensational trials, amplified by the nascent mass media, provided a platform for public statements and propelled Ulrichs and his pamphlets to the very centre of public debate. This was an opportunity for him, but it also put him at risk, for the legal/political process was in flux at the time. This chapter examines both trials and the two men who became the first of Ulrichs's followers to declare publicly that they were urnings. The first trial was held in Bremen and involved Friedrich Feldtmann, a close friend of Ulrichs who had been betrayed by a blackmailer. Months later, the second and even more sensational Zastrow trial in Berlin captured national media and public attention.

The Trial of Friedrich Feldtmann in Bremen

In 1867, the Hanseatic Free City of Bremen was the smallest and least populous state incorporated into the North German Confederation.[3] Although it was under review, the criminal law in Bremen was still a hodgepodge of local statutes based on the 1532 *Constitio Criminalis Carolina* of the Holy Roman Empire, an archaic legal code grounded in Roman law rather than Germanic common law.[4] Technically, under the terms of the *Carolina* code, same-sex relations could be punished with death by fire.[5] In practice, though, local statutes with lesser sentences had been established through precedent. There had been only five trials for same-sex crimes since 1837, although Ulrichs noted that lack of evidence and suicide often ended cases before they came to court.[6] The trial of Friedrich Feldtmann and associates in 1867 would be the next same-sex crime to come before the court in Bremen.

Friedrich ("Fritz") Conrad Anton Feldtmann was the director of the City Theatre, a post he had held since April 1864. Prior to this, he had been an actor/director at smaller theatres in Ulm in the Kingdom of Bavaria and in Zurich, Switzerland.[7] Born in Bremen on 26 January

1834, the son of a confectioner of the same name, he was connected through the marriages of his sisters to two of the most powerful families in Bremen, the Ellinghausens and the Rhodes.[8] Feldtmann was the first local man to serve as Bremen's theatre director. It was a significant position for someone who was only thirty years old, and it promised to launch him towards an illustrious career in theatre management. His three years in charge were later regarded as the City Theatre's heyday because of his innovative approach.[9]

The City Theatre of Bremen was state-owned and could seat 1,400 in the main auditorium.[10] Each year, an ensemble company of 120, including twenty-three actors, eleven operatic soloists, thirty choristers, and thirteen ballet dancers, produced a mixed winter season that included opera, classical theatre, and farces; there was also a summer season for theatre and light opera.[11] In an age before cinema, in towns of Bremen's size, theatres held a central position for entertainment. They consequently presented much fuller programs to cater to a larger potential audience. The theatre priced tickets to be affordable for the working man or woman, and several performances took place each day. In the summer season of 1867, running from 1 May to 31 August, there were 142 unique productions and 349 individual performances.[12] Most performances were of contemporary works that had been imported from the stages of Berlin. The highlights of that summer season were an operetta by Franz von Suppé, *Schöne Galathea*, which had premiered two years earlier in Berlin, and the one-act musical play *Alter Commis*, which had premiered in Berlin the previous year.[13]

Fritz Feldtmann was an urning and was likely one of Ulrichs's correspondents.[14] Even in the 1860s, the theatrical world was well known to be a haven for urnings, and actors could live relatively open lives in that narrow context.[15] As a young man holding a powerful position in a field to which urnings were drawn, Feldtmann probably had little difficulty in finding and attracting partners. In the summer season of 1867, a new actor joined the Bremen ensemble: Carl Wilhelm Otto Filsinger, who had transferred from a theatre in Berlin.[16] He was twenty-eight years old, tall (six feet, four inches), and slim of build, with brown hair and a neat blonde moustache. His clothes were elegantly stylish, and he used a modicum of face make-up. The tight grey trousers he often wore were calculated to maximize his physical appeal.[17] He must have made an impression on and off the stage. An urning himself, Filsinger had "wormed his way into Feldtmann's confidence."[18]

At some point during the summer season, Filsinger was present during an occasion when Feldtmann and three younger men were allegedly enjoying an episode of drunken intimacy. Filsinger later used this event as leverage in a blackmail attempt. He demanded 50 thalers in return for his leaving Bremen, which Feldtmann promptly paid.[19] But Filsinger did not leave the city and instead demanded 80 thalers more. When Feldtmann refused to pay the second sum, Filsinger anonymously sent a detailed denunciation to the authorities containing allegations about the event he had witnessed. Perhaps realizing that he too would be vulnerable in any investigation of his allegations, Filsinger disappeared from Bremen. In due course, the authorities arrested Feldtmann and his three associates on the following charge: "[Feldtmann] induced three young men to satisfy their sexual instincts by physical contact with him and that he masturbated with two of them. He seduced his co-defendants into the acts of lechery by giving them intoxicating drinks and touching their genitals, thus putting them in a state of great sexual excitement."[20]

Feldtmann was a popular man in Bremen, particularly in urning circles.[21] His arrest on 3 October 1867, three days after the summer season had closed, was a public sensation.[22] He was arrested alongside the three nineteen-year-old dionings he was alleged to have had relations with: Gruner of Erichsburg, Hanover, Sieb of Bremen, and Bengnot of New Orleans.[23] The authorities were also interested in the blackmailer, who was suspected of being a participant in the sexual "crimes." On 18 October, Schlodtmann, the examining magistrate, issued a warrant for the immediate arrest of Filsinger, effective across the whole of North Germany.[24] Filsinger, by that time, was no longer in North Germany and so fell outside the reach of the warrant.

When Ulrichs heard what had happened, it made a huge impression on him. There had been other trials where Ulrichs had petitioned the court on behalf of the accused, but this one had a personal dimension. Ulrichs considered Feldtmann to be "one of the best citizens" and "a loyal friend." [25] At that point, he was in the middle of writing his major work, *Memnon*. When he heard the news about Feldtmann, he gathered together the first seventy-two completed sections, had them printed, and sent copies to the judges, witnesses, state attorney, the defendant, and other legal and political authorities in Bremen.[26] Feldtmann, no doubt encouraged by Ulrichs's proactive support, requested that the court president, Herr Migault, permit Ulrichs to join his defence team.[27] Migault ruled to exclude Ulrichs, calling him "that gentleman who sent me the publication."[28] Not everybody took such a dim view of Ulrichs's writings. The court physician, Dr. Stedler, wrote back positively: "I do not believe that the practice of man-manly love is any worse than gambling, alcoholism, etc. Because these vices go unpunished, I consider this practice all the more innocent, and punishment of it all the more unjust. Intimacy with boys should, of course, be severely punished. Among adults it is a different matter. The partners in this case practice free choice."[29]

Some of the many copies that Ulrichs had mailed to Bremen passed from hand to hand, reaching a much wider audience than intended, as a rapturous correspondent prone to exaggeration wrote from Bremen:

> Your book truly has produced an uproar among the people of Bremen. Everyone is talking about it. Rumour has it that 4,000 copies of a written defence have been sent here from Würzburg. Everyone is asking to receive one from whoever is sending them. They are passing from one hand to the next … Judges, witnesses, and state attorney really appear to have different ideas on the subject. Indeed, even the public. I have already heard it said: "Only the three young people must actually be punished, not Feldtmann. The matter is indeed unnatural in their case; in Feldtmann's it is natural." Does this not prove the beginning of a turning point in public opinion?[30]

Even if the Bremen correspondent exaggerated, the Feldtmann case and Ulrichs's distribution of the booklets meant that Ulrichs's terminology and ideas about sexuality were reaching a wider audience in Bremen, including many non-urning individuals. Knowledge of the urning identity had, up to that point, not disseminated much beyond a private self-selecting minority of same-sex-attracted men. The urning identity had now become a subject of public discourse and thus a character within the public sphere. The urning was now, at least in Bremen, a public personage.

The trial began on 19 December 1867 and lasted two days. Ulrichs was particularly unhappy that even though he had sent ample material to the defence attorney, Dr. Mohr, that lawyer failed to challenge the legal assumption that urning love was "unnatural."[31] Indeed, even the prosecuting attorney, Pauli, showed some sympathy for those who felt the law was problematic: "The defendant calls it barbarism that he is accused at all. From his standpoint he may be right. In such cases, other states have abolished punishment … Until this is the case in Bremen, I have to represent the law from my standpoint."[32]

When Feldtmann took the stand, he became the second person after Ulrichs to admit on the record that he was an urning. He apparently concluded his defence with these stirring words: "Just as you, my judges, have the right to love women, I have the right to love men. We both have this right from God. If you hesitate to acknowledge this, then you are violating the justice of God, who planted the drive in my heart as he did in yours. You have the power to condemn me: I must dispute whether you have the right!"[33]

The court passed judgment on 20 December 1867. Charges against Sieb and Bengnot were dropped due to lack of evidence, Gruner was sentenced to four weeks' imprisonment, and Feldtmann was sentenced to a full year in prison.[34] While some were inclined to say this was a lenient sentence, Ulrichs was quick to point out that in most of the rest of Germany either there was no law proscribing same-sex activity or the legal system had been modernized to have laws that only criminalized anal intercourse and not non-penetrative sexual acts.[35] In 1867, mutual masturbation between men was not a crime in Bavaria, Saxony, Hanover, Württemberg, Baden, Prussia, Oldenburg, or Brunswick, and it would likely not have been considered serious enough for formal prosecution in many other places.[36] This covered most of the land area of modern Germany. If Feldtmann had been almost anywhere else in Germany, this case, which involved no penetration, would likely never have reached court.

Ulrichs was also particularly unhappy with the full text of the judgment, as it included several faulty citations and the surprising citation of Justinian's Novel 77, an archaic Byzantine legal instrument.[37] Modern legal thinking in Germany favoured replacing the Roman legal codes with Germanic common law.[38] Following the Germanist legal conferences of 1846 and 1847, all the larger states in the German Confederation had taken steps to reform their legal codes. Only a handful of small duchies and free cities had yet to reform their laws by 1867. Ulrichs was an enthusiastic advocate of the modernized Germanist legal codes, and he lionized the two intellectual advocates of the same: Paul Johann Anselm Ritter von Feuerbach and Carl Joseph Anton Mittermaier.[39] The use of the 1532 *Constitio Criminalis Carolina* of the Holy Roman Empire and citation of an archaic Byzantine law to justify Feldtmann's sentence was complete anathema to Ulrichs at a time when far superior German instruments were in circulation.

In the German and Austrian states there was likely a great deal of sympathy for Feldtmann in urning circles. This was also the case for many in the theatrical world who had worked with him professionally. Actors and opera singers were a highly mobile workforce, so it is perhaps not a surprise that expressions of support came from as far away as London. An English urning wrote to Ulrichs in English on 22 March 1868: "Though I cannot in words express my gratitude, I am true [*sic*], that, could I write with my heart instead of my hands, I should make you feel how grateful I am, not only on my own account, but for the sake of poor Fritz [i.e., Feldtmann] toward whom you have so nobly acted."[40]

Feldtmann had been on remand up until the trial. His sentence officially began on 20 December at Bremen prison. Feldtmann's two brothers-in-law, Heinrich Ellinghausen and Carl Rhode, wrote an impassioned appeal for clemency on 2 November 1868 for "a man who has rendered services to Bremen and whose work for the Bremen stage is too well known."[41] Ulrichs also sent appeals for clemency, on 17 June 1868 and then again on 13 November.[42] Feldtmann's own appeal for remission of sentence on 3 September made the point that the imprisonment was only a secondary sanction, as his primary punishment had been much harder to bear: "While I had to feel the condemnation of my fellow citizens, I was also affected by the loss of my existence, my effectiveness in my hometown – and not only in my hometown, but the condemnation destroyed my entire career, making it impossible for me to take over the leadership of any stage ever again."[43]

Feldtmann noted that his behaviour had been exemplary, which would normally result in an automatic remission of one quarter of the sentence, and that he had taken a vow of abstinence. Feldtmann also indicated his intention to set up a theatrical agency in Vienna that would need him to establish an office in advance of the close of engagements at year's end. None of this was enough for the High Court to release him three months early. On 8 September the report from the High Court stated: "In this unusual case the High Court cannot see itself obliged to recommend the pardon of the supplicant."[44]

The law apparently never caught up with Feldtmann's blackmailer, Filsinger. Soon after sending his letter of denunciation to the authorities in October 1867, he fled Bremen, and turned up again in the Grand Duchy of Hesse.[45] In Giessen, he latched on to a young urning from a wealthy family and started extorting money from him. Initially, he demanded 100 thalers. Filsinger clung to the young man "as if he had the arms of a polyp."[46] When he demanded more, the young man had nothing to give. The young urning feared his father too much to ask him for financial help. Filsinger eventually gave up and denounced the young man to his employer, who immediately dismissed him. Filsinger, although he had no pecuniary need to do so, also informed the young urning's father. This was a particularly spiteful act, calculated to inflict the greatest woe on the young urning.

In the summer of 1868, Filsinger turned up again in Frankfurt at the Hôtel du Nord, where he used the name "Feche."[47] With his good looks, elegant attire, and acting ability, he could make good money through blackmail. Under the pseudonyms "Felseck" or "Baron von

Felseck," he preyed on vulnerable urnings in the larger towns and health resorts of Europe.[48] Since he changed pseudonyms frequently and presumably had to change cities or even countries to ensure that his crimes did not catch up with him, it is not possible to find further trace of him beyond this point. Filsinger was ultimately just one of many extorters proliferating in the German states. The crime of blackmail was becoming ascendant in Germany, in part due to the greater visibility of urnings.[49]

The Feldtmann case was a tragic instance of the still prevalent application of archaic legal systems. Taking place in a small city-state, it was one of the biggest criminal cases of the year there. Through his advocacy in this case, Ulrichs had made some public impact: legal officers took note of his writings, and his texts likely reached a wider audience of non-urnings in Bremen. However, events about to unfold in Berlin comprehensively dashed any hopes that his work would have an impact on deliberations concerning the antisodomy statute.

The Zastrow Trial in Berlin

Berlin was a rapidly expanding city. In the six years prior to 1867 it had grown by 155,000 people, a 30 per cent increase; by 1871, it had grown by a further 124,000.[50] As other European cities had found, this sort of rapid growth generated stresses and strains. Policing faced an uphill struggle to maintain public order and win the hearts and minds of the public. The nascent mass media ensured that disquiet over crime reached unparalleled levels. To maintain public order, the Berlin police had to appear to be doing a good job. Intense pressure for results did not necessarily lead to good outcomes, especially in cases involving sexual violence against children.

On Sunday evening, 17 January 1869, the residents of Grüner Weg 45 heard a whimpering noise from the attic. On investigation, they discovered a badly injured five-year-old boy called Emil Handke from number 37 on the same street. The boy's attacker, thinking he was dead, had placed the body in a chimney pipe. Emil had managed to free himself and cry for help. His cries roused the neighbours, who took him immediately to the Bethanien Hospital. Two days later, Dr. Carl Liman began an examination, which, due to the child's severe injuries, he could not conclude until ten days later.[51] The examination revealed a significant anal injury, a detached rectum, partial excision of the foreskin, biting and sucking marks on the neck, and strangulation marks. The injuries were so severe that the traumatized little boy became faecally incontinent; there being no adequate antibiotic treatments, infection set in.

This meant that for much of the investigation and the court proceedings, he was too critically ill to be questioned.

As news of the crime broke, Berliners remembered a similar unsolved crime from 1867. In February of that year, passers-by on the banks of the river Panke in the Invalidenpark in central Berlin discovered the mutilated body of Ernst Corny, a sixteen-year-old baker's boy.[52] The Berlin media immediately sensationalized the case, capturing the public's attention. Kaiser Wilhelm I himself took a special interest and required daily briefings on the case.[53] Perhaps in part because of high expectations arising from media attention, the police mishandled the investigation; although they committed considerable resources to apprehending the culprit (or culprits), they were unable to solve the case. In the ensuing public outrage at this police failure, Berlin Police President Otto von Bernuth resigned on 23 March.[54] The Corny case was still fresh in the public mind when reports of Emil Handke's mutilation broke.

As they had with the Corny case two years earlier, the Berlin and national media turned the Handke case into a sensation. The Kaiser once again took an active interest. This put pressure on the police to get quick results. The nature of the injuries suggested a connection to the Corny case, yet the police first arrested the boy's father.[55] The boy had named him when asked who had caused the injuries. The police released the father one day later as he had an alibi. The investigators concluded that Emil, as a small child, had been calling his father's name just as any small child would call for their protector when threatened.

In a moment of clarity on the second day of the investigation, Emil testified that a bearded man had lured him into the attic by promising him books.[56] His eight-year-old brother, the only other real witness, said he had seen a fat man talking to his brother. Emil later said that two men had been involved. The police neglected these promising leads from eyewitnesses when far more sensational but less credible evidence broke. Although the police had searched the attic space after the discovery of Emil, neighbours who went back to look at the crime scene after the police had finished their investigation discovered a red handkerchief and a white cane, which they brought to the police. The police considered the cane to be the weapon. The police would rely on these two pieces of physical evidence in court, as Emil Handke was too ill to give evidence.

One of the first things the police did was question everyone they had interviewed over the Corny case. That included Lieutenant Carl Ernst Wilhelm von Zastrow. The police had brought in Zastrow and kept him overnight for questioning in 1867. Born in 1821, Zastrow had been living in Berlin for several years in an apartment at Potsdamer Strasse 83a.[57] He dabbled in painting and singing but had sufficient cash reserves to lead a relaxed lifestyle.[58] Physically, he was described as being of "Herculean stature."[59] This was in contrast to "the softness of his facial features."[60] He socialized with the very highest urning society, including Prince George of Prussia and the social democrat Johann Baptist von Schweitzer.[61] There was a regular club of sorts, which met in the gallery of the National Theatre, that Zastrow, Schweitzer, and Prince George all attended.[62]

Zastrow's family was from the aristocracy and prominent in the higher ranks of the Prussian military. He had served in the Prussian military himself during the revolutions of 1848–9, rising to the rank of lieutenant. According to Ulrichs, his fellow officers forced Zastrow to resign because they would not serve alongside him after he had "refused to pretend to love women" and had "defended man-manly love."[63] In civilian life, he continued to be outspoken in support of urning rights.

Like Feldtmann, Zastrow was one of the first individuals (after Ulrichs) documented as publicly acknowledging his urning nature.[64] His name appeared among Ulrichs's contacts and was probably on the lists the Prussians had confiscated from Ulrichs in Burgdorf.[65] He also had a police record in Berlin, where his name appeared on the police lists of known pederasts. The police arrested but did not charge him in Dresden in July 1852 when a man accused Zastrow of groping him on a steamship.[66] In Berlin in 1863, he became known for propositioning nightwatchmen. An attempt to entrap him resulted in his arrest but, once again, no charges.[67] In Prussia, the law proscribed only anal intercourse between men, and Zastrow had not attempted that. Later, there would be lurid media reports about his predatory sexual practices on the streets of Berlin. These possibly had more to do with sensationalized reporting than with Zastrow's actual behaviour. His arrests, and his questioning over the Corny case, meant that the police saw him as a potential suspect in the shocking assault on Emil Handke.

On 20 January 1869, within three days of the crime, Zastrow was arrested at his apartment.[68] A long-standing police informer, Ferdinand Müller, who lived on Grüner Weg, had identified him as the culprit.[69] Under interrogation, Zastrow admitted to being an urning, a member of the "third sex," but denied that he practised anal intercourse and emphatically denied that he was guilty of sodomizing the little boy.[70] Early in the investigation, Zastrow was forensically examined by Dr. Liman, who confirmed that he would not have been physically able to sodomize anyone.[71] From this point on, the police assumed that the assault had been carried out with an inanimate object, specifically the white cane retrieved from the scene that was identified as belonging to Zastrow. In addition, forensic examinations found that Zastrow's dental impression matched the bite marks on Emil Handke's neck. When the police led Zastrow into his presence, the boy began to cry. They took this to be a positive identification. Finally, the crime was supposed to have taken place at 3:30 p.m., but Zastrow had an alibi until 3 p.m. at a restaurant in Schöneberg. The police tried to re-create the journey by horse-drawn cab to the assault scene and found that it was just possible within the time frame (although the defence contested this in the trial). The police concluded their investigation in April 1869, with the investigating team, police senior management, the press, and the greater Berlin public all convinced that Zastrow was the culprit.

Journalists pored over each of these developments and reported them in meticulous detail in the newspapers, accompanied by speculative comment. They gave much attention to Zastrow's admission that he was an urning. As had happened in Bremen, the word "urning" featured heavily in the media coverage, turning what had been a private minoritized personal identity into a public personage. That coverage fuelled a surge in negative public sentiment accompanied by a ghoulish fascination with the gruesome sexual crime itself. The investigation made headlines for days, with the *Berliner Gerichtszeitung* of 26 January devoting the entire front page to the case, complete with a portrait of Zastrow. Media sensationalism often served as a substitute for accuracy.[72] Ulrichs, who might have hoped for informed public debate, commented on eyewitness reports he was receiving in correspondence from urnings in Berlin:

> The impression of the Zastrow case on the Berlin population must have been an overwhelming one. I hear some hair-raising things about it. Two new vernacular expressions have already been adopted: "a Zastrow," i.e., an Urning, but with the understanding that every Urning is possessed by demonic bloodthirstiness; and "to zastrow" (to practise Uranian rape). "I am going to zastrow you," for example, is actually supposed to have become a barracks expression.[73]

Public hysteria was becoming a problem. Ulrichs recounted a story about a senator from Freienwalde who was accused at a train station of being a "Zastrow" by a tramp with a grudge against him. The man was a dioning, but he was immediately descended on by a mob. The police arrived and dispersed the crowd. However, the police did not protect the senator himself. Paying heed to the crowd's accusations, they arrested the senator for a "Zastrow" attempt. Curiously, it was "Zastrow," the accused's name, and not the word "urning," that was used as a pejorative. Nevertheless, an association was forming in the public mind between bloodlust and sexual perversion. The hypocrisy of the sensationalizing media in provoking such reactions was apparent to Ulrichs: "Now the liberal Berlin newspapers are crying over the danger to personal freedom. Oh dear! To be honest, they had provoked the rage of the people, which got their attention and that of the police, all on their own."[74]

It took little time for the media to start making a connection between Ulrichs's ideas and Zastrow's alleged crimes. On 20 February 1869, the *Börsenzeitung* reported the discovery of one of Ulrichs's pamphlets in Zastrow's library: "He [Zastrow] publicly enjoys indulging in the acknowledgment and glorification of his love of men, a love that, according to the well-known works of the former Hanoverian lawyer Ulrichs, is to be attributed to organic reasons and psychic conditions. He often referred to the content of these writings. They discovered them, including *Memnon*, to be in his library as well."[75]

Ulrichs responded to that article with the following statement, published in the *Börsenzeitung* on 5 March:

> They dared to intimate that my writings had the tendency to gloss over the kinds of crimes that v. Zastrow is accused of. Also, there is great fear that Uranian love in itself is prone to the committing of such crimes. I detest those crimes as much as any reasonable person. Uranian love is innate to the same degree as true manly love, and, in accordance with its nature, leads just as little to crime as the other. Crimes similar to those occur also in the love of real men, whether soundness of mind be present or diminished.[76]

The nature of the terrible crime, coupled with the sensationalizing media reaction, presented a problem for Ulrichs. True, his ideas and theories were at last being discussed in public, but that discourse had become enmeshed in a dark, sensational interpretation and linked to a crime of unbridled horror. This was perhaps the first articulation of a link between a minoritized identity and brutal violence; if so, it would not be the last.[77] It couldn't have come at a worse time: the deliberations over the new criminal code for the North German Confederation were nearing their end point, and a medical commission was at that time considering the case for repeal of the antisodomy law.

Ulrichs was concerned that public hysteria had come to dominate the discourse. He decided to publish his own thoughts about the Zastrow case and how it related to his urning theories. This he published in May 1869 as *Incubus* with the subtitle "Uranian Love and Bloodthirstiness." In this pamphlet, he examined mental health and the Zastrow case through fifteen case studies. He did not intend to pronounce either way on Zastrow's guilt, nor did he seek to minimize the crime itself. Rather, his concern was that the prevailing discourse about Zastrow had linked urning love and bloodlust as if the one intimately predicated the other. This conflation threatened the prospect of a fair trial. It was as if the public took Zastrow's sexuality as proof of his guilt. Ulrichs sought to demonstrate that the assumption of a link between sexual orientation and bloodlust was faulty. Bloodlust was a case apart: "There is at times a yearning, wild, inordinate desire in certain individuals to commit cruelties and to see blood flow for no clear reason; a bloodthirstiness which, as it appears, goes far beyond a responsible state of mind, which at the moment in which it sets in seems to press heavily upon the soul of the individual as an incubus rising from the realm of darkness."[78]

Ulrichs explored three questions: 1. Was Zastrow responsible for his own sexual orientation? 2. Was the attack on Emil Handke an act of urning-love? 3. Was the crime committed in a state of diminished responsibility?[79] Ulrichs believed the answers to the first two questions were "no" and to the third was a qualified "yes." *Incubus* sold faster than any of his other publications and soon sold out.[80] Capitalizing on the interest and additional accrued evidence, he brought out an expanded new edition of *Incubus* titled *Argonauticus* a few months later, in September 1869. The public discussed Ulrichs's careful arguments but often without insight or accuracy. Later he wrote of the reaction to *Argonauticus*:

> I did not defend the horrible deed that had occurred; I did not "thrust a lance for them," as one of them challenged me. I thought that it would be easy to distinguish the two from each other: a defence of the deed and a defence of him against that which he is accused of, against injustices before the court which threaten him. And further: what has harmed us, harmed us in the eyes of the Dioning world, is the deed itself and not my explanation of the deed. You should not confuse one with the other![81]

Ulrichs was not alone in expressing an alternative perspective on the Zastrow case in 1869. Karl Maria Kertbeny, who will be discussed in the next chapter, may also have attempted to intervene. Among Kertbeny's papers at the Hungarian National Library there are three documents in draft form that he may or may not have deployed prior to the Zastrow trial.[82] These were an "anthropological report" intended as a memorandum for the prosecutor and the members of the jury, an "exchange of correspondence" that may have been intended for publication, and a "letter to an editor" that was intended to provide guidance to a certain newspaper editor.[83] In these documents, Kertbeny claimed that Zastrow was a "homosexual" and therefore could not be guilty of the crime. According to Kertbeny's letter, the "homosexual" was only "half-potent" and therefore not capable of brutal acts. Only a "normalsexual" could have assaulted Emil Handke (or Corny). If Kertbeny did deploy these arguments at one or more of these targets, there was no evidence it had any effect.

The first trial of Zastrow opened on 5 July 1869. Due to the fear of a public riot, the proceedings were conducted in a special room within the jail rather than at the courthouse.[84] The *Berliner Gerichtszeitung* devoted its front two pages to the trial.[85] The judge was W. Delius. Carl Westphal, Carl Liman, and Karl Skrzeczka were the medical examiners. W. Henke was the prosecuting attorney, and Zastrow's defence attorney was A. Holthoff.[86] Zastrow was charged with the attempted murder of Emil Handke and also with child sexual abuse under Paragraph 176 of the criminal code. In Henke's opening indictment, he argued that in addition to the evidence, Zastrow's urning nature should be seen as predisposing him to the crime. On the witness stand, Zastrow admitted his love for men and said he was a member of Ulrichs's "third sex." [87] However, he totally disavowed anal intercourse. He also said that he had never had an inclination for children, preferring mature men as sexual partners. When Holthoff called on the medical experts, they replied they were not ready and so the court adjourned.

When the court resumed for the second trial on 25 October 1869, the medical experts were ready.[88] Liman's report found Zastrow to be sane and not remotely feminine. Liman further said that Zastrow was fully convinced that his urning disposition was innate. Westphal, by contrast, declared him insane. Skrzeczka explained that even if his sexuality was innate, he was still bound by the law and his sexuality would make him capable of the crime against Emil Handke. The prosecution then guided the jury through the case with each piece of evidence. After this, a series of witnesses claimed that Zastrow propositioned strangers at night. However, no witness could place Zastrow doing so in the area where the crime took place. One witness, who knew Zastrow well, said there was another man who looked like Zastrow and was often confused with him. Attorney Holthoff then called Chief Inspector Drygalski to the witness stand. It seemed that the doppelgänger for Zastrow was a police officer, who was also an urning. Drygalski confirmed this was the case.[89] The remainder of the trial consisted of a series of witnesses whose allegations played no part in the final judgment.

On 29 October 1869, the jury unanimously found Zastrow guilty. The court sentenced him to fifteen years at the Moabit prison in Berlin. Media sensationalism and public hysteria may have played a part in the final verdict. Pressure on the police and the courts to secure a conviction came from the Kaiser himself, and expectations were fanned by the daily press. However, the evidence was at best circumstantial and at times highly questionable. In a less febrile atmosphere, the jury might have focused more on the holes in the case: the white cane missed by the forensic police investigation but then "discovered" by an unnamed member of the public several days later, the implausible mad dash in horse and carriage between his lunch restaurant and the scene of the crime, and the key witness compromised by a sexual connection to the accused. Hugo Friedländer wrote of the jury verdict thirty years later:

> Although Zastrow's guilt of having committed the attempted murder of the boy Handke rested on very weak feet – Corny's murder was not on trial – the jury unanimously affirmed, according to what they heard, the questions of guilt for attempted murder and unnatural fornication. The jurors are said to have been of the opinion that, if the accused did not commit the assassination at the Grüner Weg, then he murdered Corny.[90]

Prospects for Legal Reform in a Climate of Public Uproar

The consequences did not stop with Zastrow's incarceration. Throughout the Feldtmann and Zastrow cases, deliberations on the new North German Confederation legal code had been proceeding. In June 1868, Bismarck directed the new Justice Minister, Adolf Leonhardt, to draw up a penal code for the new Northern Confederation. On 12 August 1868, Leonhardt commissioned the Minister for Education and Medical Affairs, Heinrich von Mühler, to examine whether the antisodomy statute, Paragraph 143, should be repealed, or whether it should be retained but with the section on bestiality removed. Finally, in October 1868, Mühler appointed a Royal Scientific Deputation for the Medical Profession to provide expert clarification on this question. The scientific deputation delivered its report on 22 March 1869. They recommended from a public health perspective that male–male sodomy not be regarded as a crime but that male prostitution be criminalized.[91] However, they delivered their response against a background of public Zastrow hysteria. Leonhardt transmitted the report to Mühler on 17 April 1869 as the police investigation concluded in a frenzy of press and public indignation. Mühler responded to the Justice Minister by rejecting the recommendations of the medical deputation on the grounds that the population at large would regard reform as a "legislative mistake" because the crimes fell afoul of the "laws of nature" and the "moral code."[92] It seemed extraordinary that a Bismarckian minister would be so fearful of public opinion when legislating. The media-driven public hysteria that had agitated everyone from the Kaiser down must have had an impact. Certainly, Ulrichs and Kertbeny were both convinced that the Zastrow trial and the public reaction to it had been a decisive factor in the decision that resulted.[93] However, there was another, related reason why Mühler made his quixotic decision.

In addition to Ulrichs's and Kertbeny's submissions, there were others from "affected persons," lawyers, and medical individuals. There was also a religious submission. The Central Committee of the Inner Mission, a leading Protestant revival organization, had launched a petition against public immorality that had gathered 15,000 signatures from across the North German Confederation.[94] The petition recommended against repeal of the antisodomy law: "And that even the unnatural vice, which has found its sacrilegious apologist in Hanover and Würzburg, and which is hidden in Berlin and abroad, cannot be concealed, because the depth of the damage to be combated must be marked."[95]

The reference to "Hanover and Würzburg," Ulrichs's home state and his home in exile, was unambiguous. Ulrichs was a "sacrilegious apologist," and the church was aware of his campaign. Same-sex relations were not the central feature of this petition, even with the Zastrow trial under way, but the generalized religious/moral thrust was uncompromising. The Central Committee delivered the petition to the Bundestag on 30 March 1869 while Mühler was still considering his recommendation. Mühler was sympathetic to the church cause. He was an independent conservative who sat on the Evangelical Upper Church Council and was familiar with the Central Committee. His wife, Adelheid, was a strong advocate of the same campaign.[96] Mühler knew that his colleagues in government from other less conservative or religious parties might not be receptive to a religious argument. However, his references to "sin" and the "moral code" in his response to the Justice Minister rather suggests that unspoken religious reasons were on his mind when he rejected reform. A professor who wrote to Ulrichs from Berlin on 17 March 1870 was certainly of this opinion: "The reason given by certain influential persons, it appears to me, is this, although they do not express it: to make a concession to the orthodox Church traditions."[97] Following Mühler's decision, the legislative process could commence. The debate on the second draft of the North German Penal

Code took place in the Bundestag from February to May 1870. By that time, Bismarck had made clear his plans to consolidate Prussian power by incorporating the four southern German states of Bavaria, Württemberg, Baden, and Hesse-Darmstadt. By the time it came into force on 1 January 1872 (with minor changes and the antisodomy paragraph now renumbered as Paragraph 175), the new penal code covered the whole of newly united Germany.[98]

Conclusion

Zastrow and Feldtmann were the first two men, other than Ulrichs, to make public statements about their urning identity. Public discourse and the mass media coverage of their trials transformed what had been an identity held privately by a sequestered minority into a public personage. In the eyes of the public, the urning was now a real entity on the fringes of the public sphere. The graphic, sensational coverage of the Zastrow trial meant that *Urningtum*, at the very moment it was entering public discourse, found itself closely tied to depravity and criminal violence. The trial had turned Zastrow's name, rather than the word "urning," into a pejorative. An association between deviant sexuality and unspeakable horror was forming in public discourse at precisely the point where politically, with the deliberations over the new penal code, it was most inopportune for the urnings' cause.

Feldtmann had to make his first public declaration that he was an urning in a court of law and was extremely unlucky, given the times, to be sent to prison for non-penetrative sexual activity. Zastrow had been open about his urning nature prior to his arrest, and that may itself have contributed to the guilty verdict. Was the neighbour who discovered evidence at a crime scene that had already been examined by the police part of the negative reaction to Zastrow's openness about his sexuality? The police informant, Ferdinand Müller, who turned Zastrow in, apparently did so out of sexual jealousy.[99]

Zastrow never completed his sentence: he died of acute pleurisy while still incarcerated at Moabit on 25 February 1877. One of his last visitors was the writer Paul Lindau, who claimed that Zastrow remained adamant that he was innocent. He continued to bombard the authorities with petitions.[100] His defence attorney, Holthoff, was certain of Zastrow's innocence to the very end.[101]

It is not known whether Feldtmann was able to set up his Viennese theatrical agency upon his release in December 1868. Traces of him in the years that followed are hard to find. In late 1874, he returned to the Aktientheater in Zurich as director.[102] After Bremen, this must have felt like a demotion. The Aktientheater was housed in a repurposed monastery church that could seat 800, almost half as many as the Stadttheater in Bremen. Although it had been the theatre that Wagner used while in exile, a private stock company controlled the finances and budgets were more limited than at the state-owned theatres in German cities. Feldtmann's tenure at the theatre was a success, but he was not happy there and so did not agree to a further season after 1878.[103] This is the only record of theatrical employment of Feldtmann in the relevant press for the years 1870 to 1884. Feldtmann was in Berlin under the care of Doctor Richter's Private Sanatorium, Pankow, when he committed suicide on 12 February 1884.[104] He died only sixteen days after his fiftieth birthday and apparently left no note.

Ulrichs's dreams of achieving a society, in his lifetime, where the absence of laws against urnings meant that they could live openly and freely were fading. Events had overtaken his efforts at reform, but that did not mean his approach was faulty. His objectives were grounded and achievable. Repeal of the antisodomy statute came very close to reality. In the immediate short term, the media sensation and public reaction unquestionably had negative consequences for legal reform. In the longer term, though, once public consternation had subsided, there was a possibility that the trials had attracted a growing number of people to his cause. Ulrichs observed that "the booklet *Argonauticus*, at least, has really helped our cause, and indeed of all my books, no other has brought me as many followers, Urning and Dioning, as *Argonauticus*."[105]

Feldtmann and Zastrow both made public declarations about their urning natures even though they were being persecuted. It would be wrong, however, to assume that every same-sex-attracted man who read Ulrichs's works and corresponded with him had such uncomplicated responses to his message. The next chapter turns to individuals whose established urban identities were not predicated on Ulrichs's theories but who corresponded with Ulrichs during the 1860s.

Chapter Four

Sins of the City: Karl Maria Kertbeny and the Social Cross-Dressers, 1865–1880

In the case of Urnings (extreme Mannling nature with manly temperament, desires similar to men, etc., extreme Weibling nature, and gradation of the intermediate natures), the furthest extremes in the sexual spectrum are as far apart as – not those in women or men, but rather those in men and women.[1]

The urning, in his first configuration, was a mildly effeminate man. Karl Heinrich Ulrichs did not anticipate the gendered variation from mannling to weibling when he first started writing. Among his letters, he received some from indignant masculine men who were repelled by any suggestion that they were effeminate and others from young men about cross-dressing in public. Both of these groups existed in urban settings in the period before Ulrichs started writing, and both drew on identities derived from older early modern configurations. These urban personages had managed in different ways to carve out positions in which they could function socially, sexually, and with sybaritic ease. Both groups were from the distal boundaries of the urning world.

Ulrichs had masculine men and cross-dressers among his closest allies; however, there were subsets of both who were less receptive to his ideas.[2] In chapter 2, these were characterized in the typology as the "ambivalent mannling" and the "social cross-dresser." These subsets may have felt that they would benefit little, materially or politically, from the advent of the urning as a new personage; they may even have seen it as a threat to their existence. Many of them were city-dwellers and had already arrived at a sense of sexual self in the urban context, so for them, "urning" was not an identity but just a new terminology. They found themselves both drawn to and at odds with *Urningtum.* Ulrichs did not use the terms "ambivalent mannling" or "social cross-dresser" himself. However, he was aware of individuals who could be characterized as such. As his campaign advanced, he encountered masculine critics, whom he later acknowledged in a letter to Carl Robert Egells in 1873: "Some of my comrades have already made considerable efforts to criticise and fault my booklets. They called the contents of Memnon 'nothing but cancan,' the contents of all my booklets 'sophistry,' the poems 'miserable,' and said: that all my works had only harmed our cause and that 'anyone can write something like that,' etc. I jokingly called this faction the 'Party of Grumblers,' the 'Grumbler Party.'"[3]

One of these "grumblers" was the journalist Karl Maria Kertbeny, who left a considerable written legacy of his disaffection, views that he shared with other "grumblers." In a second letter to Egells of 31 January–1 February 1874, Ulrichs all but named him: "One of the main 'Grumblers' is probably motivated by unconscious jealousy. He writes quite well, has a more rhetorical and flourishing style than I do, is also a poet, but has never had anything printed of course."[4]

The social cross-dressers, for their part, were probably not inclined to criticize. That said, some of them were pointedly unwilling to participate in the urning struggle. In his tenth pamphlet, *Prometheus*, published in 1870, Ulrichs reflected on this: "The greater masses of Urnings, particularly in such cities as Vienna, Berlin, Moscow, Paris, and London, unfortunately show little sense for the struggle that is directed toward winning freedom, justice, and a place for Uranism in human society and, at the same time, toward improving its spiritual situation. It is more important to them to be taken for women at masked balls and to be courted by unsuspecting Dionings."[5]

Ulrichs described this group scathingly as the "boneheaded herd" who were "hardly worthy of freedom."[6] This passage in particular reeks of disappointment and dislike for a class of people, the social cross-dressers, whom Ulrichs had been promoting in his earlier pamphlets. Ulrichs may have championed these individuals, but they did not derive their sense of sexual or gendered self from his theorizing. They were part of an older tradition of gender dissonance and sexual disobedience in the urban subcultures. Only one of the letters Ulrichs published came from a social cross-dresser, but he received gushing letters, which he reproduced in print, from other urnings about the cross-dressers they encountered. The excitement of successful female impersonation and the hedonistic enjoyment of the urban milieu were preoccupations for some of this group to the exclusion of anything else. Ulrichs's reaction against them needs to be seen in that context. He was not repudiating cross-dressing *per se* but lamenting the lack of support he received from that quarter.

The individuals profiled in this chapter were all city-dwellers. Karl Maria Kertbeny was an ambivalent mannling (although he probably did not apply that term to himself) who had resided in several of Europe's larger cities, while the entertaining accounts of cross-dressers came from London and Vienna, two cities with long-standing same-sex subcultures. Ulrichs received relatively few letters from city-dwellers with either of these character profiles, and there are reasons to believe that they were less receptive to his identarian sexual modernist intervention. There were, however, several who did get involved and who sent him letters. This chapter turns first to Kertbeny, who attempted to generate his own theories and who wrote works on same-sex sexuality. It then examines the escapades of social cross-dressers in London, as well as the extraordinary letter that a prominent Austrian sent to Ulrichs.

Karl Maria Kertbeny

Kertbeny was the very model of the ambivalent mannling, although he quite possibly never referred to himself as an "urning." He was the only ambivalent mannling to have left a literary imprint in this period. The ambivalent mannling was a personage of the 1860s, a decade that was examined in this book's introduction as a transitional period characterized by the coexistence of several non-hegemonic masculinities. Ambivalent mannlings, exemplified here by Kertbeny, shared an identity that emerged from older forms of aristocratic libertinage, which acquired a foothold through the militarization of the German and Austrian middle class.[7] Kertbeny's biography contains many elements that resonate with the concept of middle-class libertinage. His public image was a carefully constructed fiction; his true biography was concealed within a multitude of contradictory autobiographical accounts.[8]

Kertbeny was a former Austrian soldier and spy who had lived a peripatetic life as a versatile journalist and literary dabbler in the years before the 1860s. He had "Magyarized" his surname in 1849 to the Hungarian-sounding "Kertbeny" and wrote of his aristocratic ancestors.[9] In fact, his parents were Austrian bourgeois bohemians who raised him in comfortable circumstances in Pest, Hungary, as Carl Marie Benkert, and who apprenticed him at a young age to a bookseller.[10] On being dismissed from that apprenticeship in 1842, Kertbeny set about reinventing himself, initially through a two-year stint in the Austrian army and then as a writer and bibliographer in Pest.[11] During his years in Pest, he translated into German the works of several prominent Hungarian writers, including the national poet Sándor Petőfi, and founded a short-lived literary magazine.[12] After the revolutions of 1848–9, he followed the diaspora of Hungarian nationalists into Austria, where he worked for a brief time as a spy for the Austrians.[13]

By the 1860s he was active as a freelance journalist, specializing in short biographical pieces about literary celebrities of his day. Hounded by debts and in search of writing commissions, he rarely stayed in any city longer than a few months.[14] In the 1860s, he moved frequently but was resident mainly in Vienna, Geneva, Paris, Brussels, Munich, Hanover, Berlin, and Pest.[15] He was happiest in the big cities or capitals, where he could mix with the literary luminaries he wanted to write about.[16] It was in the big cities that he found his kind, and it is likely that his own sense of sexual self emerged in that context.

The masculine image Kertbeny presented to the world was ambiguous. Kertbeny had crafted for himself a swashbuckling, romantic, hedonistic, and amoral masculine identity that owed much more to eighteenth-century aristocratic libertinism than it did to any newly emerging ideas of bourgeois German, Austrian, or Hungarian manhood. This must be somewhat qualified, for Kertbeny in other respects was an entirely contemporary citizen of the European urban environment. The romantic image of the intellectual Hungarian exile was a common trope in the decades after 1849. He lived the marginal life of the charismatic bohemian emigré from the east. He had no university or professional qualifications, yet he affected, and frequently claimed, a deep understanding of medicine and law. He may have attended a few lectures on these subjects, but there is scant evidence in his writings that these left much impression. A little digging makes it plain that he was utterly unqualified in any subject. He was far from being a "whole man" committed to inner self-cultivation; his image was only skin deep.

In line with his carefully crafted persona, Kertbeny steadfastly presented himself as a masculine man with a "normal" sexual orientation. In letters to his mother, he suggested at various times that he was about to marry. Then in 1864 he wrote to her that he would not be marrying because his nerves could not cope with it.[17] When he later came to write about sexuality, he claimed to be "normalsexual" and devised a misleading story to explain why he was writing on the subject.[18] In private, he behaved otherwise, and his notebook diaries contain coded references to his frequent assignations with young men.[19] His carefully crafted façade protected more tender core truths about himself. His sexuality was one of the things that he realized would damage him if it was revealed. Kertbeny's public masculinity was not qualified by either his sexuality or his sociopolitical background, both of which remained ambiguous.

However interesting the twists and turns of Kertbeny's protean persona might be, they tell us very little about his more private engagement with deviant sexuality. Scott Spector recently opined that "the search for the real Kertbeny, like Stoppard's real Inspector Hound, is a red herring, a distraction from the real mystery."[20] It is easy to get bogged down in the ephemera of Kertbeny's life when the real mystery is why someone like him turned his attention to writing several major works about "homosexuality."

The "Homosexual" Question

Prior to 1864, there was no indication in Kertbeny's writings that he had thought about advocating for sexual rights. However, he did touch on same-sex sexuality several times in his writings. In his second volume of *Sillhouetten und Reliquien* (1863), he related an account of the poet Heine discussing fellow poet Platen's sexuality. In this account, Kertbeny used an ellipsis, there being no printable words to express what he meant.[21] In the same book, Kertbeny discussed the Viennese actor Wilhelm Kunst, resolving the linguistic difficulty by comparing him to a list of classical figures with male lovers.[22] He came back to the subject again in 1864 in a short biography of the Austrian-American writer Charles Sealsfield, in which he wrote: "But this belongs to the area of the former cultural history of our development of the concepts of law, morality, and *Numa Numantius'* theses."[23] "Numa Numantius" was the pseudonym Ulrichs used for his first five pamphlets, so this passage indicates that by 1864, soon after they were published, Kertbeny was acquainted with Ulrichs's first two pamphlets or had at least heard of them. Kertbeny established contact with Ulrichs on or before 20 June 1864. Ulrichs gleefully noted in the summer of 1864: "First printed reference to my theories is in *Recollections of Charles Sealsfield* by Kertbeny."[24]

Kertbeny struck up a spirited correspondence with Ulrichs thereafter, most of which has not survived.[25] The archives contain only the draft of a letter to Ulrichs that Kertbeny composed in 1868. This letter reads like a restatement of arguments the two "combat comrades" had been engaging in for some time, and he may have intended it to be a final statement of difference.[26] The opening paragraphs read like a goodbye letter. It is possible that Kertbeny never sent a final version, since Ulrichs would report six years later, in 1874, that the two of them were still on good terms.[27] However, the 1868 letter does show that there was a gulf between the two with regard to their understanding of sexuality, and much of the correspondence between them prior to that date may have focused on those differences.

At the simplest level, the two men used different terminologies. Kertbeny used his own neologisms, "homosexual" and "heterosexual." The first recorded instance of these words was in his 1868 letter to Ulrichs.[28] Kertbeny drew on several sources for these neologisms. The Greek prefixes "homo-" and "hetero-" had previously been used in eighteenth-century German literature in connection with, respectively, same-sex and opposite-sex sexual acts.[29] Appending "sexual" as a suffix was a relatively simple way to complete the neologisms even if, for purists, it was an unforgivable mix of Latin and Greek.[30] Although the terminology did not take off during Kertbeny's lifetime, by the turn of the century, both words were starting to enter common use among scientists, legislators, and activists. These two words were Kertbeny's biggest contribution to the discourse of human sexuality.

The terminology wasn't the only point of contention revealed in this letter. Kertbeny also rejected the innate argument:

> There are also people who are innately bloodthirsty, pyromaniacs, with all sorts of perverse desires, people with monomania and so on. They are not, however, allowed to exercise their innate drives or follow their instincts, and when they are punished, even though they may not be culpable, still they are incarcerated to keep society safe from their expropriations. So, the proof of innateness, even with the most undeniable evidence, would not have given us the slightest gain.[31]

Innateness in and of itself was not a sufficient argument for toleration since the contemporary understanding was that other criminal behaviours also were innate. Ostensibly Kertbeny was saying he opposed the arguments about innateness for strategic reasons: "The theory of heredity – however true it is anthropologically – as a campaign strategy also has the very great disadvantage that, while at the same time as challenging the prejudice against urnings, it also multiplies it even more by making them special, peculiar, abnormal unfortunates of capricious creation, hermaphrodites, imperfectly formed unlike other people, lopsided and lame, eliciting cries of compassionate horror from dionings."[32]

Kertbeny spent much of the letter refuting "innateness," and it is possible that he instinctively reacted against anything that would heighten the separation between the homosexual and his fellow man. He preferred to see sexuality as a matter of taste or preference: "It is a more masculine argument of total free will when I say, 'I can eat roast mutton, but I do not choose to because I do not want to and I find other roasts tastier, and nobody has a right to tell me what I should eat, what not, since I also give everyone the freedom of his taste.'"[33]

This brings us back to Sedgwick's encapsulation of the two different ways of defining sexuality as the "minoritizing and universalizing views of sexual definition."[34] Ultimately, Ulrichs's third-sex theories were anathema to Kertbeny's urban libertinism, which held that sexuality was a masculine universal attribute, a sexual preference for men and not a separate minoritizing identity. Proofs of innateness, fixed natures, and gender variance were all irrelevant when the strongest argument was that "the state has no business interfering in consenting private acts between two people."[35] Kertbeny's central argument here did have some merit: the freedom to pursue victimless sex was ultimately the argument of gay liberation in the 1970s. For Kertbeny, it was an argument drawn directly from the Enlightenment philosophers of late eighteenth-century France, who believed that consensual sex in private should remain unpunished.[36]

Much of the 1868 letter criticized Ulrichs's ideas; very little of it presented Kertbeny's own. Having established his dissent, Kertbeny intimated his intention to publish "a unique hefty manuscript."[37] He came back to this towards the end of the letter, referring to it as his "100 theses."[38] Kertbeny wrote that he had sent these documents to a Dr. M., who declared them "the most ingenious arguments he had ever read about this question so far."[39] Kertbeny intended to publish this manuscript and had already listed it among his unpublished manuscripts, a 340-page volume focused on male and female sexuality.[40] Several years later, he pitched the idea for this book to the Leipzig publisher Hermann Serbe and sent him part of a historical introduction. On 5 July 1868, Serbe replied that he was interested in the manuscript.[41] Serbe pressed Kertbeny over the next few months, but the author was unable to supply the rest of his book. Eventually, in the summer of 1869, Kertbeny, now resident in Berlin, replied to Serbe with the manuscripts for two pamphlets calling for the repeal of Paragraph 143. The pamphlets were in the form of two open letters to the Prussian Justice Minister Leonhardt, and Kertbeny published them anonymously through Serbe's publishing house in the autumn of 1869. These pamphlets contained Kertbeny's arguments against the antisodomy law and the first articulation in print of his ideas about sexuality.[42]

Kertbeny made some important observations in these pamphlets. For example, he noted that despite the prevalence of homosexuality, the Berlin authorities had successfully prosecuted only a tiny number of cases of "unnatural sex." This meant that most instances of sodomy were going unpunished apart from a few high-profile cases. Thus, the law as it stood was just a licence for blackmail. The surprisingly accurate figures he used in making this observation suggest that he had some access to official police records.[43]

Kertbeny's core thesis was rooted in liberal utilitarian arguments for law reform: "The rights of man, however, always begins with man himself, and the most important thing for man is his own love, with which he can begin completely freely and in which he can do whatever he likes to his advantage or disadvantage, as long as he does not disturb the rights of others – the individual, society, or the state."[44]

Years later, on republishing one of Kertbeny's letter pamphlets from 1869, Hirschfeld wrote that it was "considered by experts to be one of the best works on the homosexual problem and indeed contains a wealth of aspects."[45] Although they were well-argued by Kertbeny, with his universalizing rationalism, the 1869 pamphlets had a limited readership, and other writers almost never cited them in the years that followed. His publisher later wrote to him that sales of these pamphlets had been poor and that he would not be considering a second edition.[46] The only contemporary reference to the two publications came in a criminal law journal of 1870, which stated simply that they were anonymous and about "Urning-love."[47]

The two pamphlets were almost certainly the product of Kertbeny's diligent study in 1868. It is entirely possible that he intended to reuse the material in these, augmented with other work, to supply the manuscript for his "340-page" volume on sexual studies. His papers in the National Széchenyi Library in Budapest contain evidence of his efforts. In one box of papers there are bundles of close-written documents headlined variously "Onanism," "Artificial Onanism," "Platonism," "Mutual Onanism," "Tribadism," and "Pygism."[48] It is clear from this that Kertbeny had begun producing material for a substantial work on sexuality. However, he never completed the manuscript. In January 1870 he was felled by a stroke and, unable to write, retreated to the countryside. There is little evidence that he wrote much more after the stroke, although he revived his diary after one year. In 1875 he returned to Budapest,[49] where the Hungarian authorities had offered him a state pension.[50]

Kertbeny made one further attempt to publish his ideas. In late 1878, he collaborated with and ghostwrote part of *Die Entdeckung der Seele* by the Stuttgart zoologist Gustav Jäger. The short section on homosexuality in this book was a fragment from Kertbeny's earlier work on his planned book. Jäger rejected most of the content Kertbeny had supplied but promised it would be issued in a post-publication supplement once Kertbeny provided the sources.[51] Presumably Kertbeny never did so, for no supplement had been issued by the time he died on 23 January

1882.[52] The book was a commercial success, popularizing Jäger's pheromone theories and bringing Kertbeny's terminology, if not his theories, to a wider audience.

Almost twenty years later, in 1900, Jäger did publish Kertbeny's homosexuality chapter in full, in Magnus Hirschfeld's *Jahrbuch für sexuelle Zwischenstufen*.[53] The documents provided by Jäger contained the most complete published version of Kertbeny's alternative theory. This was the first time his ideas in a near complete form reached a wider audience. Other writers had, by then, started writing "masculinist" material in *Der Eigene*, so Kertbeny's twenty-year-old arguments for an alternative masculine configuration of homosexuality would be of only historic interest to the readers of the *Jahrbuch*. Kertbeny wrote to Jäger in 1878 about the scale of the manuscript and the remaining material he had not sent: "I have not yet communicated even half of the data and conclusions that have forced themselves upon me during 39 years of long observations in three parts of the world and have remained in my memory without my finding the key to this riddle."[54] Since most of the material sent to Jäger concerned homosexuality, he may have been referring to more detailed work on other facets of sexuality. It is also possible that the material published by Jäger reflected an early stage in the development of his ideas that would have benefited from revisions, had he not suffered the stroke.

In the material published by Jäger, Kertbeny maintained repeatedly that he was sexually "normal."[55] Kertbeny, who called himself a "normalsexual," claimed to be a medical doctor called "Dr M." and invented an elaborate backstory to explain why he was writing about homosexuality. This story involved the suicide of a friend who had asked him to convey a last letter to his mother and his network of same-sex-attracted friends.[56] It was because of this that the now-aged doctor had studied the subject of same-sex sexuality for thirty-nine years.[57] This dissembling was entirely consistent with Kertbeny's conception of his own masculine identity and its layers of deception. However, it possibly also stemmed from a strategic belief that his arguments would be more credible to his readers if they were perceived as coming from an objective scientist who did not share the sexual tastes of the subjects he was studying.

Kertbeny's material reproduced by Jäger focused mainly on the homosexual. There were also short sections on "tribades" (lesbians), "amphisexuals" (bisexuals) and "monosexuals" (celibate solo masturbators). Kertbeny estimated that in a population of one million men there would be around 20,000 "homosexualists," which equated to 2 per cent.[58] This figure was higher than estimates by Ulrichs and the contemporary psychiatric literature and much closer to modern estimates.[59] Using the analogy of freemasonry, Kertbeny wrote that homosexuality was distributed, largely unseen, at every level of society.[60] According to Kertbeny, homosexuals were not happy with Ulrichs's anima thesis: "Most of them feel most unhappy about the game of nature, to be condemned as *anima muliebris in corpore masculino* [sic], as their main defender called them, calling them *Urnings* – about their hermaphroditic position on the ranks of nature, about their abnormality, which they have to conceal like a murder."[61] This was Kertbeny's projection of his own disquiet, although perhaps it also reflected the opinion of some of his friends and acquaintances. Jäger in 1878 received letters from several men about the "homosexual" section, so possibly there were others who shared Kertbeny's views.[62] Kertbeny said of his position that he was "a principled opponent of all symptomatological categorizations, which are too reminiscent of the witch trials."[63] Nevertheless, he did have his own categorizing ideas about homosexuality.

In this late version of his ideas, Kertbeny had conceded some ground. First, and most importantly, he now fully accepted that homosexuality was innate. Second, he acknowledged that many, if not most, homosexuals were to some degree effeminate. However, for Kertbeny, it was the sexual practice and not gendered behaviour that subdivided the homosexual. According to Kertbeny, more than 90 per cent of homosexuals were "mutual" – that is, they practised only mutual masturbation.[64] The other group, accounting for 2–3 per cent, were the "pygists," who practised sodomy.[65] In both cases, individuals could be either active or passive.[66] Kertbeny described active pygists as young, attractive hypermasculine libertines, passive pygists as hypereffeminates, and all mutuals as weakly effeminate.[67] The gendered hierarchy of the homosexual tacitly valorized the active pygist as part of a super-virile elite, rising above all the other subclasses. Notably, Kertbeny devoted much of the text to describing the active pygist and comparatively little to describing the other subdivisions.[68] However, for all the subclasses, the homosexual was a sexual being defined solely by his sexual acts. The assumption was that all homosexuals were having sex and that none of them were celibate. Ulrichs's urning could be inexperienced or celibate, but there was no room for this in Kertbeny's homosexual configuration.[69] Kertbeny wrote that celibate solo-masturbators were an entirely different class of sexual being – the "monosexual."

Kertbeny deployed three named case studies. The first of these involved an active pygist named Valerian Schober, whom he described as a highly attractive roué in public and a sodomite in private.[70]

Schober was the archetype of the libertine masculine configuration. The second, Giovanni Campi, was another active pygist who preferred older men as partners.[71] The final case study, Heinrich Rittmann, was an extremely effeminate twenty-two-year-old passive pygist.[72] Kertbeny's selection of three elite pygist case studies excluded any that covered the majority "mutual." The use of full names for these case studies was another curious feature. The names were probably not the real names, and the idealized way in which Kertbeny described each case study suggests that they only loosely approximated real people. Named case studies had been the practice in medical texts of the early nineteenth century, particularly in teratological and forensic settings. However, that was no longer considered appropriate, and contemporary psychiatric texts used numbered cases and anonymized initials for the subjects. Kertbeny was apparently unaware of this change in practice. He did not dwell on the works of others, but briefly cited a list of forensic doctors up to Johann Ludwig Casper and August Ambrose Tardieu in 1862.[73] The quality and quantity of the works on homosexuality on this list was apparently insufficient, and Kertbeny decried the paucity of good science on the subject: "Now, forensic medicine and anthropology in general, on this occasion dug out views that were still far behind those of Paul Zachias of 1674, and which, travestied, can be summarised in the statement: 'Natural history, in spite of its alleged laws of nature, does not yet know anything about it.'"[74]

Kertbeny's field of reference stopped in the early 1860s. He promised Jäger he would send an annotated bibliography of 173 titles, but he never did so.[75] He presented himself in Jäger's texts as an enlightened scientist, yet he based none of his assertions on contemporary science, nor did he cite the scientific literature on sexuality that was by that time proliferating.[76] He was entirely unaware of the turn psychiatry had taken following Carl Westphal's paper of 1869. Kertbeny, therefore, probably wrote most of this document in the summer of 1868, when he was first negotiating with his publisher. It is unlikely that he accomplished much writing or reading following his stroke. The 1869 pamphlets and the material published by Jäger were only early drafts of what Kertbeny had intended to be a much more substantial work. Had he not had the stroke, he might have had the time to include his response to the new psychiatric texts.

Kertbeny never published a completed edition of his substantial manuscript. The anonymously published works were only fragments of a much larger and more comprehensive work. There were certain parallels between Kertbeny's half-articulated ideas in these fragments and the early twentieth-century masculinism of Benedict Friedlaender in his *Die Renaissance des Eros Uranios* (1904).[77] Similarly, the Englishmen John Addington Symonds and Edward Carpenter would formulate more masculine theories of homosexuality (see chapter 8). Kertbeny's ideas may not have circulated widely, but his "homosexual" terminology endures to this day. The popularity of Jäger's 1878 book ensured that the word "homosexual" would reach a wider audience than it had previously. In the second volume of *Psychopathia Sexualis* in 1887, Richard von Krafft-Ebing published an autobiographical letter that mentioned Jäger's "homosexual idiosyncrasy."[78] By the fourth edition, Krafft-Ebing had begun using "homosexual" himself.[79] Several years later, in 1891, the sexologist Albert Moll used the word "homosexual" as an adjective and noun alongside the word "urning" in his most important work.[80]

Kertbeny with his sexualized disposition and Ulrichs with his third-sex identity came at the subject from different ontological and epistemological positions. However, published works used the words "urning" and "homosexual" interchangeably in the late nineteenth and early twentieth centuries. Within a few decades, Germans were using the word "homosexual" so prevalently that all alternatives became relegated to historical obscurity. Manfred Herzer has powerfully argued that the paucity of definition and the lack of any concentration on origins or psychology, and thus the absence of theoretical baggage, meant that among scientists, lawyers, legislators, and activists, the terms "homosexual," and to a lesser extent "heterosexual," were versatile enough to serve as the words of choice for describing the sexual binary.[81] By contrast, the other terms had become bogged down with definitions and theoretical frameworks that conflicted with developing understandings. The two words "homosexual" and "heterosexual" are Kertbeny's legacy.

Kertbeny and his associates, the "Party of Grumblers," occupied the distal masculine boundary of the continuum of queer possibility in the European urban milieu. Kertbeny and his associates may have reluctantly used the urning terminology for want of a widely understood alternative. Or they may have resolutely persisted with Kertbeny's homosexual alternative. Masculine homosexual discourses began appearing in the late 1890s, so it is striking that only Kertbeny presented them in print in this early period.

At the other end of the gender spectrum for urnings, there were urban men whose response to dominant gendered norms was to cross over to the other side. The next section explores the effeminate distal boundary of the urning world and the social cross-dresser.

Social Cross-Dressers in London

Late nineteenth-century cross-dressing was, in part, a descendant of older forms of gender passing, overlaid and restructured by contemporary urban modernity and vaudeville/burlesque theatricality.[82] The street-walking passing woman had been a feature of larger cities as far back as the Middle Ages.[83] By the nineteenth century, the availability of cheap mass-manufactured couture had opened up the practice to a wider community.[84] These individuals were entirely an urban trope, and while they may have noticed Ulrichs's works, they did not depend on them for their sense of self. The anonymity of the big city in the nineteenth century was the backdrop for the cross-gender performances of some effeminate young men. Few of the weiblings who cross-dressed lived their whole lives in the clothing of the opposite gender – the cross-dressing was a periodic performance for young men whose figures and feminine personalities made a convincing female impersonation possible. For persistent female impersonators, the time came when it was no longer possible. Writing from St. Petersburg on 9 November 1869, one of Ulrichs's correspondents reflected on the final years of the *Knägina* (princess), a cross-dressing beauty feted by the urnings among the local aristocracy: "Now, I suppose at least in comparison to earlier times, he has to go through the school of renunciation, after having been indulged earlier with the choicest luxuries. I think now that in such a case one has to be a philosopher, i.e., to content oneself with happy days gone by. Even if his future does not look bright, his memories at least, will be beautiful."[85]

Cross-dressing was a performative expression of the effeminate urning, a means to flirt with other men in public, a disguise, and a defiant reaction to the strictures of the closet. This was the paradox of the social cross-dresser in times of extreme social hostility: it was a defiant and outrageous reaction to the closet, but it was also a means to effect invisibility and facilitate homosocial flirting. The historian Harry Cocks put it well when he wrote: "The cross-dresser was both eminently thinkable, and at the same time, unthinkable."[86]

Some of Ulrichs's most effusive and extensive correspondence came from the urban subcultures of social cross-dressers. The first of these correspondents was an intermediate urning, probably a German residing in London, who wrote to describe the urban balls and certain cross-dressing characters. He was possibly someone who had been writing to Ulrichs from other places prior to his move to Britain. Ulrichs described him as "an intermediate Urning, who has had contact with hundreds of Urnings in Germany, England, France, and Italy."[87] In his first letter, he described travelling to Brussels and visiting the theatre with one of his London friends.[88] It is not possible to fully identify this correspondent by name, but the way he is described and the fact that he was writing from London in the months January to April 1868 together offer some intriguing clues. It is possible that this individual was part of the operatic world. The mid-nineteenth century was the golden age of grand opera in Europe, and principal singers, musicians, and ballet dancers of note could expect an international career. Grand opera was expensive to produce, and in the 1860s the only places with sufficient capital and infrastructure to produce operatic seasons were the capitals and principal cities of Germany, Italy, France, and England – all the countries in which this correspondent was well known. And as for the trip to Brussels, the Royal Theatre of La Monnaie was a prominent venue for grand opera.

This German correspondent had a close friend in London whom he referred to as "Viola." Viola was "a young English Urning from a distinguished circle" and was also a correspondent of Ulrichs.[89] He was probably one of two Londoners who had written in support after the arrest of Fritz Feldtmann, who, as director of the City Theatre in Bremen, was well known to insiders in the operatic world.

Operatic London was in turmoil at the start of 1868. A fire at Her Majesty's Theatre in Haymarket on 7 December 1867 had left the opera company without a home for presenting its costly season.[90] A production of Beethoven's *Fidelio* was already in rehearsal when the fire struck, and the theatre had also planned a full program of grand Italian opera. Fortunately, the impresario James Henry Mapleson was able to lease the Drury Lane Theatre in time for the spring and summer seasons and secure a "magnificent Company," including the German soprano Thérèse Tietjens, then at the top of her profession.[91] Tietjens was the only German among the principals, but there would have been other Germans among the vast company.[92] If the German correspondent had arrived for rehearsals in December 1867 and had performed in the season from March to June, this would tie almost precisely to the period he was writing from London.

Viola, the English friend of the London correspondent, sent Ulrichs a cutting from England's *Sun* newspaper in mid-1867 regarding a magistrates' court hearing involving two cross-dressers.[93] The *Sun* article concerned two well-dressed young men who were so "painted and powdered" that it was "difficult to tell whether they were males or females."[94] The case involved a civil disturbance during which the aforesaid individuals, Claire Montague and Henry Maltravers (pseudonyms), had engaged in an altercation with prostitutes disputing the right for "Mary Anns" (a slang term for cross-dressers) to trade on their territory at Piccadilly and Haymarket. These were well-known locations for both female and male prostitution (although there is no direct suggestion that this is what the two men were doing), and confrontations between prostitutes and Mary Anns were hardly rare.[95] When asked by the magistrate, Mr. Knox, whether the defendants wore women's clothes, Sergeant Shillingford answered: "They both see gentlemen and frequent urinals."[96] The magistrate fined them each £100 and required them to post bail of £50 for six months.

Ulrichs reported this case briefly in the first section of *Memnon*,[97] which he sent to the London correspondent on 4 January.[98] The London correspondent wrote back to Ulrichs on 12 January:

> Just about the time I had completed reading the publication, six Urnings came that evening to visit us (Viola and me), among whom, unbeknown to me, were both those "Mary Anns" mentioned in the *Sun*: "Henry Maltravers" and Adamantius, the one whose beauty and diamonds I already mentioned. Viola is a close friend of both of them. Maltravers, too, is a charming young man. Naturally I told them about the book on Uranism that I had just received from Germany, and I offered to translate extemporaneously some passages into English. So, I innocently translate §15, the passage in which the *Sun* is mentioned. Everyone present was aware of the compromising nature of the article. I came to the passage. Viola was startled. The others were struck dumb. They said I was improvising. But the book went from hand to hand: they saw it printed. Viola, the one guilty of sending you the newspaper, became as stiff as a poker! Maltravers, fortunately, wore outrageous makeup; otherwise, his embarrassment would have been visible![99]

This amusing story was one of many that the London correspondent sent to Ulrichs. He was an intermediate urning but was content in the company of social cross-dressers. He wrote rapturously of a party thrown for him by Viola:

> Of the twenty persons attending, four were brilliantly dressed as ladies. You would have sworn that a true woman was standing in front of you. The first appeared in poppy-red velvet with a long train, the second in black watered silk, the third in white silk trimmed with green lace, the fourth in bright pink and white satin. Three of them wore nothing around their necks, all four had flowers in their hair. One of them even wore real diamonds. These were a present from her lover, with whom she had spent

all the preceding summer in Paris. In Paris she was seen with him always as a lady and drew everyone's attention with her incredible beauty. He is, however, also a charming young man! His beauty truly surpasses all belief.[100]

On another occasion, Viola and the London correspondent attended a glittering costume ball where there were many urnings dressed as ladies. At this ball, a wedding took place complete with minister, groom, and cross-dressing bride, who later changed into Scottish Highland dress.[101] In all these reports, both the London correspondent and Viola had been observers of, rather than participants in, the cross-dressing extravaganzas. The events themselves had almost all been private occasions, with the cross-dressing shielded from the public.

There was only one occasion the London correspondent described where the cross-dressing was in public. Maltravers and Pallienus (the pseudonym of another urning) horrified their acquaintances by appearing in "black velvet women's clothing" at Viola's home and then proceeding from there to one of the most popular cafés and on to the theatre, where they flirted with strange men.[102] This was a risky thing to do even in a city of London's size. A year later, on 28 April 1870, the actors Ernest "Stella" Boulton and Frederick "Fanny" Park were sensationally arrested and charged for ostensibly doing the same thing.[103] The thrill of the danger was part of the attraction of such risk-taking.

The descriptions from London show a city with a large same-sex subculture. The London correspondent wrote in his letter of 22 March that "the kind of life they lead, the local urnings, is almost unbelievable; it surpasses Paris by far."[104] In Ulrichs's letters, the only similar cross-dressing urning event described from Berlin was a much smaller affair that was not altogether a success.[105] As Berlin grew throughout the 1880s and 1890s, cross-dressing balls became more common. The accounts of cross-dressing that Ulrichs received mostly came from urnings witnessing female impersonators rather than from the cross-dressers themselves. In addition to the letters from London and Berlin, he received similar accounts from Paris, Moscow, and Vienna. These were cities with apparently well-developed cross-dressing subcultures. There was, however, one letter that did come directly from an effeminate urning, from Austria. This was a weibling of considerable social standing who indulged in cross-dressing escapades of staggering daring. Ulrichs received the letter in 1868 at a time when the prospects for reform in Austria were on a knife-edge.

An Upper-Class Viennese Cross-Dresser

When an upper-class cross-dresser wrote to him from Vienna, Austria was very much on Ulrichs's mind. He had taken a strong interest in the Austrian reform process for several years.[106] He had initially been optimistic, but by early 1868 his hopes were fading, and he wrote: "I have been asked repeatedly: 'Has the abolition of punishment not been enacted yet in Austria?' Unfortunately, they have been hesitating! The search for the best has hindered them there in the introduction of what is good."[107]

It was around this time that Ulrichs received the letter from Vienna. This correspondent was an individual of elevated social standing who was himself a social cross-dresser. He lived in a substantial city residence with his extended family, waited upon by servants. This individual, who was about twenty-eight, recounted an outrageous series of escapades that started with one he engaged in when he was only seventeen years old.[108] He and his similarly weibling twenty-year-old friend were helping his sisters with their wardrobe and toilette; this culminated in them trying on some of the dresses, much to everyone's amusement. They then hatched a plan to get an aunt to invite the family to her house. With the family out of the way, the two young men could take a trip to the Universe pleasure gardens dressed in the sister's finery and accompanied in a coach by their current beaux. The Universe had opened in the suburb of Leopoldstadt (now Brigittenau) in 1842 and was, by that time, extremely popular. Patrons could dance, drink, or sample the various amusements. It was possibly a haunt for same-sex-attracted men, but it was not an appropriate place for patrons dressed in such finery.[109] As the young weibling wrote:

> On the arms of our gentlemen, we proudly filed through the ranks. Our appearance in the hall attracted attention. (Our toilette was, in fact, much too elegant for the "Universe.") We took our seats. Then a strapping handsome man approached me and asked me with a pleading glance: "May I, Miss?" Hardly had one dancer left us when there were already two or three others waiting for us. We were enraptured. In the meantime, we had both lost our gentlemen. We found, however, two very gay dancers who offered us an invitation to supper, which we accepted with true delight because they were so handsome.[110]

The two handsome men apparently thought that their weibling companions were women of the demimonde, and so, after supper, invited them to join them in their hotel room:

> Of course, we now began to make every excuse possible, except that nothing helped; we had to get into the carriage. Almost fainting with fright,

we arrived at the hotel. Now we were bound to be discovered! We were impostors, and we had carried out our game with the most delicate sensibilities. When we stepped into the room with the gentlemen my friend began to cry; I fell to my knees! I pleaded for forgiveness for our evil joke; we were not young women! I begged them to let us go. Taken aback, they looked at one another. Finally, they declared flatly; It was now all the same to them; we had to stay![111]

The correspondent said that "when the young men finally did notice the deception, it did not make any difference to them, and they nevertheless amused themselves with us."[112] This invites several questions. Were the boundaries of masculine sexuality in 1860s Vienna so porous that hedonistic excess trumped sexual object choice for these men? Or were they men who knew precisely what was on offer from the very start and who consciously made a play for the cross-dressers knowing they could do so in public without fear of censure? Whatever the case, these young men saw no reason to hold back. According to the correspondent, they then shared a wonderful night together. The two weibling young men started regularly embarking on cross-dressing escapades to "the most elegant balls" and "never returned home unaccompanied."[113]

The Viennese correspondent then recounted his most outrageous escapade. He was an individual of exalted status, but he had a particular liking for lower-class environments, perhaps because the transgressive danger was greater in such settings. He wrote:

> We soon gave preference, however, to those dance bars where we met the so-called "nice fellows." ["Nice fellows," meaning handsome and gay without being high society.] They did not treat us any less kindly. We often attracted a great amount of attention there because of our provocative behaviour. Once there was a cabbies' ball in the suburbs; and some of the Viennese cab-men are nice and neat fellows![114]

He and his friend decided to attend this cabbies' ball dressed jauntily as coquettish washerwomen, with four to six petticoats, floral dresses, ribboned calves, yellow head scarves, shawls, and lurid red-and-white face make-up.[115] This was not an attempt to hide or pass; they intended to make a spectacle of themselves, and they did:

> Here is how we arrived: two washerwomen without chaperones! The women looked at us with spiteful glances. The young men, however, gushed with general admiration. Some stood up at their tables to get a better look at the pretty and brazen "things," while we were taking our seats at one of the tables. Everyone gaped at us as if we were strange, fantastic creatures …

A bold, handsome dark-eyed young man in a velvet coat approached us. In a friendly manner he said to me, "Well my dear yellow-headed one (referring to my scarf), may I have the pleasure?" I stood up, shook my petticoats and took his arm. I noticed how this set everyone off at nearby tables. They were playing a mazurka, with which few people at that time were familiar. Hardly had we danced across the hall when everyone shouted Bravo followed by thunderous applause, as in the theatre. Now the ice was broken.

…

The fellows kissed us to their hearts' content, treated us like royalty and were happy when we sat on their laps. One of them wanted to buy me a splendid shawl … Another wanted to be my steady beau. I do not know how we could have been so gay and daring at that time.[116]

The letter from the Austrian correspondent was a highly amusing read, and he appeared to have enjoyed putting pen to paper. It reads like a long and very camp set of anecdotes intended to amuse, rather than a strictly accurate rendering of events.

From the letter, one can divine that the Viennese weibling correspondent lived in a house with servants and at least one courtyard and that he travelled to each of his escapades in a carriage belonging to the household. If the account is reliable, this individual was taking extraordinary risks. However, except for a mild family scene after the first escapade, he mentioned no other negative repercussions. Either the correspondent embellished the events described and stripped them of their negative consequences or he was of such high status that the law could not touch him.

Vienna was still a small city of less than half a million people in 1860, and its same-sex subculture was small and very discreet. A modernized criminal code, introduced in 1852, proscribed all same-sex relations (male and female), with harsher sentencing guidelines than in Prussia and the other Germanic states. The targeted persecution of sexual minorities by the police in Vienna in the early 1860s was reflected in the rising number of arrests, if not in actual court convictions.[117] As was the case in other German states, Vienna also had a significant blackmail problem, particularly for people of high status.[118] Set against that reality, it is surprising that there had been no fall from grace for this correspondent, and no indication that he feared exposure or blackmail.

There is one individual whose unique circumstances and known proclivities make him a plausible candidate for this Viennese correspondent. Archduke Ludwig Viktor of Austria was the beloved younger brother of Emperor Franz Josef I. He has been described as "homosexual to such an extent that he did not even bother to cover up this weakness."[119] Ludwig Viktor, who was twenty-six years old in 1868 (Ulrichs said the Viennese correspondent was "about twenty-eight"), was known as "Lutziwutzi" by friends and family and had a penchant for dressing in women's clothes.[120] He did not have a sister, but in the 1850s he was so extremely close to his sister-in-law, the young Empress Elizabeth, known as "Sisi," that his mother thought he was in love with her.[121] They were less close as the years went on, but it is not inconceivable that he would have assisted her toilette in 1860 when he was seventeen years old. Ludwig Viktor was an inveterate gossip, and many of the unverifiable rumours about him in the royal palace were self-instigated.[122] So he was probably the source for the rumours that he got up to frequent escapades in women's clothes and that he had at one time had a sexual relationship with a cab driver.[123]

These life details of Archduke Ludwig Viktor tie reasonably neatly to the details in the letter from the Viennese correspondent. But he becomes an even more compelling candidate when we consider the disposition of the Viennese correspondent, who feared neither the authorities nor blackmail. The reasons for this are several. First, it was not possible to arrest members of the immediate imperial family, all the Habsburg archdukes and archduchesses, or to subject them to trial in a criminal court. Technically, only Emperor Franz Josef I himself could censure them, and he was reluctant to interfere with or discipline his relatives. Their oft-repeated bad behaviour prompted one Austrian prime minister to exclaim: "What these archdukes and archduchesses do is downright outrageous!"[124] Ludwig Viktor may also have benefited from several additional layers of protection. He was the Empress Sophia's favourite as her youngest child, and she fiercely shut down any criticism of the young archduke.[125] Ludwig Viktor idolized his older brother, the emperor, and that closeness seemed to be reciprocated.[126] The emperor valued his brother's sharp, gossipy wit and drew on his advice in matters of the palace household.[127] Various senior members of the household, including Lord Chamberlain Rudolf Prince Liechtenstein, were also same-sex-attracted and suppressed criticism of the archduke because of their fear that he would expose them in return.[128] As well, the emperor was inclined to dismiss criticism of Ludwig Viktor even when it did come his way. Finally, Archduke Ludwig Viktor's escapades were trivial compared those of his even more outrageous relatives: Archduke Ludwig Salvator, with his polysexual adventures in the Balearic Islands, and his uncle, the Archduke Otto, a serial philanderer who had once appeared in the foyer of the Hotel Sacher clad only with a sabre.[129] For all the above reasons, Ludwig Viktor's scrapes went unpunished, and he never suffered the consequences.[130]

For all this, there is no compelling proof that Archduke Ludwig Viktor was Ulrichs's Austrian correspondent. Ulrichs quoted one other letter from the same author in 1867, but there is no evidence of any other letters. Had these letters not been anonymous, and had they been written openly by the brother of the Austrian emperor, Ulrichs would have immediately seen an opportunity to use that leverage. Even if it was not him and was instead another prominent Austrian, there may still have been an opportunity. However, the archduke was generally known to think "conservatively, dynastically and ultramontanously," and thus he took a dim view of anyone seeking to tap his influence.[131] If it had been Ludwig Viktor, Ulrichs would have had to proceed without royal help.[132] Austria ultimately failed to reform its antisodomy laws.[133] So it was perhaps this cross-dressing Viennese correspondent whom Ulrichs had in mind when he wrote in his tenth pamphlet about the "boneheaded herd" who cared more about dressing up as women than they did about the urning struggle.

The letters from social cross-dressers that Ulrichs reproduced in his pamphlets were highly entertaining. They were also a window onto a distal boundary that depended not on Ulrichs's urning category but instead on an older urban trope. Cross-dressing and gender passing had a long history in European urban societies. The social cross-dresser drew on these older identities, but this quasi-public form had a shorter lifespan. He came into existence in Europe through the availability of mass-made cosmetics and couture, coterminously with the development of an urning scene. The London cross-dressers were a prominent feature of private functions, but emboldened to venture into the public sphere, they risked official censure. The Austrian correspondent was a case apart. His adventures in women's attire were made possible only because of his class privilege and were executed away from the urning scene in Vienna.

Conclusion

Both the ambivalent mannling and the social cross-dresser drew on older pre-bourgeois gendered sexual identities. They were specifically metropolitan types at home in the big cities, and thus distinct from Ulrichs and his most enthusiastic correspondents, who were mainly from small towns or the countryside. They were the masculine and feminine extremes of urning presentation, and both extremes involved subterfuge and disguise. The ambivalent mannling was more masculine than the average man, and this ensured that his sexuality would never be in question. The social cross-dresser masqueraded as an authentic woman so that he could practise his sexuality and flirt with men in public. They had found ways to exist in the city in such a way that they could be subversively sexually active while *appearing* to be conforming to normative gender standards. It was perhaps unsurprising, then, that neither Kertbeny nor the prominent Viennese individual engaged fully with the newer disruptive identarian ideas of Ulrichs.

Kertbeny may have been a "grumbler" attempting to rival Ulrichs, but he went on to partly accept Ulrichs's epistemic politics and supported Ulrichs with financial contributions well beyond the point when they supposedly broke with each other.[134] His "homosexual" works, although incomplete, were a serious attempt to counter Ulrichs's theories with an alternative. Kertbeny may have hoped that his own neologism – homosexual – would become a badge of an alternative movement of same-sex-attracted men. There is no evidence that any such alternative movement emerged. Given the direction his writing was taking, it is more likely that had he continued, his work would have become an additive contribution. Instead, his limited initial works went unread and his theories were forgotten. "Homosexual" became a synonym for urning in the literature, and although it ended up eclipsing the urning terminology, there is no evidence it ever delineated a separate group.

The prominent Viennese cross-dresser was no ordinary social cross-dresser, and he never would have faced the real danger of discovery and prosecution risked by other social cross-dressers in other settings. The London cross-dressers, Henry Maltravers and friends, did run afoul of the law, but the censures they received did not seem to deter them. They may even have relished the edge of danger that drove them to impersonate females convincingly.

The 1860s, the decade that offered such a window of opportunity for civil society, saw Ulrichs in a progressive struggle agitating for societal change. Paradoxically, the urban individuals most active in subcultural endeavours were far more cautious and conservative. They either reacted against the urning struggle or they ignored it. Yet these were individuals who invested a lot of energy in expressing their sexual selves – Kertbeny through his writing and the Viennese crossdresser through his costumed adventures. It is not a surprise that, in the end, the urban subcultures with pre-existing sexual identities on the distal boundaries of queer society found themselves at odds with the progressive centre. Even in the halcyon days of gay liberation in the late twentieth century, there were older homosexual men who objected to progressive activism.[135]

This chapter has dwelt on individuals who were less responsive to Ulrichs's activist inclinations. There were many others, though, who were very much more invested in the urning cause. Even with a larger following, the pathway to reform looked very different in the early 1870s. These were watershed years during which urnings needed to adjust to new realities. The next four chapters turn to urnings who came forward in the years after German unification and were able to effect positive change as proto-activists. The next chapter focuses on Jakob Rudolf Forster, whose response to Ulrichs's call was to mount a campaign in Zurich to build an urning community there.

PART TWO

1872–1897

Part Two of this book covers the period after the unification of Germany when Ulrichs stepped back from his campaign and, in 1880, left for exile in Italy. Between 1872 and 1897, several urnings stepped forward to continue the campaign. This was the era of urning proto-activism. These chapters detail the activism of urnings who began networking and community building, lobbying psychiatrists with autobiographical case studies, working behind the scenes in police liaison, and translating Ulrichs's ideas for an international English-speaking audience.

Chapter Five

The Matchmaker of Switzerland: Jakob Rudolf Forster's Grassroots Activism in Germanic Switzerland, 1878–1897[*]

For years I have devoted myself to the study of a class of men whose souls are so peculiar that they deserve universal notice, the more so because these men are judged quite incorrectly, unfortunately to their and their fellow men's harm. This class of people has existed since the beginning of the world and will exist as long as there are people.[1]

Karl Heinrich Ulrichs and then Fritz Feldtmann and Carl von Zastrow were the first known individuals to publicly claim an urning identity. In the decades that followed, others would do so in a variety of ways, mostly outside the drama of the courtroom. One such individual was a Swiss urning activist named Jakob Rudolf Forster. His story of activism commences in 1877, almost a decade after the events described in the previous chapter. This chapter's epigraph comes from a passage in his extraordinary autobiography, self-published in 1898.[2] Forster's book is a record of a twenty-year campaign of grassroots advocacy and homo-social networking in the cantons of Zurich and St. Gallen. The lives and accomplishments of men like Forster in other cities and towns across the German-speaking world have largely been forgotten; but the fruits of their endeavours are evident in the greater visibility and assertive-ness of communities of urnings in the final decades of their century.

Ostensibly Forster's book, *Justizmorde im 19. Jahrhundert: Wahrheitsget-reue Darstellung des fast unglaublich verfolgten Schweizers J.R. Forster* (Judi-cial Murder in the Nineteenth Century: Truthful Portrayal of an Almost Unbelievably Persecuted Swiss J.R. Forster), was about his protracted

---

[*] Jakob Rudolf Forster called himself the "Matchmaker of Brunnadern" on the cover of his autobiography. Brunnadern was the town in Switzerland where he had been born.

judicial persecution at the hands of the authorities in Zurich and St. Gallen. The reason for this persecution was Forster's indefatigable activism. Under the cover of his marriage brokerage in Zurich, he networked with urnings, produced and distributed leaflets on urning love, and lobbied the authorities. Over a decade, the state punished him for his efforts with stints in prison, a workhouse, an asylum, and a brutal work camp. The authorities never once succeeded in crushing his spirit. Right up to the point he published his memoir, Forster was still campaigning, and he likely continued doing so in the years that followed.

Forster demonstrated in his activism that he could accomplish much through basic social engagement. In the previous chapter we encountered social cross-dressers who preferred hedonism to activism. However, the hedonistic pursuit of enjoyment need not be devoid of a political dimension. Networks of recognition and friendship became mutually supportive communities over time. By 1897, leadership and formal organization were able to emerge with a groundswell of support only because grassroots activists had devoted so much time to homosocial networking in the preceding years. At the grassroots level, in the 1870s, 1880s, and 1890s, such networking was probably taking place in towns and cities across the German-speaking world. The community organizers of this era were arguably a necessary component of urning emancipation. As the only account that is known to historians, Forster's must serve as a representative example of homosocial activism in this period.

This chapter explores the life of Jakob Rudolf Forster as an important example in the history of grassroots urning activism. It begins by evaluating the utility of Forster's biography as a historical source before turning to Forster's own story, which is presented in four sections: the first introduces his initial encounter with Ulrichs in 1877; the second covers his first periods of activism and incarceration in Zurich (1879–84); the third moves to the troubled years he spent back in his home canton of St. Gallen (1885–9); and the final section examines his return to business and activism in Zurich (1890–8). In this account, Forster emerges as a loveable rascal who, although he sometimes lacked judgment, often falling foul of the laws and frequently in conflict with the authorities, was nevertheless a tireless campaigner for the rights of urnings to live and love in freedom.

Forster's Autobiography as a Historical Source

As a source, Forster's 175-page autobiography is problematic. Forster was not a natural or gifted writer. He left school barely literate, and he acquired reading and writing skills in one of his first jobs rather than in a classroom. The book is a collection of material from several sources arranged in two parts. As there has been no apparent attempt to introduce each document, letter, or passage, the whole work gives the impression of a bundle of papers bound together as a manuscript rather than of a carefully curated narrative.

The first part has more polish and is possibly a melding of texts from his urning leaflets, which were self-published documents that he apparently used for outreach purposes. He referred obliquely to these leaflets in the second section of his autobiography – if the leaflets he references are those that appear in the first part of his book, then this publication is the only surviving record of their content.[3] The quality of writing in the first section suggests that Forster may have turned to some form of editorial support when producing his leaflets. The section includes a long passage on Ulrichs and his ideas accompanied by disquisitions on religion, the history of sexuality, and the contemporary treatment of urnings in St. Gallen and Zurich.

The second section, where most of the biographical details reside, is a picaresque gallop through his life up to the time of publication. Forster wrote a large part of this section as a memoir while detained in the St. Pirminsberg mental asylum.[4] The memoir was then added to in the years that followed up to 1891, when he first planned to publish it.[5] This section seems to have been written without editorial input and reads in some parts as if he were dictating it. There are frequent long digressions, and stories overlap and repeat themselves. He gets bogged down at some points with bureaucratic details. Forster interrupts the flow of the narrative frequently with reproductions of official letters, newspaper reports, certificates, a leaflet defending himself to the authorities, and other documents relevant to the matters he is writing about. Many of these documents appear in the text with no explanation. Finally, he includes some of his own poetry. He decided not to publish in 1891, so there are two additional short sections updating the biography to 1898.

Distilling the pertinent material from this was not a simple matter. Forster's autobiographical perspective had a singular purpose, which was to expose the years of state persecution he experienced. Official sources corroborate some of his incarcerations and his tangles with authority. At other points, the corroboration comes from the official letters he includes in the book. He is sometimes coy when it comes to explaining the grounds for his arrests and detentions or offering details of his urning-related activities. This suggests he may have feared the legal consequences of giving away too many details. Sometimes all Forster gives are hints about, for example, urning community outreach from the Zurich office of his marriage business and the use of his marriage newspaper to deliver covert urning messages. At other points, he refers in detail to personal vendettas against him by certain official figures in St. Gallen as the cause of his travails. The sections about St. Gallen and the St. Pirminsberg asylum are all very fresh in his mind, so the details in these passages are intense. The fact remains that the authorities in Zurich and St. Gallen must have seen him as enough of a threat to the status quo that they made strenuous efforts to keep him out of circulation. That alone is good reason to suppose that Forster was more effective an activist than he was willing to divulge. All of this makes *Justizmorde* a problematic historical source. It is, however, a unique historical document and thus a valuable primary source. Most of the biographical details unrelated to urning activities can probably be relied on up to a point. This chapter cites the autobiography only for significant events and pertinent quotations.

Meeting Ulrichs

In 1877, Switzerland and Germany were coming to the end of a four-year economic depression, part of a global depression that had started with "the Panic of 1873," which had been triggered by the collapse of the Vienna Stock Exchange on 9 May of that year. That panic had brought about an international banking collapse across Europe and North America. The sweeping geopolitical change that had characterized the years leading up to unification had promised a new economic dynamism for Imperial Germany. Instead, it had ushered in years of economic stagnation. Meanwhile, around this time, the Bismarck government pursued a policy of *Kulturkampf* to impose Protestantism forcefully over Catholicism.

In Switzerland in the 1870s, there were tensions between progressive liberal cantons like Zurich, which pushed for reforms, and more conservative cantons like St. Gallen. The reformists prevailed, and this led to a new Swiss constitution in 1874 that augmented Switzerland's unique "direct democracy" with a stronger centralized federal government. This decade saw significant progress from an agricultural to an industrialized economy and a huge expansion of the Swiss railway system. It was a time of economic insecurity but also of political optimism.

After the failure of his honey business in St. Gallen, Jakob Rudolf Forster travelled to Stuttgart, Germany, in August 1877 to liquidate his stock, away from the prying eyes of creditors.[6] Forster came from Brunnadern in the canton of St. Gallen and was twenty-eight years old in 1877. On the way to Stuttgart, while staying the night at the Kreuz-Hotel in Friedrichshafen, he met and befriended an amiable railway official from Immenstadt in Bavaria named Wilhelm Kleber.[7] Their conversation must have touched on their sexual interests because, during their meeting, Kleber handed Forster a copy of one of Ulrichs's pamphlets. This event gives us a tantalizing glimpse into the dissemination of Ulrichs's works as they passed from hand to hand, even when they were no longer available in bookshops. Forster wrote later of how reading this pamphlet made him feel: "This scripture was a balm to my sad mind, and it was only because of it that I did not fall prey to the one to whom so many of my comrades have already fallen: suicide!"[8]

Forster arrived in Stuttgart a few days later and started a honey business there. After notifying his friends of his new address, Kleber wrote to tell him that Ulrichs was also living in Stuttgart.[9] In due course, Forster arranged to meet Ulrichs. This meeting would be the start of a fruitful sustained engagement. Ulrichs had been living in Stuttgart since 1870 and was residing at Silberburgstrasse 102 in 1872. Forster apparently met him at that address. Ulrichs was fifty-two in 1877 and had filled his apartment with mulberry and oak branches for the cultivation of silkworms, as this was his primary source of income at the time.[10] It is unknown what Ulrichs's first impressions of Forster were. Other sources from the same year state that Forster "appeared to be a lowly educated merchant."[11] Forster's class and level of education were not an issue for Ulrichs, and the two established what seems to have been mutual respect during this first meeting. So Ulrichs, who at the time was working on his final pamphlet, *Critische Pfeile*, invited Forster to join his small group of local activists. Ulrichs networked through correspondence with a small number of dedicated urning activists across Europe; meanwhile, at the local level in Stuttgart, he convened a weekly discussion on urning-related issues with close colleagues every Tuesday in a restaurant on Gymnasiumstrasse.[12] Ulrichs's close colleagues included Theodor Mandello, Eduard Fridolin Schöllhorn (also known as "Marquise Emilie de Pompadour"), and occasionally the Stuttgart police director, Siegel, who was also an urning. Forster does not give additional details about these individuals, but Schöllhorn's elaborate sobriquet strongly suggests he was a "social cross-dresser" and that Siegel was possibly a "discreet professional" using his position of influence to covertly help the urning cause. Forster relished the opportunity to be at the heart of discussions. He must have made a compelling impression on Ulrichs, who probably recognized that Forster had the qualities to take his ideas and tactics back with him to Switzerland. Forster later wrote about the things he had learned while with Ulrichs: "I heard a lot of instructive things from this gentleman and also received all his further writings about urning love, which I read and studied with pleasure many times over. I decided to also enter into this fight."[13]

In November, Forster wound up his Stuttgart business and set off back to Switzerland via Ludwigsburg.[14] He had only been in Stuttgart for a few months, but the things he had learned would change his life. In a hotel room in Ludwigsburg over the Christmas period, Forster wrote a letter to King Charles I of Württemberg commending Ulrichs and writing that he had "rendered outstanding services to the world and to posterity."[15] It is quite possible that he was aware of public rumours about King Charles's sexuality when he urged the king to read Ulrichs's pamphlets.[16] Forster was expecting to see Ulrichs one last time, on New Year's Eve, when Ulrichs travelled down to Ludwigsburg, apparently to say goodbye.[17] Ulrichs and Forster seem to have formed a special, almost pedagogical, relationship. Forster wrote: "You have to love this man when you know what he's done for us. I will never forget this man, eternally grateful to him, wanting God to keep him alive for a long, long time to come."[18] Forster now had a cause to pursue, one that would be at the forefront of his mind for at least the next twenty years:

> Supported by the shield of justice of our cause, we must dare to come boldly forth from our previous reserve and isolation! On, comrades, we expect the laws that persecute us to be revised; we wish to live as nature teaches us; we want to be free from scorn, persecution and scandalous investigations, free from unjust imprisonment, free from those scoundrels who hound us, bully us and steal from us, often suck us dry, or, if we do not give in to these people, they simply accuse us, whereby usually nothing happens to them, but we, we innocents, are subjugated "by the law."[19]

Switzerland in the 1870s

Switzerland in the late 1870s was a cantonized democratic republic with a form of government unique to itself. There was a federal government in Bern, but political power mostly rested with the twenty-five cantons, which in turn comprised around 3,000 municipal governments.[20] Each person in Switzerland was a citizen of a specific municipality within a given canton. To move and work in Switzerland in the late nineteenth century, one had to apply at the municipal and canton levels for permission to do so. One even needed permission to move from one municipality in a canton to another. Permission for both required a certificate of good conduct from the municipality of one's birth, and that document had to be updated at regular intervals. Each municipality had its own police force within a cantonal criminal and penal structure.

Uniformed "land-hunters" – most of them former soldiers – kept a keen eye on every Swiss citizen, policing even the boundaries between municipalities. The Swiss playwright Dürrenmatt famously satirized Switzerland as a prison where each citizen was both prisoner and guard.[21] As Forster's travails would soon illustrate, those who fell afoul of this system faced struggles that came perilously close to resembling Dürrenmatt's satirical Switzerland.

Forster came from the canton of St. Gallen but spent most of his professional life in the neighbouring canton of Zurich. The two cantons, although adjacent to each other, were markedly different. St. Gallen was largely rural, a collection of villages in the transalpine foothills. The capital of St. Gallen was a small but prosperous town of the same name with a world-leading position in the production of textiles and embroidered cloth.[22] It was conservative, Catholic, and rather staid. Zurich, by contrast, was a highly developed, largely Protestant canton centred on the city of the same name.[23] A succession of progressive liberal governments had governed the canton of Zurich over the preceding decades and had expanded civil liberties, broadened democracy, and fostered investment and economic growth around a new banking sector.

The legal situation for urnings was complicated by the cantonal system. Napoleon had united the Swiss cantons in the short-lived Helvetic Republic. While it existed, the Napoleonic Code had been the law of the land, and it included no antisodomy law. The legacy of that, once the country had returned to its cantonized state, was that the francophone cantons carried on with the Napoleonic Code while the germanophone cantons reverted to their own cantonal legal systems, which were based on those of the Holy Roman Empire. This meant that an urning could live a life relatively unencumbered by the law in the cantons of Geneva, Ticino, Vaud, and Valais. All the other cantons had laws that impacted the lives of same-sex-attracted people. Article 189 in the St. Gallen criminal law book of 1886, which was virtually unchanged since its restoration in 1806, covered any sexual acts between people of the same sex and imposed a maximum sentence of six years in prison or a workhouse.[24] By contrast, the progressive liberal governments of Zurich had revised and updated the criminal law book in 1871, removing an older and quite precise antisodomy law and replacing it with Article 123, a more general law criminalizing any individual who through "lewd acts arouses public anger or is such in the presence of children" as well as the publication of material that did the same.[25] The commentary in Zurich's 1871 criminal law book made it clear that "unnatural lust" of men towards the same sex or towards animals was very much what the law had in mind by this. According to the commentary, it was not specified in the statute because "it was thought that in all such cases public nuisance came to be caused."[26] Importantly, Article 123 of the Zurich criminal code of 1871 offered no minimum or maximum sentences, which probably reflected a more liberal approach to sentencing that may have played out as greater judicial leniency.[27] When Forster came to plan his campaign, Zurich may well have been a marginally safer place than St. Gallen to execute it.

Forster's First Period of Swiss Activism

Forster apparently stayed in Konstanz, on the German side of the Bodensee (Lake Constance), for most of 1878 and January of 1879. He supported himself by peddling various goods. During this period, he studied Ulrichs and the Swiss writer Heinrich Hössli and set about planning how he would advance the cause of urning rights in Switzerland.[28] In February 1879, he moved to Zurich to establish an office for a new business venture: a matchmaking brokerage for marriage, employment, and the sale of property called the Deutsch-Schweizerisches Vermittlungscomptoir (Swiss-German Mediation Office).[29] This service business was a more lucrative line of work than selling honey. It was a legitimate business with real clients, but it also provided cover for Forster to contact and educate the urnings of Zurich.[30] With the business established, Forster settled in the city's Seefeld quarter and acquired a lover, a seventeen-year-old Zuricher named Jakob Zehnder. Under cover of his matchmaking work, he started networking with and spreading leaflets on urning love to new urning comrades in Zurich and beyond: "pretty and not less pretty individuals, rich and poor, civilian and military, even an amiable Zurich policeman!"[31] The first part of Forster's autobiography may contain the text of one or more of these tracts, including long passages copied from Ulrichs's works and polemic content written by Forster himself.[32] Early on, Forster sent some of these pamphlets to the lawyer defending Adolf Näf, a wealthy merchant urning from Augarten in St. Gallen.[33] He may have been trying to emulate Ulrichs's campaign in Germany, but he added an important dimension of his own. A naturally gregarious man who revelled in the company of others, Forster made a considerable effort to encourage a sense of community among the urnings of Zurich. This was to be a feature of all his efforts to advance the urning cause.[34]

Had he confined his activities to his matchmaking business, Forster might have been able to sustain his leaflet activism and community building for a longer period. However, fatefully, he also tried to monetize his insider knowledge about the making of honey and honey-derived medicinal products.[35] He had acquired this knowledge from his father, who had been active in the honey trade in St. Gallen, where there was a well-developed and closely guarded industry manufacturing honey and specialist medicinal products that used honey as a base. Forster intended to sell the recipes, and the manner in which he set about doing so aroused the suspicion of the authorities. According to an article in *Die Ostschweiz* dated 15 November, Forster had distributed thousands of circulars to the cantons of Zurich, Thurgau, Aargau, and Solothurn offering recipients the chance to get rich if they sent three francs to Forster. After he received the money, Forster then informed them that the riches came from honey recipes and that for a further seven francs, he would send the recipes in full. The newspaper article continued: "This deliberate swindle and deception of the public could no longer be tolerated, and the honey maker would be put out of business by putting him under lock and key, especially since he had in the meantime been prosecuted by Zurich for fraud, and the interrogation of his employee and the room search that had taken place revealed other things that escape disclosure."[36]

Outraged honey manufacturers accused Forster of fraud, and the police searched his premises in Zurich. After being released from four days in jail, Forster decided it was time to leave Zurich.[37] His mother was calling him home, so, in late September 1879, after seven months in Zurich, he and his lover, Jakob Zehnder, packed up and moved to St. Gallen. That move turned out to be a disastrous mistake. With its unreformed legal code and cantonal bureaucracy dominated by religious conservatives, St. Gallen was a far more dangerous place than Zurich for Forster and Zehnder. On 6 November, the police arrested them. During a search of their lodgings, where the police were looking for evidence of fraud, they discovered evidence of Forster's urning activism.[38]

The police had found a notebook belonging to Forster with the words *Meine Geliebten* (My Beloved Ones) written on the cover.[39] This notebook, which Forster had begun to fill while in Stuttgart, contained 146 names of urnings that he knew, some of whom he had loved and with some of whom he had had intimate relations. Forster's notebook offers a tantalizing window into the love life of a young attractive urning in the late 1870s. It covered mainly the years 1877 to 1879, as well as a few remembered assignations from the years preceding, Forster listed each person he had kissed or had sex with. He also listed other urnings he admired or who had been his friends. The notebook revealed that in late nineteenth-century Germany and Switzerland, an attractive young urning like Forster had little difficulty finding sexual partners.

For some periods, he listed one partner per day. Most of these were not anonymous encounters, and in many cases Forster had written down their names, ages, and professions. During his time in Germany, more than half of his contacts (forty-four) had been soldiers, twelve of them being musicians (horn, trumpet, drums). By contrast, in St. Gallen and Zurich only one of his sixty-four contacts had been a soldier. The soldier contacts were probably transactional, and since Forster encountered them mostly in Germany, this confirms Ulrichs's contention that soldier-love and the availability of soldiers seeking transactions was a particularly German phenomenon.[40] Forster described the national origins, rather than professions, of eight of his civilian contacts; they included two Austrians, a Hungarian, a Prussian, a Bavarian, a German (in Switzerland), a Zuricher (in Germany), and a Russian Pole. Most of his civilian contacts with a recorded profession were younger men working in hospitality (nine), retail (eight), services (eight), or business administration (six). There were also two policemen, two railway officials, a lawyer, a teacher, a miller, the owner of a private sanatorium, and a well-known travelling magician.

The *Meine Geliebten* book was a staggeringly indiscreet document for an urning to keep in the 1870s, especially one embarking on a campaign of activism. Back in 1866, the Prussian authorities had discovered Ulrichs's lists at his apartment in Burgdorf. However, those were lists of correspondents, and they did not document sexual assignations. Being a private document, *Meine Geliebten* might not have presented difficulties in Zurich, but in St. Gallen, once it fell into the hands of the local police, it enabled the authorities to launch a much broader investigation. They worked their way through the list, name by name, taking notes based on interviews with Forster and then more detailed notes for the sexual partners they tracked down and questioned. The St. Gallen authorities were most interested in the forty-two contacts who fell under their jurisdiction.[41] Of these, nine came with too few remembered details to be identifiable and two were travellers from outside St. Gallen. A further twenty had only kissed or hugged Forster. That left eight individuals (plus Forster and Zehnder) for the investigators to proceed to interview. These interviews were conducted over the next ten weeks. The authorities had already detained one of the interviewed contacts in a workhouse, and three others denied successfully that they had had sex with Forster. The remaining six defendants, their cases having been established, stood trial on 12–14 January 1880 at the cantonal court in St. Gallen.[42] Besides Forster, they included Konrad Graf (sixty-three), Hermann Ambühl (twenty-seven), and Albert Baumgartner (twenty-six). These three were married men at the time of trial. St. Gallen tried Jakob

Zehnder (seventeen) and Gottleib Haab (nineteen) as minors. The court handed down guilty verdicts for each of them on 14 January 1880. They sentenced Forster to one and a half years in prison and Graf to one year. The rest received three months in the workhouse.

Before facing trial, on 12 November and then again on 6 December 1879, Forster appealed to Ulrichs to send some of his works to his defence lawyers.[43] Ulrichs, who by then was in Italy, responded with a plea on Forster's behalf, but only in July 1881 "as a result of illness and other obstacles."[44] That plea, sent to St. Gallen, arrived too late. While Forster was in detention, on 13 December 1879, his sixty-three-year-old mother died at St. Fiden, a suburb of St. Gallen. He and his mother had been very close, and Forster was convinced that the shock of his arrest had caused her death. Despite his urgent pleas, the prison administration refused him permission to attend her funeral or visit her grave.

Forster served out the bulk of his term in the St. Jakob cantonal prison in St. Gallen. This was a purpose-built prison constructed in 1839 to the modern design favoured by European nations in their efforts to reform and normalize their criminal classes.[45] The prison guards closely monitored their charges and assigned them work, shackled, on the land adjoining the prison. In this sense, it was a smaller version of the prisons at Bremen and Moabit in Berlin where Feldtmann and Zastrow had languished. The prison system did not break Forster the way it had Feldtmann and Zastrow. Part of the reason for this was that it was not his first time behind bars. The St. Gallen authorities had imprisoned him for nineteen days at the time of his bankruptcy, and he may also have spent some time in a poorhouse as a child. Forster was closer to the socio-economic mean of his fellow prisoners, so, unlike Feldtmann and Zastrow, who both came from more elevated class strata, he probably had fewer problems adjusting to prison. Forster felt that his mental strength to withstand punishment and suffering was drawn from his own sense that he was doing so for a righteous cause: "I rejoice that I possessed strength enough to hold myself upright, that I did not descend to the grave without having borne witness to a violently suppressed truth."[46] The regime at St. Jakob was brutal, according to Forster: "rough and boorish, designed to make the soft-hearted hard, the hard obdurate, the obdurate animalistic."[47] During his stay at St. Jakob, that brutality directly caused one suicide and the deaths of at least two of Forster's fellow prisoners from the physical rigours of the regime.[48]

After six months, Forster was transferred to Selnau prison in Zurich so that the authorities there could complete their own investigations. Unlike in St. Gallen, the Zurich authorities questioned but did not arrest or prosecute any of Forster's partners. When he was interrogated about his own sexual behaviour, he answered: "I was, I am and I remain an urning."[49] In Zurich, he was apparently treated better than he had been in St. Gallen, but as a result of his solitary confinement during the investigation and committal, he became anxious. He was visited by Dr. Fritschi, the prison doctor, who referred him to a Dr. von Wiss, whom he consulted, under escort, in the Talacker district of Zurich.[50] Von Wiss was a sympathetic man who seems to have been aware of Ulrichs's writings. "At least you are to be freed here," he told Forster, "and probably also soon from St. Jakob Prison."[51] His return to custody dashed any hope of that outcome. He was, however, moved to a four-bed cell, where he was able to make friends. Forster even had a very brief love affair with one of his cellmates, "a nice 20-year-old Zurich man with bad hearing, with whom I soon had a love affair, to such an extent that I even slept with him once, i.e. I languished in prison because of urning love and in the same prison I slept wonderfully with a young man, for what does love care about prison!"[52]

The Zurich hearing found Forster guilty of fraud and causing public outrage by "having sexual intercourse with male persons."[53] He was sentenced to six months, less the ten weeks he had spent in detention awaiting trial. Upon his return to St. Jakob, they treated him better than during his previous stay. Forster was set free on his twenty-ninth birthday, 21 January 1882.[54]

After only a few weeks of freedom, Forster moved back to Zurich to revive his matchmaking business. The lenient treatment in his final months of imprisonment may have emboldened him. He quickly attracted enough customers to afford a comfortable apartment in central Zurich.[55] His new lover, Gustav Edwin Boller, lived and worked with him. Boller dealt with the correspondence while Forster handled client meetings. Forster and Boller's apartment became a centre of urning life in Zurich as Forster returned to political networking: "I got to know more and more comrades (urnings) from all walks of life, as well as many misfortunes of all kinds in these circles, which spurred me on anew, to stand up for them."[56] Once again, Forster was encouraging the growth of an integrated community of comrades. By living openly with Boller, he was also setting an example of openness that others may have followed. If the Zurich authorities had noticed, they did not make any immediate move to arrest them for most of 1882. Ostensibly, neither Forster nor Boller was doing anything that might have breached Zurich laws or drawn the attention of the authorities.

Forster's business grew, but his marketing costs were high, so he decided to publish a *Weltheirathszeitung* (World Marriage Newspaper) himself, which would carry all his advertising. The gazette included matchmaking advertisements, bills for sale, and offers of employment. Forster stated that he intended to use the gazette "to make propaganda for the liberation of urning love."[57] The prison chaplain from St. Jakob, who had heard rumours of his plans, wrote to Forster on the 20 October 1883: "I warn you of the terrible danger into which you are putting yourself through the enterprise of a 'World Marriage Newspaper' and everything that goes with it." [58] It was one thing to discreetly minister to and congregate with like-minded urnings, or even distribute privately printed leaflets to the same, but the mass distribution of free newspapers to the public containing urning-related content was probably a step too far. Forster published the first issue, 2,500 copies, in November 1883, and the second on 1 December of the same year.[59]

On 3 December, three plainclothes detectives came to Forster and Boller's apartment.[60] After a search and the confiscation of the gazettes and other writings, the police arrested Forster, Boller, and "a handsome youth" from Thurgau, who was an unimplicated house guest.[61] During the investigation, the police interrogated Forster and Boller; they released the house guest without charge. The press soon got wind of Forster's arrest. On 14 December, the *Zurichische Freitagszeitung* reported: "The *Weltheirathszeitung* in Oberstraß has already gone out of business at this time – according to the *Limmat*, its editor Forster was arrested for causing public outrage."[62] Following the investigation, charges of outraging public decency through press publication were brought against Forster and his lover, as well as the printer of the gazette and the owner of the newspaper kiosk through which it had been distributed.[63] The printer and the kiosk owner were served with four days' detention and did not come to trial. The printer died suddenly in the days that followed, and Forster believed that the shock of arrest was a contributing factor.[64] On 29 December, the matter came to court. Forster defended himself at this trial, arguing that his sexuality was innate and that many states, including several Swiss cantons, had repealed their antisodomy laws. His spirited defence was not enough to avert a guilty verdict, as the *St Galler Volksblatt* reported on 19 January 1884: "The publisher of the disgraceful *WeltheirathsZeitung*, a certain Forster in Oberstraß, has been sentenced to one year's workhouse and a fine of Fr. 100 for causing public outrage in repeated offences. That's the only right thing to do."[65] They also sentenced Boller to three months' imprisonment and issued a fine of 50 francs.

This time the sentence for Forster was detention at the Zurich workhouse. In the Swiss penal hierarchy, workhouses were one rung down from penitentiaries. Forster found the workhouse a pleasant improvement on his experience of prison two years earlier. He had a cell to himself and had freedom to circulate with the other detainees. Forster used the opportunity to have "happy moments" in the courtyard or the church with this or that prisoner, and he exchanged love letters with several.[66] The discovery of these letters resulted in punishment. He was not deterred, even though he was in detention: "Fortunately I did not starve, although I only got food once a day, consisting of a piece of bread or soup, my real food was mostly next to me, also in the detention – Namely, men!"[67] Once again, he was interrogated by a physician during his incarceration: "The discussion lasted quite a long time, as the doctor made various notes and asked for urning readings that he wanted to acquire. He also gave me hope that better views would certainly soon prevail in this matter, even in Swiss legislation."[68] This was the second time Forster had encountered a sympathetic physician. It cheered him up, even though he had to return to detention.

Released on 4 January 1885, Forster set about establishing his business once again in the Oberstraß quarter of Zurich. He began getting all the necessary papers in order. While Forster awaited permission to trade, Boller joined him once again. There were no ill feelings after what they had both been through, and they were happy to revive the relationship. Unfortunately, the authorities took a dim view of their cohabitation. They saw it as a sign of recidivism. On 29 January 1885, Forster received notice that the authorities intended to deport him in eight days, and although he appealed, the police apparently put pressure on him.[69] Forster and Boller decided to transfer the management of his business to an assistant and leave Zurich. They moved briefly to Geneva, a canton that followed the Napoleonic Code, where they would be able to live without fear of the law. However, Forster was unable to speak French and therefore could not sustain a business. This placed incredible strain on the relationship between the two men, and ultimately, they decided to part ways. Forster was heartbroken. In his autobiography, he devoted seventeen pages to lamenting the end of this relationship.[70] Boller, who now returned to Zurich alone, had made a very deep impression on him: "My dear Edwin Gustav Boller! You comfort of my life, how I love you! Oh, how you suffered for me! How happy we lived in Zurich! And when I wanted to please other languishing souls with a friend, I reaped hatred, ingratitude, imprisonment for this! What a boundless poverty, even almost starvation, separated us in Geneva, so that I thought you, faithful, were lost."[71]

On 5 April, Forster moved to the Swiss capital, Bern, where he tried and failed to gain approval to establish his business. All attempts to appeal against this failed, so on 30 May he travelled back by train to St. Gallen, his home canton. There were many reasons he did not wish to be in St. Gallen, but he had few other options at that time. After only a few days, he received a letter from Boller, calling for a reconciliation. Forster, perhaps forgetting what the Zurich authorities felt about the two fraternizing, immediately planned to move back to Zurich. On 15 June he caught the train to Zurich; after conducting some business, he met with Boller at 2 p.m. They spent the next three hours together, but after saying their goodbyes, the authorities closed in:

> After we had parted, a policeman in civilian clothes came up to me, asked my name, ordered me to come with him to the police station, which I immediately agreed to do; there they recorded my details, I had to hand over all my belongings, take off my jacket, waistcoat and shoes, and then we went to the Selnau prison. A few steps ahead of us, I saw Boller taking the same route with a policeman in uniform.[72]

In his interview, conducted the following day, the interrogator informed him that they had detained him for causing public offence and revealed that the police now were in possession of love letters he had written to Boller. The interrogator compelled Forster to name twenty-five urning comrades, "among them a prince, a former public prosecutor, a prison warden, hoteliers of the highest rank, restaurateurs, tradesmen and craftsmen."[73] However, on the 18 June 1885, the police informed Forster that they would terminate the investigation; instead, he was to be deported back to his home canton of St. Gallen with strict instructions not to return to Zurich.[74]

Four Difficult Years in St. Gallen

For six years, when he was not in prison or a workhouse, Forster had focused his business and activism on the city of Zurich. That period was now at an end. At this point in Forster's account, the writing is dense with detail.[75] The persecutions by the St. Gallen authorities were arbitrary and intense, and for the next four years Forster had little opportunity to conduct either business or advocacy. His home canton, as noted earlier, had an unreformed criminal code.

Matters started off badly. The deportation orders for Forster sent from Zurich to the chief of police stated that he was a "vagrant."[76] Add to that, Forster's 1880 conviction in the St. Gallen courts meant he was a marked man. His certificate of good conduct from his home municipality issued on 25 March 1885, necessary for registering residence and business permits, stated that Forster "was not of good reputation, was sentenced in St Gallen in 1880 to 18 months in prison for fornication against nature, and in Zurich in 1883 to 12 months in the workhouse and a fine of 100 Frs."[77]

Forster was now in perilous straits. When they arrested him, the Zurich police had confiscated all his cash. The "certificate of good conduct" from Brunnadern meant it would be extremely difficult for him to register either a residence or a business anywhere in the canton. The inclusion of the word "vagrant" on his deportation papers had been a spiteful move by a Zurich official, but now it seemed to be his destiny. At this point, the absence of a federal legal system meant that the exercise of police and judicial authority varied considerably from canton to canton. In Forster's case, the prejudice of several St. Gallen officials meant that the treatment he encountered there was especially severe.[78] Because he had been classified as a pauper in St. Gallen, the police could detain him without due process. The confiscation of his assets in Zurich meant he also lacked any means to seek legal redress.

In August 1885, after learning he had been refused permission to settle in St. Gallen and hearing that the authorities intended to commit him to an insane asylum, Forster fled over the border to Bavaria.[79] He seems to have travelled mostly on foot and relied on the kindness of strangers in first Munich, then Vienna, and finally Preßburg in Hungary (now Bratislava in Slovakia).[80] He was looking for work and supported himself by begging; he was questioned over his lack of papers but managed to avoid getting arrested.[81] Forster was at the mercy of his home canton for all the official papers he would have needed. He travelled for ten weeks, but it was just postponing the inevitable. An itinerant existence was not sustainable. On 27 October 1885, he left Vienna on foot via the Austrian Tyrol, crossing the arduous Arlberg massif into Switzerland on 15 November.[82]

Forster sheltered first with his stepbrother in Mogelsberg. It wasn't long before the authorities found him. On Christmas Day 1885, two drunken soldiers arrested him and brought him in.[83] They detained him first in St. Pirminsberg psychiatric asylum in Pfäfers near Bad Ragaz. Dr. Weller, the director of St. Pirminsberg, was a kind man. He listened to Forster intently, studied all of Forster's medical notes, and then shared with him some of the latest research coming out of Germany. Forster confused the name of this publication and the date, but almost certainly Dr. Weller showed him volume 38 of the *Allgemeine Zeitschrift für Psychiatrie* (1882), which contained a long disquisition on *conträre Sexualempfindung* (contrary sexual feeling) by Richard von Krafft-Ebing.[84] Forster saw his own views on urning love reflected in the pages of that book. Dr. Weller persuaded Forster to use his time in the asylum to record his memoirs. Much of the material in his later published autobiography was probably composed from the memoir he wrote in St. Pirminsberg.

Having examined Forster thoroughly, Dr. Weller established that he was not insane and facilitated his release.[85] The authorities then tried to deport him to Argentina; when he refused to go, they sent him instead to the Bitzi labour camp. Forster's detention at Bitzi was under the charge that he was work-shy and a public danger.[86] His inability to work was entirely due to his home council's own actions in producing an unfavourable certificate of good conduct for him on 25 March 1885, and the "public danger" charge was an overstatement of the risk of him reoffending. There was no trial, no due process, and no opportunity for him to appeal the decision. Forster's sister Christine appealed to the cantonal government for clemency. They replied swiftly:

> It is only to your credit if you ask for the release of your brother Rudolf Forster, who is housed in the Bitzi forced labour institution. However, sisterly attachment must resign before the demands of public order and law. And according to these, forced labour for your brother was well founded. Needless to say, that he led an offensive way of life and harassed the cantonal and federal authorities with abusive letters; but the fact that he was idle and afraid of work was enough to justify the forced labour.[87]

Bitzi was a forced-labour camp intended for individuals the state considered outcasts: the indigent poor, prostitutes, petty thieves, the insane, the disabled, ... and Forster. The camp was little better than a concentration camp for the unwanted.[88] After one year of being brutalized, starved, and worked to exhaustion, Forster was finally released back into the community on 18 June 1887 – precisely two years to the day after Zurich had deported him.[89]

Forster had endured two wasted years separated from society. The lack of judicial process and the inappropriate charges brought against him raised several questions. Forster wanted answers and wrote to the authorities.[90] The leader of the Brunnadern municipal council told Forster that he should give up his "crazy ideas."[91] Forster replied that his ideas were "based on truth, justice and charity," and went on, "I have no 'ideas' other than that urning love is innate and that punishments of urnings are judicial murders that cause much harm."[92] The reply came back the next day that they knew of his desire to work but that he must let go of his ideas as they were "generally condemned as wrong."[93] His very *ideas* about the nature and the rights of urnings were considered so dangerous that he had to be kept out of circulation through incarceration, deportation, or committal to psychiatric institutions. Note that

Zurich had not detained him because of his "ideas," and Ulrichs had been largely free to form and disseminate his disruptive ideas in Germany. St. Gallen, however, was a conservative Catholic canton, and the authorities' attempts to silence or remove dangerous ideas were their way of managing what they considered a disruptive influence. The authorities viewed those ideas and Forster's dissemination of them to a growing and mutually supportive community as a threat to public order. By removing Forster, even though he had committed no crime, St. Gallen officials had removed the instigator and reduced the danger. In effect, he had been a prisoner of conscience.

Forster had no intention of complying with this unreasonable injunction to be silent. For the time being, there were no threats to his liberty, but he was still finding it extremely difficult to receive authorization to reopen his business. However, even though he lacked official permission to open an office, he was able to conduct some of his matchmaking business through existing contacts. Now that he had an income, Forster decided to broadcast his troubles to a wider audience. He printed 1,000 copies of a leaflet outlining the official persecution that had landed him in an impossible position.[94] In the leaflet, he was forthright about his "dangerous" ideas and included a long quote from Ulrichs's speech at the Congress of German Jurists in 1867. Forster finished with a promise to publish his memoirs in an extended volume.

The St. Gallen authorities responded negatively to the leaflet. Forster had received a deportation order from the municipal authority under which he was living on 29 January 1888 and so had applied to the neighbouring municipality.[95] He was still operating his brokerage without a state licence, and when he was on his way to a client meeting in a neighbouring canton, a land-hunter apprehended and questioned him. The land-hunter, after making the necessary investigations, advised each of Forster's clients that his business was fraudulent. This resulted in civil proceedings from two of the clients. The episode spanned the two adjacent cantons of Thurgau and Schaffhausen. Forster was arrested again on 13 June 1888 and transported to Schaffhausen, where he was detained while awaiting trial.[96] The magistrate in Schaffhausen was sympathetic towards Forster; he was also detail oriented. He examined the case thoroughly and then dismissed it as meritless. This episode was the only legal process Forster faced during the four years he was persecuted in St. Gallen, and the court proceeding had pointedly exonerated him in full. Forster was immediately released. The *St Galler Tagblatt* reported the outcome of the trial on 22 June.[97]

Forster moved to St. Gallen, where he operated his business under his brother-in-law's name. To generate new business, he revived the marriage magazine under a new title, *Glücksbote Heiraths-Anzeiger* (Lucky Messenger Marriage Gazette). Even though this time it contained no obvious compromising material, the marriage newspaper came to the attention of the municipal council. They believed that Forster was operating a business without approval. The terms of his deportation from Zurich had now expired, so after several unsuccessful appeals, he moved in July 1889 to Aussersihl, near Zurich.

Return to Zurich and Activism

The difficult four years in St. Gallen were at an end. Liberal, progressive Zurich was a welcome change after the ordeal in his home canton. Perhaps aware that his ten years of persecution were ending, he wrote defiantly:

> Some may have been treated unjustly in their country, expelled, but where is the one who has been tortured and enslaved by his fatherland as innocently as I, Forster. Who, in conviction and out of the deepest love for his fatherland, drew the attention of the authorities to numerous victims of an unjust justice system, but who, for a full decade, has been repeatedly punished for the same, with imprisonment, labour and penitentiary, which cures, however, have confirmed me anew in the truth. [98]

On 16 April 1890, Forster made a pilgrimage to St. Michael's Church in Munich to lay a wreath on the grave of Ludwig II of Bavaria.[99] This event marked a symbolic recommencement of Forster's urning campaign. Unmarried and probably same-sex-attracted, King Ludwig II died in mysterious circumstances at Starnberg Lake in Bavaria in 1886. His grave in Munich became almost a shrine for German urnings in the years that followed. Ulrichs published a small volume of poems dedicated to Ludwig in 1887, and Forster self-published a leaflet under the title "Ludwig II and J.R. Forster."[100] As with previous leaflets, Forster intended this new one to serve as outreach to Zurich's urnings.

In Zurich, Forster was at last given full permission to live and work. For the next few years, he was able to operate his business with minimal interference. A decade-long campaign of harassment that had seen him hounded from place to place and incarcerated for a total of four and a half years was finally at an end. It was a tribute to his mental strength that those years had not broken him. Despite all that had been done to him, Forster was still an ardent advocate of the urning cause. He had previously noted that there were more than three hundred urnings in Zurich alone.[101] Networking with these like-minded men, if they were careful, was eminently possible, and Forster revived his community-building efforts.

In 1893, the federal council appointed a commission to study the prospects for a uniform Swiss penal code. The project of unifying Germany's penal code had presented the right time for Ulrichs to lobby for change in 1869; Forster would now take the same approach in Switzerland. At his own expense, he distributed to each of the main Swiss newspapers, and to the cantonal governments, copies of Ulrichs's writings as well as a recently published work on urnings by the sexologist Albert Moll.[102] As his submission to the federal commission in Bern, Forster sent a copy of Moll's book with a petition letter:

> I myself, an urning, have been persecuted by cantonal and federal authorities because I have fearlessly stood up for my comrades for about 12 years. I wrote some of what is contained in the enclosed book to cantonal and federal authorities myself about 10 years ago. The light now comes from Germany, for the prophet is not valid in his own country. I should be very pleased if quick action is taken in these matters, especially if it means that imprisoned urnings are returned to freedom.[103]

When Forster lobbied the authorities, he always did so by sending the works of others. In his outreach, he used the contemporary urning literature, paraphrased in his leaflets. Some urnings in Zurich would have sought out these books. Early on, Forster had popularized the works of Ulrichs and of Heinrich Hössli and later the sexological work of Albert Moll. On the final page of his autobiography, Forster presented an impressively sourced list of contemporary urning-related literature. The seventeen titles he recommended to his readers included the works of Otto de Joux (Otto Rudolf Podjukl), Melchior Grohe, "Dr Ramien" (Magnus Hirschfeld), Albert Moll, Richard von Krafft-Ebing, Norbert Grabowsky, Edward Carpenter, Ludwig Frey, and Emil Laurent.[104] For a man with little schooling, Forster was surprisingly well-read in contemporary queer literature. It is noteworthy that by the 1890s, after his initial radicalization through Ulrichs and his pamphlets, Forster familiarized himself with a multitude of sources, and drew from them.

It seems that at least some of the books Forster sent to the Zurich legislators found purchase. In 1897, when the Grand Council of the canton of Zurich met *in camera* to discuss the paragraph on "unnatural lust" for a new criminal code and, apparently, the new works of sexology, Ulrichs's works and the "urning" terminology all formed part of that discussion.[105] Reformers did not carry that day, but neither were they an insignificant minority, and at least one of them was outspoken in his support of urning rights.

Forster's renewed activism, although he was being much more careful, continued to cause problems for him with officialdom. The Zurich authorities withdrew his permit to operate his marriage brokerage in January 1895.[106] Thereafter, he operated as a financial planner, and the police threatened even that business with investigations. He also had to endure one final short period of imprisonment. Forster made significant profits with his new business in 1896, enough to pay for a holiday in Geneva with his new lover, Hans Kühne.[107] On their return to Zurich, they were immediately arrested. While they had been out of the canton, a neighbour had made a complaint of child molestation against them. It seems that the accusation was malicious and false, and the magistrate dismissed the case as spurious. Kühne was released, but Forster remained in prison until 24 December; after complaining about his detention, he was committed to the Burghölzli psychiatric hospital.[108] Presumably the authorities detained him because of his past record of imprisonment and psychiatric examination. The Burghölzli was one of the most modern psychiatric hospitals in Europe at the time and was under the direction of Dr. August Forel, a progressive advocate of the new science of sexology. Forel ensured that Forster received good treatment and even presented him to thirty or forty of his students at the hospital. On 9 January 1897, Forel delivered a public lecture where he used Forster's story, including the harsh treatment he had received in St. Gallen, as a case study.[109] Forel's treatment of his life story in this lecture apparently moved Forster.

On his release, Forster set to work compiling all the material he wished to include in his autobiography. He completed his book on 1 June 1897 and published it in 1898. Between that point and his death thirty years later, there is no record of him. He died at the age of seventy-three on 8 October 1926 in Zurich.[110] Given his history up to that point, it is probable that he did not let up on his urning advocacy, although no material corroborates this assumption. The new federal code he had been so hopeful about influencing with his petition took almost fifty years to complete. The federal government finally implemented a new Swiss legal code in 1942; it did not include an antisodomy law.[111] While the legal systems of the francophone cantons did much to influence the final decision not to include an antisodomy law in the 1942 code, the growth of an urning scene in Zurich as a legacy of Forster's homosocial outreach likely also played a part. It is also possible that scientific understanding, including the sexological ideas of Ulrichs, Westphal, Krafft-Ebing, and Moll, played a strong role.[112] Forster, by promoting these ideas so relentlessly for many years, undoubtedly helped popularize the views of these authorities.

Conclusion

Forster is unique among ordinary urnings of this period in leaving such a complete, if picaresque, account of his activist life. He was not an educated man and did not mix in the elevated circles that some of Ulrichs's followers did. His rather lowly position may have set him at a disadvantage with the authorities, but his steely determination saw him through ten years of persecution. Forster's autobiography strongly suggests that he was a lovable rascal, but he was also a man with incredible strength of character who emerged uncowed from a decade of state persecution. Forster's pamphlets, his petitions, and his advocacy for at least one urning facing trial all seemed to follow in Ulrichs's footsteps. Forster emphasized the pivotal importance of his time with Ulrichs. Something in Stuttgart had inspired this man of limited education to work tirelessly for urning rights in Switzerland. It is not known what Ulrichs had imparted to Forster in 1877; perhaps he tutored him on what he considered the core principles of activism.

The effort to build an urning community in Zurich, so important in advancing the cause of minoritized sexual rights, was a distinct feature of Forster's campaign. He and his lovers, Jakob Zehnder, Edwin Boller, and Hans Kühne, lived and loved openly. They appeared to have done so within a widening community to whose development they contributed. By the turn of the century, there were ordinary men across the cities of Switzerland, Austria, and Germany who were starting to live openly and assertively. There were almost certainly individuals in other cities and towns who were pivotal in advancing homosocial networks in those places. Perhaps they left no traces because they were less likely to face censure in other settings and because they did not consign their experiences to an autobiography.[113] Their efforts, however, were slowly transforming society. A growing number of urnings would be prepared to say publicly, as Forster did, "I was, am and remain urning."

During Forster's struggle, one group of professionals consistently showed him open-mindedness and understanding: psychiatrists. The Swiss authorities had thought they could commit Forster to an insane asylum and forget about him, but, repeatedly, this was thwarted by psychiatrists abreast of recent research from Germany. The attitudes of Drs. von Wiss, Weller, and Forel towards Forster reflected a transformation in psychiatry largely localized in Germany, Austria, and Switzerland. The next chapter examines that transformation and the role of discreet professionals in fomenting it.

Chapter Six

Queering Psychiatry: Autobiographical Lobbying of Richard von Krafft-Ebing, 1864–1901

But in my heart a voice spoke so loudly that I thought I heard it in the room: "Go to the linden trees!" – Rarely or never had I entered the inner promenade; it was before forty-eight and the lighting was probably not as bright as it is today. I walked over consciously and had long forgotten the words. – After some time, a gentleman joined me; he spoke kindly to me, and we were able to enjoy the Tiergarten. I felt a wonderful blissful feeling when he pulled me to himself, kissed me passionately and finally touched me and satisfied my nature with onanism.[1]

The opening quotation comes from the first known instance of a "pederast" using sexual autobiography to influence a sexual scientist.[2] Sometime in the 1850s, a German living in Italian exile sent a letter to Berlin forensic examiner Ludwig Casper, who would publish it in 1863.[3] The letter had had the desired effect on Casper, convincing him that same-sex sexuality was innate. At the end of the eighteenth century, Samuel Auguste Tissot's holy war against masturbation had also generated a flood of desperate confessions from men and women seeking therapeutic solutions.[4] However, the above letter from "a pederast" and many of the urning autobiographies surveyed in this chapter were qualitatively different. The men who wrote them were not trying to secure therapeutic intervention. Rather, they were deploying their autobiographies in a tactical attempt to correct the scientific record.

In the previous chapter, Jakob Rudolf Forster found that the psychiatrists he encountered were the only professionals who were consistently sympathetic to him. Some of the strongest independent voices in favour of legal reform and the humane treatment of urnings in the final decades of the nineteenth century in Germany, Austria, and Switzerland were psychiatrists. This set them strikingly apart from all the other professional disciplines, including other medical fields. German psychiatry was also distinctly more vocal in its advocacy for sexual minorities than was the case in France, Britain, and the United States at that time. In part, this was because the Germans had pioneered a new research-focused psychiatry grounded in empirical science. But it was also the result of a concerted campaign by urning men, who lobbied psychiatrists with autobiographical accounts of their sexual awakenings. Germanic psychiatry became progressively inclined to the urning cause specifically because urnings lobbied, collaborated, and educated them over several decades. This chapter is the story of that campaign.

There are two significant scholarly works that examine the collaboration between urnings and psychiatrists in the late nineteenth century: Klaus Müller's *Aber in meinem Herzen sprach eine Stimme so laut* (1991) and Harry Oosterhuis's *Stepchildren of Nature* (2000).[5] Both these books are impressive in scope and beautifully executed; together they provide a comprehensive examination of an engagement between psychiatry and urnings/homosexuals in the final two decades of the nineteenth century. Müller examined the role of the sexual autobiography in the development of a *scientia sexualis*, while Oosterhuis focused on the life and work of Richard von Krafft-Ebing through the lens of his patients. Both books relied on the same primary materials used here. This chapter draws from both these works but examines the engagement from an alternative perspective. Müller focused on the role of autobiography and Oosterhuis on the patient perspective of Krafft-Ebing; this chapter looks instead at the urning men themselves and their agency in the psychiatric engagement. This fresh analysis will reveal a concerted campaign to influence the scientific discourse on same-sex sexuality. The engagement with psychiatry this chapter describes was the longest-lived urning campaign as a continuous and sustained effort, one that ran from the 1860s right up to the 1890s.[6] It was also the only campaign that Karl Heinrich Ulrichs initiated; it continued to progress after he left Germany through the attentive advocacy of several other individual urnings.

This chapter examines the progress of psychiatric thinking as it encountered increasingly vocal minoritized urnings. It starts with Ulrichs's early engagement with psychiatry, then turns to the followers of Ulrichs who launched their own campaigns of autobiographical advocacy, chiefly with the Austro-German psychiatrist Richard von Krafft-Ebing, who engaged with and encouraged this autobiographical advocacy as he published the many editions of *Psychopathia Sexualis*. The central part of the chapter will include an analysis of the dissenting autobiographical case studies published in *Psychopathia Sexualis*. This chapter ends with the emergence of a non-pathologizing model in sexology. The picture thus painted is of a community inspired by Ulrichs, working in concert, and collaborating with Krafft-Ebing to repurpose and redirect the scientific discourse.

Ulrichs's Advocacy and the Seeds of an Urning Campaign

In the 1860s, Ulrichs aimed some of his works at medical opinion leaders and lobbied them directly in a scientific pamphleteering strategy.[7] The copies of his scientific theories sent to medical thought-leaders were in some cases read and considered. Ulrichs almost certainly received some help in identifying the doctors to target, perhaps from a medical friend or a medical individual among his readers. That guidance was prescient enough for Ulrichs to contact a young psychiatrist named Richard von Krafft-Ebing, whom we will return to later, straight after his first publication in 1866.[8] So, it is probable that Ulrichs had sent his pamphlets to most of the prominent psychiatrists and forensic doctors by the end of the 1860s. Unknown to Ulrichs, his lobbying coincided with the development of a new research-driven psychiatry in Berlin, and his efforts soon succeeded in capturing its attention. In 1865, Wilhelm Griesinger was appointed to the new chair of psychiatry at Berlin's Humboldt University, which had a dedicated psychiatric wing in the Charité Hospital where he could conduct research.[9] This was a pivotally important development for psychiatry in Germany and also, ultimately, for the development of psychiatric research globally. Griesinger's research interests up to that point had been brain-focused, and he heralded a "new psychiatry" where every mental illness or aberration would be localized in the brain: "Psychiatry has undergone a transformation in its relation to the rest of medicine ... This transformation rests principally on the realization that patients with so-called 'mental illnesses' are really individuals with illnesses of the nerves and brain."[10]

The "new psychiatry" was research-based and brain-centred. It also extended itself to domains well beyond the psychiatric institution. In particular, the realm of expert witnesses in the court system was increasingly being colonized by forensic psychiatrists, thus blocking out and marginalizing the forensic examiner. Thereafter, the psychiatric examination of pederasts facing trial would localize sexuality no longer in the genitals but instead in the brain.

Griesinger and his colleagues at the Charité were strongly influenced by the hereditary degeneration theories promoted by Benedict Morel and expanded by Valentin Magnan. Those theories posited that mental disorders, indeed any deviations from the norm, were the result of some ancestral pollution or stimulation – an alcoholic parent, for example – that generated lapses and deviations in the next generation. In this way, facets of behaviour or personality that had attracted legal censure were now reclassified as brain diseases. In 1868, Griesinger redefined sexual orientation to the same sex as a constitutional pathology.[11] He died only a few months later, after contracting diphtheria following an appendix operation. Griesinger was succeeded by his deputy, Carl Westphal, who became professor just at the time the department was launching a new psychiatric research journal: *Archiv für Psychiatrie und Nervenkrankheiten*.

It is unclear whether Ulrichs was aware of all these developments, but if he wasn't, then his targeting of the relevant psychiatric individuals with copies of his pamphlets was fortuitous. Westphal had read and absorbed Ulrichs's works by the time he decided to convene a seminar at the hospital to discuss the subject. On 15 December 1868, the Berlin Medical Psychology Society met to discuss the psychiatry of sexuality. The report of this meeting shows that two of the speakers, Drs. Skrzeczka and Liman, focused on Ulrichs's ideas in their papers.[12] Only a couple of months later, Westphal published a research paper with two case studies in the first issue of his new psychiatric journal.[13] This is the paper that Foucault later credited as the "date of birth" of homosexuality.[14] Westphal didn't use Ulrichs's terminology, preferring the term *contrāre Sexualempfindung* (contrary sexual feeling), but he quoted him extensively, and his theory owed much to Ulrichs's own outline of identity. Unlike Ulrichs, but in line with the new psychiatry, Westphal located the aetiology of contrary sexual feeling in a pathological process resulting from hereditary degeneration.

In the decade that followed, research psychiatry embedded pathological contrary sexual feeling as a resilient and widely accepted scientific model. Westphal's paper inspired other psychiatrists to approach the subject and publish their own pathologizing case studies.[15] Most of these papers either ignored or dismissed Ulrichs's contribution even as they deployed his parameters of identity.[16] Only the paper from psychiatrist Karl Stark fully acknowledged that "for many years, Ulrichs's publications remained the only information on the topic."[17] Within months, psychiatrists overseas had translated Westphal's neologism *contrāre Sexualempfindung* into English as "contrary sexual feeling/instinct" and papers started appearing in other languages.[18] By the end of the decade, the concept of contrary sexual feeling was well entrenched across the psychiatric discipline in Germany and acknowledged by some psychiatrists internationally. Ulrichs's intervention had embedded an ontological turn right at the inception of serious psychiatric research. This was a big step forward in the scientific study of sexuality. The identity Ulrichs had originally described in 1864 had become a psychiatric category by the 1870s. A forensic examiner in Hamburg wrote to Ulrichs in 1879: "You may rightfully point to the fact that your publications have had a significant effect on shaking the false belief that vice and wickedness always have been at the root in the one in whom these perverse drives appear. Under the term 'contrary sexual feeling,' the fact which you emphasise, i.e., the fact of the congenital nature of that drive, has been assumed as absolute by the other side."[19]

Ulrichs's lobbying had captured the attention of psychiatry, which went on to colonize the study of human sexuality in Germany largely using the framework he had established. However, in the process it had reduced the happy, healthy urning to a contrary sexual beset by a pathological condition caused by hereditary degeneration. Psychiatrists accepted that the law should change, but only if the contrary sexual became a subject for their therapeutic interventions. Ulrichs felt that the problem lay with the patients they were using in their studies: "My scientific opponents are mostly psychiatrists. They are, for example, Westphal, Krafft-Ebing, and Stark. They made their observations on urnings who were in institutions for the mentally ill. They appear never to have seen mentally healthy urnings."[20]

In this passage, Ulrichs criticized the use of mentally ill subjects in case studies. Psychiatrists then used their findings to claim links between mental illness and sexuality. The sentiment expressed here is contiguous with other instances when Ulrichs emphasized the good mental and physical health of urnings, implicitly omitting those whose mental or physical condition fell short. This exclusionary approach to mental and physical defects in urnings was probably adopted by Ulrichs for strategic reasons; nevertheless, it was coterminous with widespread negative ideas about disability being a product of social degeneration. There is a curious irony about objecting to degenerative pathological theories about sexuality while implicitly upholding the same attitudes towards disability. In the previous chapter, Forster was incarcerated twice in psychiatric hospitals, and in the period under consideration, many others were detained in institutions because of their sexual practices. Some of these will also have had psychiatric or physical illnesses. They were just as much in need of Ulrichs's advocacy as healthy urnings, so it is problematic that he was so quick to abandon them.

However, Ulrichs's point about the psychiatric practice of only using patients with comorbidities does have some merit. Degeneration theory as an explanatory heuristic in psychiatry thrived precisely because psychiatrists were relying on patients with comorbidities that could be associated with sexuality. In Westphal's 1869 paper, the woman had a pronounced case of chronic depression, and the young man was an epileptic. This selection of patients with florid symptomatology or interesting family histories of major psychiatric disorders was typical of the case studies of contrary sexuals in the medical literature prior to 1880. The clinician would then use the expression of comorbidities in the patients or their close relatives as evidence of a degenerative disease process and as a causative factor in the generation of the inverted sexuality. The circularity of this reasoning was apparently not questioned by anyone except Ulrichs. For the psychiatric perspective to change, it would need to engage directly with urnings from outside the psychiatric system.

Krafft-Ebing and the Initial Stages of the Autobiographical Turn

In his final pamphlet, *Critische Pfeile* (1879), Ulrichs pointed the way for his followers. In a passage taking stock of what his scientific campaign had achieved, he included a letter from Krafft-Ebing: "From that day when you sent your writings – I believe it was in 1866 – I have turned my full attention to this phenomenon, which was just as puzzling as it was interesting to me; and it was only the knowledge of your books which motivated me to study this highly important area."[21]

Ulrichs first encountered Krafft-Ebing through an essay the psychiatrist had published as a student.[22] Just as Ulrichs was a lawyer promulgating scientific theories, Krafft-Ebing was a scientist with progressive ideas about the practice of law: "The endless series of judicial murders, witch hunt trials, and persecutions came to an end only when the administrators of justice stopped treating research as if it were the angel of death … Laws and rights must comply with the results of research."[23]

Ulrichs and Krafft-Ebing struck up a reciprocal correspondence over the years, exchanging their published works. Shortly before Ulrichs left for Italy, Krafft-Ebing sent him his 1877 contribution to Westphal's *Archiv für Psychiatrie und Nervenkrankheiten*.[24] This paper surveyed all the psychiatric and forensic research to date, including Ulrichs's works, and presented three new case studies. Krafft-Ebing's and Ulrichs's mutual respect did not mean there were no real differences between them, and the conclusion to Krafft-Ebing's paper retained the pathologizing framework of his psychiatric contemporaries: "Contrary sexual feeling, where it is congenital, can be clinically regarded as the partial appearance of a neuropsychopathic, mostly hereditary condition and has the significance of a functional symptom of degeneration."[25] Even this most responsive and receptive of Ulrichs's psychiatric correspondents was nevertheless scrupulous in his adherence to contemporary psychiatric thinking, and he located his clinical analysis in degeneration theory.

Ulrichs's promotion of this psychiatrist in his final pamphlet may have prompted some of his readers who could access psychiatric literature to start following Krafft-Ebing's writings. The first unsolicited sexual autobiography Krafft-Ebing received was published in 1884 and came from Mr. X, a thirty-eight-year-old merchant in American exile who was familiar with Ulrichs's works. The author opened his letter with "I read your work in the *Journal of Psychiatry*."[26] References to Krafft-Ebing's works proliferated in the unsolicited sexual autobiographies that were sent to him, which is surprising given how inaccessible psychiatric journals and books were to the wider public. Otto de Joux wrote in 1897: "A truly epochal phenomenon of scientific literature, which unfortunately seems inaccessible to the lay public, is Prof. Dr v. Krafft-Ebing's *Psychopathia Sexualis*, a work which, because of its clarity, its unquestionable truthfulness, can be recommended to every man thirsting for knowledge."[27]

Krafft-Ebing's works were available in university or hospital libraries, and it is likely that a number of the people who followed his writings were students, doctors, or university teachers. They could have shared what they found with friends. Others with sufficient capital possibly accessed the publications through specialist booksellers. A critic from forensic medicine later remarked scathingly on the phenomenon of urnings following works of psychiatry: "Each of the unfortunates who suffer from sexual anomalies is in the habit of following the corresponding literature with attention arbitrarily or involuntarily modelling his own history after the views he finds there, especially if they make him appear morally justified and a scientifically interesting personality." [28] Beliefs such as this located the generation of the urning identity in imitation; the suggestion, then, was that urnings copied the words of psychiatrists. But it was precisely the other way round: many of the men sending sexual autobiographies generated them specifically to persuade Krafft-Ebing to change his scientific conclusions.

At least in the first few years, the urning readers of Krafft-Ebing's works followed quietly, studying his ideas and how he structured his case studies. They would have noticed a substantial change in the class of people he presented in case studies over this time. During the 1870s Krafft-Ebing focused his research on the patients in the Feldhof asylum, where he was director. These were psychiatric patients, many of them with significant levels of mental illness and most of them from the lower socio-economic classes. Krafft-Ebing resigned from the Feldhof in 1880 to focus on his academic position at the University of Graz and the small private clinic he had in the same city.[29] He would go on, in 1886, to open the upmarket Mariagrün sanatorium in suburban Graz.[30] The patients he saw in these settings in the 1880s were drawn from the upper professional classes and the aristocracy, and Krafft-Ebing became viewed as a "society doctor."[31] Himself the scion of a venerable German aristocratic family, he had greater personal rapport with this patient group. They were also, importantly, considerably less likely to have serious mental illnesses: the Mariagrün explicitly excluded "mentally disturbed patients," and his walk-in patients at the clinic tended to have only mild complaints. A qualitative change in his published case studies was the result, particularly for contrary sexual feeling.

In 1882, the three case studies he presented in the *Allgemeine Zeitschrift fuer Psychiatrie und psychisch-gerichtliche Medizin* were of three upper-class men: two aristocrats and a writer/private tutor with a doctoral degree.[32] The three patients in this paper came from a class background similar to that of Krafft-Ebing. The first of these, Count Z., was a thirty-six-year-old aristocrat who so impressed Krafft-Ebing with his outlook that the psychiatrist was inclined towards sympathy rather than pathologization:

> The patient is neither unhappy about the reversal of his sexual sensation, nor is he able to recognise it as a pathological one. He is all the less able to do so because he feels morally uplifted, happy and relieved by contact with men. How could that be morbid which makes a man happy and inspires him to beauty and nobility! His only misfortune was that social barriers and penal regulations stood in the way of the "natural" expression of his impulse. This is a great hardship.[33]

The second case study featured the fifty-year-old writer/tutor "G. Dr phil." The police referred this patient to Krafft-Ebing after his arrest following an assignation with a soldier. G. was not somebody that Krafft-Ebing warmed to. He used the words "vagabond," "crazy," and "madman" to describe G. in the case study and recounted his militant defence of his sexuality and intention to carry on as before. G. lived in Italy, where he had a measure of sexual freedom as there was no law against same-sex sexual conduct. He was also the first of Krafft-Ebing's subjects to use the word "urning" to describe himself. G. elaborated on this by relating a garbled account of Pausanias's speech in Plato's *Symposium*, the source of Ulrichs's terminology:

> He thinks that there is nothing left for him and his comrades but to elevate the unnatural that dwells in them to the supernatural. He recognises urning love as the higher, ideal, as the god-like, abstracted love ... For the

justification and explanation of his abnormal sexual sensation, G. draws on Plato "who was certainly no filthy swine." Plato already made the allegorical statement that people used to be spheres; the gods separated them into two slices. Mostly man fits on woman, but sometimes also man on man.[34]

G. Dr phil was familiar with Ulrichs's works and had taken on the minoritized identity and terminology. Both this case study and that of Count Z. were from men who rejected Krafft-Ebing's pathologizing approach. The third case study, about a patient who sought a therapeutic intervention and regarded his own sexuality as pathological, was consistent with Krafft-Ebing's discourse on sexuality, which was embedded in pathologizing degeneration theory. The presence of the dissenting case studies in conjunction with the orthodox psychiatric position gave this paper a curious ambivalence. This would become a feature of Krafft-Ebing's scientific output in the coming years.

In 1883, Krafft-Ebing persuaded one of his clinic patients, Mr. X, a thirty-three-year-old Hungarian businessman, to jot down his life experiences and sexual history. He had consulted Krafft-Ebing originally because of other psychiatric complaints and insomnia and only revealed his sexuality during a subsequent clinical interview. Krafft-Ebing turned this self-penned account, topped and tailed with his own clinical observations, into a case study, which he published in 1883 in the second edition of his textbook of psychiatry.[35] In this same volume, Krafft-Ebing also quoted several of his patients. Other psychiatrists had at times quoted patients, but Krafft-Ebing did so here in a systematic way. There were obvious reasons to do this for the psychiatric evaluation of sexual behaviour. While psychiatrists could observe the symptoms of most psychiatric complaints in the clinical setting without drawing on their patients' own accounts, in case histories of abnormal sexuality, the doctor could not be present when the patient was sexually active.[36] Patients' voices would acquire far greater prominence in Krafft-Ebing's publications from this point on.

The personal details in the two dissenting case studies, followed by the deployment of autobiographical accounts, may have had some resonance with Krafft-Ebing's urning readership. It is possible that the urnings with sufficient resources to follow such elevated psychiatric texts came from similar backgrounds and had the intellectual and financial capacity to do so. As noted earlier, some may have had access to university or hospital libraries and others would have accessed the articles as monograph reprints ordered from publisher catalogues. These readers were therefore among the educated and upper-class followers of Ulrichs and included individuals from the "discreet professionals" urning subgroup (see chapter 2). Due to their elevated class status, these individuals were targets for blackmailers and had much to lose if exposed. Writing anonymous autobiographical letters to a potentially receptive psychiatrist in another country was a relatively simple and risk-free form of activism.

As discussed in chapter 2, after Ulrichs published his first two pamphlets, *Vindex* and *Inclusa*, in 1864, readers responded to him with their life stories in the four years that followed. Ulrichs then deployed these in a process of coordinated community self-definition. What Ulrichs's readers had learned from that process was the power of self-disclosure as a means to correct the record. The curated life account, suitably medicalized, was the primary research material of the sexual scientist.[37] Urnings could write accurate and authentic accounts of themselves – something that clinicians could not do. By supplying the material for case studies themselves, urnings could commandeer the messaging and influence the discourse of sexuality in their favour. From this point on, that is what some of them started to do.

In 1884, Krafft-Ebing published a paper in the journal *Irrenfreund* that included six case studies: five men and one woman.[38] The first case study in this paper was an autobiographical letter written by Mr. X, a thirty-eight-year-old masculine German businessman.[39] As noted earlier in this chapter, he had read Krafft-Ebing's paper in the *Allgemeine Zeitschrift für Psychiatrie* and had been struck by the sympathy the author had demonstrated for his patients. Legal difficulties following a case of blackmail had caused Mr. X to flee to exile in America. Mr. X was familiar with Ulrichs's works, mentioning him twice in the letter, and was strikingly forthright in his advocacy for the rights of urnings: "One thing remains true. Our love, too, produces the most beautiful, noblest blossoms, unfolds all the nobler instincts, stimulates the spirit, just as it does in a young man who loves his girl. They find the same devotion, the same willingness to sacrifice, even if life is put on hold, the same pain, the same sorrow, the same joy, the same happiness as in the true man."[40]

This was the first published example of an urning follower of Ulrichs turning to the works of Krafft-Ebing and then contributing with an autobiographical letter for use as a case study. The man had no intention of seeking a cure, and, setting aside his legal situation and exile, he was quite content with his sexual orientation. The other five case studies, four men and one woman, were clinical studies of patients who had sought therapeutic interventions from Krafft-Ebing.

In 1885, Krafft-Ebing reproduced two more autobiographical accounts he had received in unsolicited letters from individuals who rejected any notion of pathology and who traced their sexual awakening back to Ulrichs's writings.[41] These two accounts follow the structure and content of Krafft-Ebing's published case studies, which suggests that both urnings had keenly read them. Their letters provided all the kind of content Krafft-Ebing could easily use. This was not a case of inventing content so as to align it with Krafft-Ebing's theories; if anything, the two urnings intended to persuade Krafft-Ebing he was wrong to pathologize them. However, they had been attentive to the way Krafft-Ebing constructed his case studies and so included details about parental physical and mental illness, masturbation as a teenager or young adult, and other features that Krafft-Ebing included in standard clinical evaluations.

The first such letter was from a thirty-five-year-old weibling who was attracted to soldiers. He wrote: "About the age of 24, I learned through the reading of Ulrichs's writings that I was not the only man of that kind. I received the writings from a friend who, like me, loves male beings, albeit in a different way."[42] This man was highly intelligent, well-educated, and a senior civil servant. Commenting on his mental health, he wrote: "I cannot find the love for men pathological. I would therefore be psychologically completely healthy were it not for a strange mania that haunts and torments me in my sexual life."[43] The mania to which he referred was a relentless drive for sexual satisfaction, which he often had to relieve with masturbation: "This mania is the only side of my sexual life that embarrasses me; my love for men only makes me feel some gloomy hours as far as I am often afflicted by a sudden fear that my inclinations might become known in public, an event that would bring me almost to the brink of despair."[44] He closed his letter with an appeal: "When will we be able to approach the matter without prejudice, even in the public arena? In any case, science must not pause for a moment to disseminate the results obtained as far as possible and make them understandable even to the layman."[45]

The second letter case study, from a forty-eight-year-old married intermediate urning, showed the same concern to proffer his case study to advance scientific research. He wrote: "You want the biography of different urnings. In the interest of science, I take the liberty of giving you an autobiography as detailed as possible in the following, in which I will try to give all the data that come to mind here with the greatest possible objectivity."[46] This was the man whose quotation about how he encountered Ulrichs's works was used in the introduction to this book. He did not simply attest to his mental health; he also located the origins of his well-being in his sexual awakening: "Since I let my urning nature run free, I am happier, healthier and more efficient!"[47]

These early self-penned case studies are a strong expression of the liberating experience of finding a name, and with it, a sense of belonging afforded by the urning identity. While they complied with all of Krafft-Ebing's requirements for case-study content, they also implicitly challenged Krafft-Ebing's assumptions and pushed him to change his position. In his preamble, Krafft-Ebing speculated that some urnings, possibly a minority, could be mentally healthy. However, he was still of a mind that the urning sexual disposition was pathological in origin and called for correction: "Unfortunately, the cache of medical case histories of these individuals is still quite small for obvious reasons, in order to be able to finally cure this abnormal natural phenomenon, and it would be up to the affected persons to step out of their reserve in order to enable science to make a safe judgment."[48]

Here, again, Krafft-Ebing stuck to the orthodox psychiatric position, but this time the contrast with the two urning autobiographies that followed was particularly stark. While many of the patients Krafft-Ebing saw at his clinic were looking for a "cure," this was not the case with the individuals who were sending him their autobiographies. Whatever Krafft-Ebing's scientific stance about urnings, his appeal for case studies did resonate with urnings who were following his writings, and many of them would respond in the years to come.

In his introduction to the 1885 case studies, Krafft-Ebing listed thirty-two such studies of same-sex-attracted men and women found in the psychiatric literature, including Casper's "self-confession of a pederast," Westphal's papers, and many psychiatric studies from the 1870s.[49] He had assembled all of these as well as other case studies relating to additional sexual conditions and practices for the purpose of writing what would become his career-defining work: *Psychopathia Sexualis*.

Psychopathia Sexualis

Krafft-Ebing published *Psychopathia Sexualis*, the foundational text of sexology, in eleven editions during his lifetime. After his death, there were a further six editions under other editors. The book was an encyclopedic listing of sexual categories, illustrated with case studies, and included a disquisition on the legal status of each category. Krafft-Ebing published the first edition of *Psychopathia Sexualis* in 1886; it ran to 110 pages.[50] For the next fifteen years this would be Krafft-Ebing's principal work; it would extend to multiple volumes and serve as the repository of most of his urning case studies. There were only three case studies of same-sex-attracted individuals in the first edition; that number would increase significantly, relative to the other categories, in all the editions that followed. From the second edition onwards, he included the subtitle *Mit besonderer Berücksichtigung der conträren Sexualempfindung* (With Special Consideration of the Contrary Sexual Sensation).

Perhaps as a result of the dissenting autobiographies he had received in 1884 and 1885, Krafft-Ebing introduced an important modification to his theory in the first edition of *Psychopathia Sexualis*. He classified his cases as either "congenital" or "acquired." This distinction underpinned his therapeutic approach. He believed that therapeutic intervention could work only for an individual with an "acquired" sexual instinct, and he was adamant that it could not work for those born with that instinct: "The possibility asserted by Tarnowsky (op. cit. p. 17 u. flP.) that a real urning, with a congenital perversion of the sexual life can be freed from his pathological sexual direction by education and brought to normal sexual sensation, I must deny on the basis of my experience."[51]

Krafft-Ebing now considered that while those with an "acquired" sexual disposition could be treated using hypnotherapy, those with a "congenital" sexual disposition could not. To differentiate the latter, Krafft-Ebing referred to the "acquired" cases as "Psychic Hermaphrodites," a neologism that never really found purchase.[52] Therapeutic intervention could only educate such patients towards abstinence, thus alleviating psychiatric comorbidities or curing addictions to masturbation. Krafft-Ebing's clinic offered fourteen-hour baths at 25–28°C and cold plunges to cure addictions to masturbation, the sedative potassium bromide for genital fixation, and hypnotism to dispel homosexual thoughts.[53] Most of the autobiographical case studies in *Psychopathia Sexualis* were supplied by "congenital" urnings who did not attend the clinic at all. From 1889 onwards, Krafft-Ebing used the following four headings to divide the growing corpus of case studies and commentaries on contrary sexuality:

1 *Psychische Hermaphrodisie* (Psychic Hermaphrodisia)
2 *Homosexuale oder Urninge* (Homosexuals or Urnings)
3 *Effeminatio und Viraginität* (Effeminacy and Viraginity)
4 *Androgyne und Gynandrier* (Androgynes and Gynandres)

As indicated above, "Psychic Hermaphrodites," included all the cases that Krafft-Ebing judged as being most amenable to therapeutic intervention;[54] "Homosexuals and Urnings" included all those congenitally attracted to members of the same sex with no marked gender variance; "Effeminates and Viragines" included all those congenitally attracted to their own sex but also gender nonconforming. This last section included feminine men and masculine women but also at least two individuals whose presentation was closer to what Magnus Hirschfeld would later call *seelischen Transsexualismus* (mental transsexualism).[55] These were, in many cases, arbitrary categorizations with substantial overlaps for the letter autobiographies, as Krafft-Ebing had not met or clinically assessed those men. The final section, "Androgynes and Gynandres," included only three case studies – one man and two women – judged to resemble the opposite sex physically and psychologically.[56]

There were thirty-four original autobiographies in Krafft-Ebing's works, as well as two polemic letters about urning rights and activism that contained autobiographical elements. All of these were from men. With repeats omitted, the distribution of original autobiographical case studies started with the *Lehrbuch der Psychiatrie* in 1883 and concluded with the 1892 edition of *Psychopathia Sexualis*. Editions after 1892 carried no original autobiographical case studies from same-sex-attracted men. More than half the autobiographies appeared for the first time between 1888 and 1890. Seventeen of these were supplied by men seeking treatment or undergoing treatment in the clinic. A further seven were sent "for the good of science" by individuals who either did not mention or tacitly accepted pathological explanations. These will not be included in the following discussion. The rest consisted of ten dissenting autobiographical letters and two polemics that rejected any notion of pathologization. These twelve "dissenters" will be the focus of the rest of this chapter.

Dissenting Autobiographies

Overwhelmingly, the dissenting autobiographies came from individuals in the upper and educated classes. Eleven of the dissenters disclosed their age and profession. The average age was thirty-seven, with a range between twenty-two and forty-nine. Regarding professions, there were two medical doctors, two civil servants, two merchants, two independently wealthy writers, an engineer, a concert musician, a world traveller, and a student. Most came from Austria, although there were a few Germans, one Pole, one Belgian, and one Englishman. However, all of those who sent him their sexual autobiographies were probably all themselves germanophone.[57]

The dissenting case studies were autobiographies intended to influence the discourse of psychiatry. As with the case studies supplied in 1884 and 1885, these individuals were not seeking therapeutic intervention. Their disagreements with Krafft-Ebing were usually polite but clearly articulated. A thirty-four-year-old Austrian concert musician wrote in 1890: "I do not consider contrary sexual sensation to be a nervous disease." [58] This sentiment was encountered in all the dissenting case studies. A forty-nine-year-old Belgian businessman wrote in 1888: "Even I cannot admit, in spite of being urning, that my nature is a 'morbid' one, or you must call other whole categories of people, usually considered normal, morbid. Nobody sees anything morbid in me, I have never heard that there is something sick about me, nor that I have a peculiarity that could suggest or degenerate into something morbid."[59]

The men accompanied their rejection of pathologization with an emphatic desire not to change their sexual natures. Indignantly, in 1891, a thirty-seven-year-old engineer rejected pathological causes and went on to say that "no power in the world can take away an urning's perverted natural disposition."[60] In another account, the writer expressed a personal desire never to change. A twenty-year-old medical student argued in 1890 that "although I am aware of my abnormal inclinations, I do not want any change in them; I only long for a time when I can pursue them more comfortably and with less danger of discovery."[61] Using the slang term for an older urning, a middle-aged doctor from Germany wrote in 1890:

> Most "aunts," including myself, do not consider our abnormality to be a misfortune, and would regret it if this condition were to change. In my opinion and that of all others, the congenital condition cannot be influenced. We hope that the relevant paragraphs of the penal code will be amended to the effect that only rape or causing public nuisance, if these are simultaneously to be observed, should be considered criminal offences.[62]

Five of the men attributed their education in urning matters to Ulrichs. The forty-nine-year-old Belgian businessman referred to earlier stated: "A few books of Numa Numantius had fallen into my hands and from these I received the explanation of my until then still completely inexplicable condition."[63] Some even knew him personally: "I got to know a large number of people like me or similar to me, among them Karl Ulrichs (Numa Numantius)."[64] Sometimes it was friends who enlightened them. One upper-class Austrian man of thirty-six, who had travelled the world, declared that he "had no idea of the existence of the urnings," but that a friend "initiated me into all mysteries."[65] In other cases, although a link to Ulrichs was unstated, the writers expressed their understanding of their own urning nature in Ulrichsian terminology. A thirty-four-year-old Austrian businessman described the character of the urning in 1888 as "an individual who, despite his masculine physique, feels thoroughly feminine, whose senses are not in the least excited by women and whose sexual longing is always directed toward men."[66] This definition appeared to be a version of Ulrichs's anima thesis, articulated in his first two pamphlets.

In one or two autobiographies, the men were articulating their sexuality for the first time. Remarkably, an inner conviction that theirs was a fixed and not morbid sexual orientation characterized even these individuals. A young artist in Vienna who had tortured himself in a series of chaste passionate friendships wrote: "No one suspects my true nature, – only you, a stranger, you alone know me now, and in the main, as precisely as not father and mother, not friend, not wife, not lover. It has been a blessing for me to be allowed to reveal that oppressive secret of my own nature for once."[67] The Belgian businessman, who had indulged in anonymous sex, declared, "You are the first to whom I open myself," and then explained why he was sending his life account to Krafft-Ebing: "Make use of this letter in any way you wish, perhaps it will one day contribute to making the fate of those born later, to whom nature has given the same feelings as me, easier."[68]

The writers often articulated their commitment to furthering scientific understanding. An Austrian businessman in his early thirties wrote: "I hand over these lines to you in the interest of future fellow sufferers – in the interest of science, truth and justice, publish whatever seems suitable to you."[69] A thirty-seven-year-old engineer opened his letter as follows: "I am writing down, as best I can, the story of my suffering, guided solely by the desire to contribute, through this autobiography, a little to the elucidation of the misunderstanding and the cruel misconceptions about 'contra sexual sensation' that unfortunately still prevail in so many circles."[70] A thirty-four-year-old merchant from Vienna earnestly stated his purpose in writing: "Imbued with the conviction that the mystery of our existence can only be solved or at least illuminated by men of science who think without prejudice, I describe my life solely with the intention of perhaps contributing something to the elucidation of this cruel error of nature and thus possibly being of use to my fellow men of fate of a later generation."[71]

The faith these men had in the power of science to uncover truths that would benefit them was a feature of late nineteenth-century Germany, where science and progress were valorized. Scientific method, predicated on impartiality, had a strong appeal in a world where partiality and prejudice were the alternatives.

Several of the men spoke of their experience of or desire for long-term loving relationships. One thirty-year-old physician wrote of a succession of relationships: "In the same year, I made a formal covenant of love with a 34-year-old merchant. We lived like husband and wife."[72]

This lasted a few years before breaking down and then "after a few months I fell in love with a 40-year-old civil servant. For a year I remained faithful to him. We lived like lovers."[73] This man was a serial monogamist who appeared to be happiest in a secure relationship: "If I am without love, I fall into deep melancholy, which, however, immediately gives way to the consolations of the first handsome man."[74] A Polish factory official of thirty-one was convinced that "if there would be a marriage between men, I believe, I would not shy away from a lifelong union, which on the other hand with a consecration seems to me something impossible."[75] These frank outpourings of personal details were being deployed as evidence that urnings could be happy and healthy and were capable of committed, loving relationships.

Krafft-Ebing later credited the commitment to marriage-like relationship types as convincing proof of moral seriousness: "A more striking proof of the depth and sincerity of such a sexual sentiment on the part of numerous fellow citizens who are to be taken seriously and who feel themselves to be martyrs of their organisation and of social conditions could not be provided."[76] That remark followed Krafft-Ebing's observation that Ulrichs had advocated for urning marriage; it also suggests that he was particularly impressed with commitments to long-term, mutual, loving relationships.

Two of Krafft-Ebing's correspondents were less concerned with autobiography and instead wrote detailed polemic arguments. The first, whom Krafft-Ebing described as "a highly placed man in London," was written by John Addington Symonds (see chapter 8), at the time a forty-nine-year-old English writer living in Davos, Switzerland. Symonds's letter echoed the sentiments of the dissenting case studies: "So, as much as I believe that the view you hold is one that is as beneficial as possible for us, in the interest of science I am not able to accept the word 'pathological' so readily."[77] The other polemic letter came from a forty-five-year-old senior civil servant and used the new terminology: "homosexual." This letter included an autobiographical section that concluded: "In any case, the abnormal should not be identified with the pathological, otherwise a far more pathological phenomenon would have to be seen in the psyche of a Rafael or Mozart in relation to that of the normal average man, than in the urning in relation to the normal sexual."[78] He went on to make a detailed legal and legislative examination of Germany and the prospects for reform. Krafft-Ebing was so impressed with this analysis that he republished it twice, because "the general remarks on the legal and social position of the contrary sexes, even if written by a layman, seem to me to be of great value."[79]

The Impact of the Autobiographies

The men who sent the bulk of the autobiographies, old and young, looked to Krafft-Ebing as a sympathetic researcher and committed their autobiographies to him in the hope that doing so would further science. In this way, they were continuing a campaign that had begun with Ulrichs's lobbying. It was Ulrichs's advocacy that had first captured the attention of psychiatry. Each of the dissenting autobiographies deviated from Krafft-Ebing's central pathologizing thesis and made the case for a more accurate and normalizing scientific model.

In 1892, when the last dissenting letters were coming in, there was little evidence that Krafft-Ebing had changed his mind on the matter. Publishing the dissenters alongside clinical case studies and autobiographies of men seeking cures did lend a productive ambivalence to *Psychopathia Sexualis*, which Krafft-Ebing perpetuated by repeating the dissenters' remarks in all subsequent editions. In fact, he was more likely to repeat the dissenting case studies (an average of three repeats) than the non-dissenting case studies (an average of two). This meant there were dissenting case studies in every single edition of *Psychopathia Sexualis* under Krafft-Ebing's editorship except in the 1886 first edition. Krafft-Ebing, then, implicitly approved of the dissent. Indeed, his language did soften over time, and he alluded less often to degeneration theory. However, degeneration had been the organizing principle of research psychiatry since Griesinger's time, and in his conclusions, Krafft-Ebing found it difficult to abandon that principle.

Krafft-Ebing did become much more vocal in his opposition to the antisodomy laws in Austria and Germany. On 24 May 1894, seemingly unexpectedly, he sent Ulrichs, by then in Italian exile, a pre-publication manuscript of a forthcoming publication, *Der Conträrsexual vor dem Strafrichter*.[80] Ulrichs was at that time editing a Latin newspaper, *Alaudae*, and he devoted a large section of the July 1894 edition to a discussion of that manuscript.[81] Krafft-Ebing's publication, illustrated with fifty summarized urning case studies, was an argument for Austria to scrap its antisodomy law. Once again, however, he maintained his adherence to degeneration and the pathological explanation.[82] Ulrichs, by then in his final months of life, was so enthusiastic about this publication from Krafft-Ebing that, after giving it a positive review in his Latin newspaper, he wrote a petition, his final letter, calling for the repeal of the Austrian antisodomy law.[83]

Many urnings regarded Krafft-Ebing positively. The contemporary urning writer Otto de Joux wrote in 1893 about a "larger Urning

Association" in Germany led by "a famous actor."[84] That group had composed a letter of heartfelt thanks to Krafft-Ebing:

> It is our sacred duty to give spontaneous expression to our gratitude for that excellent man (Dr von Krafft-Ebing) who stimulated the question of our social salvation, that noble researcher who has at last raised the Urning question in our gloomy times, so that we may strive courageously forward on the thorny path that leads to the final equality of all, and a lifting of the undeserved law that is destroying us. [85]

Krafft-Ebing published no new autobiographical case studies after 1892. By then, other sexologists were beginning to make a mark.

At the very end of his life, in his final publication on contrary sexuality, Krafft-Ebing concluded that although it was an abnormality and possibly the result of degenerative processes, it was not after all a pathological phenomenon. He published this paper in Hirschfeld's *Jahrbuch*, a sexological publication. Krafft-Ebing acknowledged that

> contrary sexual sensation in and of itself is not a disease, but only an anomaly … In this way, scientific knowledge comes closer to the point of view of the contrarily sexual people themselves, who never tire of emphasising, in contrast to the views of researchers, that their peculiar sexual sensation is indeed in contradiction with that of the vast majority of their sexual comrades and does not correspond to the purposes of nature, but nevertheless presents itself to them in their consciousness as an adequate, natural and thus justified one.[86]

Krafft-Ebing acknowledged that his patients and autobiographical correspondents had influenced his views. He died the following year. By then, the field of sexology was expanding on a platform where clinicians no longer saw homosexuality as being the result of degenerative processes or disease. For those of his correspondents who were still reading the literature, perhaps this reassured them that their autobiographical efforts had not been in vain.

Conclusion

The urnings who sent Krafft-Ebing their dissenting case studies had prevailed. The scientific edifice they had taken on had tilted their way. This was the result of a continuous campaign started by Ulrichs in 1864 and extended by his followers to 1892. The scale of their achievement needs to be fully appraised. When Ulrichs's campaign started, medical

researchers who wrote about the subject were mostly hostile to the pederast.[87] "New Psychiatry" had taken Ulrichs's theories as its starting
point, but it was the urnings who persisted in sending dissenting accounts that finally swept away the last vestiges of pathologization. By
the 1890s, leading figures in the psychiatric profession were supportive
of law reform. Krafft-Ebing's works and their autobiographical content
would inspire a new generation of sexual scientists: the sexologists.

Krafft-Ebing had been, throughout his engagement with human sexuality, a vociferous advocate for law reform. Perhaps that is how he
came into communication with the Berlin police official Leopold von
Meerscheidt-Hüllessem; Krafft-Ebing may then have introduced him
to Albert Moll. In 1891, Moll published *Die Conträre Sexualempfindung*,
his first edition of a landmark work of sexology. Moll's work did not include case studies. Instead, through multiple interviews he developed
a detailed social-anthropological analysis of the urning and the social
and sexual topography of urning Berlin, as well as a comprehensive
clinical and forensic evaluation of the literature. This was an early foray
into the cross-disciplinary studies that would characterize the burgeon-
ing field of sexology in the coming decades, as a new science that offered interested urnings a modern outlook on their sexuality. Moll's
book was written with the collaboration of von Meerscheidt-Hüllessem
and a prominent urning. The next chapter centres on that prominent
urning, Adolf Glaser, and his friendship with the police official, and
includes their collaboration with Moll.

Chapter Seven

Belling the Cat: Adolf Glaser's Discreet Police Liaison in Berlin, 1878–1897

Once upon a time all the Mice met together in Council and discussed the best means of securing themselves against the attacks of the cat. After several suggestions had been debated, a Mouse of some standing and experience got up and said, "I think I have hit upon a plan which will ensure our safety in the future, provided you approve and carry it out. It is that we should fasten a bell round the neck of our enemy the cat, which will by its tinkling warn us of her approach." This proposal was warmly applauded, and it had been already decided to adopt it, when an old Mouse got upon his feet and said, "I agree with you all that the plan before us is an admirable one: but may I ask who is going to bell the cat?"[1]

With the prospects for reform looking bleak in Germany after 1871, it seemed that there were few options left for urning advocates who wanted to create legislative and administrative change. The antisodomy law, Paragraph 175, loomed over Germany's urnings and encouraged a brisk trade in blackmail. In Berlin, blackmailers thrived with little police intervention; indeed, the police relied on the blackmailers for intelligence when pursuing urnings to arrest. Berlin's urnings were suffering and wanted to see an end to this collaboration with criminals. But who was going to persuade the police to change? Who was going to bell the cat?

Blackmail was by far the biggest complaint made by Karl Heinrich Ulrichs's correspondents. Across Germany, unscrupulous criminals were ruining the lives of young men and older discreet professionals. In 1869, Ulrichs discussed a solution of sorts upon hearing that the Berlin police were maintaining lists of 3,000 urnings: "I request that all Urnings send to the police authorities the name, age, occupation, and personal notes of rogues they know – decoy and ambusher alike. (They will probably also take note of unsigned correspondence, as long as the sender will indicate that he is wary of unmasking himself as an Urning.)"[2] There is no evidence that any urning took up Ulrichs's suggestion over the following decade. If they had, it might not have turned out as they hoped. In the 1870s and early 1880s, the police were more likely to rely on blackmailers as informers than investigate them as suspects. Urnings who wanted to do something about blackmail therefore needed to gain the support of senior officers who might be willing to challenge the institutional culture. Someone needed to liaise with the police and enlighten them about the predicament of Berlin's urnings.[3]

In late nineteenth-century Germany, urnings who sought to petition officials within state apparatuses such as the judiciary or the police had to be careful. Even men who were in a relatively privileged position to effect changes to improve the lives of urnings were at risk of imprisonment and social and economic ruin. As examined in chapter 6, the urnings who lobbied psychiatrists with autobiographies maintained their anonymity so as to protect their identities. Magnus Hirschfeld wrote that "more than one intelligent official has been enlightened through direct contact with urning personalities."[4] Because of the discreet manner in which men of influence went about their advocacy, almost none of it was recorded, so it is unavailable today to scholarly analysis. However, there was one occasion when advocacy effecting real change left an imprint, which we find in the archival traces of Adolf Glaser, who was a prominent figure in the literary world and an active participant in the transformation of the policing of urning Berlin. As a discreet professional, he conducted all his advocacy strictly in private while maintaining a public profile of respectability.

This chapter explores Glaser's involvement in the transformation of Berlin policing in the final two decades of the nineteenth century. The principal sources – Glaser himself, and Magnus Hirschfeld – present this as a leadership-driven process of internal reform. The first-hand reports used in this chapter make the case that the principal officer, Leopold von Meerscheidt-Hüllessem (hereafter "Hüllessem"), experienced a Damascus-like conversion from standard police hostility to full-throated support for urning rights. This narrative of police self-reform has at times been received uncritically by some historians.[5] One exception is the chapter on Hüllessem in Jens Dobler's meticulous history of the Berlin police department and its policing of urning Berlin.[6] Dobler provides a quite detailed account of Glaser's friendship with the police chief and the collaboration the two men entered into with the sexologist Albert Moll.[7] Robert Beachy devoted a full chapter to Hüllessem's reforms of the police department in his book *Gay Berlin* but made only a single mention of Glaser in that chapter relating to the collaboration with Moll.[8] What Dobler and Beachy do not explore is the role Glaser played in educating and persuading senior figures in the police department. Dobler's account sticks close to the primary sources, and he writes from the perspective of the long-term transformation of Berlin policing practice, whereas Beachy's account seems more preoccupied with aggrandizing the policeman. This chapter uses some of the same sources but takes the point of view of Glaser himself to reconstruct a pivotal engagement that contributed to some of the transformations that Dobler and Beachy have outlined.

The scenario in Berlin was rather different from the post-legislation setting seen in more recent instances of LGBTQ+ police liaison. There had been no substantial legal reform process, and Paragraph 175 was still very much in force. The transformation of the policing of queer Berlin was largely independent of legislative developments. Hüllessem's period in the Berlin police is well documented, and at least three sources describe the transformation of policing during his tenure.[9] However, Glaser's contribution to the reform process is absent from each of the accounts. This was not just a case of the police claiming all the credit. One of the accounts was Glaser's own, and he deliberately left out any mention of his own contribution.[10] Even so, it is usually possible through close reading to identify what Glaser's contributions were. Glaser was a deeply private man who preferred to keep his activism secret. Instead of reading Glaser's obituary of Hüllessem as a hagiographic account of the policeman's exploits, it is possible to read it instead as an implicit account of the influence Glaser himself wielded in the police department. Recreating the productive relationship between the two men on the basis of this account involves a modicum of speculation. However, the argument uses corroboration from more than one source in each case.

This chapter covers the years 1885 to 1897, when the language applied to sexual orientation was in transition. In 1885, the word "urning" was still dominant, but by 1897, "homosexual" had gained currency in the scientific and related literature.[11] Both words will be used as they were in the various sources in the course of the narrative, although it should be noted that even where the word "homosexual" was used in this period, it was usually used as a synonym for "urning." The chapter opens with an assessment of the policing of Berlin's urning scene in the years prior to 1885 and then turns to Glaser's biography and the "Glaser scandal" of 1878. The main part of the chapter reconstructs Glaser's friendship with Hüllessem and evaluates this as an early example of police liaison. The chapter closes with an analysis of the net effects of Glaser's intervention. Although he was reluctant to take the credit, Glaser had succeeded by 1897 in aiding the transformation of policing through his advocacy. Glaser had "belled the cat."

Policing Berlin's Urnings

By 1879, Germany's criminal code, in force since 1872, had been in operation long enough to assess whether its provisions were effective. There was some concern in political circles that the police and the legal profession had a poor grasp of the antisodomy law, Paragraph 175. Too many cases that stood no chance of conviction were appearing before the courts, and it often happened that even jurists did not understand the law. Ulrichs wrote of this muddle in 1879:

> There is a lack of unanimity among the jurists on the question: Which acts of man-manly sexual love fall under the Paragraph and which do not? In Bavaria, Saxony, Württemberg, and in the smaller states of Germany, the decision on it is often – perhaps almost always – left to a toss of the dice. Namely, it is dependent on the legal debates and the makeup of the deciding court, as well as on the legal opinion of the majority of its members at that time. This uncertainty of rights is a direct and dangerous promoter of blackmail.[12]

Ostensibly, legislators had intended Paragraph 175 to only prosecute men for same-sex anal coitus. However, there was a growing awareness in the medical literature that most urnings did not practise anal intercourse and instead preferred mutual masturbation or oral or inter-femoral sex.[13] With the establishment of the Reichsgericht (Supreme Court) in Leipzig in 1879, legislators scrutinized and broadened the definition of *widernatürliche Unzucht* (unnatural fornication) in Paragraph 175. The definition now included all acts "similar to sexual intercourse," hinging on "thrusting movements" for that similarity, thus incorporating oral and inter-femoral sex.[14] Mutual masturbation, the most common sexual practice of urnings, remained unpunished. The court also reiterated that both participants in the sexual act were culpable for each of the criminalized practices under the definition.[15]

Although the legal definitions were now more specific and more uniform across the country, few people fell afoul of or faced conviction under Paragraph 175.[16] We find that between 1890 and 1905, when we remove convictions for bestiality (covered under the same act), there were between two hundred and three hundred convictions annually for male same-sex activity in Imperial Germany.[17] Hans von Tresckow, looking back over the thirty years he had spent policing Berlin's homosexuals, wrote about Paragraph 175 in 1922: "As I can testify from my many years of practice, it is almost never applied, since it is very seldom possible to convict persons who violate it. This is in the nature of things, for in the case of the offence, the persons acting will not involve a third party as a witness, and since both are liable to prosecution, one cannot accuse the other."[18]

The low tally of convictions under Paragraph 175 was also because policing was reactive rather than proactive when it came to sexual criminals. Most cases that came to the notice of the police did so because of tip-offs from blackmailers. Although the blackmailers were breaking the law, and some faced the consequences for doing so, urnings exposed in this way were easy to convict. A corroborating witness to the sexual act, the blackmailer, would be on hand to give evidence in exchange for clemency. Urnings caught this way were facing court and even prison despite being blackmail victims, while their extorters walked free.

During this period, urning life became more visible in Berlin. By 1880, according to Hugo Friedländer, an urning scene had developed around the eastern end of the Tiergarten that included bars, restaurants, and ballrooms.[19] Men who used the park for sexual assignations had been meeting in bars in that neighbourhood since the mid-nineteenth century. Some of these bars became regular meeting places, and businesses started to appear that catered specifically to the urning crowd. The elevated Stadtbahn, which opened in 1882, meant that patrons could easily travel in from far-flung suburbs.[20] The most exclusive of these establishments was a large restaurant called "Urania" on Leipziger Platz, where "balls were often held to which only the more respectable urnings had access."[21] It was one of several ballrooms that held regular events for urnings during an annual season that ran from October to Easter. Hugo Friedländer recounted a long list of the venues he remembered from his youth as an urning on the Berlin scene:

> At these balls, where the most exuberant cheerfulness prevailed, the most elegant and chic ladies' dresses, whose wearers were mostly men, could be admired. – Very famous, but less noble, were the balls in the "Deutscher Kaiser," a larger dance hall on Lothringerstraße. The Kiechs-Balls were very noble and comfortable. These balls, which mostly took place in a noble restaurant in Potsdamerstraße, sometimes also in the "Altes Architektenhaus" (Wilhelmstraße), near Buggenhagen at Moritzplatz, or in the "Philharmonie" (Bernburgerstraße), were arranged by a lingerie dealer called Kiechs.[22]

Friedländer listed a wide variety of bars and meeting places from the 1880s, including a Parisian cellar underneath the French embassy; a cellar bar on the corner of Markgrafenstraße and Jägerstraße; the Renztunnel – a large restaurant that hosted concerts with a "young people's band"; the Reichshallen, a concert venue; and Seger's, one of the best-known urning venues, a ground-floor restaurant on Jägerstraße with an urning proprietor.[23] In all, Friedländer listed around fifteen bars, ballrooms, and restaurants that were urning meeting places in the early 1880s. Given the large number of venues, and the long-running sexual trade in the Tiergarten, it is probable that at least in this part of Berlin, the footprint of urning life was considerable and quite visible by the 1880s.

With the increase in urning venues in this part of Berlin, the police department focused on keeping public order. Under a succession of leaders, the Berlin police responded to the growing challenge through innovation, strategic organization, and gradually increased staffing. Jens Dobler's research tracked the department from 1848, when Wilhelm Stieber was police chief, up to the first Nazi government in 1933. He was able to show that the Berlin police evolved from being instigators of persecution to quasi-allies of the homosexual movement in the Weimar Republic. This chapter will focus on the central period of transformation of the Berlin police, beginning in 1885.[24]

The transformation of the police department in its treatment of urnings/homosexuals over several decades was largely undocumented; we would know very little about it today had it not been for the research efforts of two French investigative journalists, Henri de Weindel and F.P. Fischer, who in 1908 published their investigation into the policing of homosexuality in Berlin.[25] Weindel and Fischer described three stages of development. The first phase, which roughly covered the period when Prussia was consolidating its gains in the North German Confederation, was mostly a period of observation and fact gathering, during which lists of potential offenders were compiled.[26] Rumours at the time, reported in Berlin's *Gerichtszeitung* of 6 June 1869, suggested there were 3,000 names on Berlin's police lists.[27] Some arrests were made during this period to legitimize the department's operations.[28] The second phase, which began in 1872 under the new, Prussian-dominated Imperial Germany, saw a stepping up of activities, with the department using spies and *agents provocateurs* to entrap urnings. [29] This period also saw the department collaborating with blackmailers. Prior to 1885, a separate division from the one targeting urnings handled blackmail, and the lack of cooperation between the two divisions meant that convictions for extorting urnings were extremely low. As noted earlier, the pattern of arrests suggested this was about managing urning society in Berlin rather than eradicating it. This was the situation in the early 1880s. Periodically, there would be raids on urning venues. For example, in 1880, the police raided a street-level restaurant called "Die Lachmine" at the corner of Brüderstraße and Neumannsgasse.[30] According to Friedländer, the venue was far too visible as a known haunt of urning men, and the police sought to shut it down without any apparent arrests or charges.

In the third phase, after 1885, police tactics shifted towards far greater tolerance of urning Berlin. The catalyst for this was a reorganization of the Criminal Investigation Department (CID). In 1883, a murder case exposed deficiencies in the organization of the department around the policing of both blackmail and urnings. As a result, the Chief of Police signed off on a new structure, which was in place by early 1885.[31] The CID was now reconfigured into three new groups: Inspectorate A supported the investigation of cases arising from divisional police stations; Inspectorate B focused on larger investigations and the professional criminal class; and Inspectorate C dealt with white-collar crime. The Pederast Department was now within Inspectorate B, as was the investigation of blackmail, and the department now had new leadership.[32] Leopold von Meerscheidt-Hüllessem moved from the Political Police to take a position as a criminal inspector in Inspectorate B with responsibility for investigating both blackmail and urnings/homosexuals. This chapter examines the forces that came into play to produce the transition to a more tolerant police approach to the sexual lives of urnings.

Adolf Glaser – the Scandal

The son of an apothecary, Adolf Glaser was born on 15 December 1829 at Wiesbaden in the Duchy of Nassau.[33] Both his parents were Jewish, but Glaser was raised in the Protestant faith. He studied philosophy and art history at Berlin and attained a doctorate in philosophy at Jena in 1856. On graduation, he assumed the editorship of the newly founded *Westermannschen Illustrirten Deutschen Monats-Hefte*.[34] Modelled loosely on the American *Harper's* magazine, this was Germany's leading literary publication. The *Monats-Hefte* published short stories and serialized literary works, and Glaser wielded considerable influence over the development of literary careers. Glaser was, at the same time, a commissioning editor for the Westermann publishing house. Authors promoted and encouraged by Glaser and Westermann included Theodor Storm, Wilhelm Raabe, and Paul Heyse.[35] Glaser was also an author of some considerable note at the time.[36]

Glaser's background and position as a wealthy intellectual with an enviable public reputation meant he was a "discreet professional." According to Hirschfeld, Glaser had been in "lively correspondence" with Ulrichs.[37] In Glaser's obituary, Hirschfeld added that "he formed a bridge between the first and second period of the literary struggle against the persecution of the urnings, between Ulrichs and our WhK Committee."[38] While his public image was probably strictly professional, he may have been more open about his sexual nature with close friends such as the writer Wilhelm Raabe. He might have maintained this comfortable, discreet existence except for an unfortunate event that changed the course of his life.

On 11 March 1878 at 7:30 a.m., a nineteen-year-old waiter named Karl Duberke was arrested in the stairwell of Fruchtsraße 22.[39] Duberke had spent the night in the stairwell "for want of another roof" and because he had been trying to speak to one of the residents, the retired railway official Herr E. Rettschlag.[40] Under intense questioning, Duberke admitted to repeated sexual contact with Herr Rettschlag and named several others with whom he had engaged. One of the names Duberke mentioned was Adolf Glaser. The following day, Glaser, Rettschlag, the Polish actor Ladislaus Baronche (Władysław Barącz), two merchants, "J." and "H.," and a pensioner, Scheibe, were all arrested and brought in for questioning.[41] A few days later, on the 18 March, Duberke came to Glaser's apartment to plead with him. Apparently, Duberke feared that Glaser would now sue him for defamation. Word was sent for the police to attend, and, in the presence of an officer, Duberke fully retracted the allegation against Glaser.[42] In this document, Duberke wrote that he had originally applied unsuccessfully to work with Glaser, who then supported him financially until he found employment.[43] As a result of this and further statements by Duberke to the police, Glaser and the two businessmen had all charges withdrawn. In the end, the entire case collapsed because of Duberke's unreliability as a witness.[44] Glaser later wrote to Wilhelm Raabe about the ordeal:

On Sunday, 10 March, I was still in Spielhagen's house in the midst of the most cheerful company, and on Monday, as a result of the lying accusation of an insane thug, I was struck by this blow. The police lieutenant thought he had discovered some kind of conspiracy and acted accordingly, although I had never seen any of the other accused. It did not help that the rascal came afterwards to ask me not to prosecute him, whereupon I had him interrogated and arrested immediately. It was too late. Although all the decent newspapers had waited, two or three Berlin journals carried the whole scandal with my name, and the provincial papers followed suit.[45]

The withdrawal of charges would have brought an end to the matter had the press not latched onto the case. The story appeared first in the *Berliner Gerichtszeitung* on 14 March, and then in the populist *Volks-Zeitung* six days later. The media presented the matter as a major sex scandal involving men of influence.[46] The *Volks-Zeitung* named Glaser as the most prominent individual in the case, so even though he faced no charges and never went to trial, the scandal became known as the "Glaser Scandal." It was the media coverage, rather than the arrest, that did the most damage.

Professionally, all of this was a disaster for Glaser. He told Wilhelm Raabe that the papers that had named him in the scandal "had been sent to Westermann from various quarters, and many literary people had submitted requests to take over the editorship."[47] Glaser realized that although he had done nothing wrong, the bad press generated by the scandal could damage his employer. In what he later regretted as a hasty decision, he immediately resigned as editor.[48] Psychologically, the scandal took a terrible toll on him, as he confided to Raabe on 30 April:

> You can imagine, dear friend, that I thought a lot about suicide at that time, but I would like to experience for myself how such an unheard-of story goes on. When I can tell you everything in detail orally, you will understand. It is a pity that the whole thing cannot be published with complete openness: How differently I now understand the persecution of the Jews, the witch trials and everything else in which fanaticism and blind prejudice brought people to the greatest rage, without any real reason.[49]

A traumatic experience of this kind, causing public humiliation and professional ruin, was hard to recover from, although Glaser was not, at least, financially exposed. Within months he had secured an income writing a column in the *Berliner Bürgerzeitung*.[50] And his closest friends in Berlin had not deserted him, as he wrote on 4 July: "I have found my stay here without any difficulties, and since I have already met up with a large number of my friends and acquaintances, I can already judge how my life will turn out."[51] Glaser was possibly the author of a letter to Ulrichs sent in late 1878. Ulrichs reproduced part of the letter in his twelfth pamphlet, *Critische Pfeile*, introducing it as coming from "a Berlin man of knowledge of society and experience": "Urnings are tolerated at all levels of society here, and in no way do they consider the Urning's inclination dishonourable. But people do indeed consider it a dishonour as soon as court proceedings begin. Not the thing itself, no! only the intervention by the courts works to the dishonour of the Urning in the eyes of the public."[52]

Glaser was in a perplexing position. His sexuality was probably an open secret with his closest friends in Berlin and with some sympathetic literary colleagues. In that context, it presented few problems. But the moment there was the whiff of scandal from criminal proceedings, the public appetite for sexual sensationalism damaged him professionally.

Glaser kept up lines of communication with his former colleagues. When George Westermann died in late 1879, Glaser began making moves to get reinstated, and this finally happened in early 1882.[53] Although he returned in a more junior position, by the close of the decade he had recovered his old position.[54] In parallel to this, and perhaps as a consequence of the fallout from the scandal, Glaser began taking steps to make a difference in the way Berlin's urnings were policed.

Adolf Glaser and His Friendship with Hüllessem

Glaser's public "outing" in 1878 should have diminished his need for discretion. However, he still preferred not to take a public role, and he was assiduously secretive about his behind-the-scenes activism. He went to considerable efforts to maintain the public face of a discreet professional. Hirschfeld later described him as "a gentleman already old at the beginning of the movement, of excellent intelligence, who, as editor of one of Germany's leading magazines, enjoyed universal recognition. He was one of the not exactly frequent but very meritorious Urnings, who, without ever stepping out with their name, worked tirelessly 'behind the scenes,' inspiring and encouraging all, who, in word and writing, sought to improve the living conditions of homosexuals."[55]

At some point in the 1880s, Glaser managed to gain an introduction to the most important man in the policing of homosexuals: Hüllessem. It is unlikely that Glaser met Hüllessem during the events of 1878. At that time, Hüllessem's attention was on an impending trial in Marpingen in the Saarland on the other side of Germany, where he had been enforcing Bismarck's anti-socialist laws and the policy of *Kulturkampf* as an officer of the Political Police.[56] It is much more likely that Glaser met Hüllessem later, when he returned to Berlin, and that he did so socially. The Prussian police had a practice of appointing upper-class or aristocratic individuals to senior positions, often drafted in from higher officer ranks in the army. Hüllessem was a prime example: he came from an aristocratic family and initially pursued a military career. Thus, it is possible that Glaser and Hüllessem moved in similar elevated social circles in Berlin. The introduction was probably made at some point after 1885, when Hüllessem transferred to Inspectorate B and took over the CID division responsible for the policing of urnings.[57]

Hüllessem's first big case in his new position was a raid on Seger's Restaurant, which was, according to Friedländer, one of the most popular urning venues.[58] There was nothing particularly overt about this establishment: it was a ground floor bar-restaurant at Jägerstraße 10, in a quiet, middle-class neighbourhood.[59] The bar's façade was discreet and unobtrusive. Following an anonymous tip-off, Hüllessem deployed a plainclothes police officer to investigate in January 1885. The officer reported back that the bar was indeed a haunt of *warme Brüder* (warm brothers – a slang term for urnings). Although he had observed intimacy between patrons and profane language, he had seen no evidence of illegal behaviour.[60] Despite this, Hüllessem proceeded with a raid. On a Sunday night in early February, Detective Inspector Wolff entered the pub with seven colleagues while uniformed officers formed a cordon outside.[61] The bar had two rooms, both of which were bustling with a cheerful crowd when the police entered. The patrons in the bar were all men, but they came from a wide variety of backgrounds. Twelve people were arrested that night: the restaurateur, Carl August Seger; his lover and barkeep, Paul Bock, also referred to by his customers as *Die schöne Paula* or *die Fuchtel* (the shrew); and ten patrons, including a dressmaker called "Engel," another whose nickname was "Rebekka," merchants, skilled workers, a manservant, a man of private means, and a schoolteacher.[62] The case came to court in November at the third criminal division of the Berlin I Regional Court. The police charged Seger with procurement and sentenced him to eight months; Bock was charged as his accomplice and sentenced to four months. The patrons were each charged with causing a public nuisance and received between three to four months, except for the schoolteacher, who walked free.

If Hüllessem had intended the raid on Seger's as a warning shot to urning Berlin, it didn't have the desired effect. According to Friedländer, within months of the closing of Seger's, five new venues opened in the same district.[63] The raid on Seger's had been set in motion by a tip-off from a blackmailer or someone with a grudge against Seger, and the plainclothes surveillance had uncovered nothing illegal. It was hardly a compelling justification for a raid that required a heavy deployment of officers. Finally, although Seger's was an urning venue, the police had brought no charges under Paragraph 175. The Pederast Department's effectiveness ostensibly hinged on its success at securing convictions under that paragraph. Instead, this extremely expensive and labour-intensive operation had secured only a handful of prosecutions for procurement or public nuisance. This would be the last time in the nineteenth century that an urning venue in Berlin was targeted specifically to secure prosecutions under Paragraph 175.[64]

Hüllessem was a criminologist and a modernizer to the core of his being.[65] Had he looked objectively at the raid on Seger's and the wider operations of the Pederast Department, he would have struggled to assess these positively. The use of career-criminal blackmailers as informers was grubby business, and the results were equivocal. Glaser later wrote about Hüllessem's thoughts about this style of policing: "His police-trained insight made it particularly intolerable that several disreputable raffish subjects took advantage of the error of the law and applied an exploitation system against the urnings, to which many unfortunate people became and still come to be victims."[66]

Even when tip-offs led to arrests, the burden of proof that Paragraph 175 had been contravened was such that many cases collapsed when they reached the criminal court. Hüllessem realized that an all-out campaign to shut all the venues and arrest all the patrons would have required an enormous deployment of officers and that the outcomes at court would have been uncertain at best. There seemed to be no political will among city politicians to force such an approach or to facilitate it with regulatory changes. Nor did the vast army of blackmailer/informers have any interest in closing down urning Berlin, given that it was their primary source of income. All the Berlin police could do, then, was disrupt and harass the urning community on its fringes, with targets and priorities entirely at the whim of the blackmailers. This must have rankled with Hüllessem, who was more interested in transformative results and, perhaps, his own legacy.

There is no concrete evidence as to when Glaser and Hüllessem became friends. Dobler rather conservatively places their meeting as taking place, "at the latest," during their mutual collaboration with Albert Moll in 1890.[67] It is more likely that Glaser and Hüllessem met much earlier than that, probably not long after the events of 1885. Several of the points where Glaser influenced Hüllessem probably occurred well before 1890. The collaboration with Moll, described below, relied on Hüllessem changing his outlook, reading the literature, and establishing contact with the psychiatrist Richard von Krafft-Ebing. Since this chapter places Glaser as pivotal in influencing these outcomes, he would have had to develop a position of trust well before 1890. It probably took some time for Glaser to become the kind of influential friend Hüllessem needed. If they had met in 1885, the questions about policing raised in the aftermath of the Seger's raid would have provided an opening.

Magnus Hirschfeld, who knew both of the men personally after 1896, observed that their friendship "went so far that he consulted with the Urning about his heterosexual heartache as much as the Urning

spoke to him about his homosexual needs."[68] Glaser later recalled Hüllessem's state of mind when they first met: "He saw pederasty as an
unnatural debauchery, largely produced by sexual over-saturation, and
his abhorrence of it left nothing to be desired."[69] They made an unlikely
pair: Glaser, an intellectual urning of Jewish descent, and Hüllessem,
an aristocratic former military lieutenant from a family steeped in Prussian military tradition. Hüllessem, unlike Glaser, did not appear to be
an urning himself.[70] Glaser later wrote that although Hüllessem was a
man "who was able to recognize the Uranian being without prejudice,
[he] was himself such an admirer of the female form."[71]

Interpreting the Sources

There are three principal sources for Glaser's engagement with Hüllessem. The first is the obituary of Hüllessem, "In Memoriam," that
Glaser wrote and published in 1902.[72] The other two accounts were
written by Magnus Hirschfeld in 1914 and in 1922.[73] Glaser's account
was probably the source for Hirschfeld's accounts. Hirschfeld did not
know the two men until after Glaser had written to him in 1896 following the publication of Hirschfeld's *Sappho und Socrates*.[74] Hirschfeld
commented extensively on the strong friendship between the two
men and Glaser's wise counsel and made several observations that
reinforced the interpretation that Glaser's influence in the police department was far greater than Glaser had acknowledged in his own account. Glaser's account omitted any reference to a connection between
himself and Hüllessem. Glaser, ever the discreet professional, had no
intention of inserting himself into the narrative. Instead, the document
contains only one subject, Hüllessem, and details each of the significant
things the policeman accomplished on behalf of urnings. It reads as if
Hüllessem went through a spontaneous and unexplained conversion
away from standard police hostility to pederasty to becoming a strong
supporter of urning emancipation in only a few short years. It was as
if he were implying that Hüllessem had changed his own mind and
that all Glaser had done was observe the change. This lends a certain
implausibility to the account.

However, if we read Glaser's obituary of Hüllessem instead as an
account of each of the points of contact Glaser had with Hüllessem
and the police department, then a very different picture emerges. This
is not an unreasonable interpretation, since Hirschfeld attested to the
close friendship and Glaser's account was written entirely from the
perspective of his own knowledge of Hüllessem. Read in this way,
it becomes possible to reconsider the points of contact and influence

between Glaser and Hüllessem over the years as pivotal episodes of urning activism.

From Glaser's own account, there are several recorded activities that we can now ascribe to the productive relationship between Glaser and Hüllessem. These activities included providing general advice and consultancy, guiding police reading of urning literature, cooperation with sexologists, introducing Hüllessem and his colleagues to the Berlin urning scene, and, finally, providing access to Hüllessem for certain persecuted urnings. In each case, these activities were an extension of the close friendship the two men developed, rather than formalized engagement between activist and policeman. Following the Seger's raid, Hüllessem was probably taking stock of his new departmental responsibilities. If, at that point in time, he had been mindful that policing needed to change, Glaser's advice and guidance would have been timely. The reconstruction of each of these activities from Glaser's own account draws on corroborating observations from Hirschfeld, the sexologist Albert Moll, and one of Hüllessem's successors, Hans von Tresckow.

Adolf Glaser and Police Liaison

The closeness of Glaser's friendship with Hüllessem offered opportunities to provide counsel. Hüllessem probably gained many personal insights and pieces of advice from his good friend. Referring to Glaser with the pseudonym "N.," Magnus Hirschfeld made precisely this point in 1922: "The experiences, observation and conclusions gained from personal relationships, such as with N., could have given most reliable insights that far outweighed the 'official material.'"[75] Albert Moll later claimed that Glaser had "rare objectivity."[76] Hirschfeld characterized Glaser's consultative style as an "intimate relationship of trust."[77] Glaser would have been able to offer Hüllessem clarifications and guidance from the urning perspective.

Glaser was also able to advise on contemporary sexual theories and urning works, and he may have been in a position to lend the police some of the relevant texts. Glaser, in a typical instance of erasing his own role, claimed that Hüllessem "researched the relevant writings of Ulrichs, Krafft-Ebing, Schrenck-Notzing."[78] Hirschfeld also noted that Hüllessem "delved into the literature of the time on the subject, including Ulrichs's partly confiscated writings *Über die mann-männliche Liebe*, Krafft-Ebing's *Psychopathia Sexualis*, Moll's *Die Conträre Sexualempfindung*, in whose publication he himself had taken a certain part, as well as my first works."[79] Ulrichs's pamphlets were extremely difficult to get hold of at this time, according to Hirschfeld, and they would not have been an obvious first choice for a non-initiate in the urning cause.[80] Krafft-Ebing's *Psychopathia Sexualis* did achieve a certain popularity, but it would also not have been an obvious starting point for the police. Unguided by Glaser, Hüllessem would probably have begun his "homosexual" reading closer to home. The police department employed forensic physicians, and the copious contemporary literature in forensic medicine was mostly hostile to the pederast. It is far more likely that somebody with the requisite knowledge, such as Glaser, introduced Hüllessem to Ulrichs and Krafft-Ebing. Hüllessem was not the only police inspector to read these books, and he may have directed colleagues and subordinates to do so as well. Hans von Tresckow, who began working for Hüllessem in 1892, wrote: "I eagerly studied the scientific works on this subject by Dr von Krafft-Ebing, Dr Albert Moll, Dr Magnus Hirschfeld and others. I got to know the latter two personally, and I had many conversations with them, where we exchanged our experiences in this field, which at that time was still little researched."[81]

Hüllessem's introduction to contemporary sexology also led him to meet and collaborate with sexologists. Hüllessem had corresponded with Krafft-Ebing, to whom he offered valuable insights about policing. Krafft-Ebing later alluded to some of this correspondence: "From communications from a senior police officer in Berlin, I see that the Berlin police know the male demimonde of the German capital very well and are doing everything they can to prevent blackmail among the pederasts, which in many cases does not even shy away from murder, with all means at their disposal."[82]

It was probably through this correspondence that Krafft-Ebing introduced Hüllessem and Moll, who was working on his 1891 book, *Die Conträre Sexualempfindung*. Moll recruited Hüllessem as a collaborator on the book to provide insights from the perspective of policing. This was a significant engagement, as Moll's preface made clear:

> The gentleman, who thereby helped me to obtain a very large amount of material, is Mr. Criminal-Police-Inspector von Meerscheidt-Hüllessem in Berlin. He himself was my companion for the most part and helped me in my researches in a tireless way and without saving time or effort. It is a pleasant duty for me to express my sincere thanks to the Berlin Royal Police Headquarters and to Mr von Meerscheidt-Hüllessem for this.[83]

Moll's work was a landmark publication on the psychology, sociology, history, forensic pathology, diagnosis, and therapeutic treatment of the urning.[84] The most salient feature of the work was a detailed description of urning Berlin, including male prostitution in the Tiergarten, places prominent in the urning scene, and the day-to-day life of the Berlin urning. Moll also recruited Glaser as a consultant, perhaps at the suggestion of Hüllessem, and his quotes peppered the book. As ever, Glaser shunned publicity and used the pseudonymous initials "N.N.," perhaps an allusion to Numa Numantius, the pseudonym Ulrichs had used for his first four pamphlets.[85] Moll's remarks in the preface of the book indicate that Glaser's input into this book was significant:[86]

At last, a gentleman whom I would like to call N.N., and who will be quoted more often with these letters. N.N., who is himself Urning, lives in a larger city in western Germany and is a personality well known through work in other fields: he has given me numerous reports not only about his own *Vita sexualis*, but also about contrary sexual feeling in general: since Mr N.N. had also lived in Berlin for several years in the past and is characterised by a rare objectivity, his reports were particularly valuable to me.[87]

The initials N.N. appeared throughout the book in bracketed remarks and footnotes where Glaser clarified or illustrated his points.

In his forensic chapter, Moll included an assessment of Paragraph 175, concluding that it was a difficult piece of legislation to achieve convictions under and that it tended to target the "wrong" urnings.[88] He noted that there was no law against male prostitution despite the flagrant hustling in the Tiergarten and a notorious bordello. He proposed that Paragraph 175 be scrubbed from the criminal code and that Paragraph 361, the prostitution paragraph, be expanded to cover both male and female prostitution.[89] In Moll's view, the urning was pathologically affected and not criminal. Other sexual scientists concurred with that view; by then, so did some urnings. In Krafft-Ebing's works there were autobiographic urning case studies, in addition to the dissenting case studies profiled in the previous chapter, where the individuals accepted pathological explanations but rejected therapeutic input.[90] Perhaps this was a strategic position taken by some urning advocates. Moll reported a discussion that Glaser had with another urning about the objectives of activism:

The following passage from the conversation between two urnings, Mr. N.N. and a certain X, was of interest. N.N., a thoroughly objective, calm gentleman, said to X: "If only we could at least get it accepted that the contrary sexual sensation is considered pathological, so that we are no longer considered criminals." X replied: "I can never agree to that; I would rather choose the present state. We are quite simply outvoted by the rest, and if they do consider the affection to be a disease, then it would land us all in the madhouse."[91]

Although several sources noted Glaser's level-headed objectivity, it is perhaps a surprise to see him take such a conservative line regarding what could be achieved through activism. He approached police liaison as a pragmatist rather than an idealist.

By 1885, the police had raided urning venues on several occasions, and relations with the owners and operators, as well as the patrons, were probably poor. The raids stopped after the one on Seger's establishment; in the wake of that event, it was going to take a concerted effort on the part of the police if relations were to improve. According to several observers, by the 1890s the police enjoyed genial relations with the urning venues and were frequent visitors to the balls. Glaser probably played a pivotal role in fostering good relations between the Berlin police and the city's urning venues, as well as with the leading urning entrepreneurs who organized them. Hirschfeld wrote that when Hüllessem was initially exploring the homosexual question, "he personally visited the sometimes relatively rare and hidden events of homosexuals, especially their more revealing than veiled costume festivals, and studied individuals who turned to him with their threatened and hardened fear in their heart, the psychological life of the 'fallen to the Urning demon.'"[92]

It seems unlikely that the well-known head of the (at that point) hostile Pederast Department could have ventured unnoticed onto Berlin's queer scene without creating a stir. Unless, that is, someone of unquestioned credentials as a trusted insider introduced him to the scene. Again, Glaser would have been able to facilitate such an introduction. He later introduced other police officials to the urning scene and instilled similarly high levels of trust. As time passed, they were more likely to attend urning venues in a friendly capacity.

Homosexual balls were held in other cities such as Paris and London, but it was only in Berlin that members of the public, accompanied by police, could visit these venues as "tourists" to observe cross-dressing and men dancing together.[93] By the 1890s, Berlin's senior police had established cooperative lines of engagement with the organizers of these events, in a manner that was unique for the period. In due course, the police even started providing guided tours of the leading urning venues and balls to the great and good as well as "journalists, authors and other urban ethnographers."[94] A retired Prussian officer, Paul von Hoverbeck, recalled that "as we entered the brightly lit hall, the entire crowd knew that we were curiosity seekers accompanied by police officials."[95] The patrons were used to the presence of the "tourists" and accepted it, probably because there was a more serious purpose to the police presence. Hirschfeld observed later that the police had become very tolerant of these venues because it allowed them "supervision of the homosexuals and those elements that enrich themselves at their expense by blackmail and theft."[96]

The final activity in which Glaser was involved during his police liaison was facilitating access for certain urnings to senior police officers if they needed help and advice. In his obituary of Hüllessem, Glaser wrote of his counselling style:

> It gradually came to be known, even in Urning circles, that the criminal inspector von Meerscheidt-Hüllessem was not a fundamental opponent of uranism, some hard-pressed people turned to him in their heartfelt fear of the future. Never in such cases did he abuse his official position in any direction; and, when the private citizen asked for advice or poured out their hearts, he gave benevolent advice, or, where the opportunity presented itself, he encouraged the threatened and oppressed to take legal action against the ghastly vermin of the blackmailers.[97]

At least at first, most of these urnings in distress were associates brought in by Glaser and were probably upper-class men uncomfortable with presenting themselves at the counter of the police station. It may also have been the case that Hüllessem was engaging with them in a personal capacity where the risk of self-incrimination was off the table.[98] For urnings visiting Hüllessem, but also for those less privileged individuals reporting cases of blackmail, the police had developed various tools to help. Hans von Tresckow recalled one of these in his memoirs: "The criminal police had been paying attention to the goings-on of homosexuals for some time and had collected a wealth of material. The volume of the crime book *Homosexual Blackmailers* had many photographs taken at police headquarters of those brought in for punishment. Detective Inspector von Meerscheidt-Hüllessem, the founder of the crime album and the identification service, had rendered outstanding services in this regard."[99]

Tresckow also described an instance of blackmail where the legation secretary, Count Fritz Hohenau, had been preyed on by a young man called Aßmann and a gang of other extorters: "In the end, he didn't know what to do anymore and turned to me. I presented him with the volume of homosexual blackmailers from the crime album and he recognised several of his tormentors in the photographs. It was easy to arrest these fellows."[100] Mugshot albums and card indexes were specific innovations of Hüllessem's before he knew Glaser, but the police only developed the blackmailers album after 1885.[101] Men who were being extorted by blackmailers, and whom Glaser introduced to Hüllessem, would have been able to find a resolution to their situations.

This section has attempted to reconstruct the relationship of trust between Glaser and Hüllessem that enabled an early instance of police liaison. Inevitably, in the absence of any direct account of Glaser's role, this has involved a degree of speculative analysis. The principal piece of solid evidence is Glaser's strong friendship with Hüllessem, which Glaser confirmed in his account and which Hirschfeld corroborated in his. Once we accept the friendship between the two men, the outline of Glaser's influence is not difficult to trace between the lines of his own account in the obituary. As any friend would, he advised and consulted with Hüllessem; he may have recommended books to him, and even lent them. Glaser also introduced his friend to other urnings, some of whom Hüllessem was able to help, and probably accompanied him on his first trips to urning venues. Finally, the work they both did with Moll was an extension of their cooperative engagement. The outcome was a police department more inclined towards tolerance.

How the Transformation Played Out

Between 1885 and 1900, the policing of Berlin's urnings was transformed. However, it is likely that some elements of this change were on the cards before Glaser befriended Hüllessem. As noted earlier, the single biggest driver of transformation was the 1885 reorganization that assigned blackmail to Inspectorate B, where the homosexual department was also located. Hirschfeld later credited this consolidation of blackmail and homosexuality investigations into a single department as having "proven extremely beneficial for the criminal assessment of homosexuality."[102] Meanwhile, new technologies such as photography, and the development of mugshot albums and card indexes in the late 1870s, greatly improved police effectiveness.[103]

The increased effectiveness in targeting blackmailers was a welcome development. In addition to that, the new organization of the Pederast Department and the use of crime albums meant the police were becoming more effective at investigating cases relating to Paragraph 175. Even though they were no longer relying on tip-offs from blackmailers, the number of investigations in Berlin rose continuously from an average of fewer than 10 in 1885 to 60 to 100 per year – 132 cases in 1899 alone.[104] That did not in itself lead to an increase in convictions, as many cases did not reach court; indeed, the tally of guilty verdicts stood at only ten to fifteen per year throughout this period.[105] This suggests that in the majority of cases, fines or other alternatives were used rather than court proceedings. Even if Hüllessem himself supported the repeal of Paragraph 175, his department was duty bound to uphold the law.

Glaser was not lobbying for change from outside a static institution; he was influencing outcomes while change was happening. This made nineteenth-century Berlin qualitatively different from more contemporary examples of police liaison. In Berlin at the time, the police perspective and practice changed most notably with regard to community relations. Glaser's quiet counsel and his literature recommendations helped Hüllessem gain knowledge and insight. Introductions to the urning scene afforded the opportunity to extend urning networks to, and further educate, the police. According to Glaser, once he had read, consulted, and networked sufficiently, Hüllessem started to ponder what his new understanding meant for policing: "But he came to his senses when he had the opportunity to observe in direct traps that many of the accused were clear-thinking people, often in high social positions or in generally respected professions, and that almost everywhere the miserable rabble-rousing of the lowest money-grubbers appeared as accusers. Once he came to wonder, the matter did not leave him alone."[106]

The aristocratic Hüllessem had been most influenced by urnings of his own patrician class. Glaser and his urning friends were from the upper professional classes. The class parity between the two men had likely made Glaser's influence more salient than the opinions of Hüllessem's rank-and-file police colleagues. The owners of large urning venues were wealthy and influential, and the sexologists were intellectually elevated correspondents and collaborators. Class was the medium that made all this cooperation possible, but in the world of policing that class exclusivity could also present problems. The changes Hüllessem envisaged would have an impact on urnings of all classes. To bring about these changes, he would have to overcome the well-founded suspicion of the police among less patrician Berlin urnings. Hirschfeld later wrote that many ordinary urnings were leery of engaging with the police and that there were rumours of a secret list: "Also contrary to what Urnings assume, the 'Pederast Lists' kept by the police officials – the Berlin list alone contains 20,000 to 30,000 names – are not meant to intimidate but to keep police informed. As v. Meerscheidt-Hüllessem said, in cases of crimes committed by or against homosexuals, they are used to let authorities know whether those concerned are suspected of having a same-sex orientation."[107]

The lists did exist, but that was in the context of albums and card indexes, and they were not used primarily to prosecute urnings. The police cross-referenced those lists with a parallel database of blackmailers – a technique that would play a part in the evolution of a more pragmatic and tolerant style of policing. In the new dispensation, the crimes of the legion of blackmailers were of far greater concern than the largely victimless "crimes" under Paragraph 175. Hüllessem's department could not change or disregard the law, even if he himself was in favour of reform; but it could change the practice of policing. Instead of cooperating with blackmailers, his department tracked them down and brought them to book, earning the trust of Berlin's urnings. From a policing point of view, tracking down and prosecuting the gangs of extortionists was a more productive contribution to public well-being. Looking back on this work, in 1922, Magnus Hirschfeld evaluated the transformative impact the change in the police approach to blackmail had wrought:

> Surely in our time in a year not as many homosexuals will be blackmailed as earlier in a week. Just a generation ago, almost every Urning had his blackmailer. He belonged to him as the parasite to the living being in whom and from whom he lives. Like a bodily threat, the accessory of a weak hour accompanied the Urning throughout his life. There were affluent homosexuals who in their annual budget from the outset had a sizable column called "extortionist," though mostly under some code name.[108]

Blackmail did not disappear completely and would be a feature of the homosexual scene well into the twentieth century. However, the police succeeded in markedly reducing its prevalence in Berlin.

The other change that Berlin's urnings would have experienced as substantial was the apparently unthreatening presence of police in urning venues. Prior to 1885, the only time police uniforms appeared in an urning venue would have been during a raid. As noted earlier, the raids stopped after the one on Seger's in 1885, when instead, senior police officers started attending urning venues in the company of Glaser. With time, as the police and the urnings became more used to each other, the police presence became normalized as a recognizable part of the Berlin scene.

As a product of the police department of the German capital, the Berlin reforms became templates for growing urban centres such as Hamburg, Cologne, and Leipzig.[109] These reforms would persist after Glaser and Hüllessem were gone. Looking back in 1914, Hirschfeld noted that his successors maintained the reforms that Hüllessem had introduced:

> Another legacy remains intact and undiminished ... the humane and scientific spirit he implanted in the Department for Homosexual Affairs, which, beginning with him has been joined with the department that handles blackmail. He instilled these views into his co-workers and successors, into Hans von Tresckow I, the present Chief of Detectives, who from 1900 to 1910, like his predecessor, saved hundreds of homosexual persons from despair and suicide. Detective Commissioner Dr Heinrich Kopp had already been standing by his side for a long time when on 1 January 1911, he took over his position and ever since then has run his difficult office with equal understanding.[110]

The changes Hüllessem had brought in, supported by Glaser's advice, would extend well beyond Berlin and well into the twentieth century.

Conclusion

Urnings in Berlin and beyond were still vulnerable to blackmail but at far lower levels than had been the case before. Unlike in the preceding decades, they could now inhabit the urban urning scenes largely without fear of blackmail. Now the police were pursuing the blackmailers on behalf of urnings instead of using blackmailer informants to target urnings. This was an important shift that delivered material benefit to urnings in the 1890s. Adolf Glaser's role in encouraging and fostering this shift in focus was an early, effective instance of police liaison. Crucially, the police were now allies with whom some urnings could collaborate. Glaser, in his well-timed association with Hüllessem, had succeeded in turning the police into allies in the struggle against blackmail. He had succeeded in "belling the cat."

Glaser was already elderly when he began working with senior police officers. He lived on to 1915, when he died at the age of eighty-six.[111] He should have been proud of his contribution to these lasting changes in policing. Instead, right up to his death in 1915, he made certain that no person who knew his urning nature ever published his name in connection with any of his actions. In their subsequent works, neither Moll nor Hirschfeld revealed Glaser's role.[112] It was only after he died that an obituary in the *Jahrbuch für sexuelle Zwischenstufen* could finally name him: "Especially through his scientific relations with two men – v. Meerscheidt-Hüllessem and A. Moll – he contributed to maintaining the tradition ... The beautiful obituary to v. Meerscheidt-Hüllessem in the *Jahrbuch für sexuelle Zwichenstufen*, Jahrg. IV, p. 948 ff., was penned by him; it was probably the last work of the old man, then already almost 80 years old."[113] The obituary finally identified Glaser's engagement with Hüllessem and Moll.[114]

Glaser's use of pseudonymous initials to conceal his identity has made it easier for historians to overlook his unique and far-reaching contribution. Glaser probably wasn't the only uncelebrated urning advocate of the period. Other contemporaries, such as Eduard Oberg, also preferred to remain in the background, and homosexual writers such as Otto de Joux (Otto Rudolf Podjukl) and Numa Praetorius (Eugen Wilhelm) continued to use pseudonyms. Today, Glaser's professional position remains obscure, and his reputation as a prominent writer has faded. Until Jens Dobler revealed Glaser's friendship with Hüllessem in 2008, queer historians had mostly ignored Glaser.[115] There were almost certainly other urnings of greater or lesser influence who were even better than Glaser at covering their tracks. Within the institutions of the German state, there were discreet individuals trying to make a difference for their fellow urnings. Hirschfeld, who probably knew several, wrote that Glaser was "one of the not exactly frequent but very meritorious Urnings."[116] We should understand Glaser's achievements in the context that he was probably one of several unnamed individuals who contributed to the transformation of Germany from positions of influence.

As a modern metropolis in the late nineteenth century, Berlin was not alone in having a thriving scene for same-sex-attracted men. What set it apart was the, at that time, uniquely Germanic urning identity. All the developments in grassroots homosocial organization, scientific study, and, in the present chapter, police liaison, stemmed from that first articulation of the urning identity in the 1860s. That sexual identity became a feature in Zurich, especially through the activism of Jakob Rudolf Forster, and in Vienna, in the work of psychiatrist Richard von Krafft-Ebing. There was also some evidence that it was beginning to spread to other continental cities. Yet the identity did not cross the channel to England until relatively late. The next chapter follows the migration of the urning identity to England and the English-speaking world.

Chapter Eight

The Comradely Uranian: John Addington Symonds and the English Translation of the Urning, 1889–1893

I will make inseparable cities with their arms about each other's necks,
By the love of comrades,
By the manly love of comrades.[1]

For a small number of men in England, there were opportunities for homosocial association in the 1880s among followers of the American poet Walt Whitman. Small associations of men who were fans of Whitman had flourished across the English-speaking world in the decades that followed the publication of his 1855 book *Leaves of Grass*.[2] These were men who espoused Whitman's notions of spiritual comradeship and "adhesiveness."[3] Whitman never wrote about sexuality *per se*, but the "Calamus" poems in *Leaves of Grass* were replete with homoerotic longing for the trust and love of urban working men. Whitman's verse ennobled homoeroticism with a kind of spirituality but eschewed any explicit articulation of a sexual ethic. Consequently, while many Whitmanites were same-sex-attracted and resonated with this literature, others were not and read the poems as evocative of socialist comradeship. Whitmanite homosociality allowed same-sex-attracted individuals to shift their ineffable and unnameable desires to a spiritual plane.[4] Under the cover of Whitman's poetic thesis, this inchoate spiritual yearning was the closest the English had come to a modern proto-queer consciousness in the 1880s.[5]

While there were small numbers of men discussing same-sex comradeship, England at that time had no general discourse on same-sex sexuality. The previous three chapters discussed, among other things, the development of urning society in Germany, Austria, and Switzerland up to the 1890s. There were also people calling themselves urnings/homosexuals in neighbouring countries, including the Netherlands,

Belgium, France, Hungary, Italy, and likely several others. However, the urning identity had not crossed the English Channel and populated Britain in the same manner. Karl Heinrich Ulrichs received several letters from London, but these were mainly from German-speaking visitors to the city and their friends.[6] England in the late nineteenth century was a more industrially advanced nation than Germany, bourgeois masculinity was more hegemonic, and the "two spheres" separation of the sexes was dominant. The Criminal Law Amendment Act of 1885, commonly known as the Labouchere Amendment, made "gross indecency" a crime with severe penalties for any same-sex sexual activity between men. By the 1890s, London had a very sizeable subculture of same-sex-attracted and cross-dressing men; but for men in much of the rest of Britain, even for Whitmanites, same-sex desire even when possible was practised mostly in secret as a nameless crime.[7]

From 1889, that would change. The agent of translation who popularized the discourse of a fixed sexual orientation in England was John Addington Symonds. Symonds, an English writer living with his family in Davos in the 1880s, drew his sense of sexual self from the poetry of Walt Whitman and his knowledge of Ancient Greek literature and history; yet he found it hard to express his inchoate sense of sexual self until he encountered the works of Ulrichs and European sexual science. Having neglected the issue for most of his adulthood, Symonds dedicated the last four years of his life to writing almost exclusively about sexuality. In the process, he changed some of the parameters of the identity, thus ensuring the Anglo-Saxon uranian identity that emerged in the 1890s was distinct from that of continental Europe. This chapter provides an account of how the German urning became an English uranian.

Two Early Influences

In March 1857, when Symonds was seventeen years old and in his final year at Harrow, he encountered Greek *paiderastia* for the first time. He later characterized the experience as "one of the most important nights of my life."[8] On that night, Symonds was reading Henry Cary's translations of Plato when he "stumbled on the *Phaedrus*":

> Here in the *Phaedrus* and the *Symposium* – in the Myth of the Soul and the speeches of Pausanias, Agathon and Diotima – I discovered the true *Liber Amoris* at last, the revelation I had been waiting for, the consecration of a long-cherished idealism. It was just as though the voice of my own soul spoke to me through Plato, as though in some antenatal experience I had lived the life of a philosophical Greek lover.[9]

The book absorbed Symonds so much that he stayed up all night reading it. Plato's account offered sanction for what he had up to that point believed to be illicit and unthinkable. The effect on him was profound but did not yet offer him any way to express the sexual and sensual components of his desires.[10]

Symonds encountered his second major influence a few years later, in 1865, while visiting a friend in Cambridge.[11] His friend recited a poem from Walt Whitman's 1855 *Leaves of Grass*:

> This fine poem, omitted from later editions of *Leaves of Grass*, formed part of "Calamus." The book became for me a sort of Bible. Inspired by "Calamus" I adopted another method of palliative treatment and tried to invigorate the emotion I could not shake off by absorbing Whitman's conception of comradeship. The process of assimilation was not without its bracing benefit. My desires grew manlier, more defined, more direct, more daring by contact with "Calamus." I imbibed a strong democratic enthusiasm, a sense of the dignity and beauty and glory of simple healthy men.[12]

Whitman's "Calamus" poems elevated "comradeship" between men to an intensity and spiritual ineffability that meant Symonds could "now declare with sincerity that my abnormal inclinations, modified by Whitman's idealism and penetrated with his democratic enthusiasm, have brought me into close and profitable sympathy with human beings even while I sinned against law and conventional morality."[13] Whitman advanced the idea of "adhesiveness" to describe the emotional attachment between men but was silent on the potential physical components of such relationships. This omission did not apparently concern Symonds at that moment, but it would do so in the years that followed. Through Whitman's manly comradeship, Symonds now had a means to express same-sex sensuality in an "affirmative context," although it left him unable to articulate the full nature of his sexual being.[14] It was not yet a full discourse of an integrated sexual identity; rather, it was a proto-identity where the sensual and sexual components were imprecise.

Symonds was nevertheless excited by the possibilities afforded by his acquired insights. The combination of the two influences, Greek *paiderastia* and Whitman's adhesive comradeship, led Symonds to write: "The immediate result of this study of Walt Whitman was the determination to write the history of paiderastia in Greece and to attempt a theoretical demonstration of the chivalrous enthusiasm which seemed to me implicit in comradeship."[15]

Symonds's first foray into writing about same-sex desire showcased his passion for Hellenism, which he imbued with a Whitmanesque sensibility. His essay *A Problem in Greek Ethics*[16] ran to one hundred pages, divided into twenty sections on Homer, *paiderastia* in Hellas, Phoenician Orientalism, *paiderastia* in Greek poetry, art, and philosophy, and Athenian, Attic, and Dorian *paiderastia*. In section X, Symonds described the Dorians, who "gave the earliest and most marked encouragement to Greek love."[17] The Dorians were one of the four ethnicities in ancient Greece, and in the isolationist, militaristic society of Sparta they practised communal living and encouraged same-sex romantic and sexual bonds in both men and women. Symonds enthused about Dorian masculine bonds between adult equals that were quite distinct from the Athenian age-disparate ritualized pairings. It is notable that the language he used to describe these bonds used the Whitmanesque terminology of comradeship:

Most illustrious Spartans are mentioned by their biographers in connection with their comrades.[18]

The Dorian warriors had special opportunity for elevating comradeship to the rank of an enthusiasm.[19]

For Symonds, the Dorians embodied the ideals of Whitman's masculine valour, in stark contrast to the effeminate examples emanating from what he called "half-savage nations" where "this assumption of feminine duties and costume, would have been abhorrent to the Doric custom."[20] According to Symonds, the "true Hellenic manifestation of the paiderastic passion" was separate from the "effeminacies, brutalities and gross sensualities which can be noticed alike in imperfectly civilized and in luxuriously corrupt communities."[21] Symonds was drawn to this valorous masculine comradeship but was repelled by effeminacy and licentiousness. This division between masculine manly love and effeminate debauchery would be characteristic of all Symonds's writing on the subject.

Having written the essay at some point in 1873, Symonds did not initially publish it. Two years later, in 1875, he tried to use the essay in a modified form as the final chapter in a second edition of *Studies of the Greek Poets*.[22] While it was at the printers, a shocked compositor wrote him an indignant letter rebuking him for his iniquity. Symonds had hoped his book might become a school textbook, but this hope was dashed when his inclusion of the chapter on *paiderastia* provoked a letter from an enraged schoolmaster and several negative reviews in the press.[23] In particular, an article by Richard St. John Tyrwhitt in *The Contemporary Review* argued that certain Greek passages had a corrupting influence on youth and should never be entertained in an educational setting.[24] England was not ready for the subject, even when it was framed in this conservative manner, and Symonds sat on the essay for a decade before he published it privately in an edition of only ten copies, which he circulated among friends.[25] The reception of this initial attempt to write on sexuality in 1873 had been so discouraging that he would not return to writing on the subject for another sixteen years.

The Memoir

In 1889, Symonds was living with his wife and daughters in Davos, Switzerland.[26] By this time, he had established a reputation in England as a popular writer on esoteric subjects. He had recently translated and published the autobiographies of two Italian men of flamboyant sexuality. Their frank openness about their sexual histories so took him that it made him think he should write something similar: "My occupation with Cellini and Gozzi has infected me with their *Lues Autobiographica*; and I have begun scribbling my own reminiscences ... You see I have 'never spoken out.' And it is a great temptation to speak out, when I have been living for two whole years in lonely intimacy with men who spoke out so magnificently as Cellini and Gozzi did."[27]

In March 1889, Symonds started writing a sexual autobiography, quite unlike anything contemporary in English.[28] This would be his second attempt to express his sexual being on paper, but this time the exercise would focus on his own self-conception. Urnings in Germany and Austria were at the time using sexual autobiography to influence sexual scientists, but Symonds arrived at his decision to write his own independently after translating the Italian biographies. This memoir occupied him for the next eighteen months. It was during this exercise that he encountered Ulrichs and the works of sexology. These works, particularly Ulrichs's ideas, would be his third major influence and would transform his understanding of his own sexual orientation and of sexuality in general.

Initially, he was under the misapprehension that he was a uniquely abnormal individual and also the first to write on the subject: "There does not exist anything like it in print; and I am certain that 999 men out of 1000 do not believe in the existence of a personality like mine."[29] An uneasy sense of his uniqueness was evident even before he started writing; so was his discomfort with describing sex. At this point, he expressed his sense of self with the inchoate masculinity of a follower of Whitman. The exercise of writing a sexual autobiography would eventually expose the absolute limits of explanatory discourses derived from Hellenic and Whitmanite sources and drive him to seek out more credible answers from continental sexual science.

Symonds was in Venice in March 1889 when he commenced writing his autobiography. The memoir was largely a chronological narrative extracted from diaries and supplemented with accounts written by his wife, Catherine, and his childhood nanny, Sophie Girard. There were also several "thematic" chapters. The second of these, "Containing Material Which None But Students of Psychology and Ethics Need Peruse," related his sexual development in childhood and adolescence. It opened with the admission that the memoirs contained therein were "intended to describe the evolution of a somewhat abnormally constituted individual."[30] In this chapter, he described his first inkling of sex as "peculiar and uneasy" and his reaction to the sexual awakening of other boys with words like "marked repugnance," "powerful disgust" and "horror."[31] At times he seemed to be pathologizing his early experiences, with the result that a certain depressive religiosity underpinned this part of his memoir. He was more comfortable describing his youthful idealized "love" for the character Adonis in Shakespeare's poem "Venus and Adonis."[32] This established a distinction between base carnal instinct, which he was ashamed of, and idealized platonic devotion, which he saw as a quasi-spiritual ideal. The prism of Whitman's ethic shone light upon the romantic, leaving the sexual in a morass of shame. On a personal level, Symonds did not seem to be at all at ease with his sexual being.

The fifth chapter, which dealt with the sexual exploits of his contemporaries at Harrow, was similarly suffused with disgust: "In my own mind I felt sure that these vices were pernicious to our society; and I regarded them as sins which ought to have been harshly dealt with."[33] In stark contrast, his first chaste romantic affection for Willie Dyer, described at the end of the same chapter, was portrayed more favourably. The balance of sexual negativity and romantic idealization continued in the chapters that followed. At the end of chapter 12, Symonds introduced Roden Noel, an aristocratic friend who had introduced Symonds to a male brothel in 1877. The "grossness" of Noel's passions revolted Symonds, but he nevertheless felt that Noel was "superior" to base voluptuousness because he was married and therefore attracted to women.[34] Symonds had internalized a hierarchy of sexual mores where married heterosexuality was superior to Whitmanesque idealization of platonic/romantic male friendship, which, in turn, was superior to any effeminate or licentious sexual activity with the same sex.

In the remaining chapters, Symonds continued to elevate the romantic while expressing his discomfort with the sexual, although the tone softened as he described his adult being. Chapters 13 to 18 covered his adult life from 1868 onwards and included thematic chapters on his literary and intellectual development (14), his spiritual development (15), and his early married life in Bristol (16). The remaining three chapters covered three love affairs. In chapter 13 he described his passionate friendship with Norman Moore, a former pupil of Clifton School whom Symonds encountered while teaching there, between 1868 and 1872. Chapter 17 covered his move to Davos and his intimate friendship with the son of a local hotelier named Christian Buol from 1878. Finally, in chapter 18, Symonds described a romantic sexual relationship with a Venetian gondolier named Angelo Fusato from 1881. Each of these relationships was described with care and attention to detail, with the focus persistently on the romantic even where, in the case of Fusato, there was a sexual dimension.[35] Symonds's first contact with the Buol family was apparently "like a scene out of one of Whitman's poems."[36] On a trip to Italy, he shared a bed with Buol but "neither in act, nor deed, far less in words, did the least shadow of lust cloud the serenity of that masculine communion."[37] His Whitman-inspired personal philosophy allowed him to venerate and romantically pursue men of diverse classes, yet he was silent on the subject of sexual consummation. Consequently, he referred to the purely sexual engagement with a brawny soldier at a male brothel on Regent's Park in the company of Noel briefly and imprecisely before scoring it out with pencil.[38] Symonds still regarded sex for its own sake as immoral and base, but he conceded that the same-sex attraction within romantic love was acceptable. This was consistent with Whitman's concepts of "comradeship" and "adhesion," but it did not resolve what the fully sexual expression of that romantic love could mean in the final Fusato chapter. In that chapter, Symonds wrote of his "honour, rooted in dishonour," and his friendship with Fusato "originating in my illicit appetite and his compliance."[39] It is surprising that these two insinuations were all that he could muster to describe the sexual component of his relationship with Fusato. He could not resolve or adequately describe a positive integration of his sexual being.

Writing the memoir may have been a cathartic experience in and of itself; perhaps doing so gained him insights and understanding, thus stimulating his interest in further inquiry. Now that he had it on paper, he realized that the Whitman thesis he had applied to his life could not adequately account for any sexual expression of romantic love. This motivated him to look for literature that could resolve the sexual question. An undated marginal handwritten note on the reverse of one of the memoir manuscripts for his final chapter revealed the three texts that Symonds consulted at this time: "When I wrote the above, I had not yet read the autobiographies of Urnings printed in Casper-Liman's *Handbuch der Gerichtlichen Medicin*, in Ulrichs's 'Numa Numantius' various tracts, notably in *Memnon*, and in Prof. Krafft-Ebing's *Psychopathia Sexualis*. I have recently done so and am now aware that my history is only one out of a thousand."[40] Those three texts, in particular Ulrichs's *Memnon*, were Symonds's third major influence. Each contained the self-penned accounts of men who had embraced their sexual being in a more integrated manner than Symonds had in his Whitman-inspired attempts.

Krafft-Ebing's *Psychopathia Sexualis* was already in its third edition (1888).[41] If this was where Symonds started, he would have seen ten autobiographical case studies, in seven of which the men called themselves urnings, recounted their sexual histories with clarity, and rejected any notion that their disposition was pathological.[42] Both Johann Ludwig Casper's 1863 publication and Ulrichs's works were cited in the preamble to Krafft-Ebing's urning case studies.[43] Had he sought out the Casper reference, he would have found the long sexual autobiography we first encountered in chapter 2 titled "Self-Confession of a Pederast," which was sexually frank.[44] Finally, Ulrichs's works opened up for him the full conceptualization of a minoritized integrated sexual identity. In these works, Symonds at last found the elements of a sex-positive integrated account of male–male love. This was his first contact with the third-sex "urning" conception of sexuality, and it appears to have been a life-changing experience.

Symonds's transformative encounter with Ulrichs's urning identity spurred him to write a letter to Krafft-Ebing midway through 1889 (the same polemic letter already described in chapter 6).[45] Krafft-Ebing published the full text of that letter in the fourth edition of *Psychopathia Sexualis* (1889) as well as in the following edition (1890), writing that the author was "a man of high position in London."[46] Krafft-Ebing presented the letter in a discussion about the rights and wrongs of the antisodomy laws in Germany and Austria. The letter itself argued against Krafft-Ebing's pathologizing of the urning and his tendency to use arguments around morbidity to advance reformist views.[47] This was a fully assertive polemic assault on prevailing prejudice, with Symonds combining what he had learned from Ulrichs with the autobiographies and using Ulrichs's terminology to describe himself and his fellow "urnings." Symonds outlined all the difficulties that arose from a world where the law proscribed urning sexual expression, where blackmailers preyed on him, and where society denigrated the urning, leaving him vulnerable to suicide and pathologized by psychiatry. He wrote his letter from the perspective of someone who had embraced the minoritized identity for himself. By partly accepting Ulrichs's urning identity, Symonds had found the way to integrate the Whitman ethic with his sexual being.

When he returned to the manuscript of his memoir, he set about writing additional passages to detail his new accommodation with his sexual being. Several of these were indicative of his changed outlook. He attached a new "ethical formula" to chapter 15, the religious chapter, in which he presented the Greek concepts of equilibrium and moderation in all human activity, including sexual, as superior to the Christian ethic.[48] In the final chapter, where he had had so much trouble describing the sexual relationship with Fusato, he added a new passage that addressed same-sex sexual activity head on: "As the final expression of mutual love and liking, I see no harm to society or character in sensual enjoyment between man and man."[49] Symonds's engagement with the works of continental sexology had completed his understanding and acceptance of his sexual being. In a passage he appended to the second chapter, he articulated his thinking on the sexual scientific and polemic works he had just encountered:

> When I wrote these recollections of my earliest sexual impressions, I was not aware how important they were for the proper understanding of *vita sexualis*, and how impossible it would have been to omit them from a truthful autobiography. I had not then studied the works of Moreau, Tarnowski, Krafft-Ebing, who attempt to refer all cases of sexual inversion to neurotic disorder inherited or acquired. I had not read the extraordinary writings of Ulrichs, who maintains that the persons he calls Urnings form a sex apart – having literally a feminine soul included within a male body.[50]

Symonds then examined his family history of mental frailty as if it were a Krafft-Ebing case study before trying on Ulrichs's urning identity:

> With regard to Ulrichs, in his peculiar phraseology, I should certainly be tabulated as a Mittel Urning, holding a mean between the Mannling and the Weibling; that is to say, one whose emotions are directed to the male sex during the period of adolescence and early manhood; who is not marked either by an effeminate passion for robust adults or by a predilection for young boys; in other words, one whose comradely instincts are tinged with a distinct sexual partiality. But in this sufficiently accurate description of my attitude, I do not recognize anything which justifies

the theory of a female soul. Morally and intellectually, in character and taste and habits, I am more masculine than many men I know who adore women. I have no feminine feelings for the males who rouse my desires.[51]

Symonds described Ulrichs's writings as "extraordinary" but was not enamoured with his anima thesis. His lingering commitment to Whitman and idolization of Dorian comradeship meant that he could see nothing positive in the idea of effeminacy in the male. Reinforced by his sense of bourgeois masculinity, it did not square with his experience or his world view.

Symonds never published his memoirs himself. In a letter to Horatio Brown, his executor, on 29 December 1891, Symonds told him: "I want to save it from destruction after my death, and yet to reserve its publication for a period when it will not be injurious to my family ... I have sketched my wish out that this autobiography should not be destroyed."[52] He was, however, not averse to the idea of certain family members reading it after his death, writing to his daughter Margaret in 1892: "Think well of me, when all is over. I have been a very unhappy man, as you will find out if you read the history of my life."[53]

Symonds closed this initial assessment of the literature by stating that the "abnormality in question" could not be adequately explained by Ulrichs's theory or by the pathological psychologists but that "its solution has to be sought far deeper in the mystery of sex, and in the variety of type exhibited by nature. For this reason, a detailed study of one subject, such as I mean to attempt, may be valuable."[54]

The Synthesis

When Symonds had finished his memoir, he decided to write something he could share with others in a limited way. First, he had to find a way to accommodate the more integrated model of sexuality he had encountered in Ulrichs and the writings of German sexual science with his Hellenistic insights and Walt Whitman's conceptions of manly comradeship. He had already discussed this briefly in correspondence with a young, medically qualified writer, Henry Havelock Ellis. Around the time Symonds was pondering the works of sexual science, Ellis unexpectedly sent Symonds a copy of his book *The New Spirit*.[55] Briefly in a footnote, Ellis expressed some doubts about Whitman's understanding of science: "I think this defective scientific perception is perhaps as responsible as any failure of moral insight for the vigorous way an element of 'manly love' flourishes in 'Calamus' and elsewhere."[56] On 6 May 1890, Symonds wrote back to thank Ellis. In this letter, Symonds said he wished Ellis had written more about "Calamus" and about whether Whitman would "condone or ignore the physical aspects of the passion."[57] Symonds had by then written to Whitman several times, trying unsuccessfully to elicit an answer to this question. He decided to put the matter more directly and wrote to Whitman on 3 August 1890. Symonds referred to Ellis's doubts about Whitman's approach to "manly love," then went on to write: "In your conception of Comradeship, do you contemplate the possible intrusion of those semi-sexual emotions and actions which no doubt do occur between men? I do not ask, whether you approve of them, or regard them as a necessary part of the relation? But I should much like to know whether you are prepared to leave them to the inclinations and the conscience of the individuals concerned."[58]

Symonds was insistent that he needed an answer from Whitman, as "ignorance on the subject prevents me from forming a complete view of your life-philosophy."[59] Whitman's response came quickly but was not what Symonds had hoped. On 19 August 1890, Whitman wrote back:

> About the questions on "Calamus," &c., they quite daze me. *Leaves of Grass* is only to be rightly construed by & within its own atmosphere and essential character – all its pages and pieces so coming strictly under. That the Calamus part has ever allowed the possibility of such construction as mentioned is terrible. I am fain to hope the pages themselves are not to be even mentioned for such gratuitous and quite at the time undreamed and unwished possibility of morbid inferences, which are disavowed by me and seem damnable.[60]

While it is possible that Whitman was wary of mail censors or did not trust the questioner enough to be open on the subject, the repudiation must have stung Symonds. He wrote to another Whitman fan, Ernest Rhys, that although he was glad to get such a clear statement, he was "surprised at the vehemence of the language."[61] After twenty years of puzzling about "Calamus," Symonds finally had his answer.

Over a twelve-day period, he wrote an extended essay outlining his own interpretation of "Calamus." In the introduction to this work, Symonds wrote of Whitman that "the ways he chose for pushing his gospel and advertising his philosophy put a severe strain on patience."[62] In a central section on "adhesiveness," Symonds noted first that Whitman's descriptions of this attachment had a "passionate glow, a warmth of devotion, beyond anything to which the world is used in the celebration of friendship," within which "the inheritors of sexual anomalies, will recognise their own emotion."[63] He acknowledged

Whitman's denial of the sexual component but remarked that he had failed to perceive the "inevitable points of contact between sexual anomaly and his doctrine of comradeship."[64] Whitman's omission of a full clarification left the articulation of adhesiveness deficient. Symonds speculated that he might find a solution in a synthesis of adhesiveness and male–male sexual desire when elevated with chivalric and Hellenic ideas of manhood.[65] This was the germ of an idea from which he would draw in his next work. For the moment Symonds put the manuscript for his Whitman book aside. Whitman was ailing, and the time would not have been right to publish what Whitman's loyal supporters would perceive as an attack.[66] Symonds's uncritical adherence to the Whitman thesis was at an end, but neither was he convinced by Ulrichs's theory of the female soul in the male body.

Symonds intended to synthesize his own theory by drawing from all three of his major influences. He started work on a modern polemic on the subject: *A Problem in Modern Ethics*.[67] The year of writing was a transitional one for the language used in the psychiatric literature to describe same-sex sexuality. Symonds was grappling with the preferred psychiatric term and introduced it to his readers as "inverted sexual instinct" or "sexual inversion," which he commended as suitably "neutral nomenclature."[68] These were Symonds's translations of the psychiatric terms *conträre Sexualempfindung* and *Verkehrung der Sexualempfindung*. Elsewhere in the book, Symonds used Ulrichs's "urning" neologism. However, Krafft-Ebing had just revised his own terminology in a new 1889 edition of *Psychopathia Sexualis*, where he used Karl Maria Kertbeny's "homosexual" for the first time as a psychiatric term. When Symonds came to quote from Krafft-Ebing, he footnoted the word "homosexual" with the following clarification: "The adjective *homosexual*, though ill-compounded of a Greek and a Latin word, is useful, and has been adopted by medical writers on this topic. Unisexual would perhaps be better."[69] After years of having no non-pejorative terms to use in English, Symonds was presenting a veritable smorgasbord of new words.

A Problem in Modern Ethics was a polemic work, a booklet of ninety pages in a style "arid and severe" making the case for law reform in England, with its sights set on the recent Labouchere amendment of 1885.[70] This new work included a survey of all the existing European literature on sexuality that Symonds could find. Symonds's facility with languages, his location in Switzerland (out of reach of British censors), and his three major influences of Hellenism, Whitman, and sexual science were all deployed in the writing of this book. Sections V to X contained the literature reviews; sections VI and VII focused on the medico-forensic and medico-psychological literature. These sections comprised the first scholarly review in English of the continental fields of forensic medicine and psychiatry regarding sexual inversion. The section on medico-forensic literature included reviews of Auguste Ambroise Tardieu and Johann Ludwig Casper and his nephew Carl Liman, while the section on medico-psychological literature surveyed Paul Moreau, Benjamin Tarnowsky, Richard von Krafft-Ebing, and Cesare Lombroso. For a non-scientist, Symonds showed an impressive grasp of this material; he did not just summarize the findings but engaged with each and assessed its validity. It was not a complete review of all the extant work – notably, he referred to Carl Otto Westphal's work in a quoted section by Carl Liman, but otherwise not at all. It was, however, a good starting point for the first sexological review in English of the continental literature on sexual science.[71]

Although Symonds rejected any notion of a female soul in a male body, he nevertheless rated Ulrichs's contribution highly. Within the review of the scientific literature, he repeatedly compared the findings with Ulrichs's theories as if they were the gold standard. This was striking; it seems that Symonds saw Ulrichs's contribution as at least on a par with those of the leading psychiatrists of the day. He may even have seen it as superior: "Presently we shall be introduced to a theory (that of Ulrichs) which is based upon a somewhat grotesque and metaphysical conception of nature, and which dispenses with the hypothesis of hereditary disease. I am not sure whether this theory, unsound as it may seem to medical specialists, does not square better with ascertained facts than that of inherited disorder in the nervous centres."[72]

Following this section, Symonds added a "Note to the Foregoing Section," where he reproduced in its entirety the polemic letter he had sent to Krafft-Ebing in 1889, writing that he translated it "from the original document published by Krafft-Ebing."[73] Symonds did not admit that he had been the author of the letter, but in the discussion that followed, he praised the letter as "powerfully and temperately written" and added that it "confirms what I have attempted to establish while criticising the medical hypothesis."[74] It was probably this postscript to the medical literature section, rather than the section itself, that prompted Havelock Ellis to write after reading it: "When reading the Problem, I obtained the impression that you are inclined to pooh-pooh the medical view altogether."[75]

Section IX, "Literature – Polemical" was devoted entirely to a discussion of Ulrichs's works. The section opens with fulsome praise: "It can hardly be said that inverted sexuality received serious and sympathetic treatment until a German jurist, named Karl Heinrich Ulrichs, began his long warfare against what he considered to be prejudice and igno-rance upon a topic of the greatest moment to himself."[76] Symonds then presented a summary of Ulrichs's outline of identity, and the physio-logical explanation and innate nature of the urning. He then summa-rized Ulrichs's legal arguments. Using translated excerpts from the case studies he found in the works of Krafft-Ebing and Liman, Ulrichs's own life account, and short statements from five of his same-sex-attracted friends, Symonds corroborated Ulrichs's claim for innateness.

Symonds's account of Ulrichs's theories was not a didactic trans-mission. He may have appeared to be diligently and comprehensively summarizing Ulrichs's arguments, but there was one facet that he selectively omitted. Thus, he presented the gendered subgroups of urnings from Ulrichs's later theories in a curious way: "Among Urn-ings, those who prefer effeminate males are christened by the name of Mannling; those who prefer powerful and masculine adults receive the name of Weibling; the Urning who cares for adolescents is styled a Zwischen-Urning."[77]

Symonds nowhere mentioned the gendered behaviour or self-iden-tification of urnings. He defined the subgroups solely in terms of their sexual preferences. By presenting them in this way, he erased the var-iation in gendered expression of the urning himself. Symonds did not address this omission and was clearly not sympathetic to Ulrichs's gendered conception of the urning. It wasn't just in the assessment of Ulrichs's works that Symonds's reworking was apparent. When dis-cussing Krafft-Ebing's case studies, he stated: "A large majority felt like men in their relations to men."[78] Symonds then stated that less than 10 per cent of the case studies exhibited any hint of effeminacy. This was a direct instance of misrepresentation: Symonds deliberately minimized the number of effeminate case studies.[79] At this stage, the subtle reshap-ing was not a point he reinforced; still, this selective distortion gave the impression that he was intent on minimizing and excluding the effemi-nate urning so that the weibling was implicitly an extreme that was not representative of urnings in general. Symonds was building up to his theoretical synthesis, in which he would interweave Hellenism, Whit-man, and sexual science. There would be little room for the effeminate urning in that reworking.

Reading Symonds's writings now, it is striking that he repeatedly denigrates effeminacy but also the feminine in a manner that appears quasi-misogynistic.[80] Arguably he was drawing on a much older Eng-lish repudiation of effeminacy that had become pointedly directed to-wards same-sex desire in the closing decades of the nineteenth century.[81] Symonds was a late Victorian gentleman steeped in the hegemonic masculinity of bourgeois England. Nevertheless, he was at pains to eschew any sense that he was a bourgeois conformist, instead casting himself as a bohemian rebel.[82] He had arguably reframed English bourgeois masculinity with Whitman's poetic ideology. He may have been less class-conscious and more democratically minded than his fellow Englishmen, but his attitude towards the feminine urning betrayed a deeper conservatism about sex and gender. For Symonds, manly comradeship, adhesion, and even manly love were resolutely masculine endeavours. His misogyny may have been less marked than that of other English upper-class men of his generation; even so, it infused his interpretation of Whitman to the point that Symonds believed that manly comradeship ratified the total separation of the two spheres.[83] Symonds's and other English interpretations of Whitman were distinct from his reception in America due to both rigid class divisions and a sharper distinction between male and female, masculine and feminine.[84] In Symonds's interpretation, the "natural" man, in touch with himself and virilized through contact with other men, was free of the unnatural artifice of effeminacy and free of womankind.

Symonds wrote at the start of the next section that "to speak of Walt Whitman at all in connection with Ulrichs and sexual inversion seems paradoxical."[85] According to Symonds, Whitman assumed that the love of man for man coexisted with the love for woman in the same individual and that "neuropathical urnings are not hinted at in any passage of his works."[86] The universal bisexuality of this conception of Whitman's sexual ethic was not just incompatible with Ulrichs's minoritizing theory, it was its diametric opposite. Symonds then presented an interpretation of "Calamus" before quoting from Whitman's letter rejecting the sexual interpretation. He went on: "No one who knows anything about Walt Whitman will for a moment doubt his candour and sincerity. Therefore, the man who wrote 'Calamus,' and preached the gospel of comradeship, entertains feelings at least as hostile to sexual inversion as any law-abiding humdrum Anglo-Saxon could desire. It is obvious that he has not even taken the phenomena of abnormal instinct into account."[87]

Symonds quoted all the instances where he interpreted Whitman's verse as implying sexual inversion. By presenting these alongside comparable passages from Hellenistic sources, Symonds undermined Whitman's disavowal.[88] Symonds accepted that Whitman intended to see no connection between the adhesiveness of comradeship and the amativeness of sexual love. He speculated that this was because Whitman stressed "fine restraint and continence, the cleanliness and chastity, which are inseparable from the perfectly virile and physically complete nature of healthy manhood."[89] This is where Symonds's Hellenistic perspective was so important: "Still, we may predicate the same ground-qualities in the early Dorians, those martial founders of the institution of Greek Love; and it is notorious to students of Greek civilisation that the lofty sentiment of their chivalry was intertwined with singular anomalies in its historical development."[90]

Symonds believed that Whitman's democratic instincts coupled with Dorian masculine chivalry "may be destined to absorb, control, and elevate those darker, more mysterious, apparently abnormal appetites, which we have seen to be widely diffused and ineradicable in the ground-work of human nature."[91] He was synthesizing all three of his influences into a single theory that combined Dorian masculine chivalry with elements of Whitman's and Ulrichs's ideologies.

This was a first attempt to articulate what James Wilper later called "Uranian comrade love."[92] In his summation, Symonds stressed that Whitman regarded "what he calls 'manly love' as destined to be a leading virtue of democratic nations, and the source of a new chivalry."[93] While the new chivalry was a visionary matter for a future society, Symonds's synthesis envisioned a future heroic manly uranian elite. This was his substantive contribution to the translation and transformation of the urning in an English context.

Symonds finished the first draft of *A Problem in Modern Ethics* on 6 December 1890, when he wrote to his daughter Margaret: "If I were to publish it now, it would create a great sensation. Society would ring with it. But the time is not ripe for the launching of *A Problem in Modern Ethics* on the world. The MS lies on my table for retouches; & then it will go to slumber in a box of precious writings, my best work, my least presentable, until its Day of Doom."[94] He was not ready to expose himself to the damage such a publication could do to his reputation. He did, however, print the manuscript in January 1891 in a short run of fifty copies in plain covers, which he distributed among his friends.

Symonds's reshaping of the urning theory was not indicative of any antipathy to the rest of Ulrichs's theory or the man himself. Even after articulating his synthesis in *Problem in Modern Ethics*, he was fulsome in his praise for Ulrichs's work: "Ulrichs is the only European who has maintained this view in a long series of polemical and imperfectly scientific works. Yet facts brought daily beneath the notice of open-eyed observers prove that Ulrichs is justified in his main contention. Society lies under the spell of ancient terrorism and coagulated errors. Science is either wilfully hypocritical or radically misinformed."[95] Ulrichs, more than any other writer in sexual science, had given Symonds the ability to accept and articulate his sexual self. It was now possible for him to step forward as a self-confident, integrated sexual being.

As soon as *A Problem in Modern Ethics* was complete, Symonds traced Ulrichs to Aquila, establishing contact with him in the first week of January 1891.[96] Symonds was probably one of the last same-sex-attracted people to communicate with Ulrichs. One draft of a possible letter survives from their correspondence. This was the reply to Symonds's initial inquiry, and it showed that Ulrichs had probably been neglected by his urning followers for several years by that time: "Why did you not write to me 10 or 15 years earlier? If I had received two or three such letters at that time, they would probably have had a decisive influence on my work and my activity."[97] Symonds and Ulrichs probably exchanged correspondence for at least one year. On 27 October 1891, while travelling in Italy, Symonds took a detour to visit the old man in Aquila, accompanied by Angelo Fusato. They spent an afternoon and evening with Ulrichs and left the next day. The correspondence continued for some months after the visit, with the last reference to contact with Ulrichs in a letter to Horatio Brown on 23 February 1892.[98]

Sexual Inversion

In parallel to the prolonged letter engagement with Ulrichs, Symonds was making plans for his next book about inverted sexuality. He wrote to Henry Dakyns in May 1891 about the response to *A Problem in Modern Ethics*: "I sorely need to revise, enlarge, & make a new edition of my essay; & I am almost minded to print it in a PUBLISHED vol: together with my older essay on Greek Morals & some supplementary papers."[99] *A Problem in Modern Ethics* may not have been available in bookshops, but it changed hands many times among a small group of like-minded men in London.

As Ulrichs had found in the 1860s, this initial push generated letters of self-disclosure from several people. On 10 May 1891, he commented on the same to Dakyns: "I have received a great abundance of interesting & valuable communications in consequence of sending out a few copies of that 'Problem in Modern Ethics.' People have handed it about. I am quite surprised to see how frankly ardently & sympathetically a large number of highly respectable persons feel toward a subject which in society they would only mention as unmentionable."[100]

Symonds secured the agreement of a young doctor, Henry Havelock Ellis, to collaborate on England's first sexological work: *Sexual Inversion*.[101] Ellis had corresponded previously with Symonds about Walt Whitman (referred to earlier in this chapter). For the sexological collaboration, Ellis wrote an introduction and the four medico-psychological main chapters that would draw on the literature review that Symonds had executed in *A Problem in Modern Ethics*. Symonds gathered twenty-seven case studies of men with the help of Edward Carpenter, another Whitmanite invited by Ellis. Ellis's wife, Edith Lees, supplied four case studies of women. Symonds rewrote his *Problem in Greek Ethics*, replacing the *paiderastia* with the modern terms "homosexual passion" and "sexual inversion." This appeared as the third chapter in the first edition of *Sexual Inversion*. He wrote extended essays on soldier love and the Roman *concubinus* and edited and augmented the discussion of Ulrichs from *A Problem in Modern Ethics*.[102] These three formed appendices to the book alongside an essay by Josiah Flynt on "Homosexuality among Tramps."[103] Symonds set about gathering case studies in late 1892 and early 1893, using a questionnaire: "You will observe my method in eliciting these confessions. I framed a set of questions upon the points which seemed to me of most importance after a study of Ulrichs and Krafft-Ebing."[104]

Symonds never completed his contribution to *Sexual Inversion*. In the second week of March 1893, he set out with his daughter Margaret on an extended Italian holiday. In Rome, influenza struck him down and his tubercular lungs were too weak to cope with it. He died on 19 April 1893 on the fifth floor of the Hotel D'Italia in the company of Margaret and his lovers Angelo Fusato and Christian Buol.[105]

Symonds's death had been quite unexpected and meant that Ellis was no longer dealing with Symonds as a collaborator but instead with Symonds's literary executor, Horatio Brown, acting with and on behalf of Symonds's surviving family. They had been largely unaware of what Symonds had been writing with Ellis, and to complicate matters further, before he could finish the manuscript, in 1895 the sensational Oscar Wilde trial made publication in England impossible. Ellis therefore first published *Sexual Inversion* in Germany as *Das Konträre Geschlechtsgefühl*, translated by Hans Kurella in 1896.[106] The first English edition of *Sexual Inversion* did not appear until 1897, although Horatio Brown acted to prevent its dissemination.[107] There was a second edition in 1897 and then an American edition in 1901. Percy Babington showed that with each successive edition, there was a commensurate reduction in Symonds's contribution, and in the last two, his name did not appear at all as co-author.[108] Symonds's biographer, Phyllis Grosskurth, saw ill intent on the part of Ellis in this. However, more recent commentators have pointed out that there was substantial pressure from the family and from Horatio Brown to expunge Symonds from the book.[109]

Sexual Inversion ensured that some of Symonds's synthetic ideas and Ulrichs's arguments reached a wider audience in English. However, the chapters that had the greatest impact were mostly Ellis's work. Ellis, in the chapter that followed the case studies, "Nature of Sexual Inversion," took a moderate line, perhaps mindful of his need to present himself as a reputable scientist and not advance the envelope much beyond the work of Moll.[110] He referred to gender only very briefly, and what he wrote was broadly in agreement with his continental colleagues: "Although the invert himself may stoutly affirm his masculinity, and although this femininity may not be very obvious, its wide prevalence may be asserted with considerable assurance, and by no means only among the small minority of inverts who take an exclusively passive *rôle*, though in these it is usually most marked."[111]

Ellis took a similar view of female sexual inverts: "The chief characteristic of the sexually inverted woman is a certain degree of masculinity."[112] However, in footnoting the section about male effeminacy, Ellis quoted from one of Symonds's letters disagreeing strongly with this position: "'The majority [of inverts],' wrote Symonds, 'differ in no detail of their outward appearance, their physique, or their dress, from normal men. They are athletic, masculine in habit, frank in manner, passing through society year after year without arousing a suspicion of their inner temperament: were it not so society would long ago have had its eyes opened to the amount of perverted sexuality it harbours.'"[113]

By footnoting the opposing viewpoint, Ellis was possibly signalling his own doubts. In the footnote, Ellis qualified Symonds's remark by saying that Symonds was refuting a "vulgar error" that conflated the typical invert with cross-dressers.[114] In the next chapter, Ellis presented his ideas on sexual inversion. Ellis described Ulrichs's theory of a female soul in a male body. This was the theory implicit in the concept of "sexual inversion" from Westphal through to Krafft-Ebing, but Ellis rejected that concept entirely.[115] In the process of rejecting the Ulrichsian discourse, Ellis downplayed the effeminacy of inverts. This was, in part, because the cohort of case studies in *Sexual Inversion* included so few effeminate men. In the concluding chapter, Ellis outlined a therapeutic approach with an overt Whitmanesque purpose: "The 'manly love' celebrated by Walt Whitman in *Leaves of Grass*, although it may be of more doubtful value for general use, furnishes a wholesome and robust ideal to the invert who is insensitive to normal ideals."[116]

This passage goes on to suggest that homosexual men or women could use methods of self-treatment to achieve well-being; it concludes that "a man should be enabled to make the best of his own strong natural instincts, with all their disadvantages, than that he should be unsexed and perverted, crushed into a position which he has no natural aptitude to occupy."[117] Ellis may not have fully reproduced Symonds's chivalric elite of "uranian comrades," but his account was still Whitmanite. Symonds had reluctantly accepted Ellis's cautious line over the book, so it is hard to know what he would have made of Ellis's chapters. However, Edward Carpenter wrote to Ellis that he thought it was "one of the best things you have done – clear and balanced – yet leading to definite conclusions."[118]

Symonds's death made a big impression on Edward Carpenter, who seemed to have made a commitment to Symonds that he would carry on his literary advocacy.[119] Carpenter was a socialist political writer based in Leeds, and, like Ellis and Symonds, he was a Whitmanite. When he wrote on sexuality, he didn't take it to the synthetic idealist extreme that Symonds did; his writing drew on both Whitman and Ulrichs in a more naturalistic manner. Arguably, it was Carpenter, rather than Symonds or Ellis, whose "uranian comrade" writing generated the strongest following among ordinary homosexual men. In 1893, he wrote a short pamphlet, *Homogenic Love and Its Place in a Free Society*, a beautifully written and carefully argued document surveying historical, anthropological, and scientific literature to advocate what he called "homogenic" love as a valuable social force. Like those of Symonds and Ellis, this discussion hardly touched on gendered expression. A single sentence was all that he devoted to the subject: "It has become pretty well established that the individuals affected with inversion in marked degree do not after all differ from the rest of mankind, or womankind, in any other physical or mental particular which can be distinctly indicated." To this he added a footnote: "Though there is no doubt a general tendency towards femininity of type in the male Urning, and towards masculinity in the female."[120]

Carpenter tried but failed to publish his pamphlet in 1894. He had it privately printed and circulated it through the networks of Whitmanite groups. Harry Cocks demonstrated, using the letters and diaries of a group of Lancashire Whitmanites, that the ideas in Carpenter's pamphlets were engaged with and applied to the lives and desires of these men.[121] Carpenter did manage to publish related tracts in the early twentieth century, ensuring that the social, political, and scientific discourses in England took a different course those relating to the continental urning.

Conclusion

The social impacts of Symonds's foray into sexual writing were various. First, circulation of the fifty copies of *A Problem in Modern Ethics* possibly led to a brief flowering of "uranian" culture among a certain, mostly upper-class, circle of men. This anglicized version of the "urning" appeared in print in books by E.M. Forster and Marc Andre Raffalovich. It was even the name applied to a group of upper-class homophile poets.[122] In March 1892, *Love in Earnest*, a book of homophile poetry by John Gambril Nicholson, made a play on the word "earnest," which sounded not unlike "Uranist."[123] Oscar Wilde used a similar wordplay in *The Importance of being Earnest*.[124] After his release from prison, Wilde wrote to Robert Ross: "To have altered my life would have been to have admitted that Uranian love is ignoble. I hold it to be noble – more noble than other forms."[125] Partly because of the Wilde prosecution, but partly also due to the dissemination of sexological texts that used the word "homosexual" in English, the brief flowering of English uranian subculture faded in the new century.

John Addington Symonds was a significant personality in English queer history. In 1889, late in his life, he started a four-year intellectual and literary journey of identity formation. Over that time, he broke with Whitman and discovered the works of sexual science. In Ulrichs's theories, Symonds found a way to reconcile his Whitmanite self so as to form an integrated sexual being. Symonds could not accept, and did not see in himself, Ulrichs's female soul in a male body, so instead he synthesized a new theory from his three strongest influences: Hellenism, Whitmanism, and Ulrichs's "urning." The result was a new identity, the "uranian comrade." Symonds had downplayed gendered variation and replaced it with masculine Dorian chivalry and Whitman's virile comradeship.

Sexual Inversion had a more enduring impact. It established Ellis as one of Europe's leading sexologists. Unlike in Symonds's writings, there is no sense that Ellis took a rigid view of effeminacy. However, his Whitmanite instincts meant that he drew the focus of English sexology away from the variation of gendered expression among homosexual men. Other historians have noted the subtle but profound change that occurred in the English discourse of sexology as a result. Commenting approvingly on this divergence from the German model, David Halperin wrote: "That sexual object-choice might be wholly independent of such 'secondary' characteristics as masculinity or femininity never seems to have entered anyone's head until Havelock Ellis waged a campaign to isolate object-choice from role-playing."[126] The English normative model of homosexuality may have seemed more appealing in late twentieth-century America than the German third-sex model. That may be less true now that more fluid gender identities are prevalent. However, the tradition of English-language sexology from that point on decoupled gender entirely from sexual orientation.

The intellectual and ontological consequences of Symonds's translation would play out in the decades to come. While Carpenter was a Whitmanite influenced by Symonds, he did not espouse his idealistic language. Carpenter's pamphlets nevertheless promulgated gentler versions of the uranian comrade that found some following among English homosexuals. The urning identity that had passed from individual to individual in continental Europe since Ulrichs first wrote of it in the 1860s was now passing, in modified form, among the Whitmanite followers of Edward Carpenter. In Germany itself, new configurations of the homosexual identity were, in due course, proposed by "masculinists" such as Benedict Friedlaender, Adolf Brand, John Henry Mackay, and others with commitments to Hellenism, communism, and anarchism. But whether the new theorists acknowledged it or not, they all owed an intellectual and political debt to the urnings who had preceded them. The age of the urning was drawing to a close.

The End of the Urning Age

If someone had prophesied at that time that in fifty years one would be able to publish a magazine in many thousands of copies every week, destined to represent the interests of homosexuals at home and abroad, an invisible bridge from city to city, from country to country, verily, according to his experience poor Ulrichs should have supposed that the visionary who prophesied this confused the land of Urania with the land of utopia. How did this unlikely event occur? Not by chance, not by the effectiveness of a person or a cause, but by many people and circumstances working together to gradually bring these seeds to maturity in the lap of time.[1]

On the evening of 15 May 1897, a group of patrician men gathered in an apartment in Berlin's Charlottenburg. The apartment belonged to the sexologist Magnus Hirschfeld, and his guests included the publishers Max Spohr and Adolf Glaser, the railway administrator Eduard Oberg, and the writer Franz Joseph von Bülow. They were meeting to discuss the incorporation of the Wissenschaftlich-humanitäres Komitee (WhK), the world's first homosexual rights organization. However, at that point in time, these men probably did not self-describe as "homosexual," and it is unlikely that the unpublished first draft of the articles of the WhK contained the word either.[2] Instead, they called themselves "urnings."

The year 1897 was a pivotal one in queer history. In May of 1897, two other things happened almost simultaneously with the foundation of the WhK: Oscar Wilde was released from prison, and John Addington Symonds and Henry Havelock Ellis's *Sexual Inversion* was published for the first time in English. Karl Heinrich Ulrichs died two years before these events and Symonds two years before that. Karl Maria Kertbeny, Carl von Zastrow, and Fritz Feldtmann had all died many years before.

Adolf Glaser, Jakob Rudolf Forster, and Archduke Ludwig Viktor all had many years still to live.

What had started with two pamphlets on law reform in 1864 had become a community so developed that it could support a formal campaign for reform. This was part of the "utopian future" inherent in the first proposition of the "urning." When Magnus Hirschfeld set up the WhK, he could do so against a background of literary support, visible communities of urnings, a scientific discourse backing their political claims, and a police force committed to their cause. Hirschfeld's WhK heralded a new beginning for homosexual rights. However, its existence was only possible because of crucial developments in the decades that preceded it. Ulrichs and his followers had transmitted the urning from paper to personage in the 1860s, and in the decades that followed, they had emerged as a visible component of society. The trials of 1867 and 1869 turned that privately held collective identity into a public universal presence. Grassroots community organizers such as Jakob Rudolf Forster ensured that urnings came together in socially and politically engaged networks of support. A campaign of autobiographical advocacy started by Ulrichs, and continued by his followers, persuaded psychiatry to depathologize its appraisals of sexual orientation. A measure of their success was the new discipline of sexology, of which Hirschfeld himself was a part. Glaser worked behind the scenes with the Berlin police to redirect them to tackle blackmail, and, in the process, Leopold von Meerscheidt-Hüllessem became a strong supporter of homosexual rights. Glaser's police liaison meant that the WhK's foundation had police blessing. Finally, the translation and transformation of the urning identity into English by John Addington Symonds meant that in England and the English-speaking world, a different model prevailed. All of these developments and the growing number of men who called themselves urnings, uranians, or homosexuals are ultimately the legacy of Ulrichs's original campaign.

By the time the Whk was founded, Ulrichs and his campaign had been largely forgotten. Hirschfeld's book *Sapho und Sophocles* (1895) made scant mention of Ulrichs because Hirschfeld was largely unaware of his predecessor, and his fifteen-year campaign was no longer a reference marker for the present queer generation. He was soon corrected by colleagues and made up for his omission by republishing an edited version of all of Ulrichs's pamphlets in 1898. A year later, he obtained from one of Ulrichs's surviving sisters four beautiful letters, in which Ulrichs had told his family of his plans.[3] Hirschfeld published these in the first volume of the *Jahrbuch für sexuelle Zwischenstufen* (1899)[4] and made a pilgrimage to Ulrichs's grave in Aquila in 1909. Hirschfeld recounted all of this in 1914, as part of a hagiographic rendering of Ulrichs's life and works, in a long passage in *Die Homosexualität des Mannes und des Weibes*.[5] Although this was not a historical work, the basic biographical details Hirschfeld used for his account were sound. At the end of that passage, Hirschfeld wrote of his visit to Aquila, where he met the man who had written Ulrichs's funeral oration, Marquis Nicolò Persichetti. According to Hirschfeld, Persichetti remarked that "the people whom he [Ulrichs] fought for no longer bothered themselves about him."[6] When Hirschfeld visited Ulrichs's grave, the "aged groundkeeper" had told him he was the first person in fourteen years to look for it. Hirschfeld added that Ulrichs's books "had found only a relatively small readership."[7] These observations may each have been true, but the way Hirschfeld presented them together created an impression that when Ulrichs ceased his activism, few remembered him and most forgot about his works until Hirschfeld rediscovered him. At the end of his campaigning, Ulrichs walked into exile in Italy, and many of his correspondents may have ceased writing to him. Yet his ideas lived on in the men who self-identified as urnings back in Germany. Hirschfeld's account effectively erased the men who called themselves urnings in the closing decades of the nineteenth century.[8]

Ulrichs's influence had shifted over time, and his unstable legacies were not necessarily apparent in the 1890s. What this book has shown is that the urning identity, an ontological turn to sexual modernity, was his most lasting legacy. This identarian legacy has not necessarily been revealed by other methodologies but is readily apparent in an epistolary history of this kind. The urning identity was on the move from the moment it was first disseminated. It became the personal identity of other individuals passed on lover by lover, friend by friend, and through the writings and activism of future generations. It ceased very quickly as an identity directly linked to Ulrichs. Ulrichs stopped writing in the 1870s, apart from one final book before he left for Italy. By then the identity was firmly embedded and had entered another stage – a proto-advocacy stage. The actions of the case-study writers and of individuals like Forster and Glaser advanced the "cause" after Ulrichs had left the scene and foreshadowed the emergence of more formal activism. Arguably, the identity was the necessary precursor to proto- and then formal activism. This happened earlier in Germany than anywhere else precisely because of the early transmission of the terms of the urning identity by Ulrichs.

By the 1890s there were people who called themselves urnings in the principal cities of Germany, Austria, Switzerland, and Hungary. It was also possible that proximity and diaspora meant that the identity had some small purchase in Poland, Bohemia, Denmark, Sweden, the Low Countries, France, and Italy. According to a contemporary writer, Otto de Joux, there were secret societies of urnings "imbued with the spirit of uranianism" in Rome, Brussels, and Vienna by the early 1890s.[9] A "uranian" community of sorts had also briefly surfaced in London before the Wilde trial. The Symonds translation operated as a formal transmission of sexual modernity for England, and it would be interesting to see if any similar staging into proto-activism and then formal organization took place there, perhaps over a longer timeline. If I could speculate, the decision to exclude homosexuals and interrogate all recruits about their sexuality in the 1942 mass draft in the United States could have acted as a similar transmission event. In both these cases, the mode and source of transmission were less crucial than the wide dissemination of the terminology and way of living.

There were, of course, those who chose not to identify as "urnings." Kertbeny was foremost among them with his alternative "homosexual" neologism, but there may have been others. As the century drew to a close, new discourses of masculinist Greek love echoed Kertbeny's rejection of the anima thesis. For example, the masculinist Elisar von Kupffer wrote at the turn of the century about the urning terminology with contempt in the introduction to an anthology of homoerotic literature:

It has become fashionable in human-scientific circles and in other circles close to the subject to speak of a "third" sex whose soul and body are not supposed to be in harmony. The Hanoverian jurist K.H. Ulrichs, admittedly a courageous and honourable character, but not exactly a prudent head, even invented a term for this third sex, to which he counted himself; this word "Urning" (from Venus Urania), "uranian" has spread like a generalising epidemic. It has been taken up by scientists, such as the well-known psychiatrist Professor Freiherr von Krafft-Ebing in Vienna. The matter has been investigated, criticised, classified, hypnotised, popularised and God knows what else. In the end, people set about it, who wanted to make their little sheep with pious and impious sensations; in short, we have a whole jumble of morbid and silly stories, which are of no use to our culture. And what was most dreadful about it was that the tips of our entire human history were distorted in the process, so that one could hardly recognise these rich spirits and heroes in their uranian petticoats.[10]

The slang terms *schwule* and *warme Bruder* tended to be more common among working-class Berliners, with terms like "urning," "homosexual," or "contrary sexual feeling" largely restricted to the educated classes. That should be balanced with the observation that by the 1890s, all of these words had achieved a fluid discursive practice so that they could be, and were, used interchangeably. Inevitably, by the twentieth century, each term began to accrue meanings and qualities that went beyond its original meanings. In Germany, "homosexual" gradually became the preferred term. Florian Mildenberger plots the supplanting of "contrary sexual feeling" with "homosexual" in the German general medical press between 1903 and 1907.[11] Kurt Hiller, who was a Jewish fifteen-year-old embracing communism, pacifism, and homosexuality at the turn of the century, penned an essay from London for the Swiss journal *Der Kreis* in 1946 titled "Zur Frage der Bezeichnung" (On the Question of Terminology). In that essay, Hiller surveyed the German terms used to describe same-sex-attracted people, rejecting each as deficient in its own way. When he came to the word "urning," this was what he had to say: "When one thinks of 'urning' in particular, one thinks of something quite morbid and quite effeminate. The ultra-feminine type may be covered by the term by association; It compromises the middle, even the virile type."[12]

Hiller's formative early adult years covered the period in which the "urning" neologism fell out of use. It is likely that in the final years of its use, "urning" became most associated with the people who still used it as a self-description. If weiblings were more loyal to the older terminology than mannlings were, it is not hard to see how that might destabilize what had, at one time, been a unifying terminology.

Finally, a few words on other categories and parameters of sexuality and gender. This book has been a decidedly "male" history. While this has been necessary for the focus of the narrative, it is also true that none of the letters or other sources made anything more than passing reference to same-sex-attracted women.[13] There were, of course, same-sex-attracted women in Germany at the same time, but apparently their circles did not overlap with the campaigns of homosexual men until much later. Only a few years after Ulrichs had left for his Italian exile, Anita Augsburg and her lover Sophia Goudstikker would set up a photography studio together in Munich and pioneer a new wave of feminism in the German women's movement. Campaigns around prostitution and birth control by feminists at the same time as the WhK was popularizing discourses around sexual rights ensured that as the new century began, sex had reached the mainstream of political action.[14] Many of the leading feminist activists of this period were lesbian, and for them, gender equality was of more immediate concern than sexual equality.[15] Anna Rüling in a speech to the WhK in 1904 observed that "if we weigh all the contributions that homosexual women have made to the women's movement, one would be astounded that its large and influential organizations have not lifted a finger to obtain justice in the state and in society for the not so small number of its Uranian members."[16] Rüling's speech would usher in a new era during which the homosexual rights movement came to serve as a new and obvious "bridge between man and woman."

Similarly, the existence of transgender individuals in and around urning society has been touched on only slightly in this book. The "consummate weibling" discussed in chapter 2 indicates that a small number of Ulrichs's correspondents tentatively suggested that they felt themselves to be women. I left unmentioned the extraordinary 1875 pamphlet *Urningsliebe* from Dr. Heinrich Marx that extended the Ulrichian discourse onto a much more gender-nonconforming footing.[17] Marx did not quite suggest a new category, but his description of the urning anticipated a category ordered primarily by gender rather than sexuality: "It is not the urning's fault that the Creator created him with an organ that defiles his body and is completely useless for the Urning."[18] Marx was a sympathetic doctor, but he did not quote any autobiographical content from gender-nonconforming urnings. That would not come until Richard von Krafft-Ebing's autobiographical case studies in *Psychopathia Sexualis*, which contained three gender nonconformists: the passing man Count Sandor/Sarolta Vay, who was sensationally tried in 1889 in Vienna by the family of a woman he had married; another from a psychotically gender-dysphoric gynaecologist; and the last from a medical student who preferred to live as a woman and was convinced she was in the wrong gender.[19] However, the category was still indistinct and would not be differentiated systematically until well into the twentieth century, when Magnus Hirschfeld described *seelischen Transsexualismus* (mental transsexualism).[20]

In closing, how can one characterize the thirty-three-year history of the urnings? Between 1864 and 1897 the lives of urning men were far from easy. Most lived in fear of blackmail and ruination. Even in the cities, where liberal tolerance may have prevailed, they were still vulnerable. They were not, however, passive victims buffeted by events. These were men who had taken control of their destinies. They owned an identity and social identification that defied society's norms. Some of these men, the ones profiled in this book, took that a stage further and demonstrated agency in their attempts to improve the lot of their fellow urnings. These self-identified and self-constructed urnings were now a body of men ready to support the world's first homosexual rights organization. At the very point the age of the urning was ending, a new era of formal queer campaigning was about to begin.

Timeline of Events

1864

- April/May – Karl Heinrich Ulrichs publishes *Vindex* and *Inclusa* under the pseudonym Numa Numantius.
- April – Friedrich ("Fritz") Conrad Anton Feldtmann is appointed director in charge of the City Theatre, Bremen.
- 23 May – Ulrichs's publisher, H. (Heinrich) Matthes, forwards the first letter-responses. Urnings begin writing to Ulrichs in large numbers.
- Summer – Karl Maria Kertbeny publishes *Erinnerung an Charles Sealsfield*, which references Ulrichs. They establish contact soon after.

1865

- Wilhelm Griesinger becomes the new chair of psychiatry at Berlin's Humboldt University with a dedicated psychiatric wing in the Charité Hospital.
- January/February – Ulrichs publishes *Vindicta*, *Formatrix*, and *Ara Spei* under the pseudonym Numa Numantius.
- September – Ulrichs writes and circulates a constitution for a Federation of Urnings (never incorporated).
- John Addington Symonds first encounters the works of Walt Whitman while visiting a friend in Cambridge.

1866

- Ulrichs starts planning a periodical, *Uranus* (the idea of the periodical is later abandoned, and the first issue is later published as *Prometheus*).
- Ulrichs writes to young psychiatrist Richard von Krafft-Ebing, and they maintain a regular correspondence in the years that follow.

- May–September – Prussia invades and then annexes Hanover in the German–Danish War.

1867

- January – Ulrichs is arrested for agitating against the Prussian occupation and is detained at Minden fortress.
- February – The mutilated body of sixteen-year-old baker's boy Ernst Corny is discovered in Berlin. Police investigation is inconclusive.
- 24 April – A search of Ulrichs's apartment uncovers incriminating material, including all his urning work. The press reveals that Ulrichs is Numa Numantius. He is detained once again at Minden fortress.
- May – Carl Wilhelm Otto Filsinger joins the cast for the summer season at the City Theatre Bremen. At some point over the summer, Filsinger witnesses Feldtmann with three younger men and starts blackmailing him.
- 26 June – Austrian Minister of Justice von Komers proposes a new criminal code without any antisodomy law.
- 5 July – Ulrichs is released from detention and exiled to Bavaria. He settles in Würzburg.
- 29 August – Ulrichs addresses the Congress of German Jurists at the Odeon Theatre in Munich. This is the first public protest on behalf of queer rights in history.
- October – Henry Maltravers and Claire Montague, two London crossdressers, face trial in London. One of their friends sends Ulrichs the newspaper cutting.
- 3 October – Fritz Feldtmann is arrested with three younger men in Bremen. Filsinger flees North Germany and poses as Baron von Felseck in Giessen, where he continues to blackmail urnings.
- December – Ulrichs sends the first section of *Memnon* to Bremen in support of Fritz Feldtmann's trial.
- 20 December – Fritz Feldtmann is found guilty in Bremen and is imprisoned for one year.

1868

- Griesinger redefines sexual orientation to the same sex as a constitutional pathology. He dies only a few months later.
- January–April – an intermediate urning, possibly involved in grand opera, writes to Ulrichs about social cross-dressers in London.
- April – A high-ranking Austrian, possibly the Archduke Ludwig of Austria ("Lutziwutzi"), writes to Ulrichs about cross-dressing escapades in his youth.

- April – Ulrichs publishes *Gladius Furens*, his account of the Munich protest, under his own name.
- 6 May – Kertbeny uses the words "homosexual" and "heterosexual" for the first time in the draft of a letter to Ulrichs.
- July/August – Ulrichs publishes *Memnon I* and *II*.
- 12 August – Justice Minister Leonhardt appoints Minister for Education and Medical Affairs, Heinrich von Mühler, to examine the repeal of the antisodomy statute, Paragraph 143.
- Summer – Filsinger poses as "Feche" in the Hôtel du Nord, Frankfurt.
- December – Fritz Feldtmann is released from prison.
- 15 December – Berlin Medical Psychology Society meets to discuss the psychiatry of sexuality, including Ulrichs's ideas.

1869

- Early 1869 – Carl Friedrich Otto Westphal publishes a paper on *conträre Sexualempfindung* with two case studies.
- 17 January – A badly injured five-year-old boy, Emil Handke, is discovered in the attic of Grüner Weg 45, Berlin. A police investigation begins.
- 20 January – Lieutenant Carl Ernst Wilhelm von Zastrow is arrested and detained in connection with the Handke case.
- 22 March – Deputation for Medical Affairs is invited to give an expert opinion to Justice Minister Leonhardt regarding the new North German legal code – recommends decriminalization.
- 30 March – The Central Committee of the Inner Mission delivers a 15,000-signature petition against the repeal of the antisodomy law.
- April – Von Mühler rejects the conclusion of the medical deputation and recommends instead that the antisodomy statute, Paragraph 143, be retained.
- May – Ulrichs publishes *Incubus*.
- 5 July – The first trial of Zastrow for the attack on Emil Handke begins in Berlin.
- Autumn – Kertbeny anonymously publishes two open letters to the Prussian Justice Minister Leonhardt calling for the repeal of the antisodomy law.
- September – Ulrichs publishes *Argonauticus*, an updated and extended version of *Incubus*.
- 25 October – The second trial of Zastrow begins in Berlin.
- 29 October – Zastrow is found guilty and sentenced to fifteen years at Moabit Prison in Berlin.
- December – A new criminal code for North Germany is published; it retains Paragraph 143, renumbered as Paragraph 175, as the antisodomy provision.

1870

- January – Kertbeny suffers a stroke and retreats to the country to recover.
- January – Ulrichs publishes *Prometheus*, originally intended to be the first issue of a periodical, *Uranus*.
- January – New Austrian Justice Minister Dr. Herbst rejects his predecessor's proposed new legal code and thus retains a criminal code that proscribes same-sex sexual contact for both sexes.
- March – Ulrichs publishes *Araxes*, a polemic addressed to the Diets of Austria and North Germany.
- 31 May – New North German legal code with the antisodomy Paragraph 175 comes into force.
- July – France and Prussia at war.
- Late 1870 – Ulrichs moves to Stuttgart in the Kingdom of Württemberg.

1871

- January – North German victory over the French. Wilhelm I is proclaimed emperor of all Germany apart from Austria.
- April – Germany decides to adopt the North German legal code.
- October – Symonds begins his correspondence with Walt Whitman.

1872

- 1 January – The new German legal code with Paragraph 175 is extended to Bavaria, Württemberg, and Baden in the south.

1873

- 9 May – Collapse of the Vienna Stock Exchange ignites the "Great Panic" and a global recession.
- Symonds writes but does not publish *A Problem in Greek Ethics*.

1874

- Late 1874 – Fritz Feldtmann becomes director at the Aktientheater, Zurich.
- New Swiss constitution.

1875

- January – Ulrichs publishes a book of poetry, *Auf Bienchens Flügeln* (On the Wings of the Little Bee).

- July – Symonds tries to publish his Greek essay as the final chapter in a second edition of *Studies of the Greek Poets*. It is very poorly received.
- Kertbeny returns to Budapest, where the Hungarian authorities offer him a state pension.
- Heinrich Marx publishes *Urningsliebe*.

1876

- Berlin police start developing photographic card indexes for the investigation of pederasts.

1877

- February – Roden Noel takes Symonds to a male brothel in London.
- 25 February – Zastrow dies from acute pleurisy at Moabit Prison in Berlin.
- August – Symonds and his family settle at Davos Platz in the canton of Graubünden, Switzerland.
- August – Jakob Rudolf Forster travels from St. Gallen in Switzerland to liquidate his honey business in Germany. At the Kreuz-Hotel in Friedrichshafen, he meets Wilhelm Kleber, who introduces him to the works of Ulrichs. In Stuttgart, Forster contacts Ulrichs and joins his small group of activists.
- November/December – Forster winds up his business in Stuttgart and travels to Ludwigsburg.

1878

- Symonds begins a chaste relationship with Christian Buol in Davos.
- 11 March – Karl Duberke is arrested in Berlin and implicates a circle of men including the writer and publisher Adolf Glaser in a sexual scandal.
- 20 March – *Volks-Zeitung* names Glaser as the most prominent member of the circle so that even though he is acquitted, the scandal becomes known as the "Glaser Scandal." Glaser resigns from his position at the Westermann publishing house.
- June – Fritz Feldtmann leaves the directorship at the Aktientheater, Zurich.
- Late 1878 – Gustav Jäger publishes *Die Entdeckung der Seele* with a short section supplied by Kertbeny that contains the word "homosexual."

1879

- The Supreme Court in Leipzig scrutinizes and broadens the definitions of the offences covered by Paragraph 175.

- February – Forster opens a matchmaking business in Zurich and uses it as a cover for urning outreach. He settles down with his new seventeen-year-old boyfriend, Jakob Zehnder.
- September – Ulrichs publishes *Critische Pfeile*.
- October – An attempt by Forster to monetize his knowledge of honey recipes ruffles feathers and results in four days' detention. Forster and Zehnder move back to St. Gallen.
- November – Ulrichs publishes a volume of Latin poetry, *Apicula Latina*.
- 6 November – Forster and Zehnder are arrested in St. Gallen. The police discover Forster's notebook of lovers and use it in their investigation.

1880

- 12–14 January – Trial of Forster, Zehnder, and four other defendants in St. Gallen. Forster is sentenced to eighteen months' detention at St. Jakob's prison, St. Gallen.
- Ulrichs walks over the Brenner Pass into Italy.
- Krafft-Ebing resigns from the Feldhof to concentrate on his private clinic in Graz.

1881

- Symonds starts a sexual relationship with Angelo Fusato in Venice.
- July – Ulrichs settles in Naples, Italy.

1882

- Glaser manages to get reinstated at Westermann.
- 21 January – Forster is released from prison and moves back to Zurich and his matchmaking business. He settles down with his new lover, Gustav Edwin Boller.
- 23 January – Kertbeny dies in Budapest.

1883

- Krafft-Ebing persuades a thirty-three-year-old Hungarian to write a sexual autobiography, which he then publishes.
- June – Ulrichs moves to Aquila in the Abruzzo region of Italy.
- Symonds prints privately and circulates ten copies of *A Problem in Greek Ethics*.
- November/December – Forster publishes the *World Marriage Newspaper* with covert urning material. He and Boller are arrested on 3 December, along with the printer and the newsagent.

- 29 December – Forster and Boller are tried in Zurich. Forster is sentenced to a year in the workhouse.

1884

- Mr. X, a thirty-eight-year-old masculine German businessman self-exiled in America due to blackmail, sends a sexual autobiography to Krafft-Ebing.
- 12 February – Fritz Feldtmann commits suicide in Berlin.
- October – Ulrichs publishes a book of short stories, *Matrosengeschichten* (Sailor Stories: Manor, the Monk of Sumbö, Sulitelma, Atlantis).

1885

- The Berlin police department reorganizes and appoints Leopold von Meer-schedit-Hüllessem as the inspector in charge of the policing of homosexuals and of blackmail. Photographic card indexes now extended for use in the policing of blackmail.
- Two followers of Ulrichs send sexual autobiographies to Krafft-Ebing, which he then publishes.
- 4 January – Forster is released from the workhouse.
- 29 January – After receiving a deportation order in Zurich, Forster and Boller move to Geneva. This does not work out, and Forster and Boller separate.
- February – The Berlin police raid Seger's restaurant.
- 15 June – Forster and Boller attempt a reconciliation in Zurich; both are arrested after only a few hours.
- 18 June – Forster is deported to St. Gallen.
- August – Forster hears that the authorities wish to detain him in an insane asylum. He flees on foot to Germany and over the next few months walks to Munich, then Vienna and Preßburg (now Bratislava).
- 27 October–15 November – Forster walks from Vienna through the Austrian Tyrol and over the Arlberg massif to Switzerland.
- November – Trial of the publican, staff, and patrons of Seger's restaurant.
- 25 December – Forster arrested and detained at St. Pirminsberg asylum.
- The Labouchere amendment introduced in the UK criminalizes "gross indecency" between men.

1886

- Krafft-Ebing publishes his first edition of *Psychopathia Sexualis*. He will issue eleven editions of this book with an ever-growing number of urning case studies.

- 12 March – Forster released from St. Pirminsberg; after refusing to accept a one-way ticket to Buenos Aires, he is detained at the Bitzi work camp.
- 13 June – Bavarian King Ludwig II drowns at Lake Starnberg near Munich.
- Krafft-Ebing opens the Mariagrün sanatorium in Graz.

1887

- January – Ulrichs publishes a book of Latin poems in memory of King Ludwig II: *Cupressi: Carmina in Memoriam Ludovici II Regis Bavariae.*
- 18 June – Forster is released from the Bitzi work camp.

1888

- June – Forster is arrested for suspected fraud, detained, and then tried in the canton of Schaffhausen. He is found not guilty.

1889

- March 1889 – Symonds begins to write his memoirs as a sexual autobiography and, in the process, encounters the works of Ulrichs, Krafft-Ebing, and others.
- May – Ulrichs starts writing and publishing a Latin newspaper called *Alaudae.*
- July 1889 – Forster moves back to Zurich and re-establishes his matchmaking business.
- Symonds sends a polemic letter in German to Krafft-Ebing, who publishes it in *Psychopathia Sexualis.*
- 4 November – Arrest of Count Sandor (Charlotte Sarolta Vay), a "passing man" from Hungary who had married a Viennese heiress. Sandor then faces trial in Vienna but is acquitted.

1890

- Glaser and Hüllessem collaborate with Albert Moll.
- 16 April – Forster makes a pilgrimage to Ludwig II's grave in Munich.
- Mid-1890 – Henry Havelock Ellis sends Symonds a copy of his book *New Spirit*, in which he criticizes Whitman's understanding of science. Symonds is emboldened to write to Whitman and ask him about his sexual ethic.
- 19 August – Whitman writes to Symonds to reject any sexual interpretation of adhesiveness and comradeship in his poetry.
- October – Symonds writes *Walt Whitman: A Study*, in which he criticizes Whitman's sexual ethic. However, he does not publish it.
- December – Symonds finishes *A Problem in Modern Ethics.*

1891

- January – Symonds publishes privately and circulates fifty copies of
  A Problem in Modern Ethics.
- Albert Moll publishes *Die Conträre Sexualempfindung*.
- January – Correspondence between Symonds and Ulrichs begins.
- 27–8 October – Symonds, accompanied by Angelo Fusato, visits Ulrichs in
  Aquila.

1892

- February – The last known contact between Symonds and Ulrichs.
- March – Walt Whitman dies in Camden, New Jersey.
- June – Symonds and Ellis decide to collaborate in writing *Sexual Inversion*.
  In the closing months of 1892, Symonds gathers case studies with the
  help of Edward Carpenter and Edith Lees, while Ellis writes the major
  chapters.

1893

- Symonds publishes *Walt Whitman: A Study*.
- On hearing that the Swiss Federal Council is about to start preliminary
  consultations on a uniform Swiss penal code, Forster composes and
  sends each council member a petition and copies of works by Ulrichs and
  Albert Moll.
- 19 April – Symonds dies in Rome.
- 27 April – Ulrichs's apartment in Aquila has a fire.
- Edward Carpenter writes *Homogenic Love and Its Place in a Free Society*.
  Although he fails to get it published until later, the privately printed
  manuscript circulates among groups of Whitmanites.

1894

- 24 May – Krafft-Ebing sends Ulrichs a copy of *Der Conträrsexuale vor dem
  Strafrichter*.
- 18 June – Ulrichs sends a petition to the Austrian Parliament.

1895

- February – Ulrichs publishes his final issue of *Alaudae*.
- 25 May – Trial and conviction of Oscar Wilde.
- 14 July – Ulrichs dies in Aquila.

1896

- Magnus Hirschfeld publishes *Sappho und Socrates*, after which he meets and gets to know Glaser and Hüllessem.
- The first edition of Symonds and Ellis's *Sexual Inversion* is published in German as *Das konträre Geschlechtsgefühl*.
- Forster goes on a holiday in Geneva with his new lover, Hans Kühne, and is arrested on his return to Zurich. Forster is detained until 24 December and is then sent to the Burgholzli asylum.

1897

- The English edition of *Sexual Inversion* is published and then banned.
- 9 January – Dr. August Forel uses Forster's life story as a case study in a lecture.
- 14 May – Hirschfeld launches the Wissenschaftlich-humanitäres Komitee (WhK) during a meeting at his apartment in Charlottenburg, Berlin.
- 18 May – Oscar Wilde is released from prison.
- 1 June – Forster finishes his autobiography, which he publishes in 1898.

Notes

Acknowledgments

1 Pretsell, *The Correspondence*.

Notes on Terminology

1 Ulrichs derived the term from Plato's Symposium as the source for his neologism: "My terminology is derived from the names of the gods Uranus and Dione. A poetical piece of fiction by Plato traced the origins of man-manly love to Uranus, the love for women to Dione." Ulrichs, *Vindex*, §2, 1; Lombardi-Nash (tr.) *The Riddle* vol. 1, 34.
2 Westphal, "Die conträre Sexualempfindung," 92–4.
3 Draft letter, Kertbeny to Ulrichs, 6 May 1868. Budapest, National Széchényi Library, Manuscript Collection, Oct. Germ. 302, ff225–7. Translated as letter 160 in Pretsell, *The Correspondence*, 199–205.
4 Curiously, in the 1889 edition, Krafft-Ebing did not discuss why he started using the new terminology. Krafft-Ebing, *Psychopathia Sexualis*, 4th ed., 74ff.
5 Albert Moll, writing in 1891, attested to the "very conspicuous agreement" in self-descriptions and the use of the urning terminology in biographies and autobiographies. Moll, *Die conträre Sexualempfindung*, 7.
6 Kunzel, "The Power of Queer History," 1565.

Introduction: The Age of the Urning

1 Krafft-Ebing, "Die conträre Sexualempfindung," 46. An English translation can be found in Pretsell, *Queer Voices*, 59.
2 Heinrich Hössli wrote and published a two-volume treatise titled *Eros. Die Männerliebe der Griechen, ihre Beziehungen zur Geschichte, Erziehung,*

Literatur und Gesetzgebung aller Zeiten. Hössli used his knowledge of classical literature to prove that eros between people of the same sex is an innate, immutable, natural, universal, and timeless phenomenon that should not be socially or legally persecuted. Robert Deam Tobin, "Die Quellen der Innovation: Heinrich Hössli und sein Zeitalter," in Thalmann, *"Keine Liebe ist an sich Tugend oder Laster,"* 149. Ulrichs was not aware of Hössli's treatise when he first started writing, but a correspondent in Switzerland sent the volumes to him on 12 February 1866. Ulrichs felt that they were "too detailed and tedious" but "in parts rich and brilliant." Ulrichs, *Memnon, Abtheilung II*, §134 (8), 129; Lombardi-Nash (tr.), *The Riddle*, vol. 2, 428–9.

3 In 1849, Claude-François Michéa published an essay on the case of a Sergeant Bertrand, who had raped newly buried corpses. Michéa, "Des déviations maladives." Following the case study, there was a long discussion of "Greek love" that was an early attempt at a more modernist approach to understanding perversion. Hekma, "'A Female Soul in a Male Body,'" 215. Michéa called the attraction for the same sex *philopœdie* (this was the word used in French for "pederasty") in men and *tribadisme* in women. Michéa defined these as fixed, innate, and instinctive identities. He even suggested a biological cause for same-sex desire in men, citing Ernst Heinrich Weber's 1836 discovery of the *uterus masculinus* – a vestigial cavity found in the abdomen of some men that Michéa thought might be the cause of *philopœdie*. Michéa, "Des déviations maladives," 339. This was a theoretical discussion rather than one based on clinical observation, and it appears to have been largely ignored. Michéa was a forensic psychiatrist, but he was also a *philopede* himself, and that probably motivated him to write. The French police in the nineteenth century maintained a register of pederasts in which both Michéa and his lover, Pierre Edouard Vallerand de la Fosse, were listed. Féray, *Le Registre infamant*, 348–9, 430–1. Although Michéa put forward a proto-modern identity, it was nevertheless positioned as pathological.

4 In Michéa's case, a paper in a medical periodical was unlikely to be read by anyone other than medical professionals, but Hössli's books should have been available to a wider audience. Unfortunately, attempts to ban the books by the Glarus authorities and a later fire in a warehouse meant it was extremely difficult to find copies of either volume. Ferdinand Karsch, "Auszüge aus Heinrich Hössli (1784–1864)," in Thalmann, *"Keine Liebe ist an sich Tugend oder Laster,"* 27–34.

5 Sedgwick, *Epistemology of the Closet*, 44.

6 In particular, three volumes edited by Wolfram Setz: *Die Geschichte der Homosexualitäten; Karl Heinrich Ulrichs zu Ehren;* and *Neue Funde und Studien zu Karl Heinrich Ulrichs.*

7 Pretsell, *The Correspondence of Karl Heinrich Ulrichs*.

8 Pretsell, *Queer Voices*.

9 Beachy, *Gay Berlin*, 3.

10 Watson, *The German Genius*, 50–1, 228.

11 The universities that emerged in Germany in the early decades of the nineteenth century resembled modern research universities at a time when comparable universities in France, the United Kingdom, and the United States did not. Osterhammel, *The Transformation of the World*, 803–5.

12 Szporluk, *Communism and Nationalism*, 25.

13 Beachy, *Gay Berlin*, 8, 12.

14 Goschler, *Rudolf Virchow*, 58–9.

15 Galassi, *Kriminologie im Deutschen Kaiserreich*, 17–18.

16 Verheyen, *The German Question*, 8; Davies, *Europe*, 824.

17 Even before the revolutions, a customs union treaty of 1833 saw the removal of tariffs in trade between all the German states; also, the postal service and the train network expanded to form quasi-state communications infrastructures in the 1850s; Segal, *The Political Fragmentation of Germany*, 96.

18 Segal, *The Political Fragmentation of Germany*, 11.

19 Hull, *Sexuality, State, and Civil Society*, 349–59.

20 Hull, *Sexuality, State, and Civil Society*, 357.

21 In practice during this period, although it was in statute, the death penalty was never used in these jurisdictions. Friedrich Feldtmann was tried using these laws in Bremen and received one year's imprisonment (see chapter 4).

22 The Austrian criminal code was subsequently reformed in 1803 and again in 1852. In Paragraph 129 of the *Strafgesetzbuch* same-sex sexual activity was punished with imprisonment: "Als Verbrechen werden auch nach-stehende Arten der Unzucht bestraft: I. Unzucht wider die Natur, das ist a) mit Thieren; b) mit Personen desselben Geschlechts" (The following types of fornication are also punished as crimes: I. Fornication against nature, that is a) with animals; b) with persons of the same sex). *Allgemeines Reichs-Gesetz- und Regierungsblatt für das Kaiserthum Österreich* 1852, my translation.

23 Hull, *Sexuality, State, and Civil Society*, 340–1. The minimum sentence was reduced to six months in 1851.

24 Dobler, *Zwischen Duldungspolitik*, 197.

25 Galassi, *Kriminologie im Deutschen Kaiserreich*, 94.

26 Dobler, *Zwischen Duldungspolitik*, 44–5.

27 Robb, *Strangers*, 30.

28 In 1862, only 4 per cent of Germans in the Confederation lived in cities with more than 100,000 inhabitants. A further 3.5 per cent lived in towns

with a population between 25,000 and 100,000. Ninety-two per cent of Germans lived in small towns of fewer than 25,000 people. Kolb, *Grundriss der Statistik*, 47–8.

29 Kolb, *Grundriss der Statistik*, 1–2.
30 Beachy, *Gay Berlin*, 48.
31 Derks, *Die Schande der heiligen Päderastie*, 103.
32 Dobler, *Zwischen Duldungspolitik*, 44.
33 Stieber, *Die Prostitution in Berlin*, 209, my translation.
34 Hugländer, "Aus dem homosexuellen Leben," 47, my translation.
35 Otto de Joux, *Des Enterbten des Liebesglückes, oder Das dritte Geschlecht* (Leipzig: Spohr, 1893), 99.
36 Brunner and Sulzenbacher, "Donauwalzer," 39.
37 Brunner and Sulzenbacher, "Donauwalzer," 40.
38 Brunner and Sulzenbacher, "Donauwalzer," 39.
39 Brunner and Sulzenbacher, "Donauwalzer," 39.
40 The Zentralbad was popular with Archduke Ludwig Viktor and the scene of the scandal that saw him banished from Vienna (see chapter 3).
41 Ulrichs, *Ara Spei*, §135, 71n60; Lombardi-Nash (tr.) *The Riddle* vol. 1, 241.
42 Pederast was the German word for sexually active same-sex attracted men. Strictly speaking, it referred directly to the act of sodomy, although its usage as a word to describe individuals or categories of individuals sometimes suggested a broader meaning.
43 In a meticulous study of German etiquette books, Martina Kessel demonstrated that the German nineteenth century had been dominated by a masculine concept of the "whole man" that incorporated *Bildung* and balance, facets that could be considered feminine in more modern conceptions of masculinity. By the 1860s, that was giving way to a "soldier of labour" model of masculinity; there was no dominant "hegemonic" masculine role in that decade. Kessel positions the masculine identities of late nineteenth-century Germany as "Janus-like," straddling Enlightenment and modern models of masculinity. Kessel, "The 'Whole Man,'" 2–23.
44 Tobin, *Warm Brothers*, 23.
45 Vick, "Liberalism, Nationalism, and Gender Dichotomy," 584.
46 Vick, "Liberalism, Nationalism, and Gender Dichotomy," 582.
47 Tobin, *Warm Brothers*, 195.
48 Palmowski, "The Politics of the 'Unpolitical German,'" 678.
49 The Social Democratic Party of Germany (Sozialdemokratische Partei Deutschlands; SPD) was founded in 1863. The General German Cigar Workers Society (Der Allgemeine Deutsche Cigarrenarbeiter-Verein), established in Leipzig in 1865, was the first centrally organized union in Germany, and the first independent German feminist organization, Der Allgemeine Deutsche Frauenverein, was founded in 1865 at a women-only conference in Leipzig.

50 Chapter 1 presents a full biographic account of Karl Heinrich Ulrichs as the first urning.
51 Sedgwick, *Epistemology of the Closet*, 86.
52 Foucault, *The History of Sexuality*, vol. 1. All quotations in this book are taken from this English edition.
53 Foucault, *The History of Sexuality*, vol. 1, 43.
54 Foucault, *The History of Sexuality*, vol. 1, 101.
55 Foucault, "The Gay Science," 387.
56 Eribon, *Insult*, 279.
57 See, for example, Halperin, *One Hundred Years of Homosexuality*, 16; Greenberg, *The Construction of Homosexuality*, 408–13; and Weeks, *Sexuality and Its Discontents*, 66.
58 See, for example, Oosterhuis, *Stepchildren of Nature*, 10; Leck, *Vita Sexualis*, 221–5; and Tobin, *Peripheral Desires*, 22.
59 Serious German scholarship on the queer nineteenth century did not start appearing until after the Berlin "Eldorado" exhibition in 1984. Bollé and Bothe, *Eldorado*. Prior to 1976, there had been only two publications relating to events in Germany, and both were American. Lauritsen and Thorstad, *The Early Homosexual Rights Movement*; Steakley, *The Homosexual Emancipation Movement*.
60 See discussion in, "Forgetting Foucault," 97–8.
61 Before the 1860s, same-sex acts were the subject of works by forensic examiners like Ambroise Tardiue and Johann Ludwig Casper; such works focused on legal prohibition and the physical evidence for certain sexual acts. After 1870, psychiatrists began looking at the sexual invert as a person with an interior psychology. In the earlier quoted passage, Foucault credits Carl Westphal's 1869 paper, the first of these psychiatric papers, as "the birth certificate of homosexuality." Foucault, *The History of Sexuality*, vol. 1, 43.
62 Eribon, *Insult*, 270.
63 Boswell, *Christianity, Social Tolerance and Homosexuality*; Eribon, *Insult*, 315.
64 Foucault, *The History of Sexuality*, vol. 2, 18.
65 Eribon, *Insult*, 248–9.
66 Martin, Gutman, and Hutton, eds., *Technologies of the Self*, 19.
67 Eribon, *Insult*, 337.
68 Foucault, *The History of Sexuality*, vol. 1, 43.
69 Fraser, "Rethinking the Public Sphere," 67.
70 Richter, "Winckelmann's Progeny," 39.
71 Letter from Ulrichs to Carl Robert Egells, 31 January–1 February 1874, quoted in Ferdinand Karsch-Haack, 1922. *Carl Heinrich Ulrichs. Die Freundschaft*, 29, 4. 20 May. Translated as letter 202 in Pretsell, *The Correspondence*, 237.

72 When Ulrichs was arrested in 1867, the authorities seized a quantity of letters; Ulrichs claimed there were letters from 150 individuals in Berlin alone. Ulrichs, *Argonauticus*, §5, 12; Lombardi-Nash (tr.), *The Riddle*, vol. 2, 477. There were only eighty-two urning letter fragments from sixty-six individuals quoted in his books, and they came from all over the German-speaking world and beyond.

73 Ulrichs, *Formatrix*, §83, 39; Lombardi-Nash (tr.), *The Riddle*, vol. 1, 162.

74 Eder, *Kultur der Begierde*, 161.

75 Dagmar Günther, "'And Now for Something Completely Different,'" 31.

76 Günther, "'And Now for Something Completely Different,'" 35.

1. The First Urning: Karl Heinrich Ulrichs, 1825–1895

1 Ulrichs, *Vindex*, §34, 15; Lombardi-Nash (tr.), *The Riddle*, vol. 141.

2 CV contained in a letter from Ulrichs to Board of the Free German Academy, 19 February 1861. Frankfurt, Freies Deutsches Hochstift/ Frankfurter Goethe-Museum, Mitgliedsakte von Karl Heinrich Ulrichs ff65–9. Translated as letter 62 in Pretsell, *The Correspondence*, 104.

3 Letter 62 in Pretsell, *The Correspondence*, 104.

4 Ulrichs was particularly close to his mother, his grandfather (whom he lived with while at school), his younger sister Ulrike, and his paternal uncle, Pastor Otto Ülzen. When he announced his intention to mount the urning campaign, it was his sister and his uncle to whom he wrote at length about his plans. Both tried to dissuade him; nevertheless, they encouraged him to explain his arguments to them. Both must have saved the letters Ulrichs sent back to them, as Magnus Hirschfeld was able to acquire them from Ulrike in the 1890s. This suggests they cared for him even if not for his ideas.

5 Ulrichs, *Memnon, Abtheilung II*, §77, 54; Lombardi-Nash (tr.) *The Riddle* vol. 2, 377.

6 Letter 62 in Pretsell, *The Correspondence*, 106.

7 Letter from Ulrichs to the Royal Hanoverian Ministry of Justice, 30 November 1854. Niedersächsisches Landsarchiv, Hannover, Hann. 26a Nr 6206: ff35–6. Letter 31 in Pretsell, *The Correspondence*, 74.

8 There was no antisodomy law in Hanover, but Paragraph 276 of the General Criminal Code of Hanover punished "unnatural lust under circumstances which cause public annoyance" with up to six months' hard labour. Art. 276, Allgemeines Criminal-Gesetzbuch für das Königreich Hannover vom 8. August 1840. Cited in Hoffschildt, *Olivia*, 18.

9 Letter 62 in Pretsell, *The Correspondence*, 107.

10 Ulrichs, "Das deutsche Postfürstenthum"; Ulrichs, *Der Nassau-Taxis'sche Postvertrag*.

11 Ulrichs, *Großdeutsches Programm.*
12 Kennedy, *Karl Heinrich Ulrichs*, 40.
13 Kennedy, "Johann Baptist von Schweitzer," 75.
14 Ulrichs, *Vindicta*, xvii; Lombardi-Nash (tr.), *The Riddle*, vol. 1, 105.
15 Segal, *The Political Fragmentation of Germany*, 11.
16 Interestingly, Ulrichs and the urnings were not the only people to see this period in German history as an opportunity for progressive advancement. In 1865, the year after Ulrichs published his first urning books, Louise Otto Peters, Auguste Schmidt, Henriette Goldschmidt, Ottilie von Steyber, and Mina Cauer founded the first independent German feminist organization, Der Allgemeine Deutsche Frauenverein, and participated in the first women-only conference, held in Leipzig. In the years that followed, several prominent lesbians played leading roles in the German feminist movement.
17 Four of those letters survive: one to his sister, one circular to the whole family, and two to his maternal uncle. Ulrichs, "Vier Briefe." Translations of all four letters can be found as letters 80, 82, 85, and 86 in Pretsell, *The Correspondence*, 120–40.
18 The etymology of Ulrichs's pseudonym Numa Numantius is obscure, and Ulrichs never told his readers why he chose the name. The Numa part of the pseudonym possibly alludes to Numa Pompilius, who was the second king of Rome. Numa Pompilius was the king of peace: he ruled for forty years, established the religious institutions of Rome, and was reputed to have written sacred texts. When these texts were later discovered they were burned, "since in them there were many things subversive of religion" (Titus Livius [Livy], *The History of Rome* 40.29). Thus, "Numa" carries an association with forbidden and profane texts. Numantius was an honorific used by certain prominent figures in medieval Rome, and Ulrichs may have chosen it for its alliterative link to Numa. I am grateful to my colleague Lauren Murphy for these insights.
19 Letter from Ulrichs to his sister Ulrike, 22 September 1862. Translated as letter 80 in Pretsell, *The Correspondence*, 124.
20 In this letter, Ulrichs uses the word *uranier* – an earlier version of his urning terminology. Letter from Ulrichs to his maternal uncle, Pastor Otto Ülzen, 12 December 1862. Translated as letter 85 in Pretsell, *The Correspondence*, 134.
21 Letter from Ulrichs to his maternal uncle, Pastor Otto Ülzen, 12 December 1862. Translated as letter 85 in Pretsell, *The Correspondence*, 134.
22 Ulrichs, *Inclusa*, §16, 14; Lombardi-Nash (tr.), *The Riddle*, vol. 1, 59.
23 Kennedy, *Karl Heinrich Ulrichs*, 59.
24 Ulrichs, *Inclusa*, §17, 15; Lombardi-Nash (tr.), *The Riddle*, vol. 1, 59–60.
25 Ulrichs, *Formatrix*, §108, 55n46; Lombardi-Nash (tr.), *The Riddle*, vol. 1, 172.

26 Hirschfeld, *The Homosexuality of Men and Women*, 150.
27 Ulrichs, *Vindex*, §§12–13, 6; §53, 26–27; Lombardi-Nash (tr.), *The Riddle*, vol. 1, 36–7; 47–8.
28 Letter from Ulrichs to his maternal uncle, Pastor Otto Ülzen, 12 December 1862. Translated as letter 85 in Pretsell, *The Correspondence*, 136.
29 Müller, *Aber in meinem Herzen*, 57. The current German court system does not use juries; however, they were used widely following the revolution of 1848, and Ulrichs would have been used to juries in the courts of the Kingdom of Hanover. Koch, "C.J.A. Mittermaier," 350.
30 Singy, "Sexual Identity," 397.
31 Patrick Singy wrote that the "historical significance of Ulrichs's argument cannot be overstated: for the first time in history, someone used a legal reasoning to call for an 'anthropology' of same sex desire." Singy, "Sexual Identity," 400.
32 These three books were *Vindicta*, *Formatrix*, and *Ara Spei*.
33 In September 1865 he circulated the by-laws for this federation to his closest correspondents. Only one copy of these by-laws survives, in the papers of Karl Maria Kertbeny, Budapest, National Széchényi Library, Manuscript Collection, Oct.Germ. 301, f37. Translated as letter 126 in Pretsell, *The Correspondence*, 173–4. When Ulrichs was arrested in 1867, these lists were discovered by the police; they were found to contain at least 150 names from Berlin alone. Ulrichs, *Argonauticus*, §5, 12; Lombardi-Nash (tr.), *The Riddle*, vol. 2, 477.
34 Ulrichs, *Memnon, Abtheilung II*, §134, 122; Lombardi-Nash (tr.), *The Riddle*, vol. 2, 424.
35 Kennedy, *Karl Heinrich Ulrichs*, 99.
36 Report from Minden, containing the confession of Ulrichs, to the Royal General Government, 26 January 1867. Berlin, Geheimes Staatsarchiv Preußischer Kulturbesitz I. HA Geh. Rat, Rep. 90A, no. 3773, ff36–9. Translated as letter 132 in Pretsell, *The Correspondence*, 180.
37 Letter from Ulrichs to the Royal Prussian Fortress Commander at Minden, May 1867. Berlin, Geheimes Staatsarchiv Preußischer Kulturbesitz I. HA Geh. Rat, Rep. 90A, no. 3773, ff41–2. Translated as letter 133 in Pretsell, *The Correspondence*, 181.
38 Ulrichs later wrote to the ministry listing all the materials that had been confiscated and asking for their return. Letter from Ulrichs to Royal Prussian State Ministry, 12 February 1874. Berlin, Geheimes Staatsarchiv Preußischer Kulturbesitz I. HA Geh. Rat, Rep. 90A, no. 3773, ff58–62. Translated as letter 205 in Pretsell, *The Correspondence*, 239–41.
39 Ulrichs listed the dates of his incarceration in a letter to the President of the State Ministry Behrmann, 8 November 1870. Berlin, Geheimes Staatsarchiv Preußischer Kulturbesitz I. HA Geh. Rat, Rep. 90A, no. 3773, ff19–22. Translated as letter 197 in Pretsell, *The Correspondence*, 233.

40 Jens Dobler, *Zwischen Duldungspolitik*, 62.

41 Letter from Lieutenant General Voigts-Rhetz to the Royal Minister President and Minister of Foreign Affairs, Knight of the Supreme Order, His Excellency Count of Bismarck-Schönhausen, 31 July 1867. Berlin, Geheimes Staatsarchiv Preußischer Kulturbesitz I. HA Geh. Rat, Rep. 90A, no. 3773. ff9,10.

42 Ulrichs, *Gladius Furens*, 2; Lombardi-Nash (tr.), *The Riddle*, vol. 1, 263.

43 Ulrichs, *Gladius Furens*, 4; Lombardi-Nash (tr.), *The Riddle*, vol. 1, 264.

44 Ulrichs, *Gladius Furens*, 4; Lombardi-Nash (tr.), *The Riddle*, vol. 1, 263.

45 Letter from an eyewitness to Karl Maria Kertbeny. Cited in Kennedy, *Karl Heinrich Ulrichs*, 118.

46 Ulrichs, *Gladius Furens*; Lombardi-Nash (tr.) *The Riddle*, vol. 1, 259–88.

47 Ulrichs, *Gladius Furens*, 15–16; Lombardi-Nash (tr.), *The Riddle*, vol. 1, 270–1.

48 Ulrichs, *Memnon, Abtheilung II*, ix; Lombardi-Nash (tr.), *The Riddle*, vol. 2, 355–6.

49 The two Irrenfreund reviews, one from Dr. F. and one from Dr. D. Lissauer, can be read in Dworek, "'Ist diese Krankheit heilbar?,'" *CAPRI* 2, no. 90 (1990): 45–6.

50 Ulrichs, *Incubus*, 34; Lombardi-Nash (tr.), *The Riddle*, vol. 2, 447.

51 [Geigel], *Das Paradoxon der Venus Urania*.

52 It is mildly amusing that Geigel pinpointed by chance the exact year, 2000, that Dutch politicians legalized gay marriage: a first in the entire world. [Geigel], *Das Paradoxon*, 14, my translation.

53 [Geigel], *Das Paradoxon*, 34.

54 Letter from Rudolf Virchow to Ulrichs, 19 August 1864. Ulrichs, *Ara Spei*, §89, 45; Lombardi-Nash (tr.), *The Riddle*, vol. 1, 224.

55 Hirschfeld, *Memoir*, 171–2.

56 Kennedy, "Johann Baptist von Schweitzer," 71.

57 In 1869, Ulrichs published two books in response to the public reaction around the Zastrow trial. The first, *Incubus*, proved so popular that he published an extended version as *Argonauticus* a couple of months later.

58 In 1870, Ulrichs published *Prometheus* (originally intended to be the first issue of a periodical called "Uranus") and *Araxes*.

59 Kertbeny, *§143 des preussischen Strafgesetzbuches*; Kertbeny, *Das Gemeinschädliche des §143 des preussischen Strafgesetzbuches*.

60 The "Central Committee of the Inner Mission," a leading Protestant revival organization, launched a petition against public immorality, which gathered 15,000 signatures from across the North German Confederation. Dobler, *Zwischen Duldungspolitik*, 120.

61 Kennedy, *Karl Heinrich Ulrichs*, 161.

62 Kennedy, *Karl Heinrich Ulrichs*, 191.

63 Letter from Ulrichs in Aquila to an acquaintance in Germany, 6 February 1892, reproduced in *Jahrbuch für sexuelle Zwischenstufen* 5, no. 1 (1903): 44. Translated as letter 226 in Pretsell, *The Correspondence*, 260.

2. From Page to Personhood: The Transmission of *Urningtum*, 1864–1868

1 Herzer, "Zastrow–Ulrichs–Kertbeny," 78, my translation.

2 Ulrichs, *Vindex*, §1, 1; Lombardi-Nash (tr.), *The Riddle*, vol. 1, 34.

3 Booksellers in Germany during this period also acted as publishers, marketing the works on their shelves through catalogues that were mailed to subscribers and by binding advertisements for other books at the back of similar works. The H. Matthes catalogues survive today in a large compendium of catalogues from the decades before 1880; they are held at the Deutsches Buch- und Schriftmuseum at the German National Library in Leipzig. "H. Matthes catalogues," in *Gesamt-Verlags-Katalog des Deutschen Buchhandels*.

4 Osterhammel, *The Transformation of the World*, 74.

5 Watson, *The German Genius*, 370.

6 Ulrichs wrote in his third book, "My bookseller has sent me several letters, some of them signed, expressing their approval of both publications. Some were from Urnings, some from Dionings from Germany and abroad." Ulrichs, *Vindicta*, xxii; Lombardi-Nash (tr.), *The Riddle*, vol. 1, 107.

7 Ulrichs, *Argonauticus*, §5, 12; Lombardi-Nash (tr.), *The Riddle*, vol. 2, 477.

8 Ulrichs petitioned the government for the next two decades to recover his papers. He never received a reply, but each petition generated internal communications in the relevant ministries. These internal communications show that the letters were retained for intelligence purposes. In a letter replying to an inquiry by the Vice President of State Lord Camphausen, the now retired Privy Counsellor Wagener wrote: "The documents in question, which were confiscated from Judge Ulrichs, were conveyed to me by his Highness the Lord Minister President, Prince Bismarck, with express orders not to let them enter the proper course of affairs of the Royal State, but to keep them at my side until further orders. Among the documents which had been confiscated there are, in large numbers, photographic portraits, correspondence and lists which refer to the connections with pederasts of the aforementioned Dr. Ulrichs. These extend into the widest circles and in some cases have resulted in further steps being taken against persons who, unlike Dr. Ulrichs at that time, did not enjoy the benefit of Hanoverian legislation." Letter from Privy Counsellor Wagener to Lord Camphausen, Vice President of the State Ministry, 14 April 1874. Berlin, Geheimes Staatsarchiv Preußischer Kulturbesitz I. HA Geh. Rat, Rep. 90A, no. 3773. ff67–9, my translation.

9 Ulrichs may have disposed of many of these himself when he walked over the Brenner pass into Italian exile in 1880. Any he carried with him were probably destroyed in a fire at his apartment in Aquila on 27 April 1893. Kennedy, *Karl Heinrich Ulrichs*, 231; Ulrichs, *Alaudae*, 282.

10 Letters were classified as from urnings only where Ulrichs introduced
   them as such or where the content unequivocally identified the author as
   an urning.
11 Most of these are the letters Ulrichs introduced as being from dionings.
   Ulrichs was in the habit of publishing the names of his dioning readers but
   not his urning readers. There were two anonymous letters, and one named,
   where the author was not identified as either urning or dioning and where
   the content was non-specific. These have been included in the dioning figures.
   It is, of course, entirely possible that these and even some of the named letters
   were from urnings who chose not to out themselves to Ulrichs in a letter.
12 In the 1860s only Berlin and Vienna were large enough to be considered
   proper cities with respectively 541,000 and 580,000 inhabitants. Kolb,
   Grundriss der Statistik, 48.
13 Ulrichs received most of his letters from Frankfurt (2), Baden (1), Dresden
   (1), Leipzig (2), Hanover (2), Bremen (2), Würzburg (2), Munich (1),
   and Potsdam (1); regions such as Mittelrhein (2), Kurhessen (1), Central
   Germany (1), North Germany (2), Bavaria (1), and Saxony (1); and then
   rural locations by the Main River (1) and Oder River (2). In 1862, most of
   these locations had under 150,000 residents: Munich (148,000), Dresden
   (128,000), Leipzig (78,000), Frankfurt (75,000), Hanover (70,000), Bremen
   (65,000), Würzburg (36,119), Potsdam (33,250), and Baden (7,722). Kolb,
   Grundriss der Statistik, 40, 48–9, 52, 55–6.
14 Once he was in exile in Bavaria and then in Württemberg, Ulrichs did
   socialize with other urnings.
15 Ulrichs, *Memnon, Abtheilung II*, §123, 116; Lombardi-Nash (tr.), *The Riddle*,
   vol. 2, 419.
16 Sedgwick, *Epistemology of the Closet*, 86.
17 See the discussion of Enlightenment discourses on sexuality in
   Oosterhuis, *Stepchildren of Nature*, 25–31.
18 Pederasty was the word used in German for the practice of anal
   intercourse, which was proscribed by the Prussian legal code. Casper,
   Klinische Novellen, 35–9.
19 Casper, *Klinische Novellen*, 38, my translation.
20 Casper, *Klinische Novellen*, 38, my translation.
21 Casper, *Klinische Novellen*, 39, my translation.
22 Casper, *Klinische Novellen*, 39, my translation.
23 Casper, *Klinische Novellen*, 39.
24 Hugländer, "Aus dem homosexuellen Leben," 47.
25 Chauncey, *Gay New York*, 3.
26 Kolb, *Grundriss der Statistik*, 47–8.
27 This animal magnetism theory appeared in a short document
   enclosed with his CV in a letter from Ulrichs to Board of the Free German

Academy, 19 February 1861. Frankfurt, Freies Deutsches Hochstift/ Frankfurter Goethe-Museum, Mitgliedsakte von Karl Heinrich Ulrichs ff65–9. Translated as letter 62 in Pretsell, The *Correspondence*, 107.

28 In a letter to his relatives of 28 November 1862, Ulrichs noted that "only recently I have picked this thought up again: partly because, strangely, it appears that the feminine bearing of all Uraniers I have observed repeats itself." Translated as letter 82 in Pretsell, *The Correspondence*, 128.

29 Orientation of desire is a running refrain through the first two pamphlets and is initially articulated in the first numbered paragraph in his first pamphlet, where Ulrichs describes the urning solely in terms of the orientation of his desire towards his own sex. Ulrichs, *Vindex*, §1, 1; Lombardi-Nash (tr.), *The Riddle*, vol. 1, 34.

30 Ulrichs, *Inclusa*, §§6–11, 7–12; Lombardi-Nash (tr.), *The Riddle*, vol. 1, 55–8.

31 The converse was also true, and Ulrichs described the urnind/urningin, or same-sex attracted woman, as coming from a female embryo with a male love drive.

32 Ulrichs was not well versed in this literature and apparently only became aware of most of his scientific knowledge and sources "by a scientific authority" on 23 and 26 November 1862, just a few months before he wrote his first books; letter from Ulrichs to his relatives, 28 November 1862. Translated as letter 82 in Pretsell, *The Correspondence*, 127.

33 Ulrichs, *Inclusa*, §38, 29; Lombardi-Nash (tr.), *The Riddle*, vol. 1, 68.

34 Ulrichs, *Inclusa*, §§12–21, 12–19; Lombardi-Nash (tr.), *The Riddle*, vol. 1, 58–62.

35 Ulrichs, *Inclusa*, §§18–19, 16–18; Lombardi-Nash (tr.), *The Riddle*, vol. 1, 60–1.

36 This is also the shorthand term Klaus Müller used in German. Müller, *Aber in meinem Herzen*, 129.

37 The "anima muliebris virili corpore inclusa" has been taken by some to suggest that Ulrichs is more relevant to trans than to gay history. For a thorough examination of Ulrichs's theorizing of sexuality and gender non-conformity and his use of trans and intersex examples to describe the urning, see chapter 2 in Joyce, *LGBT Victorians*, 71–109.

38 Krafft-Ebing, "Die conträre Sexualempfindung," 46; English translation in Pretsell, *Queer Voices*, 59.

39 It may seem pre-emptive to refer to these men as "urnings" in the period before Ulrichs published his first books. However, in a letter to his uncle Ulrichs refers to this small group of six men several times, mentioning that he had discussed all his ideas with them and that several of them "considered publication to be absolutely necessary." This group can therefore be seen as Ulrichs's first "urning followers." Letter from Ulrichs to his maternal uncle, Pastor Otto Ülzen, 12 December 1862. Translated as letter 85 in Pretsell, *The Correspondence*, 136.

40 Ulrichs, *Formatrix*, §81, 37; Lombardi-Nash (tr.), *The Riddle*, vol. 1, 161.

41 Ulrichs, *Memnon, Abtheilung I*, §14, 10; Lombardi-Nash (tr.), *The Riddle*, vol. 1, 306.

42 Ulrichs also postulated, as he had done in each version of his theories, that the diverse categories of the male urning were replicated in reverse for the female "urningin" (lesbian) (Ulrichs, *Memnon, Abtheilung II*, §148, xxv; Lombardi-Nash (tr.), *The Riddle*, vol. 2, 365). He also gave names to men who have sex with men only because of situations where women are not available (uraniaster), as well as to urning men who are forced into conventional marriages (virilized urnings) (Ulrichs, *Memnon, Abtheilung II*, §81, 61–2; Lombardi-Nash (tr.), *The Riddle*, vol. 2, 381). The final category he included in the urning taxonomy was people with a type of intersex variation. (Ulrichs, *Memnon, Abtheilung II*, §101, 85; Lombardi-Nash (tr.), *The Riddle*, vol. 2, 398–9).

43 Goldstein, "Organizing and Arguing Sex and Gender," 61.

44 Foucault, *The History of Sexuality*, vol. 1, 43.

45 Martin, Gutman, and Hutton, eds., *Technologies of the Self*, 19.

46 Muñoz, *Cruising Utopia*, 64.

47 Nancy, *Being Singular Plural*, 28.

48 Ulrichs, *Vindicta*, §57, 25; Lombardi-Nash (tr.), *The Riddle*, vol. 1, 123.

49 "Proto-activism," as opposed to "formal activism," includes forms of personal advocacy that are ad hoc, individual, and not executed to any preconceived plan. Proto-activism refers to the assertive advocacy of individuals and small unincorporated groups who are seeking to change their circumstances. The proto-activist urge is an inevitable and necessary foregrounder to more formal arrangement of activist groups.

50 Chauncey, *Gay New York*, 5.

51 More recently, in the third decade of the twenty-first century, that scaffold has arguably started to crumble as a result of more fluid conceptions of queerness.

52 Leck, *Vita Sexualis*, xvi.

53 Karl Zastrow did publicly admit to his urning nature in the 1860s (see chapter 3).

54 Ulrichs, *Ara Spei*, xxii; Lombardi-Nash (tr.), *The Riddle*, vol. 1, 192.

55 Principal among these was Hugo Friedlander, who pseudonymously wrote a historical overview of five decades of queer Berlin. Hugländer, "Aus dem homosexuellen Leben"

56 Müller, *Aber in meinem Herzen*, 231.

57 The first five types comprise the individuals who responded to Ulrichs's call and were most committed to the urning identity. Types 6 and 7 were individuals in the larger cities who had found their own identities independently prior to Ulrichs's intervention and did not necessarily warm to his efforts. Finally, the last two types were distally related to the urning

in that they either transacted sex with urnings or preyed on them as a source of income.

58 Letter from Ulrichs to his maternal uncle, Pastor Otto Ülzen, 12 December 1862. Ulrichs, "Vier Briefe." Translated as letter 85 in Pretsell, *The Correspondence*, 136.

59 In the twentieth century, Magnus Hirschfeld recategorized them as individuals with *seelischen Transsexualismus* (mental transsexualism). Hirschfeld, "Die intersexuelle Konstitution," 14.

60 Ulrichs, *Prometheus*, §64, 71–2; Lombardi-Nash (tr.), *The Riddle*, vol. 2, 592–3.

61 Ulrichs introduced the letter as coming from "a Berlin man of knowledge, society and experience." This letter possibly came from the writer and publisher Adolf Glaser (see chapter 7). Letter from a Berlin man of knowledge, of society and experience, to Ulrichs, July 1878. Ulrichs, *Critische Pfeile*, §57, 39; Lombardi-Nash (tr.), *The Riddle*, vol. 2, 651. Letter 213 in Pretsell, *The Correspondence*, 247.

62 Ulrichs, *Memnon, Abtheilung I*, §38, 24, 24n24; Lombardi-Nash (tr.), *The Riddle*, vol. 1, 316, 316n108.

63 It may also have been a relief for some women that they no longer felt obligated to have sex with their husbands. That was the case with Catherine, the wife of John Addington Symonds (see chapter 8). In 1890, one of Krafft-Ebing's patients came to a remarkable accommodation with his wife: "The patient recently confessed the true facts to his wife. She pitied him and urged him to seek medical advice, partly because she feared that the projected abstinence from sexual intercourse with persons of his own sex could come to harm her husband. The patient appeared again for a medical consultation with his beautiful wife, who spoke of her husband's suffering with the greatest sympathy, emphasized the hopelessness of treatment and declared that she would continue to live with him in harmony under the present conditions. She would not come to tease him with his 'man-loves' in the future." Krafft-Ebing, *Psychopathia Sexualis*, 5th ed., 154.

64 Abrams, "Crime against Marriage?," 120.

65 Cocks, *Nameless Offences*, 78.

66 Garber, *Vested Interests*, 10.

67 Symonds, *Soldier Love*, 9; Ulrichs, *Ara Spei*, §135, 71; Lombardi-Nash (tr.), *The Riddle*, vol. 1, 241.

68 Symonds, *Soldier Love*, 9–10.

69 Ulrichs, *Critische Pfeile*, §§75–85, 50–62; Lombardi-Nash (tr.), *The Riddle*, vol. 2, 658–66.

70 Ulrichs, *Argonauticus*, §64(b), 117; Lombardi-Nash (tr.), *The Riddle*, vol. 2, 523.

3. Two Trials: Sensation, Horror, and the Urning in the Public Sphere, 1867–1870

1 Hirschfeld, *Memoir*, 26.
2 Spector, *Violent Sensations*, 4.
3 The city of Bremen itself had 67,217 citizens in 1862. Kolb, *Grundriss der Statistik*, 61.
4 Vick, "Liberalism," 551.
5 Hull, *Sexuality, State and Civil Society*, 62.
6 Ulrichs, *Memnon, Abtheilung II*, §118(1), 108–9; Lombardi-Nash (tr.), *The Riddle*, vol. 2, 415.
7 "Theater in Zürich," *Neue Zürcher Zeitung*.
8 Fricke, "Der Theater-Direktor Friedrich Feldmann," 103; Germany, *Select Births and Baptisms, 1558–1898*: Bremen, Germany, 26 January 1834, FELDTMANN, Friedrich Conrad Anton, FHL Film Number – 1344155, ancestry.com.au.
9 Fricke, "Der Theater- Direktor Friedrich Feldmann," 103.
10 Schmidt, *25 Jahre*, iii–iv.
11 Roeder, *Theaterkalendar auf das Jahr 1865*, 164–6.
12 Schmidt, *25 Jahre*, 327–32.
13 Schmidt, *25 Jahre*, 329–30.
14 Ulrichs quoted from only one Bremen individual, and it is possible that this was Feldtmann. Over three letters in October and November 1864 the Bremen correspondent, who was described as a mannling, recounted his discovery of a naive young effeminate urning, whom he took as a lover before discarding him on discovering infidelity. Letter from a mannling to Ulrichs, 1 October 1864. Ulrichs, *Formatrix*, §117, 60–1; Lombardi-Nash (tr.) *The Riddle* vol. 1, 176. Letter 108 in Douglas Pretsell, *The Correspondence*, 155.
15 Hugländer, "Aus dem homosexuellen Leben," 53.
16 Filsinger's name appears for only one season at the City Theatre: the summer season of 1867. Schmidt, *25 Jahre*, 326.
17 The details in this description are taken from Ulrichs's account and also from an arrest warrant issued on 18 October 1867. The two accounts contradict each other on several points – his build and the colour of his hair. For these, Ulrichs's description is used. Ulrichs, *Argonauticus*, §64(c), 118–19; Lombardi-Nash (tr.), *The Riddle*, vol. 2, 523; Schlodtmann, Steckbrief, Filsinger 18 October 1867, Der Wächter. *Polizeiblatt für Norddeutschland*, Schwerin, 30/81 (23 October 1867), 319.
18 Ulrichs, *Argonauticus*, §64(c), 117; Lombardi-Nash (tr.), *The Riddle*, vol. 2, 523.
19 The currency in Bremen at this time was the Bremen Thaler (Bremen dollar).

20 Letter refusing Feldtmann's appeal, 10 September 1868, Staatsarchiv Bremen 2-D.17.d.10, my translation.

21 Ulrichs, *Memnon, Abtheilung II*, §118, 110; Lombardi-Nash (tr.), *The Riddle*, vol. 2, 416.

22 Ulrichs, *Memnon, Abtheilung I*, §69, 48; Lombardi-Nash (tr.), *The Riddle*, vol. 1, 331.

23 Ulrichs, *Memnon, Abtheilung I*, 48n46; Lombardi-Nash (tr.), *The Riddle*, vol. 1, 331n130.

24 Schlodtmann, Der Wächter, 319.

25 Ulrichs, *Memnon, Abtheilung I*, §69, 48; Lombardi-Nash (tr.), *The Riddle*, vol. 1, 331.

26 This is the reason why *Memnon* ended up being published in two parts. Ulrichs, *Memnon, Abtheilung II*, §114, 101; Lombardi-Nash (tr.), *The Riddle*, vol. 2, 410.

27 Ulrichs, *Memnon, Abtheilung II*, §134(4), 124–5; Lombardi-Nash (tr.), *The Riddle*, vol. 2, 426.

28 Ulrichs, *Memnon, Abtheilung II*, §134(4), 125; Lombardi-Nash (tr.), *The Riddle*, vol. 2, 426.

29 Letter from Dr. Stedler of Bremen to Ulrichs, January 1868. Ulrichs, *Gladius Furens*, 26n25; Lombardi-Nash (tr.), *The Riddle*, vol. 1, 278n72. Letter 147 in Pretsell, *The Correspondence*, 191.

30 Letter from a dioning to Ulrichs, 21 December 1867. Ulrichs, *Memnon, Abtheilung II*, §118, 110; Lombardi-Nash (tr.), *The Riddle*, vol. 2, 416. Letter 142 in Pretsell, *The Correspondence*, 189.

31 Ulrichs, *Memnon, Abtheilung II*, §114, 101; Lombardi-Nash (tr.), *The Riddle*, vol. 2, 410.

32 Ulrichs, *Memnon, Abtheilung II*, §117, 106; Lombardi-Nash (tr.), *The Riddle*, vol. 2, 414.

33 Ulrichs, *Memnon, Abtheilung II*, §116, 106; Lombardi-Nash (tr.), *The Riddle*, vol. 2, 413.

34 Ulrichs, *Memnon, Abtheilung II*, §114, 101; Lombardi-Nash (tr.), *The Riddle*, vol. 1, 410.

35 Ulrichs, *Memnon, Abtheilung II*, §114, 101–2; Lombardi-Nash (tr.), *The Riddle*, vol. 2, 410–11.

36 Hull, *Sexuality, State, and Civil Society*, 357.

37 Novel 77 was a section of Justinian's legal code of the year 538 that sought to punish men who practised "the most disgraceful lusts and act contrary to nature" because these acts caused "cities [to] perish with all their inhabitants." Bailey, *Homosexuality and the Western Christian Tradition*, 73–4.

38 Vick, "Liberalism," 546.

39 See Appendix II to *Gladius Furens*, where Ulrichs writes approvingly of both these legal philosophers. Ulrichs, *Gladius Furens*, 19–26; Lombardi-Nash (tr.), *The Riddle*, vol. 1, 274–8.

40 Letter from English urning to Ulrichs (in English), 22 March 1868. Ul-
     richs, *Memnon, Abtheilung II*, §130, 119; Lombardi-Nash (tr.), *The Riddle*,
     vol. 2, 422. Letter 152 in Pretsell, *The Correspondence*, 195–6.

41 In a letter sent by Heinrich Ellinghausen and Carl Rohde to the Bremen
     Senate on 2 November 1868 and quoted in Fricke, "Der Theater-
     Direktor," 104, my translation.

42 Letters from Ulrichs with appeals for clemency on 17 June 1868 and 13
     November. Staatsarchiv Bremen: 2-D.17.d.10. Translated as letters 163
     and 166 in Pretsell, *The Correspondence*, 206–8, 210–12.

43 Letter of appeal from Friedrich Feldtmann to the Court of Appeal,
     Staatsarchiv Bremen 2-D.17.d.10, my translation.

44 Report from High Court to the Minister of Justice, 8 September 1868,
     Staatsarchiv Bremen 2-D.17.d.10, my translation.

45 Ulrichs, *Argonauticus*, §64(c), 118; Lombardi-Nash (tr.), *The Riddle*, vol. 2,
     523.

46 Ulrichs, *Argonauticus*, §64(c), 118; Lombardi-Nash (tr.), *The Riddle*, vol. 2,
     523.

47 Ulrichs, *Argonauticus*, §77, 153; Lombardi-Nash (tr.), *The Riddle*, vol. 2, 539.

48 Ulrichs, *Argonauticus*, §64(c), 119; Lombardi-Nash (tr.), *The Riddle*, vol. 2, 523.

49 It would be several decades before the police turned their attention to the
     blackmailers rather than their victims. See chapter 7 for the first attempt
     to bring this about.

50 The population had increased from 547,541 in 1861 to 702,437 in 1867 and
     was 826,341 by 1871. "Statistik und Sehenswürdigkeiten von Berlin," in
     Berliner Adreßbuch, 183.

51 Liman, *Practisches Handbuch*, 204–6.

52 Dobler, *Zwischen Duldungspolitik*, 127.

53 Hugländer, "Aus dem homosexuellen Leben," 48.

54 Dobler, *Zwischen Duldungspolitik*, 130.

55 *Berliner Gerichtszeitung*, 19 January 1869, 17 Jg. Nr 7, 2.

56 Dobler, *Zwischen Duldungspolitik*, 131.

57 Dobler, *Zwischen Duldungspolitik*, 133.

58 Hugo Friedländer reported that even though he had been sued for sub-
     stantial amounts, he still had an estate of 60,000 thalers when he died.
     Hugländer, "Aus dem homosexuellen Leben," 52.

59 Hugländer, "Aus dem homosexuellen Leben," 48.

60 Ulrichs, *Argonauticus*, §4, 10; Lombardi-Nash (tr.), *The Riddle*, vol. 2, 476.

61 Hugländer, "Aus dem homosexuellen Leben," 53, 54.

62 Hugländer, "Aus dem homosexuellen Leben," 54.

63 Ulrichs, *Argonauticus*, §5, 12–13; Lombardi-Nash (tr.), *The Riddle*, vol. 2, 477.

64 Ulrichs's first public protest took place in 1867, which would have been
     after Zastrow's acknowledgment of his nature. However, Ulrichs dis-
     cussed his own sexual nature at length with his family by letter and in

person in 1862 and with his friend August Tewes at the same time. It is
probable that he was reasonably open about it among friends.

65 Dobler, *Zwischen Duldungspolitik*, 128; Ulrichs, *Argonauticus*, §5, 11–12;
Lombardi-Nash (tr.), *The Riddle*, vol. 2, 477.

66 Dobler, *Zwischen Duldungspolitik*, 128.

67 Dobler, *Zwischen Duldungspolitik*, 129.

68 There is some uncertainty in the literature over the date of the arrest. Ulrichs does not date the arrest, but his account makes it sound as if it happened on the same day as the assault, 17 January. Ulrichs, *Argonauticus*,
§65, 122; Lombardi-Nash (tr.), *The Riddle*, vol. 2, 526. Herzer places the
arrest as happening on the 18th. Herzer, "Zastrow–Ulrichs–Kertbeny,"
61. Both these accounts drew mainly on press reports. Dobler, however,
places the date as 20 January, and since he was drawing on Berlin police
records, it is most likely to be accurate. Dobler, *Zwischen Duldungspolitik*,
133.

69 Müller was rewarded with 50 thalers for his testimony, but Zastrow
claimed at the trial that he had had a sexual encounter with Müller, and
this was an act of revenge. Dobler, *Zwischen Duldungspolitik*, 132–3.

70 Herzer, "Zastrow–Ulrichs–Kertbeny," 64.

71 Zastrow had an extremely tight foreskin (phimosis) and would not have
been able to penetrate without causing himself injury. There was no evidence of foreskin injury. Liman, *Practisches Handbuch*, 207.

72 Kennedy, *Karl Heinrich Ulrichs*, 145.

73 Ulrichs, *Incubus*, 87; Lombardi-Nash (tr.), *The Riddle*, vol. 2, 469.

74 Ulrichs, *Incubus*, 88; Lombardi-Nash (tr.), *The Riddle*, vol. 2, 469.

75 *Börsenzeitung*, 20 February 1869. Cited in Ulrichs, *Argonauticus*, §5, 12;
Lombardi-Nash (tr.), *The Riddle*, vol. 2, 477.

76 Ulrichs, *Incubus*, 27; Lombardi-Nash (tr.), *The Riddle*, vol. 2, 444.

77 Spector, *Violent Sensations*, 101.

78 Ulrichs, *Incubus*, 49; Lombardi-Nash (tr.), *The Riddle*, vol. 2, 453.

79 Kennedy, *Karl Heinrich Ulrichs*, 148.

80 Kennedy, *Karl Heinrich Ulrichs*, 144.

81 Notes written by Ulrichs on 3 September 1872 from Stuttgart on the back
of a proof copy of *Argonauticus*. Sigusch, "Unbekanntes aus dem
Nachlaß," 250, my translation.

82 Herzer, "Zastrow–Ulrichs–Kertbeny," 71–2.

83 Karl Maria Kertbeny, unpublished assorted papers, Hungary, National
Széchényi Library, Manuscript Collection, Oct. Germ. 296 ff371–6, ff377–
87; Oct. Germ. 297, ff440–443.

84 Ulrichs, *Argonauticus*, §65, 120; Lombardi-Nash (tr.), *The Riddle*, vol. 2, 525.

85 *Berliner Gerichtszeitung*, 6 July 1869, 17 Jg. Nr 76, 1–2.

86 Dobler, *Zwischen Duldungspolitik*, 135.

87 Dobler, *Zwischen Duldungspolitik*, 135.

88 *Berliner Gerichtszeitung*, 30 October 1869, 17 Jg. Nr 126, 1.

89 On the next day of the trial, Police Lieutenant von Stutterheim claimed that this person was not known to be an urning. Dobler, *Zwischen Duldungspolitik*, 137.

90 Hugländer, "Aus dem homosexuellen Leben," 52, my translation.

91 Marhoefer, *Racism and the Making of Gay Rights*, 30.

92 Hirschfeld, *The Homosexuality of Men and Women*, 1073.

93 Notably, Manfred Herzer, uniquely among historians of the period, does not see the trial as a significant factor. Herzer, "Zastrow–Ulrichs–Kertbeny," 62.

94 Dobler, *Zwischen Duldungspolitik*, 120.

95 Cited in Dobler, *Zwischen Duldungspolitik*, 121, my translation.

96 Ulrichs, *Critische Pfeile*, §107, 76; Lombardi-Nash (tr.), *The Riddle*, vol. 2, 674.

97 Ulrichs, *Critische Pfeile*, §107, 76; Lombardi-Nash (tr.), *The Riddle*, vol. 2, 674.

98 Kennedy, *Karl Heinrich Ulrichs*, 191.

99 Dobler, *Zwischen Duldungspolitik*, 132–3.

100 Dobler, *Zwischen Duldungspolitik*, 137.

101 Hugländer, "Aus dem homosexuellen Leben," 52.

102 "Theater," in *Neue Zürcher Zeitung* 31 December 1874, Nr 633, 5.

103 "Feuilleton 1878: Theater," *Neue Zürcher Zeitung*, 1 June 1878, Nr 252, 1–2.

104 Berlin, Germany, Deaths, 1874–1955: FELDTMANN, Friederich Conrad Anton, 12 February 1884, Pankow, Berlin, Certificate number 11, Erstregister C, ancestry.com.

105 Notes written by Ulrichs on 3 September 1872 from Stuttgart on the back of a proof copy of *Argonauticus*. Sigusch, "Unbekanntes," 250, my translation.

4. Sins of the City: Karl Maria Kertbeny and the Social Cross-Dressers, 1865–1880

1 Ulrichs, *Memnon, Abtheilung II*, §114, xx; Lombardi-Nash (tr.), *The Riddle*, vol. 2, 362.

2 Ulrichs had several masculine and cross-dressing close supporters. For example, Carl Robert Egells, an enthusiastic correspondent of Ulrichs who was in contact with activists in the Scientific Humanitarian Committee late in his life, considered himself to be a mannling. Eduard Fridolin Schöllhorn, whose alter ego was the "Marquise de Pompadour," was a close colleague of Ulrichs in Stuttgart in the 1870s.

3 Letter from Ulrichs to Carl Robert Egells, 20–1 December 1873, quoted in Ferdinand Karsch-Haack, 1922. Carl Heinrich Ulrichs, *Die Freundschaft*, 29, 4, 20 May. Translated as letter 200 in Douglas Pretsell, *The*

Correspondence, 236. Ulrichs used the terms *Partei des Mops* and *Mopspartie*, both of which literally mean "party of pug dogs." It is likely that this was a reference to an old saying: "Was kümmert es den Mond wenn der Mops ihn anbellt" (Does the moon really care if a pug barks at it?). In other words, one disregards the grumbling, complaining, and criticism of a person as equal to a (small-minded) dog's barking at the moon. Ulrichs saw the *Mopspartei* in that way, always "barking" about something or other. The clause that follows this said that he did not wish to be portrayed as the *Mond* ("ohne gerade Mond sein zu wollen" [without portraying myself as the moon right now]).

4 Letter from Ulrichs to Carl Robert Egells, 31 January–1 February 1874, quoted in Ferdinand Karsch-Haack, 1922. Carl Heinrich Ulrichs, *Die Freundschaft*, 29, 4, 20 May. Translated as letter 202 in Pretsell, *The Correspondence*, 237.

5 Ulrichs, *Prometheus*, §64, 71; Lombardi-Nash (tr.), *The Riddle*, vol. 2, 592.

6 Ulrichs, *Prometheus*, §64, 71; Lombardi-Nash (tr.), *The Riddle*, vol. 2, 592.

7 Vick, "Liberalism," 578–9.

8 This biographical tangle presents problems for the historian. Manfred Herzer charted the most definitive account of Kertbeny's life in several papers and books, which have been used in this section.

9 Herzer, "Kertbeny and the Nameless Love," 3.

10 Herzer, *Karl Maria Kertbeny*, 11–12.

11 Herzer, *Karl Maria Kertbeny*, 15–17.

12 Herzer, *Karl Maria Kertbeny*, 17.

13 Although Kertbeny followed them out of Hungary and presented himself as a nationalist, he was not himself a committed revolutionary. In 1854, while in Vienna, Kertbeny offered his services to the Austrian authorities to spy on the Hungarian diaspora. Joseph von Protmann, Police Commissioner in Pest and Buda and Kertbeny's police handler when he was a spy, characterized him as "an adventurer who does not lack in talent. Cunning and frivolous, with pleasant manners and good mimicry skills." An inability to generate substantive intelligence meant that his career in espionage may not have progressed far. Deák, "Translator, Editor, Publisher, Spy, 30, 32.

14 Between 1855 and 1875, Kertbeny lived a peripatetic life flitting from city to city in southern Germany, Switzerland, France, the Netherlands, and northern Germany. In 1860 he did settle for a couple of years in Geneva, but after that he travelled to Ouchy, Solothurn, and then Paris. After treatment for his eyesight in Corsica, he then went to Brussels, where he first wrote to Ulrichs in 1864. Thereafter he was in the Rhineland in 1866, Hanover in 1867, and finally in Berlin from 1868 to 1875. Kertbeny, "Persönliches Schlußwort."

15 Herzer, *Karl Maria Kertbeny*, 18.
16 In the 1860s, Paris (1.7 million), Berlin (1.5 million), and Vienna (0.5 million) were already large cities. Brussels, Hanover, Munich, Geneva, and Pest all had the status of regional capitals with populations between 82,323 (Geneva) and 368,973 (Hannover). Kolb, *Grundriss der Statistik*, 13, 30, 37, 52, 55, 64, 65.
17 Herzer, *Karl Maria Kertbeny*, 25–6.
18 Kertbeny wrote to the editor of an unknown newspaper in July 1869 offering his views on the Zastrow trial and signed the letter "Normal Sexualer." Kertbeny, unpublished assorted papers, Budapest, National Széchényi Library, Manuscript Collection, Oct. Germ. 297, documents 440–3. The story about how he, as a – "normalsexual," took an interest in writing about homosexuality because of the suicide of a friend was contained in a passage written by Kertbeny that Gustav Jäger published after his death. Jäger, "Ein bisher ungedrucktes Kapitel,'" 58–60.
19 In his German diaries, Kertbeny wrote in Hungarian note form for all the things he wished to keep hidden. A full listing of the instances when a Hungarian note indicated sexual activity can be found in Takács, "The Double Life of Kertbeny," 33–4.
20 Spector, *Violent Sensations*, 97.
21 Kertbeny, *Silhouetten und Reliquien*, 236. A quotation from this passage can be found in Herzer, *Karl Maria Kertbeny*, 29.
22 Kertbeny, *Silhouetten und Reliquien*, 10. A quotation from this passage can be found in Herzer, *Karl Maria Kertbeny*, 30.
23 Kertbeny, *Erinnerung an Charles Sealsfield*, 74, my translation.
24 This was written in the summer of 1864 but published in early 1865. Ulrichs, *Formatrix*, vii; Lombardi-Nash (tr.), *The Riddle*, vol. 1, 130.
25 A record of each letter can be found in Kertbeny's private diaries held at the National Széchényi Library, Budapest. The majority were sent and received between June 1864 and December 1866, with the final record of contact on 21 October 1868. Kertbeny sent thirty-seven letters to Ulrichs and received in return only sixteen. Feray, Herzer, and Peppel, "Homosexual Studies," 28.
26 Herzer, *Karl Maria Kertbeny*, 32–3.
27 Ulrichs wrote, "Incidentally, I am on a very friendly footing with him. He also pays me an annual Numa penny; he would help me and certainly help others wherever and however he could." Letter from Ulrichs to Carl Robert Egells, 31 January–1 February 1874, quoted in Ferdinand Karsch-Haack, 1922. Carl Heinrich Ulrichs, *Die Freundschaft*, 29, 4, 20 May. Translated as letter 202 in Pretsell, *The Correspondence*, 237.
28 This was the first time the two words appeared. Kertbeny used "homosexual" in his published works on the subject. However, other than this one

instance of him using the word "heterosexual," he used "normalsexual" instead in his published works. Draft letter, Kertbeny to Ulrichs, 6 May 1868. Budapest, National Széchényi Library, Manuscript Collection, Oct. Germ. 302, ff225–7. Translated as letter 160 in Pretsell, *The Correspondence*, 202.

29 See, for example, Kant's 1795 discussion on moral philosophy: "Zweytens gehört zu den Criminibus carnis contra naturam die Gemeinschaft des sexus homogenii, wenn der Gegenstand der Geschlechts-Neigung zwar unter den Menschen bleibt, aber verändert wird, wo die Gemeinschaft des sexus nicht heterogen, sondern homogen ist, d. i. wenn ein Weib gegen ein Weib, und ein Mann gegen einen Mann seine Neigung befriediget." (Secondly, to the *criminibus carnis contra natur*am belongs the community of *sexus homogenii*, when the object of sexual inclination remains among men, but is changed, where the community of *sexu*s is not heterogeneous, but homogeneous, that is, when a woman satisfies her inclination against a woman and a man against a man). Kant, *Gesammelte Schriften*, 391, my translation.

30 Ellis and Symonds, *Sexual Inversion*, 96n1.

31 Draft letter, Kertbeny to Ulrichs, 6 May 1868. Budapest, National Széchényi Library, Manuscript Collection, Oct. Germ. 302, ff225–7. Translated as letter 160 in Pretsell, *The Correspondence*, 203.

32 Draft letter, Kertbeny to Ulrichs, 6 May 1868. Budapest, National Széchényi Library, Manuscript Collection, Oct. Germ. 302, ff225–7. Translated as letter 160 in Pretsell, *The Correspondence*, 204.

33 Draft letter, Kertbeny to Ulrichs, 6 May 1868. Budapest, National Széchényi Library, Manuscript Collection, Oct. Germ. 302, ff225–7. Translated as letter 160 in Pretsell, *The Correspondence*, 204.

34 Sedgwick, *Epistemology of the Closet*, 86.

35 Draft letter, Kertbeny to Ulrichs, 6 May 1868. Budapest, National Széchényi Library, Manuscript Collection, Oct. Germ. 302, ff225–7. Translated as letter 160 in Pretsell, *The Correspondence*, 204.

36 The legal philosopher Montesquieu is principal among these, although Nicolas de Condorcet and Anacharsis Cloots made similar arguments.

37 Draft letter, Kertbeny to Ulrichs, 6 May 1868. Budapest, National Széchényi Library, Manuscript Collection, Oct. Germ. 302, ff225–7. Translated as letter 160 in Pretsell, *The Correspondence*, 202.

38 This is almost certainly a reference to Martin Luther's ninety-five theses at the time of the German Reformation. Draft letter, Kertbeny to Ulrichs, 6 May 1868. Budapest, National Széchényi Library, Manuscript Collection, Oct. Germ. 302, ff225–7. Translated as letter 160 in Pretsell, *The Correspondence*, 204.

39 Draft letter, Kertbeny to Ulrichs, 6 May 1868. Budapest, National Széchényi Library, Manuscript Collection, Oct. Germ. 302, ff225–7. Translated as letter 160 in Pretsell, *The Correspondence*, 204.

40 In the bibliography, he lists the following: "77. Sexualitäts Studien. Psychologische Untersuchung über Nachtseiten des Geschlechtstriebes bei Mann und Weib, 340S." This, and a second listing of unpublished manuscripts in 1873, are the only two places that Kertbeny's name appeared in connection with any "sexuality studies" in print. Karl Maria Kertbeny, "Bibliografie der Werke, publizirt von K.M. Kertbeny, 1846–1866," in Kertbeny, *Hundertsechsig Lyrische Dichtungen*, 240.

41 Feray, Herzer, and Peppel, "Homosexual Studies," 29–30.

42 Kertbeny, *§143 des preussischen Strafgesetzbuches*; Kertbeny, *Das Gemeinschädliche*. The texts of both these publications have been reproduced in facsimile in Herzer, *Karl Maria Kertbeny*, 63–150, 151–229.

43 Kertbeny, *§143 des preussischen Strafgesetzbuches*, 20, reproduced in facsimile in Herzer, *Karl Maria Kertbeny*, 82.

44 Kertbeny, *§143 des preussischen Strafgesetzbuches*, 21, reproduced in facsimile in Herzer, *Karl Maria Kertbeny*, 83.

45 Hirschfeld, "Vorbemerkung des Herausgebers," I.

46 In a letter from the publisher Hermann Serbe to Kertbeny dated 7 January 1870, Serbe indicated that there would be no interest in a second edition. Herzer believed this was because the first editions had been financial failures. Herzer, *Karl Maria Kertbeny*, 35.

47 Sontag, "Drei Bemerkungen zu dem Entwurf," 26; see also Herzer, "Kertbeny and the Nameless Love," 4. The pamphlets were believed to have been written by Ulrichs and were only publicly acknowledged as Kertbeny's work in 1905 in Hirschfeld, "Vorbemerkung des Herausgebers," 7, no. 1 (1905): I–II.

48 Feray, Herzer, and Peppel, "Homosexual Studies," 31; Karl Maria Kertbeny, unpublished assorted papers, Budapest, National Széchenyi Library, Oct. Germ. 296, pp. 371–6.

49 The Hungarian twin capitals of Buda and Pest were formally united as Budapest in 1873.

50 Kertbeny, "Persönliches Schlußwort," 29–30.

51 Herzer, *Karl Maria Kertbeny*, 45.

52 Herzer, *Karl Maria Kertbeny*, 41.

53 Jäger [Kertbeny], "Ein bisher ungedrucktes Kapitel," 53–125.

54 Jäger [Kertbeny], "Ein bisher ungedrucktes Kapitel," 82, my translation.

55 Kertbeny repeatedly asserted his "normal" sexual instincts throughout the chapter. Jäger, "Ein bisher ungedrucktes Kapitel," 58, 59, 60, 63, 65, 82.

56 Jäger [Kertbeny], "Ein bisher ungedrucktes Kapitel," 58–60.

57 Jäger [Kertbeny], "Ein bisher ungedrucktes Kapitel," 64.

58 Jäger [Kertbeny], "Ein bisher ungedrucktes Kapitel," 69.

59 When Magnus Hirschfeld conducted a questionnaire study of steelworkers and students in 1903, he found a prevalence of between 1.5 and 2 per cent. Hirschfeld, "Das Ergebnis der statistischen Untersuchungen," 151.

Modern estimates of prevalence are fraught with methodological difficulties, but the reported range is between 2 and 10 per cent. Kertbeny's estimate would be at the lower end of these. See ACSF, "AIDS and Sexual Behaviour in France"; Semenyna et al., "Familial Patterning"; Bailey et al., "Sexual Orientation."

60 Jäger, "Ein bisher ungedrucktes Kapitel," 70–1.
61 Jäger,"Ein bisher ungedrucktes Kapitel," 72, my translation.
62 Jäger, "Ein bisher ungedrucktes Kapitel," 116.
63 Jäger,"Ein bisher ungedrucktes Kapitel," 118.
64 Jäger,"Ein bisher ungedrucktes Kapitel," 65.
65 Jäger,"Ein bisher ungedrucktes Kapitel," 97. Kertbeny did not write what the sexual practices of the remaining 8 to 9 per cent were.
66 While sodomy has an obvious separation between active and passive, this is less clear with mutual masturbation. According to Kertbeny, there was always an age disparity between mutuals: one was more active and assertive while the other was passive and effeminate. Jäger,"Ein bisher ungedrucktes Kapitel," 93.
67 Jäger,"Ein bisher ungedrucktes Kapitel," 102, 106–7.
68 There is absolutely no way to corroborate this, but Kertbeny's valorizing of the masculine active "pygist" prompts the question: Was this the preferred sexual practice of his own younger years?
69 The isolated urning was one of the character types described in chapter 2.
70 Jäger,"Ein bisher ungedrucktes Kapitel," 103–5.
71 Jäger,"Ein bisher ungedrucktes Kapitel," 110.
72 Jäger,"Ein bisher ungedrucktes Kapitel," 110–11.
73 Jäger,"Ein bisher ungedrucktes Kapitel," 66.
74 Jäger,"Ein bisher ungedrucktes Kapitel," 62–3, my translation.
75 Jäger,"Ein bisher ungedrucktes Kapitel," 83.
76 Spector, *Violent Sensations*, 98.
77 Friedlaender, *Die Renaissance des Eros Uranios*.
78 Krafft-Ebing, *Psychopathia Sexualis*, 2nd ed., 88; English translation can be found in Pretsell, *Queer Voices*, 132.
79 Krafft-Ebing, *Psychopathia Sexualis*, 4th ed.
80 In the first edition, he used various forms of the word "homosexual" 234 times and the word "urning" 753 times. By the third edition at the end of the decade, he was using various forms of the word "homosexual" (1,669 times) and "urning" (696) times. See Moll, *Die conträre Sexualempfindung*; and Moll, *Die conträre Sexualempfindung*, 3rd ed.
81 Herzer, "Kertbeny and the Nameless Love," 16.
82 Cocks, *Nameless Offences*, 78.
83 Bray, *Homosexuality in Renaissance England*, 88.
84 Cocks, *Nameless Offences*, 96.

85 Letter to Ulrichs from an urning in Petersburg, 9 November 1869. Ulrichs, *Prometheus*, §62(m), 67; Lombardi-Nash (tr.), *The Riddle*, vol. 2, 588–9. Letter 182 in Pretsell, *The Correspondence*, 222.

86 Cocks, *Nameless Offences*, 114.

87 Ulrichs, *Memnon, Abtheilung II*, §92, 69; Lombardi-Nash (tr.), *The Riddle*, vol. 2, 387.

88 Letter to Ulrichs from an intermediate urning in London, 1868. Ulrichs, *Memnon, Abtheilung II*, §97, 76; Lombardi-Nash (tr.), *The Riddle*, vol. 2, 392. Letter 149 in Pretsell, *The Correspondence*, 193.

89 Ulrichs, *Memnon, Abtheilung II*, §97, 75; Lombardi-Nash (tr.), *The Riddle*, vol. 2, 391.

90 Mapleson, *Memoirs*, 109.

91 Mapleson, *Memoirs*, 117.

92 "MUSIC – Beethoven's *Fidelio*," *London Illustrated News*, 2 May 1868, 20.

93 Ulrichs, *Memnon, Abtheilung I*, §15, 11; Lombardi-Nash (tr.), *The Riddle*, vol. 1, 307.

94 "POLICE INTELLIGENCE – This day, Marlborough-Street," *Sun*, Evening, 18 October 1867, 7.

95 Thomas Ernest "Stella" Boulton had been arrested twice in similar confrontations at the same location while cross-dressing that same summer. McKenna, *Fanny and Stella*, 102–5.

96 "POLICE INTELLIGENCE – This day, Marlborough-Street," *Sun*, Evening, 18 October 1867, 7.

97 Ulrichs, *Memnon, Abtheilung I*, §15, 11–12; Lombardi-Nash (tr.), *The Riddle*, vol. 1, 307.

98 Letter to Ulrichs from an intermediate urning in London, 12 January 1868. Ulrichs, *Memnon, Abtheilung II*, §97, 75; Lombardi-Nash (tr.), *The Riddle*, vol. 2, 392. Letter 149 in Pretsell, *The Correspondence*, 192.

99 Letter to Ulrichs from an intermediate urning in London, 12 January 1868. Ulrichs, *Memnon, Abtheilung II*, §97, 75–6; Lombardi-Nash (tr.), *The Riddle*, vol. 2, 392. Letter 149 in Pretsell, *The Correspondence*, 192–3.

100 Letter to Ulrichs from an intermediate urning in London, 12 January 1868. Ulrichs, *Memnon, Abtheilung II*, §97, 74–5; Lombardi-Nash (tr.), *The Riddle*, vol. 2, 391–2. Letter 149 in Pretsell, The *Correspondence*, 192.

101 Letter to Ulrichs from an intermediate urning in London, 22 March 1868. Ulrichs, *Memnon, Abtheilung II*, §97, 77; Lombardi-Nash (tr.), *The Riddle*, vol. 2, 393. Letter 149 in Pretsell, *The Correspondence*, 194.

102 Letter to Ulrichs from an intermediate urning in London, 22 March 1868. Ulrichs, *Memnon, Abtheilung II*, §97, 76; Lombardi-Nash (tr.), *The Riddle*, vol. 2, 392–3. Letter 149 in Pretsell, *The Correspondence*, 193.

103 McKenna, *Fanny and Stella*, 10.

104 Letter to Ulrichs from an intermediate urning in London, 22 March 1868. Ulrichs, *Memnon, Abtheilung II*, §97, 77; Lombardi-Nash (tr.), *The Riddle*, vol. 2, 393. Letter 149 in Pretsell, *The Correspondence*, 194.

105 A costume ball arranged by a Polish count in a restaurant involved ten soldiers and a number of urnings, six of whom were dressed as women. It ended ignominiously in a brawl between the drunken soldiers and the musicians. Letter to Ulrichs from a weibling in Berlin, 23 February 1868. Ulrichs, *Memnon, Abtheilung II*, §98, 77–8; Lombardi-Nash (tr.), *The Riddle*, vol. 2, 394. Letter 151 in Pretsell, *The Correspondence*, 195.

106 In 1864 a Liberal Party politician in the Austrian Parliament, Carl Giskra, requested that Ulrichs send him a suggestion for reform to the Austrian penal legislation, which he did. Ulrichs, *Formatrix*, xiv-xv; Lombardi-Nash (tr.), *The Riddle*, vol. 1, 133–4. There is no record of what became of Ulrichs's reform suggestion, but on 26 June 1867, the Austrian Justice Minister, Emanuel Heinrich Komers von Lindenbach, introduced a new modernized criminal code to the Imperial Diet with the following words: "The imperial government has attentively followed the investigations of science. The results of these investigations have been applied in this draft of the law." Ulrichs, *Memnon, Abtheilung I*, §70, 48; Lombardi-Nash (tr.), *The Riddle*, vol. 1, 332. The new criminal code had no antisodomy statute, which meant that if ratified, it would have decriminalized same-sex sexual acts. Ulrichs had received a draft copy of the new criminal code and had high hopes that the proposed Austrian reform would succeed and that this would have a positive impact on other German-speaking states. The new criminal code entered committee stage in the Imperial Diet, where it could be examined in detail and amended as appropriate.

107 Ulrichs went on, "The draft of the law concerning the abolition was issued by Minister of Justice v. Komers. The 'parliamentary' Minister of Justice Herbst appears to want to make significant revisions. He has set the year 1870 as the actual enforcement date of the new penal code!" Ulrichs, *Memnon, Abtheilung II*, §134, 123; Lombardi-Nash (tr.), *The Riddle*, vol. 2, 424.

108 Letter sent to Ulrichs from a twenty-eight-year-old weibling in Vienna, 9 April 1868. Ulrichs, *Memnon, Abtheilung II*, §§99–100, 78–84; Lombardi-Nash (tr.), *The Riddle*, vol. 2, 394–7. Letter 141 in Pretsell, *The Correspondence*, 185–9.

109 Brunner and Sulzenbacher, "Donauwalzer," 39.

110 Letter sent to Ulrichs from a twenty-eight-year-old weibling in Vienna, 9 April 1868. Ulrichs, *Memnon, Abtheilung II*, §99, 79–80; Lombardi-Nash (tr.), *The Riddle*, vol. 2, 395. Letter 141 in Pretsell, *The Correspondence*, 187.

111 Letter sent to Ulrichs from a twenty-eight-year-old weibling in Vienna, 9 April 1868. Ulrichs, *Memnon, Abtheilung II*, §100, 82; Lombardi-Nash (tr.), *The Riddle*, vol. 2, 397. Letter 141 in Pretsell, *The Correspondence*, 189.

112 Letter sent to Ulrichs from a twenty-eight-year-old weibling in Vienna, 9 April 1868. Ulrichs, *Memnon, Abtheilung II*, §100, 83; Lombardi-Nash (tr.), *The Riddle*, vol. 2, 397. Letter 141 in Pretsell, *The Correspondence*, 189.

113 Letter sent to Ulrichs from a twenty-eight-year-old weibling in Vienna, 9 April 1868. Ulrichs, *Memnon, Abtheilung II*, §99, 80; §100, 82–3; Lombardi-Nash (tr.), *The Riddle*, vol. 2, 395, 397. Letter 141 in Pretsell, *The Correspondence*, 187, 189.

114 The parenthetical information in this quote is Ulrichs's interpolation. Letter sent to Ulrichs from a twenty-eight-year-old weibling in Vienna, 9 April 1868. Ulrichs, *Memnon, Abtheilung II*, §99, 80; Lombardi-Nash (tr.), *The Riddle*, vol. 2, 395. Letter 141 in Pretsell, *The Correspondence*, 187.

115 Letter sent to Ulrichs from a twenty-eight-year-old weibling in Vienna, 9 April 1868. Ulrichs, *Memnon, Abtheilung II*, §99, 80; Lombardi-Nash (tr.), *The Riddle*, vol. 2, 395. Letter 141 in Pretsell, *The Correspondence*, 187–8.

116 Letter sent to Ulrichs from a twenty-eight-year-old weibling in Vienna, 9 April 1868. Ulrichs, *Memnon, Abtheilung II*, §99, 80–1; Lombardi-Nash (tr.), *The Riddle*, vol. 2, 396–7. Letter 141 in Pretsell, *The Correspondence*, 188.

117 Brunner and Sulzenbacher, "Donauwalzer," 30.

118 Ulrichs detailed several cases where blackmail occurred in Vienna, referring to gangs of blackmail rowdies who frequented places where urnings were known to seek assignations, including the City Park. Ulrichs, *Argonauticus*, §11, 20–1; Lombardi-Nash (tr.), *The Riddle*, vol. 2, 480.

119 Max Reversi, a contemporary of Archduke Ludwig Viktor, cited in Neuhold, *Das andere Habsburg*, 63, my translation.

120 Roschitz, *Kaiserwalzer*, 146.

121 Neuhold, *Das andere Habsburg*, 120.

122 Neuhold, *Das andere Habsburg*, 140.

123 Neuhold, *Das andere Habsburg*, 67, 109.

124 The words were spoken by Ernest von Körber, who was Austrian prime minister in 1900–4 and 1916. Neuhold, *Das andere Habsburg*, 104, my translation.

125 Neuhold, *Das andere Habsburg*, 101.

126 Neuhold, *Das andere Habsburg*, 102.

127 Neuhold, *Das andere Habsburg*, 111.

128 Neuhold, *Das andere Habsburg*, 110–11.

129 Neuhold, *Das andere Habsburg*, 104.

130 Archduke Ludwig Viktor ultimately had his downfall. His conservative influence over the emperor was not appreciated by younger members of the imperial family. They only had to wait for a scandal that they could exploit. Ludwig Viktor was in the habit, when he was in Vienna, of swimming at the Zentralbad. It seems he got into an argument with a subaltern officer there, who did not recognize the archduke in his swimming costume and slapped him full in the face in response to one of Ludwig

Viktor's sharp remarks. In the ensuing scandal, he was banished to his Castle Klessheim, just outside Salzburg, where he lived out the rest of his days. Neuhold, *Das andere Habsburg*, 158.

131   Neuhold, *Das andere Habsburg*, 92. Ultramontanism was a conservative Catholic position in Austria that positioned the Pope and the Church as more powerful than the emperor.

132   Ulrichs did have some more active allies in the Austrian legal establishment. Ulrichs's close friend and collaborator, August Tewes, was a law professor in Graz and an influential source for intelligence on legal reform in Austria. The Liberal MP Carl Giskra, who requested a reform suggestion from Ulrichs, became the Austrian Interior Minister in 1867. Ulrichs sent him a copy of his book *Gladius Furens* in 1868, but there is no record of any further correspondence. Ulrichs, *Memnon, Abtheilung II*, ix; Lombardi-Nash (tr.), *The Riddle*, vol. 2, 356.

133   Ulrichs, *Araxes*, 30; Lombardi-Nash (tr.), *The Riddle*, vol. 2, 618.

134   Letter from Ulrichs to Carl Robert Egells, 31 January–1 February 1874, quoted in Ferdinand Karsch-Haack, 1922. Carl Heinrich Ulrichs, *Die Freundschaft*, 29, 4, 20 May. Translated as letter 202 in Pretsell, *The Correspondence*, 237.

135   "The date was 24 June 1972. It was not the first gay liberation march (that happened the year before). It was a Gay Liberation Front march. About 50 of us marched to the gay ghetto of Earl's Court to publicise the first UK Gay Pride march, which was planned for 1 July 1972. As our march approached the Coleherne, we were booed and jeered by a couple of dozen drinkers who were gathered on the pavement outside. We then went inside the pub to leaflet about the upcoming Gay Pride march but were forced out by a combination of angry gay customers and bar staff. We had very little support." Peter Tatchell, email message to author, 9 August 2021.

5. The Matchmaker of Switzerland: Jakob Rudolf Forster's Grassroots Activism in Germanic Switzerland, 1878–1897

1   Forster, *Justizmorde*, 17, my translation.

2   Forster, *Justizmorde*.

3   Forster refers to "pamphlets on romantic love" being among possessions confiscated by the police when he was arrested in 1879. Because he also lists the works of Ulrichs and Hössli separately, it appeared that these were pamphlets from another source. He wrote elsewhere about composing and distributing pamphlets denouncing the authorities and defending himself, so it is probable that these romantic love pamphlets were composed and self-published by Forster himself. Forster, *Justizmorde*, 61.

4 According to Forster, a Dr. Weller at St. Pirminsberg asylum encouraged him to write a memoir, possibly for therapeutic purposes, while he was detained there. Forster, *Justizmorde*, 114.

5 The final part of the second section consists of a series of dated statements in which he wrote of his intention to publish but feared the repercussions. Forster, *Justizmorde*, 164–74.

6 Forster does not specify what month he moved to Germany, but one of his contacts, Gottlieb Haab, indicated that Forster was in St. Gallen up to August 1877, at which time he set off for Konstanz and presumably onwards into Germany. *Forsters Liebhaberheft*, Staatsarchiv St. Gallen, KA R. 182–4.

7 Forster, *Justizmorde*, 59; *Forsters Liebhaberheft*, Staatsarchiv St. Gallen, KA R.182–4.

8 Forster, *Justizmorde*, 59, my translation.

9 Forster, *Justizmorde*, 59.

10 The crucial mulberry bushes could grow easily in the southern German states, and a silk manufacturing industry in Württemberg drew on private cultivators. In Ulrichs's case, he probably bred Chinese oak silkworms, which produced a coarse thread suitable for spinning. Ulrichs wrote and published a poem about cultivating silkworms titled "Unterbrochene Häutung" (Interrupted Moulting). Ulrichs, *Auf Bienchens Flügeln*, 119–21. It was confirmed he was making a living from this in a letter from Stuttgart City Director Hofer to State Councillor von Grättner, 29 January 1878. Landesarchiv Baden-Württemberg Akte E 14 (Kgl. Kabinett) Bü 2049.

11 Letter from Stuttgart City Director Hofer to State Councillor von Grättner, 29 January 1878. Landesarchiv Baden-Württemberg Akte E 14 (Kgl. Kabinett) Bü 2049, my translation.

12 *Forsters Liebhaberheft*, Staatsarchiv St. Gallen, KA R.182–4.

13 Forster, *Justizmorde*, 59, my translation.

14 It is possible that he did not do so voluntarily, as he was being pursued for unpaid taxes while in Germany and was fined ten marks for this in Stuttgart and then again in Ludwigsburg. Letter from Stuttgart City Director Hofer to State Councillor von Grättner, 29 January 1878. Landesarchiv Baden-Württemberg Akte E 14 (Kgl. Kabinett) Bü 2049.

15 Letter from Jakob Rudolf Forster to King Charles of Württemberg, 28 December 1877. Landesarchiv Baden-Württemberg Akte E 14 (Kgl. Kabinett) Bü 2049.

16 Hergemöller, ed., *Mann für Mann: Biographisches Lexikon zur Geschichte*, 628–9.

17 Letter from Jakob Rudolf Forster to King Charles of Württemberg, 28 December 1877. Landesarchiv Baden-Württemberg Akte E 14 (Kgl. Kabinett) Bü 2049.

18 *Forsters Liebhaberheft*, Staatsarchiv St. Gallen, KA R. 182–4, my translation.
19 Forster, *Justizmorde*, 19, my translation.
20 There are twenty-six cantons in Switzerland today, but one of them, Jura, was only created in the 1970s.
21 This satirical understanding of Switzerland was contained in a 1954 radio play, *Herkules und der Stall des Augias*. An English translation of this work can be found in Dürrenmatt, *Selected Writings,* with a translation by Joel Agee.
22 The city of St. Gallen itself had 14,623 citizens in the main town and 19,000 if you included suburban municipalities in 1862. Kolb, *Grundriss der Statistik*, 64. The population rose to 26,398 in 1870, 43,296 in 1888, and finally 53,796 in 1900. "St Gallen Gemeinde," in *Historisches Lexikon der Schweiz*, 6 January 2012, https://hls-dhs-dss.ch/de/articles/001321/2012-01-06.
23 The city of Zurich itself had 20,258 citizens in the main town and 43,300 if you included suburban municipalities in 1862. Kolb, *Grundriss der Statistik*, 64. The population rose to 58,657 in 1870, 94,129 in 1888 and 150,703 in 1900. "Zurich," *Encylopaedia Britannica*, 11th ed., vol. 27, "Vetch to Zymotic Diseases" (Cambridge: Cambridge University Press, 1911), 1057, https://archive.org/details/encyclopaediabri28chisrich/page/1056/mode/2up?q=Zurich.
24 Art. 189 in Kanton St. Gallen Gesetzessammlung. Neue Folge. Fünfter Band. 1886 bis 1890 (St. Gallen: Zollikofer, 1890), 64.
25 Art. 123 in *Strafgesetzbuch für den Kanton Zürich*, StAZH OS 15 (S. 392–470), "Zürcher Gesetzessammlung seit 1803," Staatsarchiv des Kantons Zürich, 2021, https://www.archives-quickaccess.ch/search/stazh/os.
26 Cited in Martin Mühlheim, "'… dass über die Verwerflichkeit,'" my translation.
27 Mühlheim, "'… dass über die Verwerflichkeit,'" 30–1.
28 Heinrich Hössli, a hatter from Glarus in Winterthur, was one of the earliest writers on the subject of man-manly love. Hössli, *Eros*, vols. 1 and 2. Hössli's work was not well known, even in Switzerland, at this time. Ulrichs had been unaware of Hössli until 2 February 1866 and wrote then that his was a pioneering work that suffered from being too detailed and lacking strong arguments. Ulrichs, *Memnon, Abtheilung II*, §134, 129; Lombardi-Nash (tr.), *The Riddle*, vol. 2, 428. It is entirely possible that Ulrichs introduced Forster to the work of his compatriot, as Forster wrote to him that he had finally managed to find copies of both volumes. Letter from Jakob Rudolf Forster to Ulrichs, 6 December 1879. Kanton St. Gallen Staatsarchiv KA R. 182–4, ff3–4. Translated as letter 220 in Pretsell, *The Correspondence*, 251. Hössli's pioneering early foray into writing about *Mannerliebe* has been the recent subject of an excellent collection of essays

that I would recommend to interested readers: Thalmann, ed., *"Keine Liebe ist an sich Tugend oder Laster."*

29 Deutsch-Schweizerisch refers to the German-speaking part of Switzerland, which in English is "Swiss-German."

30 There is no direct evidence that the business and activism were mixed, but when the police raided the office, they found urning outreach material. Forster, *Justizmorde,* 61.

31 Forster, *Justizmorde,* 61, my translation.

32 Forster, *Justizmorde,* 7–50.

33 Letter from Jakob Rudolf Forster to Karl Heinrich Ulrichs, 6 December 1879. Kanton St. Gallen Staatsarchiv KA R. 182–4, ff3–4. Translated as letter 220 in Pretsell, *The Correspondence,* 251.

34 Another distinction was that Ulrichs drew a line at not encouraging sexual contact between his correspondents (compare with letter to Carl Robert Egells, 31 January–1 February 1874, quoted in Ferdinand Karsch-Haack, 1922. Carl Heinrich Ulrichs. *Die Freundschaft,* 29, 4, 20 May. Translated as letter 202 in Pretsell, *The Correspondence,* 237), Forster apparently had no such qualms.

35 Forster, *Justizmorde,* 60.

36 *Die Ostschweiz,* No. 264 St. Gallen, Sunday, 15 November 1879, 3, my translation.

37 Forster, *Justizmorde,* 61.

38 According to Forster, the police discovered the following in the apartment: "All the letters weighing about 50 pounds were taken away, including writings on urning love compiled by me, a list of comrades and lovers, letters on this subject in quantity, also Hössli's works on this subject and a booklet by Ulrichs which he gave me with a dedication." Forster, *Justizmorde,* 61, my translation.

39 *Forsters Liebhaberheft,* Staatsarchiv St. Gallen, KA R. 182–4.

40 The ubiquity and dominance of soldier love in Germany has already been noted in the Introduction. Ulrichs, *Ara Spei,* 71n60; Lombardi-Nash (tr.), *The Riddle,* vol. 2, 241; Symonds, *Soldier Love,* 9.

41 I am grateful to Rolf Thalmann for extracting and transcribing the interrogations from Forster's criminal file at St. Gallen, Staatsarchiv des Kantons St Gallen, Signatur GA 002/145.

42 Judgment of the Cantonal Court of St. Gallen in the Criminal Case of Forster and Consorts Concerning Fornication against Nature, 14 January 1880, Staatsarchiv des Kantons St Gallen KA R. 182–4.

43 Letters from Jakob Rudolf Forster to Karl Heinrich Ulrichs, 12 November and 6 December 1879. Kanton St. Gallen Staatsarchiv KA R. 182–4, ff1–4. Translated as letters 219 and 220 in Pretsell, *The Correspondence,* 250–2.

44 Ulrichs's Forster Petition, 11 July 1881. Kanton St. Gallen Staatsarchiv KA R. 182–4, ff01–09. Translated as letter 221 in Pretsell, *The Correspondence*, 252–7.

45 Foucault, *Discipline and Punish*, 297.

46 Forster, *Justizmorde*, 45, my translation.

47 Forster, *Justizmorde*, 67, my translation.

48 Forster, *Justizmorde*, 67–8.

49 Forster, *Justizmorde*, 69, my translation.

50 Forster, *Justizmorde*, 70.

51 Forster, *Justizmorde*, 70, my translation.

52 Forster, *Justizmorde*, 70, my translation.

53 Forster, *Justizmorde*, 71, my translation.

54 Forster, *Justizmorde*, 74.

55 Forster, *Justizmorde*, 76–7.

56 Forster, *Justizmorde*, 77, my translation.

57 Forster, *Justizmorde*, 77, my translation.

58 Forster, *Justizmorde*, 80, my translation.

59 Forster, *Justizmorde*, 77.

60 Copies of the *Weltheirathszeitung* from those months have not survived, so it is impossible to know what "urning propaganda" was contained in them. However, the swift response of the Zurich authorities suggests that the urning material was not particularly covert.

61 Forster, *Justizmorde*, 77.

62 *Züricherische Freitagzeitung*, 14 December 1883, 3, my translation.

63 Forster, *Justizmorde*, 78.

64 Forster, *Justizmorde*, 78.

65 *St. Galler Volksblatt*, 19 January 1884, 2, my translation.

66 Forster, *Justizmorde*, 82.

67 Forster, *Justizmorde*, 82, my translation.

68 Forster, *Justizmorde*, 83, my translation.

69 Forster, *Justizmorde*, 84.

70 Forster, *Justizmorde*, 85–102.

71 Forster, *Justizmorde*, 93, my translation.

72 Forster, *Justizmorde*, 106–7, my translation.

73 Forster, *Justizmorde*, 107, my translation.

74 Forster, *Justizmorde*, 108.

75 The events he was describing were fresh in his mind when he wrote them in his memoir, which was started soon after this point.

76 Forster, *Justizmorde*, 108.

77 Forster's testimony of reputation, Brunnarden, 25 March 1885, in Forster, *Justizmorde*, 66, my translation.

78 Several officials were apparently prejudiced against Forster: the municipal official Brunner, who had issued the unfavourable certificate

in Brunnadern, but also councillors Segmüller and Näf in St. Gallen.
There may have been others, but in these three cases, Forster presented
official letters indicating that these men clearly were the instigators in his
misfortune.

79 Forster, *Justizmorde*, 111.
80 Forster wrote, "In general, I found understanding noble souls in the
Empire of Germany and Austria." Forster, *Justizmorde*, 111. Preßburg was
the German name for Bratislava, now the capital of Slovakia; at that time,
however, it was in the Hungarian part of Austria-Hungary. It was a little
over 60 kilometres from Vienna, so Forster could have made it there in a
long day of walking – more quickly, if he had hitched a lift.
81 Forster, *Justizmorde*, 111.
82 Forster, *Justizmorde*, 111.
83 Forster, *Justizmorde*, 112–13.
84 Forster uses "über" instead of "für" in the title and states the year as
1881, but he gets the volume (38) and the publisher correct. Forster,
Justizmorde, 113. Krafft-Ebing and his psychiatric publications will be
examined in more detail in chapter 6.
85 Dr. Weller's report of 23 March 1886 stated plainly, "Mr Forster was taken
away from here on 16 March, after I had to give my expert opinion that
he was not suffering from a mental disorder." Forster, *Justizmorde*, 114–15.
86 Forster, *Justizmorde*, 116.
87 Letter from government councillor Segmüller, St. Gallen Department of
Interior, to Christine Forster, in Gonzenwyl-Mogelsberg, 13 September
1886. Cited in full in Forster, *Justizmorde*, 118, my translation.
88 The resemblance of Bitzi to a concentration camp was not just
coincidental. Forced labour camps had existed across central Europe for
a long time before the Second World War and became the model and
precedent for the first German concentration camps. Gibson and Poerio,
"Modern Europe," 317.
89 Forster, *Justizmorde*, 123.
90 Forster reproduces the exchange of letters in his book. Forster,
Justizmorde, 125–31.
91 Forster, *Justizmorde*, 126.
92 Forster, *Justizmorde*, 127, my translation.
93 Forster, *Justizmorde*, 128.
94 The full text of this leaflet is contained in his autobiography. "Flugblatt,"
in Forster, *Justizmorde*, 131–6.
95 Forster, *Justizmorde*, 137.
96 Forster, *Justizmorde*, 140.
97 Forster, *Justizmorde*, 140.
98 Forster, *Justizmorde*, 156, my translation.
99 Forster, *Justizmorde*, 163.

100 Carlo Ulrichs, *Cupressi*; Forster, *Justizmorde*, 163.
101 Ulrichs used to give figures for the number of urnings in principal cities that were just estimates. Forster's figures were more realistic and based on his grassroots activism. Forster, *Justizmorde*, 107.
102 Albert Moll, *Die conträre Sexualempfindung* (1891).
103 Forster, *Justizmorde*, 167–8, my translation.
104 Forster, *Justizmorde*, 176.
105 Mühlheim, "'… dass über die Verwerflichkeit,'" 18–22.
106 Forster, *Justizmorde*, 168–9.
107 Forster, *Justizmorde*, 172.
108 Forster, *Justizmorde*, 173.
109 Forster, *Justizmorde*, 174.
110 Hornung, "Jakob Rudolf Forster, 80.
111 Mühlheim, "'… dass über die Verwerflichkeit,'" 31.
112 Mühlheim, "'… dass über die Verwerflichkeit,'" 32.
113 The experience of Ulrichs with his lists and Forster with his book of loves suggests that recording things was dangerous and that others may have avoided doing so.

6. Queering Psychiatry: Autobiographical Lobbying of Richard von Krafft-Ebing, 1864–1901

1 Cited in Casper, *Klinische Novellen*, 37, my translation. Part of this quote was used in the title of Müller, *Aber in meinem Herzen*.
2 This "pederast" case study was also used in the "Urning Identity" discussion in chapter 2.
3 Casper published a series of pederast case studies in 1852, in which he speculated that some pederasts might have an innate disposition. A man living in exile sent a letter autobiography that deeply impressed Casper, who published it in full and declared he now believed that most had an innate disposition. (The opening quote in this chapter is taken from this letter.) This, in effect, was the "proof of concept" for this particular tactic. The text for this letter is found in Casper, *Klinische Novellen*, 36–9.
4 Klaus Müller, *Aber in meinem Herzen*, 176.
5 Müller, *Aber in meinem Herzen*; Oosterhuis, *Stepchildren of Nature*.
6 Magnus Hirschfeld continued this campaign of scientific sexual reform into the twentieth century, but that falls outside of the temporal bounds of this book.
7 In particular, Ulrichs sent the three books that contained his scientific theory: *Inclusa* (1864), *Formatrix* (1865)), and *Memnon I & II* (1868).
8 Letter from Richard von Krafft-Ebing, Graz, to Ulrichs, 29 January 1879. Ulrichs, *Critische Pfeile*, §125, 92; Lombardi-Nash (tr.), *The Riddle*, vol. 2, 685. Letter 214 in Douglas Pretsell, *The Correspondence*, 247.

9 Shorter, *A History of Psychiatry*, 74.

10 Shorter, *A History of Psychiatry*, 76.

11 Griesinger, "Vortrag zur Eröffnung," 651.

12 Berliner Medicinische-Psychologische Gesellschaft, 15 December 1868, *Archiv für Psychiatrie und Nervenkrankheiten* 2 (1869): 226–7.

13 Westphal, "Die conträre Sexualempfindung."

14 Foucault, *The History of Sexuality*, vol. 1, 43.

15 Schmincke, "Ein Fall von conträrer Sexualempfindung"; Scholz, "Bekenntnisse"; Gock, "Beitrag zur Kenntniss"; Servaes, "Zur Kenntniss"; Rabow, "Über angeborene conträre Sexualempfindung."

16 Mildenberger, … *in der Richtung Homosexualität verdorben*, 40.

17 Stark, "Über conträre Sexualempfindung," 209, my translation.

18 For example, Tamassia, "Sull'inversione dell'istinto sessuale"; Backman, "Ett fall af konträr sexualkänsla"; Blumer, "A Case of Perverted Sexual Instinct"; Shaw and Ferris, "Perverted Sexual Instinct"; Kiernan, "Insanity"; Shrady, "Perverted Sexual Instinct"; Krueg, "Perverted Sexual Instincts"; Savage, "Case of Sexual Perversion in a Man."

19 Letter from Dr. Erman, a forensic physician in Hamburg, to Ulrichs, 8 February 1879. Ulrichs, *Critische Pfeile*, §125, 92; Lombardi-Nash (tr.), *The Riddle*, vol. 2, 686. Letter 215 in Pretsell, *The Correspondence*, 248.

20 Ulrichs, *Critische Pfeile*, §126, 96; Lombardi-Nash (tr.), *The Riddle*, vol. 2, 688.

21 Letter from Richard von Krafft-Ebing, Graz, to Ulrichs, 29 January 1879. Ulrichs, *Critische Pfeile*, §125, 92; Lombardi-Nash (tr.), *The Riddle*, vol. 2, 685. Letter 214 in Pretsell, *The Correspondence*, 247.

22 Krafft-Ebing, "Die Sinnestäuschungen."

23 Krafft-Ebing, "Die Sinnestäuschungen," 244. Ulrichs quoted several paragraphs from this essay: Ulrichs, *Vindicta*, 124.

24 Krafft-Ebing, "Ueber gewisse Anomalien."

25 Krafft-Ebing, "Ueber gewisse Anomalien," 309, my translation.

26 Krafft-Ebing, "Zur Lehre von der conträren Sexualempfindung," 2; English translation can be found in Pretsell, *Queer Voices*, 47.

27 Otto de Joux, *Die Enterbten des Liebesglückes*, 20, my translation.

28 This was a hostile account from an individual who criticized the psychiatric approach and all those who were tolerant of homosexuality. Strassmann, *Lehrbuch der gerichtlichen Medizin*, 122. The fuller quotation in German can be found in Müller, *Aber in meinem Herzen*, 259, my translation.

29 Oosterhuis, *Stepchildren of Nature*, 85.

30 Oosterhuis, *Stepchildren of Nature*, 91.

31 Oosterhuis, *Stepchildren of Nature*, 94.

32 Richard von Krafft-Ebing, "Zur 'conträren Sexualempfindung' in klinisch-forensischer Hinsicht."

33 Krafft-Ebing, "Zur 'conträren Sexualempfindung,'" 213, my translation.
34 Krafft-Ebing, "Zur 'conträren Sexualempfindung,'" 216, my translation.
35 Krafft-Ebing, *Lehrbuch der Psychiatrie*, 85–8. Translated as Case Study 2.1 in Pretsell, *Queer Voices*, 43–6.
36 Crozier, "Pillow Talk," 375.
37 Pretsell, "The Evolution of the Questionnaire," 330.
38 Krafft-Ebing, "Zur Lehre von der conträren Sexualempfindung," 2–14.
39 Krafft-Ebing used Xs and Ys to anonymize the subjects of his case studies but wasn't careful to give each a distinctly different combination – the 1883 and 1884 autobiographies both came from individuals he called "Mr. X."
40 Krafft-Ebing, "Zur Lehre," 5; Pretsell, *Queer Voices*, 50.
41 Krafft-Ebing, "Die conträre Sexualempfindung " 34–47. Pretsell, *Queer Voices*, 50–60.
42 Krafft-Ebing, "Die conträre Sexualempfindung," 40; Pretsell, *Queer Voices*, 54.
43 Krafft-Ebing, "Die conträre Sexualempfindung," 42; Pretsell, *Queer Voices*, 55.
44 Krafft-Ebing, "Die conträre Sexualempfindung," 42; Pretsell, *Queer Voices*, 55–6.
45 Krafft-Ebing, "Die conträre Sexualempfindung," 42; Pretsell, *Queer Voices*, 56.
46 Krafft-Ebing, "Die conträre Sexualempfindung," 42–3; Pretsell, *Queer Voices*, 56.
47 Krafft-Ebing, "Die conträre Sexualempfindung," 46; Pretsell, *Queer Voices*, 56.
48 Krafft-Ebing, "Die conträre Sexualempfindung," 36, my translation.
49 Krafft-Ebing, "Die conträre Sexualempfindung," 36–7.
50 Richard von Krafft-Ebing, *Psychopathia Sexualis*, 1st ed.
51 Krafft-Ebing, *Psychopathia Sexualis*, 1st ed., 64, my translation.
52 Mildenberger, ... *in der Richtung*, 43.
53 Mildenberger, ... *in der Richtung*, 44.
54 It is interesting that Krafft-Ebing used this term for transient or acquired cases. Johann Friedrich Meckel in 1812 postulated the mental hermaphrodite as someone with the genitals of one sex and the psyche of the other, that is, an "urning." Meckel, "Ueber die Zwitterbildungen." Ulrichs also described the urning as a physio-psychic hermaphrodite. Ulrichs, *Memnon, Abtheilung II*, §142, xxi; Lombardi-Nash (tr.), *The Riddle*, vol. 2, 363.
55 Hirschfeld, "Die intersexuelle Konstitution," 14.
56 Androgynes and gynandres were categories of "pseudohermaphrodites" borrowed from teratology. In the twentieth century, they did not survive as categories once transgender and intersex were defined.

57 For example, the Englishman John Addington Symonds, who features in chapter 8, was fluent in German, lived in Davos, and probably wrote his polemic letter to Krafft-Ebing in German.

58 Krafft-Ebing, *Neue Forschungen*, 61; Pretsell, *Queer Voices*, 95.

59 Krafft-Ebing, *Psychopathia Sexualis*, 3rd ed., 82; Pretsell, *Queer Voices*, 62.

60 Krafft-Ebing, *Neue Forschungen* [1891], 131; Pretsell, *Queer Voices*, 100.

61 Krafft-Ebing, *Neue Forschungen* [1890], 66; Pretsell, *Queer Voices*, 168.

62 Krafft-Ebing, *Psychopathia Sexualis*, 5th ed., 175; Pretsell, *Queer Voices*, 83.

63 Krafft-Ebing, *Psychopathia Sexualis*, 3rd ed., 83; Pretsell, *Queer Voices*, 63.

64 Krafft-Ebing, *Psychopathia Sexualis*, 5th ed., 172; Pretsell, *Queer Voices*, 79.

65 Krafft-Ebing, *Neue Forschungen* [1890], 49–50; Pretsell, *Queer Voices*, 87.

66 Krafft-Ebing, *Psychopathia Sexualis*, 3rd ed., 87, my translation.

67 Krafft-Ebing, *Psychopathia Sexualis*, 4th ed., 138; Pretsell, *Queer Voices*, 201.

68 Krafft-Ebing, *Psychopathia Sexualis*, 3rd ed., 87; Pretsell, *Queer Voices*, 68.

69 Krafft-Ebing, *Psychopathia Sexualis*, 5th ed., 164; Pretsell, *Queer Voices*, 78.

70 Krafft-Ebing, *Neue Forschungen* [1891], 127; Pretsell, *Queer Voices*, 96.

71 Krafft-Ebing, *Psychopathia Sexualis*, 3rd ed., 87–8; Pretsell, *Queer Voices*, 138.

72 Krafft-Ebing, *Psychopathia Sexualis*, 2nd ed., 101; Pretsell, *Queer Voices*, 136.

73 Krafft-Ebing, *Psychopathia Sexualis*, 2nd ed., 101; Pretsell, *Queer Voices*, 137.

74 Krafft-Ebing, *Psychopathia Sexualis*, 2nd ed., 102; Pretsell, *Queer Voices*, 137.

75 Krafft-Ebing, *Neue Forschungen* [1891], 107; Pretsell, *Queer Voices*, 229.

76 Krafft-Ebing, "Neue Forschungen," 2, my translation.

77 Krafft-Ebing, *Psychopathia Sexualis*, 3rd ed., 167; Pretsell, *Queer Voices*, 103.

78 Krafft-Ebing, "Zur conträren Sexualempfindung: Autobiographie," 388; Pretsell, *Queer Voices*, 108.

79 Krafft-Ebing, "Zur conträren Sexualempfindung: Autobiographie," 388n, my translation.

80 None of the letters have survived (other than the one Ulrichs published himself in *Critische Pfeile*), but it seems as if the two maintained lines of communication over many years, even after Ulrichs moved to Italy. Krafft-Ebing, *Der Conträrsexuale*.

81 Ulrichs, *Alaudae*, 355–8.

82 Krafft-Ebing, *Der Conträrsexual*, 26.

83 Letter from Ulrichs to Members of the Austrian Royal and Imperial Ministry of Justice, 18 June 1894. Österreichisches Staatsarchiv/AVA Justiz JM Allgemein Sig 1 A1076/IKI, Zl.12.153 ex 1930. Translated as letter 227 in Pretsell, *The Correspondence*, 260–2.

84 De Joux does not mention the actor's name, but it was possibly Josef Gottfried Ignaz Kainz. Kainz, an Austrian, had been performing on the Berlin stage since 1883 and was one of Germany's most famous actors. Dazzlingly handsome, he had been a close favourite and possible lover of Ludwig II. Though married, Kainz was bisexual, and in Berlin, he

maintained a salon of young attractive artists and poets. Hergemöller, ed., *Mann für Mann: Biographisches Lexikon*, 619–21.
85 De Joux, *Die Enterbten*, 73, my translation.
86 Krafft-Ebing, "Neue Forschungen," 2, my translation.
87 The exception in Germany was Berlin's Forensic Examiner, Johann Ludwig Casper, who became progressively less hostile to his pederast patients after encountering, first of all, the diary of Count von Malzhan in 1852 and then later a sexual autobiography sent by letter (the quotation at the start of this chapter comes from that letter). Just as with Krafft-Ebing, his opinion about pederasts was influenced by autobiographical accounts.

7. Belling the Cat: Adolf Glaser's Discreet Police-Liaison in Berlin, 1878–1897

1 Jones, *Aesop's Fables*, 6.
2 Ulrichs, *Argonauticus*, §64(b), 117; Lombardi-Nash (tr.), *The Riddle*, vol. 2, 523.
3 Police liaison is a tactic used by activists to establish common ground between communities of sexual and gender nonconformity and police departments. In the late twentieth century, following decriminalization, some LGBTQ+ activists in developed nations took it upon themselves to engage directly with police forces. This tactic was adopted in several places, including Melbourne, Australia, where it has recently been characterized as driven by "cynical pragmatism" (Russell, "Ambivalent Investments," 379). Some scholars today regard modern police liaison as controversial. Police departments rarely volunteer changes to the policing of sexual or gender minorities (see, for example, Lamble, "Queer Necropolitics," 234; Spade, Normal Life, 34). Change, when it comes, is the result of years of patient lobbying and backroom discussion. One exasperating factor in these engagements between activists and police is that, even when they deliver results, the police tend to cast themselves as "heroes of their own story" and erase the contributions of activists (Russell, "Ambivalent Investments," 380). They present the transformation of policing as an internally generated phenomenon rather than a process of engagement with activists.
4 Hirschfeld, *The Homosexuality of Men and Women*, 1117.
5 In part, this is because it was the narrative that Glaser initiated himself in his obituary for Meerscheidt-Hüllessem and that Hirschfeld perpetuated thereafter. See, for example, Beachy, *Gay Berlin*, 64–70; and Whisnant, *Queer Identities*, 104.
6 Dobler, *Zwischen Duldungspolitik*, 205–60.

7 Dobler, *Zwischen Duldungspolitik*, 239–45.

8 Beachy, *Gay Berlin*, 58.

9 The three main independent sources are Magnus Hirschfeld in two works, Hüllessem's successor Hans von Tresckow's memoir, and Adolf Glaser's own obituary for Hüllessem.

10 G. [Adolf Glaser], "In Memoriam."

11 At this point in time, despite the use of the word in literature, "homosexual" was probably not a word that many men used to describe themselves.

12 Ulrichs, *Critische Pfeile*, §86, 62–3; Lombardi-Nash (tr.), *The Riddle*, vol. 2, 666.

13 See chapter 6 and Krafft-Ebing's case studies in *Psychopathia Sexualis*.

14 Dobler, *Zwischen Duldungspolitik*, 208.

15 Dobler, *Zwischen Duldungspolitik*, 208.

16 Fout, "Sexual Politics," 395.

17 Fout, "Sexual Politics," 395.

18 Von Tresckow, *Von Fürsten und anderen Sterblichen*, 111, my translation.

19 Hugländer [Hugo Friedländer], "Aus dem homosexuellen Leben."

20 Beachy, *Gay Berlin*, 43.

21 Hugländer, "Aus dem homosexuellen Leben," 60.

22 Hugländer, "Aus dem homosexuellen Leben," 60–1, my translation.

23 Hugländer, "Aus dem homosexuellen Leben," 58.

24 Dobler, *Zwischen Duldungspolitik*, 205–60.

25 De Weindel and Fischer, *L'homosexualité en Allemagne*.

26 The lists of correspondents that were confiscated from Ulrichs when he was arrested in 1867 were possibly among the sources drawn on to construct these lists, for they contained at least 150 names from Berlin. Ulrichs, *Argonauticus*, §5, 12; Lombardi-Nash (tr.), *The Riddle*, vol. 2, 477.

27 Ulrichs, *Argonauticus*, §67, 127–8; Lombardi-Nash (tr.), *The Riddle*, vol. 2, 529.

28 It is possible that one measure of the department's effectiveness was the number of successful investigations relating to Paragraph 175.

29 Dobler, *Zwischen Duldungspolitik*, 205.

30 Hugländer, "Aus dem homosexuellen Leben," 54–5.

31 Dobler, *Zwischen Duldungspolitik*, 211.

32 According to Hirschfeld, the department was still called the "Pederast Department" in 1885, although it may later have been called the "Homosexual Department." Hirschfeld, *Memoir*, 33.

33 Rohse, "Ein Nicht-Braunschweiger," 46.

34 Rohse, "Ein Nicht-Braunschweiger," 46.

35 Rohse, "Ein Nicht-Braunschweiger," 46.

36 Glaser wrote two plays under the pseudonym "Reinhald Reimer": *Kriemhilden's Rache* (1853) and *Penelope* (1854). He published the

following works under his own name: *Familie Schaller* (1857); *Bianca Candiano* (1859); *Geschichte des Theaters zu Braunschweig* (1861); *Galileo Galilei* (1861); *Erzählungen und Novellen* (1862); *Gedicht* (1862); *Leseabende* (1867); *Was Ist Wahrheit?* (1869); *Der Hausgeist der Frau von Estobal* (1878); *Schlitzwang* (1878); *Eine Magdalene ohne Glorienschein* (1878); *Weibliche Dämonen* (1879); *Aus dem 18. Jahrhundert* (1880); *Mulshilde* (1880); *Moderne Gegensätze* (1881); *Aus Hohen Regionen* (1882); *Savonarola* (1883); and *Cordula* (1885). Glaser also translated the works of several Dutch authors. Rohse, "Ein Nicht-Braunschweiger," 46–7.

37 Hirschfeld, *Memoir*, 35.

38 Hirschfeld, *Jahrbuch für sexuelle Zwischenstufen*, 64, my translation.

39 This account is taken from a confession of Karl Duberke from seven days after the event took place. As such, it is probably more accurate than the widely diverging accounts in the media reports, the anonymous author of "Das perverse Berlin," and the memories of Hugo Friedländer. Confession of Karl Duberke at the apartment of Adolf Glaser, 18 March 1878. Stadtarchiv Braunschweig, H III Nr 6 Glaser, Adolf Dr, 75–6.

40 Confession of Duberke at the apartment of Adolf Glaser, 18 March 1878, 76.

41 Dobler, *Zwischen Duldungspolitik*, 240.

42 Confession of Duberke at the apartment of Adolf Glaser, 18 March 1878, 76.

43 In his statement, Duberke wrote, "I was asked what I did for a living and replied that I was supported from several sides, including by Dr. Glaser." Confession of Duberke at the apartment of Adolf Glaser, 18 March 1878, 76. Duberke's income was generated either through services rendered for these individuals or through blackmailing these individuals in return for regular payments. Glaser does not provide any background, but the fact that he acted to sever all contact with Duberke and brought the police in to witness the confession tends to suggest this was possibly a case of blackmail. The police, as we shall see later in this chapter, often sought to turn blackmailers into informants in exchange for clemency.

44 Dobler, *Zwischen Duldungspolitik*, 240–1.

45 Letter from Glaser to Wilhelm Raabe, 10 April 1878. Stadtarchiv Braunschweig, H III Nr 6 Glaser, Adolf Dr, 77, my translation.

46 Dobler claims that the "Fall Glaser" was one of the four great "Homo-Skandals" in nineteenth-century Berlin, alongside the trials of Friedrich Wadzeck (1837), Alfred von Maltzan-Wedell (1852), and Carl von Zastrow (1869). Dobler, *Zwischen Duldungspolitik*, 239.

47 Letter from Glaser to Wilhelm Raabe, 10 April 1878 Stadtarchiv Braunschweig, H III Nr 6 Glaser, Adolf Dr, 77, my translation.

48 Letter from Glaser to Wilhelm Raabe, 10 April 1878 Stadtarchiv Braunschweig, H III Nr 6 Glaser, Adolf Dr, 77.

49 Letter from Glaser to Wilhelm Raabe, 30 April 1878 Stadtarchiv Braunschweig, H III Nr 6 Glaser, Adolf Dr, 78, my translation.

50 Letter from Glaser to Wilhelm Raabe, 29 August 1878 Stadtarchiv Braunschweig, H III Nr 6 Glaser, Adolf Dr, 81.

51 Letter from Glaser to Wilhelm Raabe, 4 July 1878. Stadtarchiv Braunschweig, H III Nr 6 Glaser, Adolf Dr, 80, my translation.

52 Letter from a Berlin man of knowledge, of society and experience,
   to Ulrichs, July 1878. Ulrichs, *Critische Pfeile*, §57, 39; Lombardi-Nash
   (tr.), *The Riddle*, vol. 2, 651. Letter 213 in Douglas Pretsell, *The
   Correspondence*, 247.

53 Letter from Glaser to Wilhelm Raabe, 26 January 1882, Stadtarchiv
   Braunschweig, H III Nr 6 Glaser, Adolf Dr, 89.

54 Dobler, *Zwischen Duldungspolitik Zwischen Duldungspolitik*, 241.

55 Hirschfeld, *Memoir*, 35.

56 Dobler, *Zwischen Duldungspolitik Zwischen Duldungspolitik*, 229.

57 Dobler believed that the two men got to know each other in 1890 during
   the collaboration with Moll. Dobler, *Zwischen Duldungspolitik Zwischen
   Duldungspolitik*, 242. However, that collaboration came about partly
   because Hüllessem had been in correspondence with Richard von
   Krafft-Ebing, who introduced him to Albert Moll. Since this chapter
   places Glaser as an adviser on Hüllessem's sexological education, it
   seems more likely that they established contact before 1890 and at some
   point after 1885.

58 Hugländer, "Aus dem homosexuellen Leben," 58.

59 Hugländer, "Aus dem homosexuellen Leben," 58.

60 Beachy, *Gay Berlin*, 44.

61 Hugländer, "Aus dem homosexuellen Leben," 58.

62 Hugländer, "Aus dem homosexuellen Leben," 59.

63 Hugländer, "Aus dem homosexuellen Leben," 60.

64 There was one further instance, when the police closed Wiebusch's
   tavern at Schützenstrasse 55, "der kleine Salvator," on Monday, 4 May
   1892. However, in that case the venue was targeted because transvestite
   prostitutes were operating from the venue. J.G.F., "Ein Fall von
   Effemination," 330.

65 Hüllessem's contributions to the modernization of policing in Berlin went
   well beyond the policing of homosexuals. He developed, among other
   things, photographic card indexes of criminals and suspects as well as a
   criminal museum used in the education of new recruits. He also
   pioneered the use of police dogs and armed the vice squad. Dobler,
   Zwischen Duldungspolitik, 233–7.

66 G. [Adolf Glaser], "In Memoriam," 952, my translation.

67 Dobler, *Zwischen Duldungspolitik*, 242.

68 Hirschfeld, *Memoir*, 35.

69 G., "In Memoriam," 952, my translation.

70 Hüllessem was married with children and also maintained a mistress on the side. Although there were rumours about his sexual nature later on, these usually came from hostile sources. His homosexual friends (Glaser, Hirschfeld, and others) considered him to be heterosexual.

71 G., "In Memoriam," 953, my translation.

72 G., "In Memoriam," 948–55.

73 Hirschfeld, *The Homosexuality of Men and Women*; Hirschfeld, *Memoir*.

74 Hirschfeld, *Memoir*, 35.

75 Hirschfeld, *Memoir*, 36.

76 Albert Moll, *Die Conträre Sexualempfindung*, x.

77 Hirschfeld, *Memoir*, 35.

78 G., "In Memoriam," 952.

79 Hirschfeld, *Memoir*, 34.

80 Hirschfeld, *The Homosexuality of Men and Women*, 1077.

81 Tresckow, *Von Fürsten*, 107, my translation.

82 Krafft-Ebing, *Psychopathia Sexualis*, 9th ed., 399, my translation.

83 Moll, *Die Conträre Sexualempfindung*, ix–x, my translation.

84 Moll used both words but would go on to use "homosexual" more and more in subsequent editions.

85 This abbreviation could also have been for *nomen nescio* (Latin trans. "I do not know the name") – a term that a Latin scholar might use for anonymity.

86 Hirschfeld and others adhered to Glaser's desire not to be named in connection with his urning activities right up to his death in 1915. In 1916, his identity was fully revealed in Hirschfeld, *Jahrbuch* 16, no. 2 (1916): 64–5.

87 Moll, *Die Conträre Sexualempfindung*, x, my translation.

88 Moll, *Die Conträre Sexualempfindung*, 232.

89 Moll, *Die Conträre Sexualempfindung*, 245–6.

90 Pretsell, *Queer Voices*, 23–4.

91 Moll, *Die Conträre Sexualempfindung*, 75n, my translation.

92 Hirschfeld, *Memoir*, 34.

93 Hirschfeld, *The Homosexuality of Men and Women*, 789.

94 Beachy, *Gay Berlin*, 63.

95 Schoenaich [Paul von Hoverbeck], cited in Beachy, *Gay Berlin*, 64.

96 Hirschfeld, *The Homosexuality of Men and Women*, 786.

97 G., "In Memoriam," 953, my translation.

98 G., "In Memoriam," 953; Dobler, *Zwischen Duldungspolitik*, 247.

99 Tresckow, *Von Fürsten*, 114–15, my translation.

100 Tresckow, *Von Fürsten*, 118, my translation.

101 Dobler, *Zwischen Duldungspolitik*, 214.

102 Hirschfeld, *Memoir*, 29.

103 Dobler, *Zwischen Duldungspolitik*, 214–15.

104 Dobler, *Zwischen Duldungspolitik*, 248.

105 Dobler, *Zwischen Duldungspolitik*, 248.

106 G., "In Memoriam," 952–3, my translation.

107 Hirschfeld, *The Homosexuality of Men and Women*, 1117.

108 Hirschfeld, *Memoir*, 29.

109 Hirschfeld, *The Homosexuality of Men and Women*, 786.

110 Hirschfeld, *The Homosexuality of Men and Women*, 1116.

111 Glaser was sixty-two years old when engaging with Moll, and when the sexologist mentioned that he believed there were urnings who only loved platonically and not sexually, Glaser replied that this was "known from his own experience as lasting for a long time." Moll, *Die Conträre Sexualempfindung*, 95n1. While Glaser deployed his urning advocacy in Berlin, he was also back in his old establishment position at the *Monats-Hefte* where the pressure for him to conform to normative standards was considerable. This may be the reason he decided in 1895 to marry a woman, Anna Peterson, twenty-one years his junior. Glaser wrote to Wilhelm Raabe about the marriage. A handwritten note on the corner of the marriage certificate states that this marriage ended in divorce only five years later. See Letter from Glaser to Wilhelm Raabe, 7 April 1895, Stadtarchiv Braunschweig, H III Nr 6 Glaser, Adolf Dr, 99; Marriage certificate of Adolf Glaser and Anna Peterson, Landesarchiv Berlin; Berlin, Deutschland; Personenstandsregister Heiratsregister; Laufende Nummer: 402, ancestry.com.au.

112 Moll's work went through several editions. All of them kept the initials. Even as late as 1922, Hirschfeld's account in his memoirs used initials for Glaser.

113 Hirschfeld, "Aus der Kriegzeit," 64–5, my translation.

114 Up to that point, each of them had only used pseudonymous initials in place of the author's name.

115 For example, the first edition of Hergemöller's who's who of queer Germany in 1998 had no entry for Glaser and mentioned him only in an anonymous paragraph about the 1878 scandal, mistakenly saying that the seven accused were being tried for setting up an illegal private casino. This misconstruction may have been introduced in an article in the magazine *Die Freundschaft* in 1922. Hergemöller, "Anonym: Berlin 1878," in *Mann für Mann* [1998], 95.

116 Hirschfeld, *Memoir*, 35.

8. The Comradely Uranian: John Addington Symonds and the English Translation of the Urning, 1889–1893

1 Whitman, "For You O Democracy," in *Leaves of Grass*, 99.

2 Whitman, *Leaves of Grass*. Harry Cocks wrote about one such association of Whitman followers: the "Eagle Street College" in Bolton, Lancashire, founded in 1885. Cocks, *Nameless Offences*, 157–98.

3 "Adhesiveness" was a word borrowed from phrenology. Whitman in *Democratic Vistas* positioned "adhesiveness" as a neologism for the masculine love between men. It was more ardent than friendship but stopped short of physical expression. Lynch, "'Here Is Adhesiveness,'" 89.

4 Cocks, *Nameless Offences*, 160.

5 This needs to be qualified. Alan Bray charted affective intimacy as an organizing principle for the history of same-sex relations in premodern and early modern England. Bray, *The Friend*, 35–41, 53–77, 209. Whitman's poetic thesis straddled the transition between the older friendship intimacy and a new, more modern configuration where physicality and sex were the organizing principles. However, it stopped short of articulating the full implications and outcomes of that transition.

6 Ulrichs reproduced letters he had received from four correspondents in London. Two of them were connected with the theatre and commented on Friedrich Feldtmann's arrest (see chapter 3): one of these was from an urning in London (in French), 1 January 1868 (Ulrichs, *Memnon, Abtheilung I*, xi–xii; Lombardi-Nash (tr.), *The Riddle*, vol. 1, 293), and the other from an English urning in London (in English), 22 March 1868 (Ulrichs, *Memnon, Abtheilung II*, §130, 119; Lombardi-Nash (tr.), *The Riddle*, vol. 2, 422). The third recounted a series of cross-dressing balls (see chapter 4) (letter from an intermediate urning in London to Ulrichs, 12 January 1868) (Ulrichs, *Memnon, Abtheilung II*, §97, 74–7; Lombardi-Nash (tr.), *The Riddle*, vol. 2, 391–3). The fourth was from a British urning, a member of the Anthropological Society of London, 13 April 1868 (Ulrichs, *Memnon, Abtheilung II*, §94, 72; Lombardi-Nash (tr.), *The Riddle*, vol. 2, 390). Letters 148, 149, 152 and 155 in Douglas Pretsell, *The Correspondence*, 191–7.

7 Cocks, *Nameless Offences*, 158.

8 Regis, *The Memoirs of John Addington Symonds*, 152.

9 Regis, *The Memoirs of John Addington Symonds*, 152.

10 Wilper, *Reconsidering the Emergence*, 71.

11 Grosskurth, *John Addington Symonds*, 119.

12 Regis, *The Memoirs of John Addington Symonds*, 368.

13 Regis, *The Memoirs of John Addington Symonds*, 368.

14 Wilper, *Reconsidering the Emergence*, 71.

15 Regis, *The Memoirs of John Addington Symonds*, 368.

16 Grosskurth, *John Addington Symonds*, 125; Symonds, *A Problem in Greek Ethics* [1883].

17 Symonds, *A Problem in Greek Ethics*, 19–30.

18 Symonds, *A Problem in Greek Ethics*, 20.

19 Symonds, *A Problem in Greek Ethics*, 23.

20 Symonds, *A Problem in Greek Ethics*, 26.

21 Symonds, *A Problem in Greek Ethics*, 27.

22 Grosskurth, *John Addington Symonds*, 125.

23 Grosskurth, *John Addington Symonds*, 164.

24 Funke, "'We Cannot Be Greek Now,'" 143.

25 Grosskurth, *John Addington Symonds*, 272.

26 Symonds and his wife both suffered from tuberculosis. They had moved to Davos, characterized for its dry, cold climate, for health reasons in 1887, and remained there. Grosskurth, *John Addington Symonds*, 181.

27 Letter 1709 to Henry Dakyns, 27 March 1889, in Schueller and Peters, *The Letters of John Addington Symonds*, 364.

28 Regis, *The Memoirs of John Addington Symonds*, 1.

29 Letter 1709 from Symonds to Henry Dakyns, 27 March 1889, in Schueller and Peters, *The Letters of John Addington Symonds*, 364.

30 Regis, *The Memoirs of John Addington Symonds*, 99.

31 Regis, *The Memoirs of John Addington Symonds*, 100.

32 Regis, *The Memoirs of John Addington Symonds*, 101; Shakespeare, "Venus and Adonis."

33 Regis, *The Memoirs of John Addington Symonds*, 149–50.

34 Regis, *The Memoirs of John Addington Symonds*, 371–2.

35 Symonds did not directly describe the sexual encounter with Fusato, preferring to illustrate it with a sonnet he had written. Regis, *The Memoirs of John Addington Symonds*, 516.

36 Regis, *The Memoirs of John Addington Symonds*, 499.

37 Regis, *The Memoirs of John Addington Symonds*, 502.

38 Regis, *The Memoirs of John Addington Symonds*, 492, 509n19.

39 Regis, *The Memoirs of John Addington Symonds*, 517.

40 Regis, *The Memoirs of John Addington Symonds*, 528n44.

41 Krafft-Ebing, *Psychopathia Sexualis*, 3rd ed.

42 Krafft-Ebing, *Psychopathia Sexualis*, 3rd ed., 73–129. Of the three case studies that did not use the word "urning," the subjects used no words to describe themselves, although one of these case studies mentioned the word "homosexual."

43 Krafft-Ebing, *Psychopathia Sexualis*, 3rd ed., 64–73.

44 Casper, *Klinische Novellen*, 36–9.

45 The authorship of this letter came to light after Symonds's death when the manuscript was discovered with his memoirs. It was passed to Edith

Lees, wife of Havelock Ellis, who transcribed it. Brady, *John Addington Symonds*, 209.

46 Krafft-Ebing, *Psychopathia Sexualis*, 4th ed., 216–19; translated as Case Study 4.1 in Pretsell, *Queer Voices*, 103–6.

47 Ulrichs used the word *Krankhaft*, usually translated as "pathology"; Symonds used the word "morbidity" in English to describe the same pathologizing tendency.

48 Regis, *The Memoirs of John Addington Symonds*, 471–3.

49 Regis, *The Memoirs of John Addington Symonds*, 520.

50 Regis, *The Memoirs of John Addington Symonds*, 102.

51 Regis, *The Memoirs of John Addington Symonds*, 103.

52 Regis, *The Memoirs of John Addington Symonds*, 534.

53 Letter 1997 to Margaret Symonds, 8 July 1892, in Schueller and Peters, *The Letters of John Addington Symonds*, 712.

54 Regis, *The Memoirs of John Addington Symonds*, 103.

55 Ellis, *The New Spirit*.

56 Ellis, *The New Spirit*, 104n1.

57 Letter 1791 from Symonds to Henry Havelock Ellis, 6 May 1890, in Schueller and Peters, *The Letters of John Addington Symonds*, 459.

58 Letter 1814 from Symonds to Walt Whitman, 3 August 1890, in Schueller and Peters, *The Letters of John Addington Symonds*, 482.

59 Letter 1814 from Symonds to Walt Whitman, 3 August 1890, in Schueller and Peters, *The Letters of John Addington Symonds*, 484.

60 John Addington Symonds, *A Problem in Modern Ethics*, 118–19.

61 Letter 1837 from Symonds to Ernest Rhys, 12 October 1890, in Schueller and Peters, *The Letters of John Addington Symonds*, 508.

62 Symonds, *Walt Whitman*, 7.

63 Symonds, *Walt Whitman*, 71, 75.

64 Symonds, *Walt Whitman*, 76.

65 Symonds, *Walt Whitman*, 76–7.

66 The essay was not published until 1893, one year after Whitman's death and only a few months before Symonds himself died. When it was, it was immediately angrily rejected by some of Whitman's American followers. Grosskurth, *John Addington Symonds*, 275n.

67 Grosskurth, *John Addington Symonds*, 280; Symonds, *A Problem in Modern Ethics*.

68 Symonds, *A Problem in Modern Ethics*, 3.

69 Brady, *John Addington Symonds*, 151n.

70 Letter 1847 to Edmund Gosse, 23 November 1890, in Schueller and Peters, *The Letters of John Addington Symonds*, 520.

71 There had been psychiatric papers in English on the subject of contrary sexual feeling since 1881 that included literature reviews. However, this

work by Symonds, where he translated contrary sexual feeling as "sexual inversion," and the simultaneous book from Albert Moll in Berlin together mark the first sexological works after Krafft-Ebing's *Psychopathia Sexualis*.

72 Symonds, *A Problem in Modern Ethics*, 60.

73 Symonds, *A Problem in Modern Ethics*, 68–74.

74 Symonds, *A Problem in Modern Ethics*, 74.

75 Letter from Havelock Ellis to Symonds, 3 Jan 1893, in Brady, *John Addington Symonds*, 238.

76 Symonds, *A Problem in Modern Ethics*, 84.

77 Symonds, *A Problem in Modern Ethics*, 87–8.

78 Symonds, *A Problem in Modern Ethics*, 57.

79 In reality, close to half of the case studies in *Psychopathia Sexualis* were of effeminate men. In the 1889 edition, there were thirty-five case studies, of which fifteen were in the section headed "Effeminatio"; a further three in other sections were also classified as effeminate. In the 1890 edition, there were fifty-three case studies, one third of which were included in the section for "Effeminatio." However, some effeminate urnings appeared in other sections, so a breakdown of Krafft-Ebing's comments on gendered behaviour within each case study gives a relatively even split, with twenty-four masculine, twenty-one effeminate, and five intermediate.

80 Sedgwick, *Between Men*, 211.

81 Joyce, LGBT Victorians, 119.

82 See, for example, his comparison between Henry Sidgwick and himself in Letter 1807 to Henry Dakyns, 19 July 1890, in Schueller and Peters, *The Letters of John Addington Symonds*, 476.

83 Sedgwick, *Between Men*, 211.

84 Sedgwick, *Between Men*, 204.

85 Symonds, *A Problem in Modern Ethics*, 115.

86 Symonds, *A Problem in Modern Ethics*, 116.

87 Symonds, *A Problem in Modern Ethics*, 119.

88 Symonds, *A Problem in Modern Ethics*, 116–22.

89 Symonds, *A Problem in Modern Ethics*, 118.

90 Symonds, *A Problem in Modern Ethics*, 118.

91 Symonds, *A Problem in Modern Ethics*, 124.

92 Wilper, *Reconsidering the Emergence*, 73.

93 Symonds, *A Problem in Modern Ethics*, 130.

94 Grosskurth, *John Addington Symonds*, 281.

95 Symonds, *A Problem in Modern Ethics*, 130.

96 A draft for a letter from Ulrichs addressed to an unknown recipient surfaced in the 1950s and is now held at the Staatsbibliothek in Berlin. It is possible that this was an initial draft for Ulrichs's reply to Symonds.

Letter from Ulrichs to unknown recipient (possibly John Addington Symonds), 17 January 1891, Staatsbibliothek zu Berlin – Preußischer Kulturbesitz, Handwriting Department, Signature: Coll. Autogr.: Ulrichs, Karl Heinrich, DE-611-HS-1626086, ff1–3. Translated as letter 225, in Pretsell, *The Correspondence*, 259–60.

97 Letter from Ulrichs to unknown recipient (possibly Symonds), 17 January 1891, 259.

98 Letter 1959 from Symonds to Horatio Brown, 13 February 1892, in Schueller and Peters, *The Letters of John Addington Symonds*, 663.

99 Letter 1891 from Symonds to Henry Dakyns, 20 May 1891, in Schueller and Peters, *The Letters of John Addington Symonds*, 579.

100 Letter 1891 from Symonds to Henry Dakyns, 20 May 1891, in Schueller and Peters, *The Letters of John Addington Symonds*, 579.

101 Henry Havelock Ellis and John Addington Symonds, *Studies in the Psychology of Sex*.

102 As Ellis appended a note to this section, one can assume that the editing and augmenting was Symonds's and not Ellis's work. "[Ellis:] He seems, however, to have gone further than Symonds here states, and to have advocated marriage between persons of the same sex." In Ellis and Symonds, *Sexual Inversion*, 309.

103 Josiah Flynt, an American sociologist who had pioneered the study of tramps, was the author of *Tramping with Tramps* (1900) and *The World of Graft* (1901).

104 Letter 2087 to Havelock Ellis, 12 February 1893, in Schueller and Peters, *The Letters of John Addington Symonds*, 817. This use of questionnaires by Symonds in 1893 was one stage in the development of the sexological research questionnaire. Pretsell, "The Evolution of the Questionnaire," 344.

105 Grosskurth, *John Addington Symonds*, 315–16.

106 Ellis and Symonds, *Das konträre Geschlechtsgefühl*.

107 In 1898, the bookseller George Bedborough was arrested and prosecuted for selling one copy of the 1897 English edition. Ellis moved publication of the next edition to New York.

108 Babington, *Bibliography*, 122–7.

109 Grosskurth, *John Addington Symonds*, 292; Ellis and Symonds, *Sexual Inversion*, 56.

110 Ellis had a general wish to advance science only incrementally. In a discussion concerning the issue of morbidity, Ellis wrote to Symonds on 21 December 1892, "I am quite prepared to go somewhat beyond Moll and would most certainly wish to avoid any assumption of the necessity of psychopathic conditions, or question-begging epithets of the 'morbid' class. But I do not wish to put myself in opposition to the medical psychologists, the people who have most carefully studied the question; to

do so in any case would be bad policy; I simply wish to carry their investigations a step farther." In Brady, *John Addington Symonds*, 234.

111 Ellis and Symonds, *Sexual Inversion*, 192.

112 Ellis and Symonds, *Sexual Inversion*, 173.

113 Ellis and Symonds, *Sexual Inversion*, 193n16.

114 For Ellis, this was not necessarily about erasure of the cross-dresser. Ellis may have been beginning to make a distinction between the homosexual and gender variance. Alongside Magnus Hirschfield, he would go on to pioneer the study of transvestism, gender dysphoria, and what he would later call "Eonism."

115 Ellis and Symonds, *Sexual Inversion*, 202.

116 Ellis and Symonds, *Sexual Inversion*, 214.

117 Ellis and Symonds, *Sexual Inversion*, 214.

118 Letter from Carpenter to Ellis, 28 November 1895, in Ellis and Symonds, *Sexual Inversion*, 55.

119 For discussions of Carpenter's engagement with Symonds over this publication before he died, see Rowbotham, *Edward Carpenter*, 186–9; and Bauer, *English Literary Sexology*, 73–9.

120 Carpenter, *Homogenic Love*, 19–20.

121 Cocks, *Nameless Offences*, 159.

122 Michael M. Kaylor claims, "Given that the prominent Uranians were trained Classicists, I consider ludicrous the view, widely held, that "Uranian" derives from the German apologias and legal appeals written by Karl Heinrich Ulrichs in the 1860s." However, the poets themselves were likely to either have read Symonds's polemic or know someone who did. Kaylor, *Secreted Desires*, xiiin1.

123 Nicholson, *Love in Earnest*. For a more detailed discussion of this see Smith, *Love in Earnest*, xvii–xxii.

124 Wilde, *The Importance of Being Earnest*.

125 Letter 705 from Oscar Wilde to Robert Ross, February 1898, in Holland and Hart-Davis, eds., *Wilde, Complete Letters*, 1019.

126 Halperin, *One Hundred Years of Homosexuality*, 16.

Conclusion: The End of the Urning Age

1 Hirschfeld, *Memoir*, 8.

2 When they were published in 1907, the articles of the WhK did use the word "homosexual," but this reflected a change in popular nomenclature that occurred in the decade after 1897. Contemporary texts from Hirschfeld, Moll, and de Joux indicate that "urning" was the dominant terminology in the 1890s, although the word "homosexual" was by then coming into use. Although "homosexual" was gaining ground in the

scientific literature, it may have coexisted with "urning" long before then in queer settings. As late as 1916, Hirschfeld was still using "urning" in preference to "homosexual" when writing in a sociopolitical rather than scientific context. Hirschfeld, *Jahrbuch für sexuelle Zwischenstufen*.

3 Hirschfeld, *The Homosexuality of Men and Women*, 1065.
4 Ulrichs, "Vier Briefe." For translations, see letters 80, 82, 85, and 86 in Pretsell, *The Correspondence*.
5 Hirschfeld, *The Homosexuality of Men and Women*, 1062–77.
6 Hirschfeld, *The Homosexuality of Men and Women*, 1077.
7 Hirschfeld, *The Homosexuality of Men and Women*, 1077.
8 Historical appraisal of this period in history has frequently used Hirschfeld as a source, reproducing his elision of the individuals who responded to and followed Ulrichs and collapsing the period between the end of Ulrichs's campaign and the launch of Hirschfeld's WhK. See, for example, Marhoefer, *Racism and the Making of Gay Rights*, 32.
9 De Joux, *Die Enterbten des Liebesglueckes*, 126.
10 Von Kupffer, *Lieblingsminne und Freundesliebe*, 3, my translation.
11 Mildenberger, … *in der Richtung Homosexualität verdorben*, 9–10.
12 Hiller, "Zur Frage der Bezeichnung," 3, my translation.
13 Ulrichs did appeal for, but apparently did not receive any, letters from same-sex-attracted women.
14 Herzog, *Sexuality in Europe*, 6.
15 For a survey of the sexual rights campaigns of the German feminist movements, see Treusch-Dieter "Die Sexualdebatte."
16 Rüling, "What Interest Does the Women's Movement Have," 36.
17 Marx, *Urningsliebe*.
18 Marx, *Urningsliebe*, 8.
19 Krafft-Ebing, *Psychopathia Sexualis*, 5th ed., 66–79, 213–20. Translated as Case Studies 7.1–7.3 in Pretsell, *Queer Voices*, 157–83.
20 Hirschfeld, "Die intersexuelle Konstitution," 14.

Bibliography

Primary Sources

Archival Documents

Duberke, Karl. Confession at the apartment of Adolf Glaser, 18 March 1878. Stadtarchiv Braunschweig. H III Nr 6 Glaser, Adolf Dr, 76.

Feldtmann, Friedrich. Letter of appeal to the Court of Appeal. Staatsarchiv Bremen 2-D.17.d.10.

Feldtmann, Friedrich. Letter refusing the appeal of Friedrich Feldtmann, 10 September 1868. Staatsarchiv Bremen 2-D.17.d.10.

Forster, Jakob Rudolf. Interrogations from Forster's criminal file at St. Gallen. Staatsarchiv des Kantons St. Gallen. Signatur GA 002/145.

– Judgment of the Cantonal Court of St Gallen in the criminal case of Forster and consorts concerning fornication against nature, 14 January 1880. Staatsarchiv des Kantons St. Gallen. KA R. 182–4.

– Letter to King Charles of Württemberg, 28 December 1877. Landesarchiv Baden-Württemberg. Akte E 14 (Kgl. Kabinett) Bü 2049.

Forsters Liebhaberheft. Staatsarchiv St. Gallen. KA R. 182–4.

Glaser, Adolf. Letter to Wilhelm Raabe, 10 April 1878. Stadtarchiv Braunschweig. H III Nr 6 Glaser, Adolf Dr, 77.

– Letter to Wilhelm Raabe, 30 April 1878. Stadtarchiv Braunschweig. H III Nr 6 Glaser, Adolf Dr, 78.

– Letter to Wilhelm Raabe, 4 July 1878. Stadtarchiv Braunschweig. H III Nr 6 Glaser, Adolf Dr, 80.

– Letter to Wilhelm Raabe, 29 August 1878. Stadtarchiv Braunschweig. H III Nr 6 Glaser, Adolf Dr, 81.

– Letter to Wilhelm Raabe, 26 January 1882. Stadtarchiv Braunschweig. H III Nr 6 Glaser, Adolf Dr, 89.

– Letter to Wilhelm Raabe, 7 April 1895. Stadtarchiv Braunschweig. H III Nr 6 Glaser, Adolf Dr, 99.

Kertbeny, Karl Maria. Unpublished assorted papers. Hungary, National Széchényi Library. Manuscript Collection. Oct. Germ. 296, documents 371–6, 377–87; Oct. Germ. 297, documents 440–3.

Lieutenant General Voigts-Rhetz. Letter to the Royal Minister President and Minister of Foreign Affairs, Knight of the Supreme Order, His Excellency Count of Bismarck-Schönhausen, 31 July 1867. Berlin, Geheimes Staatsarchiv Preußischer Kulturbesitz I. HA Geh. Rat, Rep. 90A, no. 3773. ff9,10.

Privy Counsellor Wagener. Letter to Lord Camphausen, Vice President of the State Ministry, 14 April 1874. Geheimes Staatsarchiv Preußischer Kulturbesitz I. HA Geh. Rat, Rep. 90A, no. 3773. ff67–9.

Report from High Court to the Minister of Justice 8 September 1868. Staatsarchiv Bremen 2-D.17.d.10.

Stuttgart City director Hofer. Letter to State Councillor von Grättner, 29 January 1878. Landesarchiv Baden-Württemberg. Akte E 14 (Kgl. Kabinett) Bü 2049.

Published Primary Sources

Carpenter, Edward. *Homogenic Love, and Its Place in a Free Society*. Manchester: The Labour Press, 1894.

Ellis, Henry Havelock. *The New Spirit*. London: Bell, 1890.

Ellis, Henry Havelock, and John Addington Symonds. *Das konträre Geschlechtsgefühl*. Leipzig: G.H. Wigand, 1896.

– *Sexual Inversion: A Critical Edition*. Edited by Ivan Crozier. London: Palgrave Macmillan, 2008.

– *Studies in the Psychology of Sex*, vol. 1: *Sexual Inversion*. London: Wilson and Macmillan, 16, John Street, Bedford Row, W.C., 1897.

Forster, Jakob Rudolf. *Justizmorde im 19. Jahrhundert: Wahrheits Darstellung des fast unglaublich verfolgten Schweizers J.R. Forster*. Zurich: self-published, 1898.

Friedlaender, Benedict. *Die Renaissance des Eros Uranios: Die physiologische Freundschaft, ein normaler Grundtrieb des Menschen und eine Frage der männlichen Gesellungsfreiheit*. Schmargendorf, Berlin: Renaissance, 1904.

G. [Adolf Glaser]. "In Memoriam." *Jahrbuch für sexuelle Zwischenstufen* 4 (1902): 947–55.

[Geigel, Alois.]. *Das Paradoxon der Venus Urania: Geschrieben für Aerzte, Juristen, Geistliche und Erzieher*. Würzburg: Stuber, 1869.

Hiller, Kurt. "Zur Frage der Bezeichnung." *Der Kreis: eine Monatsschrift = Le Cercle: revue mensuelle* 14, no. 8 (1946): 2–6.

Hirschfeld, Magnus. *The Homosexuality of Men and Women*. Translated by Michael Lombardi-Nash. New York: Prometheus Books, 2000. Originally published in German as *Die Homosexualität des Mannes und des Weibes*. Berlin: Louis Marcus, 1914.

- "Die intersexuelle Konstitution." *Jahrbuch für sexuelle Zwischenstufen* 23 (1923): 3–27.
- *Jahrbuch für sexuelle Zwischenstufen mit besonderer Berücksichtigung der Homosexualität* (Vierteljahrsberichte des Wissenschaftlich-humanitären Komitees während der Kriegszeit) 16, no. 2 (1916).
- *Memoir: Celebrating 25 Years of the First LGBT Organization (1897–1922)*. Translated by Michael Lombardi-Nash. Jacksonville: Urania Manuscripts, 2020. Originally published in German as *Von einst bis jetzt: Geschichte einer homosexuellen Bewegung 1897–1922*. Berlin: Max Spohr, 1922.
- "Vorbemerkung des Herausgebers." *Jahrbuch für sexuelle Zwischenstufen* 7, no. 1 (1905): I.
Hössli, Heinrich. *Eros. Die Männerliebe der Griechen, ihre Beziehungen zur Geschichte, Erziehung, Literatur und Gesetzgebung aller Zeiten*, vol. 1. Glarus: self-published, 1836; vol. 2. St. Gallen: in commission from C.P. Scheitlin, 1838.
Hugländer, F. [Hugo Friedländer]. "Aus dem homosexuellen Leben Alt-Berlins." *Jahrbuch für sexuelle Zwischenstufen* 14 (1914): 45–63.
Jäger, Gustav [Karl Maria Kertbeny]. "Ein bisher ungedrucktes Kapitel über Homosexualität aus der Entdeckung der Seele." *Jahrbuch für sexuelle Zwischenstufen* 2 (1900): 53–125.
J.G.F. "Ein Fall von Effemination mit Fetischismus." *Jahrbuch für sexuelle Zwischenstufen* 2 (1900): 324–44.
Joux, Otto de. *Die Enterbten des Liebesglückes, oder Das dritte Geschlecht*. Leipzig: Spohr, 1893.
Kant, Immanuel. *Gesammelte Schriften*. Band 27, Abteilung 4, Band 4, 1. Berlin: Walter de Gruyter, 1974.
Kertbeny, Karl Maria. *§143 des preussischen Strafgesetzbuches vom 14. April 1851 und seine Aufrechterhaltung als §152 im Entwurfe eines Strafgesetzbuches für den Norddeutschen Bund*. Leipzig: Serbe's Verlag, 1869. Reproduced in *Karl Maria Kertbeny: Schriften zur Homosexualitätsforschung*, edited by Manfred Herzer. Berlin: rosa Winkel, 2000.
- *Erinnerung an Charles Sealsfield*. Brussels and Leipzig: Ahn, 1864.
- *Das Gemeinschädliche des §143 des preussischen Strafgesetzbuches vom 14. April 1851 und daher seine nothwendige Tilgung § 152 im Entwurfe eines Strafgesetzbuches für den Norddeutschen Bund*. Leipzig: Serbe's Verlag, 1869.
- *Hundertsechzig Lyrische Dichtungen von Alexander Petöfi: Aus dem Ungarischen im Versmaße der Originale übersetzt von K.M. Kertbeny*. 4 völlig neu bearbeitete Auflage. Elberfeld und Leipzig: Sam. Lucas, 1866.
- "Persönliches Schlußwort." In *Bibliografie der ungarischen nationalen und internationalen Literatur. Band l: Ungarn betreffende deutsche Erstlings-Drucke 1454–1600*. Mitgetheilt von K.M. Kertbeny. Leipzig und Budapest 1880, S. CLV, CLVII, CLIX. Facsimile reproduced in *CAPRI* 4, 2/88 (1988): 29–30.
- *Silhouetten und Reliquien*, vol. 1. Prague: J.F. Kober, 1861.

Lombardi-Nash, Michael, trans. *The Riddle of "Man-Manly" Love: The Pioneering Work on Male Homosexuality*, vols. 1–2 [translation of twelve pamphlets by Karl Heinrich Ulrichs]. Buffalo: Prometheus Books, 1994.

Mapleson, James Henry. *The Mapleson Memoirs, 1848–1888*, vol. 1. New York: Belford, Clark, 1888.

Marx, Heinrich. *Urningsliebe: Die sittliche Hebung des Urningthums und die Streichung des § 175 des deutschen Strafgesetzbuches*. Leipzig: H. Marx Selbstverlag, 1875.

Nicholson, John Gambril. *Love in Earnest: Sonnets, Ballades, and Lyrics*. London: E. Stock, 1892.

Rüling, Anna. "What Interest Does the Women's Movement Have in Solving the Homosexual Problem?," translated by Michael Lombardi-Nash. In *Sodomites and Urnings: Homosexual Representations in Classic German Journals*, edited by Michael Lombardi-Nash. Binghampton: Harrington Park Press, 2006.

Sontag, C.R. "Drei Bemerkungen zu dem Entwurf eines Strafrechtes für den Norddeutschen Bund." *Archiv für preussisches Strafrecht* 18 (1870): 15–28.

Stieber, Wilhelm. *Die Prostitution in Berlin und ihre Opfer*. Berlin: A. Hofmann, 1846.

Symonds, John Addington. *A Problem in Greek Ethics*. London: self-published in ten copies, 1883.

– *A Problem in Modern Ethics* [1890]. London: privately printed, 1896.

– *Soldier Love and Related Matter*. Translated and edited by Andrew Dakyns. Eastbourne: self-published by Andrew Dakyns, 2007.

– *Walt Whitman: A Study*. London: John C. Nimmo, 1893.

Ulrichs, Carlo Arrigo [Karl Heinrich]. *Cupressi: Carmina in Memoriam Ludovici II Regis Bavariae*. Berlin: W Pinn, 1887.

Ulrichs, Karl Heinrich. *Alaudae: Eine lateinische Zeitschrift, 1889–1895*. Nachdruck mit einer Einleitung von Wilfried Stroh. Hamburg: MännerschwarmSkript Verlag, 2004.

– *Ara Spei*. Leipzig: H. Matthes, 1865. Reproduced in Lombardi-Nash as "Book Five: Ara Spei," *The Riddle of "Man-Manly" Love*, vol. 1, 181–258.

– *Araxes*. Schleiz: C. Hübscher'sche Buchhandlung, 1870. Reproduced in Lombardi-Nash as "Book Eleven: Araxes," *The Riddle of "Man-Manly" Love*, vol. 2, 601–24.

– *Argonauticus*. Leipzig: A. Serbe's Verlag, 1869. Reproduced in Lombardi-Nash as "Book Nine: Argonauticus," *The Riddle of "Man-Manly" Love*, vol. 2, 473–540.

– *Auf Bienchens Flügeln: Ein Flug um den Erdball in Epigrammen und poetischen Bildern*. Leipzig: Schaeffer, 1875.

– *Critische Pfeile*. Leipzig: Otto und Kadler, 1880. Reproduced in Lombardi-Nash as "Book Twelve: Critical Arrows," *The Riddle of "Man-Manly" Love*, vol. 2, 625–90.

- "Das deutsche Postfürstenthum, sonst reichsunmittelbar: jetzt bundesunmittelbar Gemeinrechtliche Darstellung des öffentlichen Rechtsdes Fürsten von Thurn und Taxis als Inhabers der gemeinen deutschen Post." *Archiv für das öffentliche Recht des deutschen Bundes*, edited by Dr. J.T.B. von Linde. 4(2), 41–296.
- *Formatrix*. Leipzig: H. Matthes, 1865. Reproduced in Lombardi-Nash as "Book Four: Formatrix," in *The Riddle of "Man-Manly" Love*, vol. 1, 127–80.
- *Gladius Furens*. Kassel: G. Württenberger, 1868. Reproduced in Lombardi-Nash as "Book Six: Gladius Furens," in *The Riddle of "Man-Manly" Love*, vol. 1, 259–88.
- *Großdeutsches Programm und Lösung des grossdeutschen Problems*. Frankfurt: Verlag für Kunst und Wissenschaft, 1862.
- *Inclusa*. Leipzig: H. Matthes, 1864. Reproduced in Lombardi-Nash as "Book Two: Inclusa," in *The Riddle of "Man-Manly" Love*, vol. 1, 49–95.
- *Incubus*. Leipzig: A. Serbe's Verlag, 1869. Reproduced in Lombardi-Nash as "Book Eight: Incubus," in *The Riddle of "Man-Manly" Love*, vol. 2, 435–72.
- *Memnon, Abtheilung I*. Schleiz: C. Hübscher'sche Buchhandlung, 1868. Reproduced in Lombardi-Nash as "Book Seven: Memnon I," in *The Riddle of "Man-Manly" Love*, vol. 1, 289–333.
- *Memnon, Abtheilung II*. Schleiz: C. Hübscher'sche Buchhandlung, 1868. Reproduced in Lombardi-Nash as "Book Seven: Memnon II," in *The Riddle of "Man-Manly" Love*, vol. 2, 351–434.
- *Der Nassau-Taxis'sche Postvertrag und der Braun'sche Antrag in der Nassauer 2. Kammer*. Giessen: Ferber, 1861.
- *Prometheus*. Leipzig: A. Serbe, 1870. Reproduced in Lombardi-Nash as "Book Ten: Prometheus," in *The Riddle of "Man-Manly" Love*, vol. 2, 541–99.
- "Vier Briefe." *Jahrbuch für sexuelle Zwischenstufen* 1 (1899), 36–70.
- *Vindex*. Leipzig: H. Matthes, 1865. Reproduced in Lombardi-Nash as "Book One: Vindex," in *The Riddle of "Man-Manly" Love*, vol. 1, 29–48.
- *Vindicta*. Leipzig: H. Matthes, 1865. Reproduced in Lombardi-Nash as "Book Three: Vindicta," in *The Riddle of "Man-Manly" Love*, vol. 1, 97–126.
von Kupffer, Elisar. *Lieblingsminne und Freundesliebe in der Weltliteratur*. Eberswalde: Siegfried Dyck, 1900.
von Tresckow, Hans. *Von Fürsten und anderen Sterblichen: Erinnerungen eines Kriminalkommissars*. Berlin: F. Fontane, 1922.
Weindel, Henri de, and Fischer, F.P. *L'homosexualité en Allemagne: étude documentaire et anecdotique*. Paris: Juven, 1908.

Historic Medical Texts

Backman, Johan A. "Ett fall af konträr sexualkänsla." *Finska Läkaresällskapets Handlingar* 24 (1882): 151–60.

Berliner Medicinische-Psychologische Gesellschaft. 15 December 1868. *Archiv für Psychiatrie und Nervenkrankheiten* 2 (1869): 226–7.

Blumer, G. Alder. "A Case of Perverted Sexual Instinct (Conträre Sexualempfindung)." *American Journal of Insanity* 39 (1882): 22–35.

Casper, Johann Ludwig. *Klinische Novellen zur gerichtlichen Medicin: nach eigenen Erfahrungen.* Berlin: Hirschwald, 1863.

Gock, Dr. H. "Beitrag zur Kenntniss der conträren Sexualempfindung." *Archiv für Psychiatrie und Nervenkrankheiten* 5 (1875): 564–74.

Griesinger, Wilhelm. "Vortrag zur Eröffnung der psychiatrischen Clinik zu Berlin." *Archiv für Psychiatrie und Nervenkrankheiten* 1 (1868): 636–54.

Hirschfeld, Magnus. "Aus der Kriegzeit. (VI. Teile)." *Jahrbuch für sexuelle Zwischenstufen mit besonderer Berücksichtigung der Homosexualität* (Vierteljahrsberichte des Wissenschaftlich-humanitären Komitees während der Kriegszeit) 16, no. 2 (1916): 51–65.

– "Das Ergebnis der statistischen Untersuchungen über den Prozentsatz der Homosexuellen." *Jahrbuch für sexuelle Zwischenstufen* 6 (1904): 109–78.

– *The Homosexuality of Men and Women.* Translated by Michael Lombardi-Nash. New York: Prometheus Books, 2000. Originally published in German as *Die Homosexualität des Mannes und des Weibes.* Berlin: Louis Marcus, 1914.

– "Die intersexuelle Konstitution." *Jahrbuch für sexuelle Zwischenstufen* 23 (1923): 3–27.

Kiernan, James G. "Insanity: Lecture XXVI – Sexual Perversion." *Detroit Lancet* 7 (1884): 481–4.

Krafft-Ebing, Richard von. "Die conträre Sexualempfindung vor dem Forum." *Jahrbücher für Psychiatrie* 6 (1885): 34–47.

– *Der Conträrsexuale vor dem Strafrichter.* Vienna: Franz Deutige, 1895.

– *Lehrbuch der Psychiatrie auf klinischer Grundlage für practische Ärzte und Studirende,* 2nd ed. Stuttgart: Ferdinand Enke, 1883.

– "Neue Forschungen auf dem Gebiet der Psychopathia Sexualis." *Jahrbuch für sexuelle Zwischenstufen* 3 (1901): 1–36.

– *Neue Forschungen auf dem Gebiet der Psychopathia Sexualis: Eine medicinisch-psychologische Studie.* Stuttgart: Ferdinand Enke, 1890.

– *Neue Forschungen auf dem Gebiet der Psychopathia Sexualis: Eine medicinisch-psychologische Studie.* Stuttgart: Ferdinand Enke, 1891.

– *Psychopathia Sexualis: Eine klinisch-forensische Studie,* 1st ed. Stuttgart: Ferdinand Enke, 1886.

– *Psychopathia Sexualis. Mit besonderer Berücksichtigung der conträren Sexualempfindung: Eine klinisch-forensische Studie,* 2nd ed. Stuttgart: Ferdinand Enke, 1887.

– *Psychopathia Sexualis. Mit besonderer Berücksichtigung der conträren Sexualempfindung: Eine klinisch-forensische Studie,* 3rd ed. Stuttgart: Ferdinand Enke, 1888.

– *Psychopathia Sexualis. Mit besonderer Berücksichtigung der conträren Sexualempfindung: Eine klinisch-forensische Studie*, 4th ed. Stuttgart: Ferdinand Enke, 1889.

– *Psychopathia Sexualis. Mit besonderer Berücksichtigung der conträren Sexualempfindung: Eine klinisch-forensische Studie*, 5th ed. Stuttgart: Ferdinand Enke, 1890.

– *Psychopathia Sexualis. Mit besonderer Berücksichtigung der conträren Sexualempfindung: Eine klinisch-forensische Studie*, 9th ed. Stuttgart: Ferdinand Enke, 1894.

– "Die Sinnestäuschungen und ihre Bedeutung für die gerichtliche Psychologie." *Friedreich's Blätter für Gerichtliche Medicin* 15 (1864): 243–77.

– "Ueber gewisse Anomalien des Geschlechtstriebs und die klinisch-forensische Verwerthung derselben als eines wahrscheinlich functionellen Degenerationszeichens des centralen Nervensystems." *Archiv für Psychiatrie und Nervenkrankheiten* 7 (1877): 291–312.

– "Zur conträren Sexualempfindung. Autobiographie und strafrechtliche Betrachtungen über den Paragraphen 175 des deutschen Strafgesetzbuchs von einem Conträr-Sexualen." *Friedreichs Blätter für gerichtliche Medicin* 42 (1891): 385–400.

– "Zur 'conträren Sexualempfindung' in klinisch-forensischer Hinsicht." *Allgemeine Zeitschrift für Psychiatrie* 38 (1882): 211–27.

– "Zur Lehre von der conträren Sexualempfindung." *Der Irrenfreund* 26 (1884): 1–14.

Krueg, Julius. 'Perverted Sexual Instincts." *Brain* 4 (1881): 368–76.

Liman, Carl. *Practisches Handbuch der gerichtlichen Medicin von Johann Ludwig Casper*. Berlin: August Hirschwald, 1871.

Meckel, Johann Friedrich, "Ueber die Zwitterbildungen," *Archiv für die Physiologie* 11 (1812): 263–340.

Michéa, Claude-François. "Des déviations maladives de l'appétit vénérien." *L'Union médicale: journal des intérêts scientifiques et pratiques, moraux et professionnels du corps médical* (17 July 1849): 338–9.

Moll, Albert. *Die conträre Sexualempfindung, Mit Benutzung amtlichen Materials*. Berlin: Fischer, 1891.

– *Die conträre Sexualempfindung, Mit Benutzung amtlichen Materials*, 3rd ed. Berlin: Fischer, 1899.

Rabow, Siegfried. "Über angeborene conträre Sexualempfindung." *Zeitschrift für klinische Medicin* 17 (1890): 129–43.

Savage, George. "A Case of Sexual Perversion." *Journal of Mental Science* (1884): 390–1.

Schmincke, Dr. "Ein Fall von conträrer Sexualempfindung." *Archiv für Psychiatrie und Nervenkrankheiten* 3 (1872): 225–6.

Scholz, Dr. "Bekentnisse eines an perverser Geschlechtsrichtung Leidenden."
Vierteljahrschrift für Gerichtliche Medizin 19 (1873): 321–8.
Servaes, Dr. F. "Zur Kenntniss von der conträren Sexualempfindung." *Archiv
für Psychiatrie und Nervenkrankheiten* 6 (1876): 484–95.
Shaw, J.C., and G.N. Ferris. "Perverted Sexual Instinct." *Journal of Nervous and
Mental Disease* 10 (1883): 185–204.
Shrady, George F. "Perverted Sexual Instinct." *Medical Record* 26 (1884): 70–1.
Stark, Karl. "Über conträre Sexualempfindung. Zehnte Wanderversammlung
der südwestdeutschen Irrenärzte zu Karlsruhe." *Allgemeine Zeitschrift für
Psychiatrie und psychisch-gerichtliche Medicin* 33 (1877): 209–16.
Strassmann, Fritz. *Lehrbuch der gerichtlichen Medizin*, Auflag 1. Berlin:
Ferdinand Enke, 1895.
Tamassia, Arrigo. "Sull' inversione dell' istinto sessuale." *Rivista sperimentale
di freniatria e di medicina legale* 2 (1878): 97–117.
Westphal, Karl Friedrich Otto. "Die conträre Sexualempfindung: Symptom
eines neuropathischen (psychopathischen) Zustandes." *Archiv für Psychiatrie
und Nervenkrankheiten* 2 (1869): 73–108.

Nineteenth-Century Legal Codes

Allgemeines Reichs-Gesetz- und Regierungsblatt für das Kaiserthum
Österreich 1852.
Art. 123 in *Strafgesetzbuch für den Kanton Zürich*, StAZH OS 15 (S. 392–470).
"Zürcher Gesetzessammlung seit 1803," Staatsarchiv des Kantons Zürich,
2021. https://www.archives-quickaccess.ch/search/stazh/os.
Art. 189 in Kanton St. Gallen Gesetzessammlung. Neue Folge. Fünfter Band.
1886 bis 1890. St. Gallen: Zollikofer, 1890.

Newspapers and Serials

SOURCED FROM ADELSQUELLEN.DE
Schlodtman, Steckbrief, Filsinger 18 October 1867, Der Wächter. *Polizeiblatt für
Norddeutschland, Schwerin* 30, no. 81 (23 October 1867): 319.

SOURCED FROM ZEFYS ZEITUNGSINFORMATIONSSYSTEM [ONLINE DATABASE]
Berliner Gerichtszeitung, 19 January 1869, 17 Jg. Nr 7, 2.
Berliner Gerichtszeitung, 6 July 1869, 17 Jg. Nr 76, 1–2.
Berliner Gerichtszeitung, 30 October 1869, 17 Jg. Nr 126, 1.

SOURCED FROM BRITISH NEWSPAPER ARCHIVE [ONLINE DATABASE]
"MUSIC – Beethoven's 'Fidelio.'" *London Illustrated News*, Saturday, 2 May
1868, 20.

"POLICE INTELLIGENCE – This day, Marlborough-Street." *Sun*, Evening, Friday, 18 October 1867, 7.

SOURCED FROM E-NEWSPAPERARCHIVES.CH

"Feuilleton 1878: Theater." *Neue Zürcher Zeitung*, 1 June 1878, Nr 252, 1–2.
Die Ostschweiz, No. 264, St. Gallen, 15 November 1879, 3.
St. Galler Volksblatt, 19 January 1884, 2.
"Theater." *Neue Zürcher Zeitung*, 31 December 1874, Nr 633, 5.
"Theater in Zürich." *Neue Zürcher Zeitung*, 11 April 1862, Nr 101, 393–4.
Züricherische Freitagszeitung, 14 December 1883, 3.

Reference Works and Internet Sources

"H. Matthes catalogues." In *Gesamt-Verlags-Katalog des deutscher Buchhandels, Ein Bild deutcher Geistesarbeit und Cultur, Vollständig bis Ende 1880 VII*, vol. 2, 367–82. Münster: Adolf Russels Verlag, 1882.
Kolb, G. Fr. *Grundriss der Statistik der Völkerzustands- und Staatenkunde*. Leipzig: Förstnersche Buchhandlung, 1862.
Roeder, Ferdinand. *Theaterkalender auf das Jahr 1865, Achter Jahrgang*. Berlin: W.F. Peiser, 1865.
Schmidt, Heinrich. *25 Jahre des Bremer Stadt-Theaters*. Bremen: Bremer Stadt-Theaters, 1868.
"St. Gallen Gemeinde." *Historisches Lexikon der Schweiz*, 6 January 2012. https://hls-dhs-dss.ch/de/articles/001321/2012-01-06.
"Statistik und Sehenswürdigkeiten von Berlin." In *Berliner Adreßbuch: für das Jahr 1895: unter Benutzung amtlicher Quellen* (Berlin: Loewenthal, 1895), 183.
"Zurich." *Encylopaedia Britannica*, 11th ed., vol. 27, "Vetch to Zymotic Diseases." Cambridge: Cambridge Universigty Press, 1911, 1057. https://archive.org/details/encyclopaediabri28chisrich/page/1056/mode/2up?q=Zurich.

Records Held on Ancestry.com

Berlin, Germany, Deaths, 1874–1955: FELDTMANN, Friederich Conrad Anton, 12 February 1884, Pankow, Berlin, Certificate number 11, Erstregister C, ancestry.com.au.
Germany, *Select Births and Baptisms, 1558–1898*: Bremen, Germany, 26 January 1834, FELDTMANN, Friedrich Conrad Anton, FHL Film Number – 1344155, ancestry.com.au.
Marriage certificate of Adolf Glaser and Anna Peterson, Landesarchiv Berlin; Berlin, Deutschland; Personenstandsregister Heiratsregister; Laufende Nummer: 402, ancestry.com.au.

Secondary Sources

Abrams, Lynn. "Crime against Marriage? Wife-Beating, Divorce and the Law in Nineteenth-Century Hamburg." In *Gender and Crime in Modern Europe*, edited by Meg Arnot and Cornelie Usborne, 118–36. London: Taylor and Francis, 1999.

ACSF investigators. "AIDS and Sexual Behaviour in France." *Nature* 360 (1992): 407–9.

Babington, Percy L. *Bibliography of the Writings of John Addington Symonds* [1925]. New York: Burt Franklyn, 1968.

Bailey, D.S. *Homosexuality and the Western Christian Tradition*. London: Longmans, 1955.

Bailey, J. Michael, Paul L. Vasey, Lisa M. Diamond, S. Marc Breedlove, Eric Vilain, and Marc Epprecht. "Sexual Orientation, Controversy, and Science." *Psychological Science in the Public Interest* 17, no. 2 (2016): 45–101.

Bauer, Heike. *English Literary Sexology: Translations of Inversion, 1860–1930*. London: Palgrave Macmillan, 2009.

Beachy, Robert. *Gay Berlin: Birthplace of a Modern Gay Identity*. New York: Vintage Books, 2014.

Bollé, Michael, and Rolf Bothe. *Eldorado: homosexuelle Frauen und Männer in Berlin, 1850–1950: Geschichte, Alltag und Kultur*. Berlin: Frölich & Kaufmann, 1984.

Boswell, John. *Christianity, Social Tolerance, and Homosexuality*. Chicago: University of Chicago Press, 1979.

Brady, Sean. *John Addington Symonds (1840–1893) and Homosexuality: A Critical Edition of Sources*. London: Palgrave Macmillan, 2012.

Bray, Alan. *The Friend*. Chicago: University of Chicago Press, 2003.

– *Homosexuality in Renaissance* England. London: Gay Men's Press, 1982.

Brunner, Andreas, and Hannes Sulzenbacher. "Donauwalzer – Herrenwahl: Schwule Geschichte der Donaumetropole vom Mittelalter bis zur Gegenwart." In *Schwules Wien: Reiseführer durch die Donaumetropole*, edited by Andreas Brunner and Hannes Sulzenbacher, 7–108. Vienna: Promedia, 1998.

Chauncey, George. *Gay New York: Gender, Urban Culture, and the Making of the Gay Male World*. New York: Basic Books, 1994.

Cocks, H.G. *Nameless Offences: Homosexual Desire in the 19th Century*. London: Tauris, 2003.

Crozier, Ivan. "Pillow Talk: Credibility, Trust, and the Sexological Case Study." *History of Science* 10, no. 6 (2008): 375–404.

Davies, Norman. *Europe: A History*. New York: HarperCollins, 1998.

Deák, Ágnes. "Translator, Editor, Publisher, Spy: The Informative Career of Károly Kertbeny (1824–1882)." *Hungarian Quarterly* 39 (1998): 26–33.

Derks, Paul. *Die Schande der heiligen Päderastie: Homosexualität und Öffentlichkeit in der deutschen Literatur 1750–1850.* Berlin: rosa Winkel, 1990.

Dobler, Jens. *Zwischen Duldungspolitik und Verbrechensbekämpfung: Homosexuellenverfolgung durch die Berliner Polizei von 1848 bis 1933.* Frankfurt: Schriftenreihe der Deutschen Gesellschaft für Polizeigeschichte, 2008.

Dürrenmatt, Friedrich. *Selected Writings*, vol. 1: *Plays*. Chicago: University of Chicago Press, 2006.

Dworek, Günter. "'Ist diese Krankheit heilbar?' Zwei Irrenärzte kommentieren Karl Heinrich Ulrichs." *CAPRI* 2, no. 90 (1990): 42–6.

Eder, Franz X. *Kultur der Begierde: Eine Geschichte der Sexualität*, 2nd ed. Munich: C.H. Berg, 2009.

Eribon, Didier. *Insult, and the Making of the Gay Self.* Translated by Michael Lucy. Durham: Duke University Press, 2004.

Féray, Jean-Claude. *Le Registre infamant.* Paris: Quintes-feuilles, 2012.

Feray, Jean-Claude, Manfred Herzer, and Glen W. Peppel. "Homosexual Studies and Politics in the Nineteenth Century: Karl Maria Kertbeny." *Journal of Homosexuality* 19, no. 1 (1990): 23–48.

Foucault, Michel. *Discipline and Punish: The Birth of the Prison.* Translated by Alan Sheridan. New York: Pantheon, 1977.

– "The Gay Science." Translated by Nicolae Morar and Daniel W. Smith. *Critical Inquiry* 37, no. 3 (2011): 385–403.

– *The History of Sexuality*, vol. 1: *An introduction*. Translated by Robert Hurley. New York: Vantage Books, 1990.

– *The History of Sexuality*, vol. 2: *The Use of Pleasure*. Translated by Robert Hurley. New York: Vantage Books, 1986.

Fout, John C. "Sexual Politics in Wilhelmine Germany: The Male Gender Crisis, Moral Purity, and Homophobia." *Journal of the History of Sexuality* (1992): 388–421.

Fraser, Nancy. "Rethinking the Public Sphere: A Contribution to the Critique of Actually Existing Democracy," *Social Text* 25–6 (1990): 56–80.

Fricke, Dieter. "Der Theater-Direktor Friedrich Feldmann und die mann-männliche Liebe – ein Bremer Sittenskandal aus dem Jahr 1867." *Arbeiterbewegung und Sozialgeschichte. Zeitschrift für die Regionalgeschichte Bremens im 19. und 20. Jahrhundert* 21–2 (2008): 103–8.

Funke, Jana. "'We Cannot Be Greek Now': Age Difference, Corruption of Youth, and the Making of Sexual Inversion." *English Studies* 94, no. 2 (2013): 139–53.

Galassi, Silviana. *Kriminologie im Deutschen Kaiserreich. Geschichte einer gebrochenen Verwissenschaftlichung.* Stuttgart: Franz Steiner Verlag, 2004.

Garber, Marjorie. *Vested Interests: Cross-Dressing and Cultural Anxiety.* London: Taylor and Francis, 1991.

Gibson, Mary, and Ilaria Poerio. "Modern Europe, 1750–1950." In *A Global History of Convicts and Penal Colonies*, edited by Clare Anderson, 317–48. London: Bloomsbury, 2018.

Goldstein, Anne B. "Organizing and Arguing Sex and Gender." *Law and Contemporary Problems* 85, no. 1 (2022): 57–79.

Goschler, Constantin. *Rudolf Virchow: Mediziner – Anthropologe – Politiker*. Cologne: Böhlau Verlag, 2002.

Greenberg, David F. *The Construction of Homosexuality*. Chicago: University of Chicago Press, 1988.

Grosskurth, Phyllis. *John Addington Symonds: A Biography*. London: Longmans, 1964.

Günther, Dagmar. "'And Now for Something Completely Different.' Prolegomena zur Autobiographie als Quelle der Geschichtswissenschaft." *Historische Zeitschrift* 272 (2001): 25–61.

Halperin, David M. "Forgetting Foucault: Acts, Identities, and the History of Sexuality." *Representations* 63 (1998): 93–120.

– *One Hundred Years of Homosexuality, and Other Essays on Greek Love*. New York: Routledge, 1990.

Hekma, Gert. "'A Female Soul in a Male Body': Sexual Inversion as Gender Inversion in Nineteenth-Century Sexology." In *Third Sex, Third Gender: Beyond Sexual Dimorphism in Culture and History*, edited by Gilbert Herdt, 213–39. New York: Zone Books, 1994.

Hergemöller, Bernd-Ulrich, ed. *Mann für Mann: Biographisches Lexikon*. Berlin: Suhrkamp, 1998.

– *Mann für Mann: Biographisches Lexikon zur Geschichte von Freundesliebe und mannmännlicher Sexualität im deutschen Sprachraum*, vol. 1. (A-RAS). Berlin: LIT, 2010.

Herzer, Manfred. *Karl Maria Kertbeny: Schriften zur Homosexualitätsforschung*. Berlin: rosa Winkel, 2000.

– "Kertbeny and the Nameless Love." *Journal of Homosexuality* 12, no. 1 (1986): 1–26.

– "Zastrow–Ulrichs–Kertbeny. Erfundene Identitäten im 19. Jahrhundert." In *Männerliebe im alten Deutschland: Sozialgeschichtliche Studien, Sozialwissenschaftliche Studien zur Homosexualität*, edited by Rüdiger Lautmann and Angela Taeger, 7–61. Berlin: rosa Winkel, 1992.

Herzog, Dagmar. *Sexuality in Europe: A Twentieth-Century History*. Cambridge: Cambridge University Press, 2011.

Hoffschildt, Rainer. *Olivia: Die bisher geheime Geschichte des Tabus Homosexualität und der Verfolgung der Homosexuellen in Hannover*. Hannover: Selbstverlag, 1992.

Holland, Merlin, and Rupert Hart-Davis, eds. *Wilde, Complete Letters*. London: Fourth Estate, 2000.

Hornung, René. "Jakob Rudolf Forster (1853–1926) oder Wie Ulrichs ein Leben prägte." In *Karl Heinrich Ulrichs zu Ehren: Materialen zu Leben und Werk*, edited by Wolfram Setz. Berlin: rosa Winkel, 2000.

Hull, Isabel V. *Sexuality, State, and Civil Society in Germany, 1700–1815*. Ithaca: Cornell University Press, 1996.

Jones, Vernon Stanley. *Aesop's Fables: A New Translation*. New York: Avenel, 1912.

Joyce, Simon. *LGBT Victorians: Sexuality and Gender in the Nineteenth-Century Archives*. New York: Oxford University Press, 2022.

Karsch, Ferdinand. "Auszüge aus 'Heinrich Hössli (1784–1864).'" In Thalmann, *"Keine Liebe ist an sich Tugend oder Laster,"* 27–34.

Kaylor, Michael M. *Secreted Desires. The Major Uranians: Hopkins, Pater and Wilde*. Brno: Masaryk University Press, 2006.

Kennedy, Hubert. "Johann Baptist von Schweitzer: The Queer Marx Loved to Hate." In *Gay Men and the Sexual History of the Political Left*, edited by Gert Hekma, Harry Oosterhuis, and James Steakley, 69–96. Binghampton: Harrington Park, 1995.

– *Karl Heinrich Ulrichs: Pioneer of the Modern Gay Movement*, 2nd ed. Concord: Peremptory Books, 2005.

Kessel, Martina. "The 'Whole Man': The Longing for a Masculine World in Nineteenth-Century Germany." *Gender and History* 15, no. 1 (2003): 1–31.

Koch, Arnd. "C.J.A. Mittermaier and the 19th-Century Debate about Juries and Mixed Courts." *Revue internationale de droit penal* 72, nos. 1–2 (2001): 347–53.

Kunzel, Regina. "The Power of Queer History." *American Historical Review* 123, no. 5 (2018): 1560–82.

Lamble, Sarah. "Queer Necropolitics and the Expanding Carceral State: Interrogating Sexual Investments in Punishment." *Law Critique* 24 (2013): 229–53.

Lauritsen, John, and David Thorstad. *The Early Homosexual Rights Movement (1864–1935)* [1974]. Ojai: Times Change Press, 1995.

Leck, Ralph M. *Vita Sexualis: Karl Ulrichs and the Origins of Sexological Science*. Champaign: University of Illinois Press, 2016.

Lynch, Michael. "'Here Is Adhesiveness': From Friendship to Homosexuality." *Victorian Studies* 29, no. 1 (1985): 67–96.

Marhoefer, Laurie. *Racism and the Making of Gay Rights: A Sexologist, His Student, and the Empire of Queer Love*. Toronto: University of Toronto Press, 2022.

Martin, Luther H., Huck, Gutman, and Patrick H. Hutton, eds. *Technologies of the Self: A Seminar with Michel Foucault*. Amherst: University of Massachusetts Press, 1988.

McKenna, Neil. *Fanny and Stella: The Young Men Who Shocked Victorian England*. London: Faber and Faber, 2014.

Mildenberger, Florian. … *in der Richtung Homosexualität verdorben: Psychiater, Kriminalspychologen und Gerichtsmediziner über männliche Homosexualität 1850–1970*. Hamburg: Männerschwarm Verlag, 2002.

Mühlheim, Martin. "'… dass über die Verwerflichkeit der genannten Handlungen gewiss Einheit besteht, nicht aber über die Grenze der Strafbarkeit': die Diskussion um die strafrechtliche Stellung der Homosexualität im Kanton Zürich von 1798 bis 1942." Paper presented at a seminar, University of Zurich, April 2003. https://www.es.uzh.ch/dam/jcr:b6b60323-297a-450f-bc506c230d65d14f/M%C3%BChlheim_Martin--Die_Diskussion_um_strafrechtliche_Stellung_der_Homosexualit%C3%A4t_im_Kanton_Z%C3%BCrich_von_1798_bis_1942.pdf.

Müller, Klaus. *Aber in meinem Herzen sprach eine Stimme so laut: Homosexuelle Autobiographien und medizinische Pathographien im neunzehnten Jahrhundert*. Berlin: rosa Winkel, 1991.

Muñoz, José Esteban. *Cruising Utopia: The Then and There of Queer Futurity*. New York: NYU Press, 2009.

Nancy, Jean-Luc. *Being Singular Plural*. Stanford: Stanford University Press, 2000.

Neuhold, Helmut. *Das andere Habsburg: Homoerotik im österreichischen Kaiserhaus*. Marburg: Tectum Verlag, 2008.

Oosterhuis, Harry. *Stepchildren of Nature: Krafft-Ebing, Psychiatry, and the Making of Sexual Identity*. Chicago: University of Chicago Press, 2000.

Osterhammel, Jürgen. *The Transformation of the World: A Global History of the Nineteenth Century*. Translated by Patrick Camiller. Princeton: Princeton University Press, 2014.

Palmowski, Jan. "The Politics of the 'Unpolitical German': Liberalism in German Local Government, 1860–1880." *Historical Journal* 42, no. 3 (1999): 675–704.

Pretsell, Douglas. *The Correspondence of Karl Heinrich Ulrichs 1846–1894*. Cham: Palgrave Macmillan, 2020.

– "The Evolution of the Questionnaire in German Sexual Science: A Methodological Narrative." *History of Science* 58, no. 3 (2020): 326–49.

– *Queer Voices in the Works of Richard von Krafft-Ebing, 1883–1901*. Cham: Palgrave Macmillan, 2023.

Regis, Amber, ed. *The Memoirs of John Addington Symonds: A Critical Edition*. London: Palgrave Macmillan, 2016.

Richter, Simon. "Winckelmann's Progeny: Homosocial Networking in the Eighteenth Century." In *Outing Goethe and His Age*, edited by Alice A Kuzniar, 33–46. Stanford: Stanford University Press, 1996.

Robb, Graham. *Strangers: Homosexual Love in the Nineteenth Century*. London: Picador, 2003.

Rohse, Eberhard. "Ein Nicht-Braunschweiger als Braunschweiger Autor: Der Westermann-Radakteur und Schriftsteller Adolf Glaser." In *Adolf Glaser's*

"Hennig Braband" (1857), edited by Eberhard Rohse, 43–65. Peine: Fischer Druck, 1993.

Roschitz, Karlheinz. *Kaiserwalzer: Traum und Wirklichkeit der Ringstraßenzeit.* Vienna: Ueberreuter, 1996.

Rowbotham, Sheila. *Edward Carpenter: A Life of Liberty and Love.* London: Verso, 2008.

Russell, Emma K. "Ambivalent Investments: Lessons from LGBTIQ Efforts to Reform Policing." *Current Issues in Criminal Justice* 31, no. 3 (2019): 378–95.

Schueller, Herbert, and Robert Peters. *The Letters of John Addington Symonds,* vol. 3: *1885–1893.* Detroit: Wayne State University Press, 1969.

Sedgwick, Eve Kosofsky. *Between Men: English Literature and Male Homosexual Desire.* New York: Columbia University Press, 1985.

– *Epistemology of the Closet* [1990]. Berkeley: University of California Press, 2008.

Segal, Zef M. *The Political Fragmentation of Germany: Formation of the German States by Infrastructures, Maps, and Movement, 1815–1866.* Cham: Palgrave Macmillan, 2019.

Semenyna, Scott W., Doug P. VanderLaan, Lanna J. Petterson, and Paul L. Vasey. "Familial Patterning and Prevalence of Male Androphilia in Samoa." *Journal of Sex Research* 54, no. 8 (2017): 1077–84.

Setz, Wolfram, ed. *Die Geschichte der Homosexualitäten und die schwule Identität an der Jahrtausendwende – Eine Vortragsreihe aus Anlaß des 175. Geburtstags von Karl Heinrich Ulrichs.* Berlin: rosa Winkel, 2000.

– *Karl Heinrich Ulrichs zu Ehren: Materialien zu Leben und Werk.* Berlin: rosa Winkel, 2000.

– *Neue Funde und Studien zu Karl Heinrich Ulrichs.* Hamburg: MännerschwarmSkript, 2004.

Shakespeare, William. "Venus and Adonis" [1593]. In *The Complete Poems of Shakespeare,* edited by Cathy Shrank and Raphael Lyne. New York: Routledge, 2018.

Shorter, Edward. *A History of Psychiatry: From the Era of the Asylum to the Age of Prozac.* New York: Wiley, 1997.

Sigusch, Volkmar. "Unbekanntes aus dem Nachlaß von Karl Heinrich Ulrichs." *Zeitschrift für Sexualforschung,* 12, no. 3 (1999): 187–286.

Singy, Patrick. "Sexual Identity at the Limits of German Liberalism: Law and Science in the Work of Karl Heinrich Ulrichs (1825–1895)." *Journal of the History of Sexuality* 30, no. 3 (2021): 390–410.

Smith, Timothy D'Arch. *Love in Earnest.* London: Routledge and Kegan Paul, 1970.

Spade, Dean. *Normal Life: Administrative Violence, Critical Trans Politics, and the Limits of Law.* Durham: Duke University Press, 2015.

Spector, Scott. *Violent Sensations: Sex, Crime, and Utopia in Vienna and Berlin 1860–1914*. Chicago: University of Chicago Press, 2016.

Steakley, James. *The Homosexual Emancipation Movement in Germany*. Salem: Ayer, 1975.

Szporluk, Roman. *Communism and Nationalism: Karl Marx versus Friedrich List*. Oxford: Oxford University Press, 1993.

Takács, Judit. "The Double Life of Kertbeny." In *Past and Present of Radical Sexual Politics*, edited by Gert Hekma, 26–40. Amsterdam: UvA-Mosse Foundation, 2004.

Thalmann, Rolf. *"Keine Liebe ist an sich Tugend oder Laster": Heinrich Hössli (1784–1864) und sein Kampf für die Männerliebe*. Zurich: Chronos, 2014.

Tobin, Robert Deam. *Peripheral Desires: The German Discovery of Sex*. Philadelphia: University of Pennsylvania Press, 2015.

– *Warm Brothers: Queer Theory and the Age of Goethe*. Philadelphia: University of Pennsylvania Press, 2001.

Treusch-Dieter, Gerburg. "Die Sexualdebatte in der ersten deutschen Fruaenbewegung." In *Homosexualität: Handbuch der Theorie- und Forschungsgeschichte*, edited by Rüdiger Lautmann, 19–28. Frankfurt: Campus Verlag, 1993.

Verheyen, Dirk. *The German Question: A Cultural, Historical, and Geopolitical Exploration*. Boulder: Westview Press, 1991.

Vick, Brian. "Liberalism, Nationalism, and Gender Dichotomy in Mid-Nineteenth-Century Germany: The Contested Case of German Civil Law." *Journal of Modern History* 82 (2010): 546–84.

Watson, Peter. *The German Genius: Europe's Third Renaissance, the Second Scientific Revolution and the Nineteenth Century*. New York: Harper Perennial, 2011.

Weeks, Jeffrey. *Sexuality and Its Discontents: Meanings Myths and Modern Sexualities*. London: Routledge, 1995.

Whisnant, Clayton. *Queer Identities and Politics in Germany*. New York: Harrington Park, 2016.

Whitman, Walt. *Leaves of Grass*. Boston: James Osgood, 1881–2.

Wilde, Oscar. *The Importance of Being Earnest: A Trivial Comedy for Serious People*. London: Leonard Smithers & Co., 1899.

Wilper, James. *Reconsidering the Emergence of the Gay Novel in English and German*. West Lafayette: Purdue University Press, 2016.

Index